The Playful Citizen

The Playful Citizen

Civic Engagement in a Mediatized Culture

Edited by
René Glas, Sybille Lammes, Michiel de Lange,
Joost Raessens, and Imar de Vries

Amsterdam University Press

The publication of this book was made possible by the Utrecht Center for Game Research (one of the focus areas of Utrecht University), the Open Access Fund of Utrecht University, and the research project *Persuasive gaming. From theory-based design to validation and back*, funded by the Netherlands Organisation for Scientific Research (NWO).

Cover illustration: Photograph of *Begging For Change*, MEEK (courtesy of Jake Smallman).

Cover design: Coördesign
Lay-out: Crius Group, Hulshout

ISBN 978 94 6298 452 3
e-ISBN 978 90 4853 520 0
DOI 10.5117/9789462984523
NUR 670

Contents

Part II Ludo-epistemologies

Part III Ludo-politics

1. The playful citizen: An introduction

René Glas, Sybille Lammes, Michiel de Lange, Joost Raessens, and Imar de Vries

With the emergence of digital and mobile technologies, our conceptions and hopes of what citizen participation entails have changed profoundly. It seems as though interactive, networked, and cheap technologies have greatly democratized how literacies, knowledge, and power structures are generated and perceived in everyday life and that they have increased—and have further potential to increase—the degree of civic engagement. From playing, modifying, and designing games and interactive documentaries, and using playful tools and games for the production of alternative knowledges, to becoming protest-cartographers or pollution measurers, citizens appear to engage with, alter, and probe media technologies to a far greater extent than ever before. At the same time, we should be critical of what exactly these apparently enabling technologies do, and question what the drawbacks and the possibilities of digital media are for civic engagement.

In this edited volume, we provide an overview of the potentials and limitations of citizen engagement in the digital age through a selection of contributions from various academic fields. These contributions discuss the many digital media technologies and developments that grew to prominence in the second decade of this century. From the Occupy Wall Street movement to the development of citizen science games, from new forms of participatory documentary film-making to the rise and exploits of Reddit users, unifying all these topics is a sustained focus on what we consider to be *ludic*, or *playful*, engagement. It is through this view, we argue, that forms of partaking such as DIY, journalism, research, activism, art, or politics are to be understood. We would like to share a particularly striking example here, found in the 2010 exhibition *Space Invaders*, organized by the National Gallery of Australia. Referring to the eponymous 1978 arcade video game, this playful exhibition celebrated the energy of graffiti culture and its street-based creativity (Babington 2010). Street artist MEEK's contribution *Begging For Change* shows a homeless man holding a sign that reads "Keep your coins, I want

---

Glas, R., S. Lammes, M. de Lange, J. Raessens, and I. de Vries, eds. 2019. *The Playful Citizen. Civic Engagement in a Mediatized Culture.* Amsterdam: Amsterdam University Press.
DOI: 10.5117/9789462984523/INTRO

change." This work's explicit word play exhibits powerful social comments about the inadequacy of non-binding charity and compassion, and about the need for structural change (see Mouffe 2013, 64). From this particular instance of playful social commentary, we find we can extrapolate many other clues as to how forms of public participation in the early twenty-first century can be understood. Play, we posit, is an important theoretical principle for comprehending new manifestations of civic engagement.

With this book, we therefore want to further our interdisciplinary understanding of how media and citizenship can converge in contemporary culture through the lens of play. In an era in which play has left the traditional playground and has pervaded domains traditionally perceived as non-playful, we need to get a better analytical purchase on how this shift has changed our approaches to citizenship as well as to media. The ongoing ludification of culture (Raessens 2014) and ludification of identity and self (Frissen et al. 2015) prompts us to rethink what citizenship is and how it can be understood, enacted, analyzed, and conceptualized in relation to media and play. If we have become more playful as citizens, in what ways and through which media is this manifested in our daily lives? Which media practices can we discern as evidencing and letting us understand the reciprocal relationship between ludification and citizenship? And should these practices be viewed as new ways to enhance and change the agency of citizens, or rather as facilitating and maintaining dominant hegemonies or assemblages of power (e.g. Lammes and Perkins 2016)? We set out to give a pluralistic answer to such questions by bringing together scholars from different fields. They discuss a plethora of themes and topics, from game design to politics, pertaining to playful citizenship in the digital age.

The multifaceted framework we offer in this book builds on a corpus of academic literature that has previously drawn attention to the phenomenon of the ludification of culture and how culture can be understood through a playful lens (Fuchs 2012;[1] Fuchs et al. 2014; Walz and Deterding 2015). It is important here to address the question whether the ludification of culture refers to, or is meant to be interpreted as, an ontological or an epistemological claim. The claim is ontological if it refers to a "new phase of history characterized so much by play that we can deem it a play world" (Combs 2000, 20). Or, as Eric Zimmerman declares in his *Manifesto*, if the claim is that we are living in a "Ludic Century" (2015).

In this book, we do focus on this ontological aspect of ludification of culture and society; however, our claim is also of an epistemological nature.

1 All references to online sources were current as of 5 November 2018.

We argue that the concepts of play and the ludification of culture are crucial for understanding what we call the "ludic turn in media theory" (Raessens 2014, 109), and should be used as heuristic tools to shed new light on contemporary notions of citizenship, as lenses that make it possible to see new objects and phenomena in a different light and study them in a particular way. Both concepts enable us, as theorists, to identify poignant aspects of today's media culture—and to construct a specific conceptual perspective on this culture. Zimmerman's claim that we are living in a ludic century is both too broad and too narrow: it is too broad because it seems to suggest that we should have the whole twenty-first century as our research locus, and it is too narrow because the kind of research Zimmerman advocates is restricted to a game studies perspective. Our approach is rather more finely drawn: we argue that we should become more specific by studying particular cultural, scientific, and political fields and practices, and by doing so take into account broader developments that we wish to label as the 'ludic' or 'playful' turn taking place in these domains.

In tandem with academics noting a ludification of culture, especially in the social sciences, scholars have become increasingly interested in how digital and analog media can be used to engage citizens with their environments. From local citizen science projects (Nold 2009; Gabrys et al. 2016) to experimental, creative, and embodied projects (Calvillo 2012; Last 2012; McCormack 2013), these studies shed light on how media technologies can stimulate citizen participation through their performative, experimental, and creative affordances. While such studies at times implicitly relate citizenship to the ludic, we argue that creativity, experimentation, open-endedness, and playful citizenship should be examined more directly as well.

This book is indebted to a rich array of studies that directly or indirectly examine the relation between citizenship, media technologies, and play. However, we want to take a step further in how we tie such perspectives together. What has not been thoroughly examined so far is how these three can be approached as a *triadic* relationship. Although studies about citizen science games, for example, may draw attention to the relation between science and games, they often underplay what citizenship is about. To be clear, it is often impossible to give equal attention to all three aspects and their reciprocal relations in individual studies, but it is precisely for this reason that an ordering, clustering, and contextualization of cases and analyses is needed to truly understand this triadic relation between citizenship, media, and play from a critical perspective.

We are convinced that such an ordering should go beyond disciplinary boundaries if we really want to start to understand citizenship, media, and play from a multilayered perspective. The collected texts offer the reader a pluralistic perspective: we invited scholars and collected insights from diverse fields such as (new) media studies, politics, science and technology studies, critical geography, design studies, game studies, play studies, communication studies, and urban studies. This book should speak to anyone interested in how citizenship, media, and play are unfolding in the digital age and how we can develop a multifaceted and situated perspective to understand their relations and connections in productive ways. By bringing together a plethora of historical and more recent cases, and by including authors hailing from different fields to examine such phenomena, we present a book that critically investigates manifestations of citizenship, media, and play in contemporary digital culture.

Citizenship, media, and play

Our point of departure is the changing notion of what citizenship entails in our contemporary digital media culture. As Joyce Neys and Jeroen Jansz argue in their chapter in this volume, the importance of contributing to and interacting with democracy's formal institutions is increasingly complemented by citizens who express their political and civic engagement in different, playful ways. Analyzing the notions of play and playful media should subsequently enable us to better conceptualize our idea of 'playful citizenship'.

Yet, as discussed before, this book aims to respond to the academic status quo in which the triadic relationship may have been under-theorized, but where *dual* relations have been conceptualized to a far greater extent. As will be discussed below, the relationship between certain pairs within our triad of citizenship-media-play has already been fairly well studied, namely in the case of media and citizenship, and of playful media. Our line of argumentation is as follows. First, the relationship between media and citizenship stands in a long theoretical, predominantly sociological tradition, including the more interdisciplinary field of communication studies. Therefore, discussions overwhelmingly emphasize citizenship as shaped by information and communication media (mass media and more recently social media). Recently, more attention has been paid to other technologies, practices, and approaches. This includes gaming, urban mobile media use, sensing technologies, datafication, media practices other than mostly rational and deliberative communication practices, and an emphasis on the imaginative, creative, and affective as important dimensions for understanding civic media. Second, we observe that media and associated media cultures have become more playful. Many authors point to this ludification of digital technologies, and the culture of playfulness this fosters and taps into. Accordingly, we also need to redefine citizenship as *playful* and make clear what this notion of playful citizenship means within the domains of culture, science, and politics.

New media and changing civic engagement

Civic participation can be described as the extended involvement of individuals in a collective political decision-making process (Gordon and Mihailidis 2016; Koc-Michalska, Lilleker and Vedel 2016; Skoric et al. 2016). Broadly speaking, we can discern a rights-based model of citizenship, a duty-based sense of citizenship, and a contemporary kind of actualizing citizenship (cf. Hartley 2010). Each of these models highlights a different type of civic agency and mode of participation. And, as Kligler-Vilenchik notes, each citizenship model come with its own way of understanding media in relation to citizenship (Kligler-Vilenchik 2017, 1890).

First, in the rights-based view of citizenship, instruments for civic participation include voting, campaigning, demonstrating, contacting elected representatives, joining political organizations, access to the judicial system, and so on. This emphasis on institutions underpins an understanding of citizenship in terms of what Margaret Somers calls "the right to have rights" (2008, xiv). This citizenship model highlights the power dynamics between state, market, and civil society. Governments are often the legal owners of issues and the ultimate decision-makers. Communication tends to be managed by authorities. Citizens have varying degrees of rights to obtain information and limited opportunity to voice their opinions using media. With the rise of mass media, a plethora of institutions and (global) corporations have increasingly started to lobby for their interests and likewise have become political agents that use various media strategically.

Second, in what Bennett, Wells, and Freelon (after Schudson 1998) refer to as 'dutiful citizenship,' individuals participate in civic life by joining or forming organized groups, by becoming more informed via the news, and by engaging in public life based on a sense of personal or collective duty (2011, 838). This model of citizenship understands civic participation as being driven by a sense of responsibility, or out of obedience to public authorities (Ibid., 839). Thus, citizenship is a form of socialization.

Third, digital media technologies are frequently understood as a driving force of civic participation. This would necessitate a reconceptualization of citizenship. In the context of studies of young people's use of online media, Bennett, Wells, and Freelon identify the rise of what they call 'actualizing citizenship,' in order to draw attention to the ways in which self-expression, emotional involvement, and intrinsic motivation are key elements in peer networks sustained via social media. Elsewhere, Bennett and Segerberg argue that we need to rephrase 'collective action,' based on high levels of organizational resources and the formation of collective identities, as 'connective action,' which is based on personalized content sharing across media networks (Bennett and Segerberg 2012). Other authors have similarly focused on civic involvement through various media as a way to highlight everyday practices of the political rather than formalized institutional politics. With digital media technologies, 'networked publics' can engage with shared issues and material objects of concern (Latour 2005; Marres 2007, 2012; Varnelis 2008). Technologies empower people to monitor issues collectively and act upon them. Schudson calls this kind of active civic engagement 'monitorial citizenship' (Schudson 1998, 311-312). In this changing landscape of mediated citizenship, citizens increasingly feel a sense of collective ownership of complex (urban) issues (De Lange and De Waal 2013). At the same time, John Hartley observes the emergence of a 'silly citizenship' (Hartley 2010), in which comedy, satire, viral videos, and other manifestations of playful media revolve around attracting people's attention in the mediated political landscape. Hartley observes: "It is as much dramatic and performative as it is deliberative. The play's the thing, as DIY-citizens, many of them children, perform their own identities and relations" (Ibid., 241).

Civic engagement thus is increasingly understood in this third sense, by focusing on personal experiences and affectively charged social networks. Some have argued that digital media afford more casual practices of engagement. Critics highlight how media divert attention away from real issues and trick people into pseudo-participation, bordering on 'make-believe' involvement, with 'slacktivism' and 'clicktivism' (e.g. Morozov 2011; Tufekci 2017). While these authors take a very critical perspective, Alex Gekker, in his contribution to this volume, takes into account the limitations and opportunities of this development. He reworks Jesper Juul's notion of 'casual games' (Juul 2009) and calls this new type of participation 'casual politicking'.

Most theories on media and citizenship focus on communication aspects and, by extension, community dynamics. In communication studies and sociology, a key debate in the discussion about media and civic engagement concerns reinforcement theory versus mobilization theory. The reinforcement thesis holds that media cater for more of the same and thus help to establish more firmly what someone already believes. This is frequently labeled using terms like balkanization, filter bubble, capsularization, or parochialism. Mobilization theory, by contrast, argues that media expose people to new ideas and different perspectives, and therefore allow people to become better acquainted with ideas and standpoints beyond their known world. In terms of social capital, the reinforcement thesis emphasizes the tendency of media to strengthen 'bonding capital' and 'strong ties,' while the mobilization thesis underlines the potential of media to foster 'bridging capital' and 'weak ties' (Skoric et al. 2016). Mercedes Bunz, in her contribution, uses this tension to highlight how digital media can both facilitate increased participation and, at the same time, contribute to an additional splintering of publics.

Further specifying the relationship between new media and citizenship, we can identify three groups of questions, dealing with information, communication, and action. First, an information-based understanding of citizenship looks at what constitutes 'the well-informed citizen.' The 'good citizen' is a well-informed citizen. What happens to citizenship when digital media technologies and platforms become prominent as new sources of information? For example, in their chapter, Jessica Breen, Shannon Dosemagen, Don Blair, and Liz Barry address the question of what constitutes new types of citizen-generated information and knowledge, and how this is conveyed. Second, a communication-based view approaches citizenship in terms of social identities. The good citizen is a community member, local or imagined. What happens to this communal type of citizenship with the rise of digital media technologies and practices? Digital media shape how we connect to and feel part of groups, communities, and publics. New forms of distribution and the digital self that have emerged in the digital age complicate our senses of belonging and identity. Again, play is an important element for understanding this shift in social identity. Jennifer Gabrys, for instance, analyzes community-led citizen sensing projects in her contribution as a new form of environmental citizenship. Third, a focus on action highlights how citizenship emerges by doing things collectively, often with a common purpose. The good citizen is a creative entrepreneur. How do digital media technologies afford new modes of action? For instance, in his chapter, Douglas Rushkoff analyzes these issues by focusing on the Occupy movement, while William Uricchio focuses on how people actively engage with interactive documentaries.

Play and playful media

In this introduction and throughout this book, we develop a framework for approaching citizenship in the digital age through play, with play as both a heuristic tool for understanding citizenship (a way of looking), and a set of civic practices (a way of doing). A key strength of the notion of playful citizenship is that it opens up a productive space to start reconceptualizing citizenship in a post-identitarian age, venturing beyond sedimented categories of group affiliations. Play offers a new set of terms to recast today's practices around citizenship in more dynamic and processual terms: as experimental, as rehearsal, as continual competition, as joking and mischievous, as engaging and participatory, as a type of meta-communication, and so on.

An important step in our argument is that media themselves have playful qualities that warrant a reconceptualization of citizenship. Although play has always been a constituent element of many cultural practices (Huizinga 1955), since the 1960s, a tendency can be discerned in which daily cultural practices have become far more imbued with play. This cultural shift has further accelerated with the emergence of a myriad of digital technologies, which impels us to think of the modern digital age in terms of a playful media culture (Frissen et al. 2015) where play has become increasingly connected with daily activities. This is, for example, evident in our changing attitudes to work, travel, politics, or the economy. But let us first unpack the notion of play.

Most people would associate the activity of play with games, but to engage with the notion of play in a broader socio-cultural perspective we start from a more general definition. A very basic definition is given by Salen and Zimmerman, who consider play as "free movement within a more rigid structure" (2004, 304). While some chapters in this volume do discuss play in relation to games, in other chapters play is understood in this very general form: as seeking the 'play' in an established mechanism or structure, which can be a media technology, but also politics, art, or scientific research. In both a game-related definition and a more general one, play can be considered a problem-solving force. As Salen and Zimmerman point out, "when play occurs, it can overflow and overwhelm the more rigid structure in which it is taking place, generating emergent, unpredictable results," potentially even leading to transformative play where "the force of play is so powerful that it can change the structure itself" (Ibid., 305). The notion of play having transformative power has by now been pushed far beyond games—think of notions of 'critical play' (Flanagan 2009) and 'carnivalesque play' (Sicart

2014), or of popular game designers like Jane McGonigal foreseeing "games that augment our most essential human capabilities—to be happy, resilient, creative—and empower us to change the world in meaningful ways" (2011, 14). Such lines of reasoning have since become very much in vogue as the simultaneous ludification and digitization of culture has given rise to new connections between citizenship and participatory media technologies that are shaping our culture.

The connection between media technologies and play is, of course, not new. Scholars within and well beyond the field of game studies have already established the link between various media and play (Stephenson 1967; Fiske 1987; Silverstone 1999; Kerr, Kücklich, and Brereton 2006; Raessens 2006; Simons 2007; Buckland 2009; Sicart 2014; Frissen et al. 2015), but very few of these studies focus on the sociocultural implications of this playfulness in media, let alone on citizenship.

We should be cautious, though, not to overstate the potential of play and, consequently, games and other playful media. In their critical political analysis of the digital gaming phenomenon, Nick Dyer-Witheford and Greig de Peuter remind us that we should not consider play as necessarily or inherently empowering or democratizing (2009). For them, games are also the exemplary media of 'Empire,' Hardt and Negri's concept for describing postmodern global capitalism (2000). Similarly critical views have also already been expressed about phenomena like gamification (e.g. Bogost 2011a, 2011b; Fuchs et al. 2014; Walz and Deterding 2015). The question remains in what ways we have become empowered and where the limitations of our participatory powers lie. Games can motivate citizens to engage in citizen science and make players become ecological citizens by encouraging support, sympathy, and action for a variety of scientific and ecological issues. Cheap embeddable sensors, portable wireless communications, and computation technologies, paired with crowd-sourcing, networking, and co-creation principles from online culture, may all leverage citizens' involvement in gathering, visualizing, disseminating, and producing data, information, and forms of knowledge and culture. Even though they may inspire citizens to become involved and thus help overcome asymmetries between where power is produced and where it is 'lived' (see Latour 2003), we still need to examine further where exactly their strength lies as well as the limitations of the affordances such media technologies really offer to change the way we perceive and engage in active citizenship (see also the chapters by Anne-Marie Schleiner and Ingrid Hoofd in this volume).

Another gap we aim to fill is giving attention to some of the sociocultural implications of an increasingly playful media landscape. Lievrouw and

Livingstone (2002) propose that we think of media as composed of three elements: technical devices, social practices, and institutional arrangements. This provides a useful framework to zoom in on the playful qualities of media technologies. At the level of devices, we can see that Information and Communication Technologies (ICTs) have playful affordances (see also the chapter by Joost Raessens in this volume). In addition, we observe that new technologies are often approached and understood in playful ways, opening up room for playful exploration and experimentation. At the level of practices, we similarly see a plethora of playful or lusory attitudes (Suits 1978) and uses of ICTs that can be extended to reflections about playful citizenship. Think about the origins of computing culture in the playful hacking practices of MIT students, and hardware hackers of the West Coast (see also the chapter by Stefan Werning in this volume). Thirdly, at the level of institutional arrangements and protocols, we contend that play is a productive heuristic for focusing on more structural aspects of media and citizenship. On the one hand, play provides a rich arsenal of strategies to deal with today's complexity, uncertainty, risk, and network society. We see this in new arrangements for innovation and creativity: experimentation, (urban) living labs, self-learning networks, social movements, with room for improvisation and failure (see also the chapters by Eric Gordon and Stephen Walter, and by Mark Deuze and Lindsay Ems in this volume). On the other hand, play highlights the fact of *being played*: under the moniker of participatory media, people are being nudged into compliance, as a neoliberal ploy to extract free labor veiled as creative play done of your own free will (see also the chapter by Sonia Fizek and Anne Dippel in this volume).

Playful citizenship

So far in this introductory chapter, we have discussed the dual relationships between media and citizenship on the one hand, and media and play on the other. We now want to focus on the link between play and citizenship. One of the first scholars who paid attention to this relationship was the Dutch historian Johan Huizinga, who, in his *Homo ludens* (1955), put forward the notion of play as generative and constituting the 'origin' of human civilization. He concludes his long treatise on play with the argument that "civilization is, in its earliest phases, played. It does not come *from* play like a babe detaching itself from the womb: it arises *in* and *as* play, and never leaves it" (1955, 173, emphasis in original). It is important to point out here that Huizinga was critical about the interwar period, when he saw the play element in culture turn into barbaric "puerilism" (Ibid., 205). To tie this into our argument with some poetic license, he was also aware that play could spoil the potential for civic engagement. He nonetheless pointed out that:

> [R]eal civilization cannot exist in the absence of a certain play-element, for civilization presupposes limitation and mastery of the self, the ability not to confuse its own tendencies with the ultimate and highest goal, but to understand that it is enclosed within certain bounds freely accepted. Civilization will, in a sense, always be played according to certain rules, and true civilization will always demand fair play. (Ibid., 201)

Building upon Huizinga's ethical reflections, we contend that play is an indispensable ingredient for building a civic society and citizenship. Yet, we are also critical of how Huizinga, motivated by the troubled interwar period, relates 'good' civilization to sticking to the rules of play. Instead, we also see potential in *not* playing by the rules, in bending rules, or changing rules. For Huizinga, cheating and being a spoilsport "shatters civilization" (Huizinga 1955, 201). However, there have since been many instances that demonstrate that transgressive forms of play can also present and produce new forms of civil resistance, or even ludic anarchy, the latter powerfully demonstrated by the Situationist movement in the late 1950s and 1960s. Such playful practices, in which citizens as players, political activists, artists, or provocateurs creatively engage with bending, shattering, or ignoring rules, can result in highly productive ways for citizens to engage with and give shape to their civic society.

The unruly dimension of play and citizenship is addressed by René Glas and Sybille Lammes in this volume when they discuss ludo-epistemology and meaningful citizen participation in processes of knowledge production. It is also touched upon by Ben Schouten, Erik van der Spek, Daniël Harmsen, and Ellis Bartholomeus, as well as by Stephanie de Smale, in their analyses of non-expert forms of knowledge production. Furthermore, in the contribution by Michiel de Lange attention is drawn to the destabilizing, yet productive potential of play when speaking about creative engagement with urban issues, while Sam Hind points to creative aspects of protest as a disruptive human and non-human practice.

We want to show the situatedness of playful citizenship and how specific cases either destabilize, or consolidate notions of citizenship and society through creative and playful approaches. As such, we see play as a manifold phenomenon and are critical, yet open to how it can change, stabilize, and undermine our classical notions of citizenship. We want to offer readers a kaleidoscopic view of the ludic potential of playful citizenship.

Structure of the book

Now that we have established the notion of playful citizenship, we want to present it as a productive label for bundling and identifying common threads in a variety of empirical phenomena as interrelated, from citizen science to political activism, from online gaming to urban planning. To give structure to the breadth of contributions, we have divided this book into three parts, each pertaining to the notion of play: ludo-literacies, ludo-epistemologies, and ludo-politics. These three parts, discussed below, form a new way of ordering the emerging technologies and developments of the past decade that relate to the notion of playful citizenship. The three parts of the book do not delineate strict borders; inevitably there is quite some overlap in themes and topics. The chapters in each part nonetheless point toward a specific relational context in which we can situate and understand contemporary playful citizenship.

Ludo-literacies

As indicated earlier, play is permeating our daily lives more than ever. It is not just the omnipresence of games in many people's media diet, but the ludification of culture in general that should be addressed to understand this properly. And, as Matthias Fuchs argues, "societies with high lusory attitude will turn anything into games or into toys," which results in media technologies with increasingly ludic interfaces, thus advancing the process of ludification ever further (Fuchs 2012). This makes it all the more important to be able to understand the nature of contemporary games and play as part of critical media literacy.

According to Zagal, games literacy entails having the ability to play games, the ability to understand meanings with respect to games, and the ability to make games (2010, 23). Whereas the ability to play is functional, the ability to understand games is critical. Zagal defines understanding games as "the ability to explain, discuss, describe, frame, situate, interpret, and/or position games" in the context of human culture, other games, technological platforms and their ontological components (Ibid., 24). The third ability of games literacy moves from critical to creative, as understanding turns into the more active role of designing one's own preconditions for play.

For Zimmerman, this design-oriented take on literacy is key for what he calls *gaming* literacy, a new set of cognitive, creative, and social skills that point to "a new paradigm for what it will mean to become literate in the coming century" (2009, 25). Zimmerman thinks the mischievous meaning connoted by the term 'gaming' (rather than by 'games') is deliberate: "Gaming a system, means finding hidden shortcuts and cheats, and bending and modifying rules in order to move through the system more efficiently—perhaps to misbehave, but perhaps to change that system for the better" (Ibid.). Here, we see notions of games literacy that, through their critical and creative dimensions, align with more critical takes on media literacy that focus on active citizenship. As Kellner and Share point out:

> Critical media literacy involves cultivating skills in analyzing media codes and conventions, abilities to criticize stereotypes, dominant values, and ideologies, and competencies to interpret the multiple meanings and messages generated by media texts. Media literacy helps people to use media intelligently, to discriminate and evaluate media content, to critically dissect media forms, to investigate media effects and uses, and to construct alternative media. (2005, 372)

They too stress the importance of being able not only to understand media, but also to intervene through participatory, creative media practices.

In the chapters in *Part I: Ludo-literacies*, we take these three different aspects of games-related literacies as our point of departure. Joyce Neys and Jeroen Jansz show that playing political games can contribute to an increase in political participation and political engagement. Next, Stefan Werning and William Uricchio analyze how designing, modifying, and producing games and interactive documentaries can be considered to be forms of creative, cultural, and political expression, as a means of developing the player's critical understanding of the medium. Finally, Joost Raessens, Anne-Marie Schleiner, and Ingrid Hoofd claim that making sense of games requires an understanding of the social, cultural, and political context in which these games are made and played.

Ludo-epistemologies

In the second part of this book, we look at the connections between play, media, and citizenship from the perspective of knowledge production. Using the term 'ludo-epistemology,' we have grouped together authors who use different perspectives on whether play and epistemology can form productive relations and how this is done. Under the header of ludo-epistemology, we see strategies that move away from a top-down conception of knowledge production, instead incorporating citizens' daily practices into the equation. Inspired by Feyerabend's term 'anarcho-epistemology,' which he introduced to prompt a radical transformation in how knowledge is understood and made—scientists are citizens too—we argue for a shift to focus on play in order to achieve this. Similar to Feyerabend's (1978, 1987, 1993) anarchic and somewhat 'messy' (see Law 2004), yet possibly less radical approach, play also has strong potential for overcoming asymmetrical relations between traditional bastions of knowledge production (e.g. the laboratory) and how techno-science is used in daily life by citizens (Latour 2003). However, it puts more emphasis on the creative, imaginative, subversive, and inquisitive qualities that can be part of knowledge production. This is exactly what lies at the core of this part of the book: it is through play that epistemology becomes more participatory.

We agree with Sutton-Smith (2001) that play is always ambiguous and can be attributed contradictory or paradoxical meanings. In relation to knowledge production, ambiguity affects not only play, but also a preconception regarding the distinction between science and citizenship. According to this view, citizens are considered lay people while scientists are experts. Such thinking, we argue, prevents us from developing more innovative strategies (in design, method, or thinking) for meaningful connections between citizenship and science that truly use the potential of the playful citizen as an actor in techno-scientific knowledge production. At the same time, the contributions to this part of the book show that we need to keep a close eye on critical questions about when and how modes of play, like tinkering, tweaking, reshaping, and even cheating, become tools that subvert or even clash with knowledge production in terms of usefulness and the ethics of participation and civic action.

Part II: Ludo-epistemologies aims to give answers to these questions from two key perspectives. The first three chapters of this section zoom in on citizen science projects as they are enacted in daily live. From Jessica Breen, Shannon Dosemagen, Don Blair, and Liz Barry describing the hands-on tactics advocated by the Public Lab for mapping pollution, to the sensing projects examined and compared by media and science and technology studies scholar Jennifer Gabrys, and the biohacking project discussed by game and media scholar Stephanie de Smale, these chapters offer the reader a taste of ways in which play can be used in everyday life to turn citizens into experts and give them a creative voice in producing 'artefacts' that can have a direct impact on their livelihood and well-being. The last three chapters in this section also form a triad, this time centering on the potential and pitfalls of citizen science games. René Glas and Sybille Lammes combine science and technology studies (STS) and game studies perspectives to arrive at recommendations on how to change the aforementioned asymmetries, while

Ben Schouten, Erik van der Spek, Daniël Harmsen, and Ellis Bartholomeus approach this from a design perspective. Lastly, Sonia Fizek and Anne Dippel are perhaps less optimistic when they warn how the labor involved in citizen science games can also be used to enforce neoliberal ideologies.

Ludo-politics

The third part of this book collects contributions discussing how ludic engagement with digital media technologies offers new opportunities to 'act politically.' These chapters suggest several tensions in the relationship between playful media and political agency. While acknowledging that these tensions cannot be completely resolved, the authors investigate where and how those tensions occur, and what perspectives help in understanding the limitations and opportunities in dealing with them.

The first tension frames playful media between strengthening individual and collective agency, and co-optation. Playful media can help to build networked publics around shared issues of concern, but can also consolidate existing institutional structures and corporate interests. Cloaked as fun and play, they foster pseudo-participation or 'tokenism' (Arnstein 1969), confining agency to what Müller (2009) terms 'formatted spaces of participation.' Some argue that discourses about participatory media as disruptive change agents in effect serve as simulacra for true political action. In an age of political consensus—which Chantal Mouffe (2005) has called 'post-politics'—the logic of participatory media platforms sustains the neoliberal consensus, and a 'Californian ideology' of individual responsibility and entrepreneurialism. A closely related second tension revolves around the question of whether social media platforms help to strengthen or erode collective action and public values. A growing number of authors—e.g. Trebor Scholz (2016); Van Dijck, Poell and De Waal (2018)—are critical of what is called the 'sharing economy.' Play then acts as a thin veneer for an underlying political economy of relentless extraction of free or low-paid labor and value. Recent publications (e.g. Rathenau Institute 2017) underline the possible harm this increasing reliance on participatory platforms could do to historically nurtured public values and democratic institutions. A third tension is whether playful media help to unify the public realm or further accentuate social differences. As discussed above, some people are ludo-literate and make productive use of media technologies, whereas others may not be able to. Hence civic rights are not the same for all. Playful media thus may contribute to social sorting by fragmenting the public into what we could call participation readiness levels.

Throughout *Part III: Ludo-politics*, authors explore how playful media, ludic strategies, and tactics are employed in civic contexts to deal with these tensions. Mercedes Bunz sets the scene by arguing that new and playful forms of political participation do not necessarily allow revolutionary change and may not even provide sufficient friction and debate for real changes to occur. The four chapters that follow aim to show that there *are* productive frictions that can be generated in playful citizen activities, by staging carnivalesque interventions that use Twitter as a means for organizing and disrupting activities (Sam Hind), by incorporating play-like 'meaningful inefficiencies' in all kinds of everyday societal processes and systems (Eric Gordon and Stephen Walter), by approaching political gatherings from a player/hacker's point of view, rewriting general assembly rules and prototyping new ones (Douglas Rushkoff), or by moving away from efficiency-driven plans for building 'smart cities' to more serendipity-embracing projects including the participation of people in creating 'playful cities' (Michiel de Lange). The last two chapters in the book advocate a cautionary stance in analyzing and praising playful uses of new media technologies to create fissures in power. Playful citizenship is not guaranteed to deliver on its promises when it is driven by a means-over-end attitude (Mark Deuze and Lindsay Ems), or when the political arena itself becomes a game in which people predominantly casually participate (Alex Gekker).

References

Arnstein, S. R. 1969. A ladder of citizen participation. *Journal of the American Institute of Planners* 35 (4): 216-224.

Babington, J. 2010. *Space Invaders: Australian street | Stencils | Posters | Paste-ups | Zines | Stickers*. Canberra: National Gallery of Australia.

Bennett, W. L., C. Wells, and D. Freelon. 2011. Communicating civic engagement: Contrasting models of citizenship in the youth web sphere. *Journal of Communication* 61 (5): 835-856.

Bennett, W. L., and A. Segerberg. 2012. The logic of connective action: Digital media and the personalization of contentious politics. *Information, Communication & Society* 15 (5): 739-768.

Bogost, I. 2011a. Gamification is bullshit. *Ian Bogost*. http://www.bogost.com/blog/gamification_is_bullshit.shtml.

—. 2011b. Persuasive games: Exploitationware. *Gamasutra*. http://www.gamasutra.com/view/feature/134735/persuasive_games_exploitationware.php.

Buckland, W. 2009. *Puzzle films: Complex storytelling in contemporary cinema*. Hoboken, NJ: Wiley Blackwell.

Calvillo, N. 2012. The affective mesh: Air components 3D visualizations as a research and communication tool. *Parsons Journal for Information Mapping* 4 (2): 1-8.

Combs, J. E. 2000. *Play world. The emergence of the new ludenic age*. Westport, CT: Praeger Publishers.

De Lange, M., and M. de Waal. 2013. Owning the city: New media and citizen engagement in urban design. *First Monday* 18 (11).

Dyer-Witheford, N., and G. de Peuter. 2009. *Games of Empire: Global capitalism and video games*. Minneapolis, MN: University of Minnesota Press.

Feyerabend, P. 1978. *Science in a free society*. London: New Left Books.

—. 1987. *Farewell to reason*. London: Verso Books.

—. 1993. *Against method*. London: Verso Books.

Fiske, J. 1987. *Television culture*. New York: Routledge.

Flanagan, M. 2009. *Critical play: Radical game design*. Cambridge, MA: The MIT Press.

Frissen, V., S. Lammes, M. de Lange, J. de Mul, and J. Raessens, eds. 2015. *Playful identities: The ludification of digital media cultures*. Amsterdam: Amsterdam University Press.

Fuchs, M. 2012. Ludic interfaces: Driver and product of gamification. *G|A|M|E Journal* 1 (1). http://www.gamejournal.it/ludic-interfaces-driver-and-product-of-gamification.

Fuchs, M., S. Fizek, P. Ruffino, and N. Schrape, eds. 2014. *Rethinking gamification*. Lüneburg: meson press.

Gabrys, J., H. Pritchard, N. Calvillo, N. Shapiro, and T. Keene. 2016. Becoming civic: Fracking, air pollution, and environmental sensing technologies. In *Civic media: Technology | Design | Practice*, eds. E. Gordon and P. Mihailidis, 435-440. Cambridge, MA: The MIT Press.

Gordon, E., and P. Mihailidis, eds. 2016. *Civic media: Technology | Design | Practice* Cambridge, MA: The MIT Press.

Hardt, M., and A. Negri. 2000. *Empire*. Cambridge, MA: Harvard University Press.

Hartley, J. 2010. Silly citizenship. *Critical Discourse Studies* 7 (4): 233-248.

Huizinga, J. 1955. *Homo ludens: A study of the play-element in culture*. Boston, MA: Beacon Press.

Juul, J. 2009. *A casual revolution: Reinventing video games and their players*. Cambridge, MA: The MIT Press.

Kellner, D., and J. Share. 2005. Toward critical media literacy: Core concepts, debates, organizations, and policy. *Discourse: Studies in the Cultural Politics of Education* 26 (3): 369-386.

Kerr, A., J. Kücklich, and P. Brereton. 2006. New media – new pleasures? *International Journal of Cultural Studies* 9 (1): 63-82.
Kligler-Vilenchik, N. 2017. Alternative citizenship models: Contextualizing new media and the new "good citizen". *New Media & Society* 19 (11): 1887-1903.
Koc-Michalska, K., D. G. Lilleker, and T. Vedel. 2016. Civic political engagement and social change in the new digital age. *New Media & Society* 18 (9): 1807-1816.
Lammes, S., and C. Perkins. 2016. An introduction to playful mapping in the digital age. In *Playful mapping in the digital age*, eds. S. Lammes and C. Perkins. The Playful Mapping Collective, 12-27. Amsterdam: Institute of Network Cultures.
Last, A. 2012. Experimental geographies. *Geography Compass* 6 (12): 706-724.
Latour, B. 2003. *We have never been modern*. Cambridge, MA: Harvard University Press.
—. 2005. *Reassembling the social: An introduction to Actor-Network-Theory*. Oxford: Oxford University Press.
Law, J. 2004. *After method: Mess in social science research*. London: Routledge.
Lievrouw, L. A., and S. Livingstone. 2002. *Handbook of new media: Social shaping and consequences of ICTs*. London: SAGE.
Marres, N. 2007. The issues deserve more credit: Pragmatist contributions to the study of public involvement in controversy. *Social Studies of Science* 37 (5): 759-780.
—. 2012. *Material participation: Technology, the environment and everyday publics*. Houndmills: Palgrave Macmillan.
McCormack, D. P. 2013. *Refrains for moving bodies: Experience and experiment in affective spaces*. Durham, NC: Duke University Press.
McGonigal, J. 2011. *Reality is broken: Why games make us better and how they can change the world*. London: Jonathan Cape.
Morozov, E. 2011. *The net delusion: The dark side of internet freedom*. New York: PublicAffairs.
Mouffe, C. 2005. *On the political*. London: Routledge.
—. 2013. *Agonistics: Thinking the world politically*. London: Verso Books.
Müller, E. 2009. Formatted spaces of participation: Interactive television and the changing relationship between production and consumption. In *Digital material: Tracing new media in everyday life and technology*, eds. M. van den Boomen, S. Lammes, A. Lehmann, J. Raessens, and M. T. Schäfer, 49-63. Amsterdam: Amsterdam University Press.
Nold, C. 2009. Emotional cartography: Technologies of the self. *Emotional Cartography*. http://www.emotionalcartography.net.
Raessens, J. 2006. Playful identities, or the ludification of culture. *Games and Culture* (1) 1: 52-57.

—. 2014. The ludification of culture. In *Rethinking gamification*, eds. M. Fuchs, S. Fizek, P. Ruffino, and N. Schrape, 91-114. Lüneburg: meson press.

Rathenau Institute. 2017. *Eerlijk delen: Waarborgen van publieke belangen in de deeleconomie en de kluseconomie*. The Hague: Rathenau Institute.

Salen, K., and E. Zimmerman. 2004. *Rules of play: Game design fundamentals*. Cambridge, MA: The MIT Press.

Scholz, T. 2016. *Uberworked and underpaid: How workers are disrupting the digital economy*. Malden, MA: Polity Press.

Schudson, M. 1998. *The good citizen: A history of American civic life*. Cambridge, MA: Harvard University Press.

Sicart, M. 2014. *Play matters*. Cambridge, MA: The MIT Press.

Silverstone, R. 1999. *Why study the media?* Thousand Oaks, CA: SAGE.

Simons, J. 2007. *Playing the waves: Lars von Trier's game cinema*. Amsterdam: Amsterdam University Press.

Skoric, M., Q. Zhu, D. Goh, and N. Pang. 2016. Social media and citizen engagement: A meta-analytic review. *New Media & Society* 18 (9): 1817-1839.

Somers, M. 2008. *Genealogies of citizenship: Markets, statelessness, and the right to have rights*. New York: Cambridge University Press.

Stephenson, W. 1967. *The play theory of mass communication*. Chicago, IL: University of Chicago Press.

Suits, B. 1978. *The grasshopper: Games, life and utopia*. Peterborough: Broadview Press.

Sutton-Smith, B. 2001. *The ambiguity of play*. Cambridge, MA: Harvard University Press.

Tufekci, Z. 2017. *Twitter and tear gas: The power and fragility of networked protest*. New Haven, CT: Yale University Press.

Van Dijck, J., T. Poell, and M. de Waal, eds. 2018. *The platform society: Public values in a connective world*. Oxford: Oxford University Press.

Varnelis, K., ed. 2008. *Networked publics*. Cambridge, MA: The MIT Press.

Walz, S. P., and S. Deterding, eds. 2015. *The gameful world: Approaches, issues, applications*. Cambridge, MA: The MIT Press.

Zagal, J. P. 2010. *Ludoliteracy: Defining, understanding, and supporting games education*. Pittsburgh, PA: ETC Press.

Zimmerman, E. 2009. Gaming literacy: Game design as a model for literacy in the twenty-first century. In *The video game theory reader 2*, eds. B. Perron and M. J. P. Wolf, 23-31. New York: Routledge.

—. 2015. Manifesto for a ludic century. In *The gameful world: Approaches, issues, applications*, eds. S. P. Walz and S. Deterding, 19-22. Cambridge, MA: The MIT Press.

About the authors

René Glas is Assistant Professor of New Media and Digital Culture in the Department of Media and Culture Studies at Utrecht University. With a background in film and new media studies, his primary field is game studies, in which he teaches and writes about a variety of topics, including game history and culture, fan and participatory culture, cheating and other forms of deviant play, serious and pervasive games, and media comparison. Glas is a founding member of Utrecht University's Center for the Study of Digital Games and Play. His book *Battlefields of negotiation: Control, agency, and ownership in World of Warcraft* (2012) was published by Amsterdam University Press.

Sybille Lammes is Full Professor of New Media and Digital Culture at The Centre for the Arts in Society (LUCAS) at Leiden University. She has been a visiting Senior Research Fellow at The University of Manchester, and has worked as a researcher at the Centre for Interdisciplinary Methodologies at the University of Warwick, as well as the media studies departments of Utrecht University and the University of Amsterdam. Her background is in media studies and play studies, which she has always approached from an interdisciplinary angle, including cultural studies, science and technology studies, postcolonial studies, and critical geography. She is co-editor of *Playful identities: The ludification of digital media cultures* (Amsterdam University Press 2015), *Mapping time* (Manchester University Press 2018) and *The Routledge handbook of interdisciplinary research methods* (Routledge 2018). She is an ERC laureate and has been the principal investigator of numerous research projects.

Michiel de Lange is Assistant Professor in New Media Studies, Department of Media and Culture Studies, Utrecht University. He is co-founder of The Mobile City, a platform for the study of new media and urbanism, an advisor on E-culture at Mediafonds, and works as a researcher in the field of (mobile) media, urban culture, identity, and play. He is a researcher in the NWO Creative Industries funded project *The Hackable City*, about the ways digital media shape the future of city-making.

Joost Raessens is chair and Full Professor of Media Theory at Utrecht University, and scientific director of the Utrecht Center for Game Research (gameresearch.nl). His research concerns the 'ludification of culture,' focusing on games for change in relation to global climate change and refugee and migration issues. Raessens was conference chair of the first DiGRA conference Level Up in Utrecht (digra2003.org) and leads the research project *Persuasive gaming. From theory-based design to validation and back* (persuasivegaming.nl). Among his book publications (see raessens.nl for a complete overview) are the *Handbook of computer game studies* (The MIT Press 2005), *Homo ludens 2.0: The ludic turn in media theory* (Utrecht University 2012), and *Playful identities: The ludification of digital media cultures* (Amsterdam University Press 2015).

Imar de Vries is Assistant Professor of New Media and Digital Culture in the Department of Media and Culture Studies at Utrecht University. His work primarily focuses on studying innovation discourses of wireless technologies, social media, and augmented reality. He obtained his Ph.D. in 2008 with a media-archaeological and philosophical study of how mobile phones developed to become quintessential personal communication tools, and he subsequently published on the subject in the book *Tantalisingly close: An archaeology of communication desires in discourses of mobile wireless media* (Amsterdam University Press 2012). He also published on mobile ringtones and identity performances, selfie culture, and archives in the digital age. De Vries is a member of the supervisory board of Media Lab IMPAKT and is affiliated with Media Lab SETUP.

Part I

Ludo-literacies

Introduction to Part I

René Glas, Sybille Lammes, Michiel de Lange, Joost Raessens, and Imar de Vries

In the first part of this book, we present a collection of chapters on the relationship between the design of games and other playful media on the one hand, and the politics of citizenship and participation on the other. More specifically, all the chapters relate to notions of 'ludo-literacy' as discussed in the Introduction. In what follows, various elements of games and play-related literacy—being able to play, critically understand, and create games—come into view, showing that without such literacy, citizens lack the critical skills to understand how game and playful design operates. These elements also allow game and playful media developers to enrich their work, creating more interesting, participatory experiences. Such skills, as will become clear, can be employed for political gains and needs, but also for acts of resistance. Moreover, having a critical understanding of games will allow us to think about the limitations of civic game design.

One key question asked when discussing games with political themes or goals is in what ways they facilitate civic engagement and political engagement. In the first chapter of Part I, entitled *Engagement in play, engagement in politics: Playing political video games*, media and communication scholars Joyce Neys and Jeroen Jansz ask this very question. What makes this work especially interesting as a starting point for this collection is their exploration of contemporary notions of citizenship and how these notions relate to modern (Western) democracies. They look at what constitutes a 'good citizen' in our contemporary mediatized culture and how political games arouse civic engagement and political participation in their players. Discussing both theory and empirical findings, Neys and Jansz highlight the persuasive potential of games, but they also call for further investigations of these effects.

New media and games scholar Stefan Werning is also interested in the relationship between citizenship and engaging with games, but he approaches this subject from the perspective of design rather than play. His chapter, *Analytical game design: Game-making as a cultural technique in a gamified society*, highlights an aspect of ludo-literacy—game design—that is key to understanding how games and playful media operate. According to Werning, being an independent citizen requires a basic knowledge of how software and programming operates due to our society's heavily reliance on digital media. Game-making, he argues, should be seen as a cultural technique. By engaging with 'analytical' game design experiments, the process of game creation allows citizens to understand and give shape to their surroundings, moving beyond enhanced ludo-literacy toward active civic engagement.

Moving away from games, media scholar William Uricchio focuses on interactive documentaries as a playful format in his chapter entitled *Rethinking the social documentary*. In this chapter, he stresses the potential of this new documentary film format for increasing the participation of viewers in the creation of documentary productions. He shows that through playful participation, viewers can collaborate and co-create with makers, influencing the final product. It allows viewers to pick and reorder content that they find relevant for their own personal engagement with a certain topic. This creates individual experiences and is a move away from having a strong authorial voice. For social impact documentaries, he points out, being able to trace and collect such individual experiences could also provide further insight into how civic engagement through contemporary media actually works. Uricchio's chapter presents a strong case for the civic potential of allowing viewers to play with the documentary film format, foregrounding the interactive documentary as a potent challenger for its traditional linear and author-driven counterpart.

In contrast to the previous chapter, new media and game scholar Joost Raessens focuses on a close reading of one particular example of a political game, the ecology-themed online production of *Collapsus – Energy Risk Conspiracy*. In his chapter, entitled *Collapsus, or how to make players become ecological citizens*, he aims to tackle the psychological climate paradox, namely the observation that the more climate facts people hear, the less likely they are to take action. The question is whether climate communication can be channeled through a game in such a way that it actually manages to change citizens' thinking and behavior regarding climate change issues.

The contributions by Neys and Jansz, and Werning provide more general overviews of the potential of playing and making politically charged games, while Uricchio and Raessens focus on the potential of a new playful genre and a specific production respectively. The final two chapters in this section of the book take a more critical stance on the often alleged or implied emancipatory or empowering potential of such productions. In her chapter *The broken toy tactic: Clockwork worlds and activist games*, media artist and theorist Anne-Marie Schleiner takes the procedurality of games as her focal point. She examines what she refers to as the 'toyness' of activist simulation games, a ludic abstraction of the real world that can negate a game's potential critical impact. It reminds us that we should not take the persuasive capacity of procedural rhetoric as a given: the clockwork logic of a game can be so enchanting to the player that he or she can lose track of its argument. To confront players with the inner workings of a game, and consequently its inner argument, might require such toys to be broken by disruptive game design or deviant player strategies.

Finally, new media theorist Ingrid Hoofd tackles the civic potential of digital play head-on in a chapter entitled *Video games and the engaged citizen: On the ambiguity of digital play*. With a critical reading of a key piece of empirical research on the civic potential of games, she unpacks the overly positivist undertones of such research. By situating political games in a larger framework where digital play meets global neoliberal capitalism, she points out that games that might look empowering or emancipatory actually make such notions part of the pre-shaped and predicated mechanical logic of games. Taking cues from Baudrillard, who discusses the seductive nature of games that try to divert energy away from efforts to actually change a system, Hoofd considers playing games as engaging with the highest-order demands of cybernetic capitalism. This, she argues, applies to most civic games as well. Like Schleiner, though, she recognizes ways for resistance and subversion through playful self-reflexivity and hacking practices.

2. Engagement in play, engagement in politics: Playing political video games

Joyce Neys and Jeroen Jansz

Abstract

It is a widely shared value in Western democracies that citizens should engage with political and social issues. This engagement is not necessarily confined to party politics, but includes other aspects of citizenship as well, from commitment to a local cause to supporting the global campaign of an NGO. Video games are arguably an excellent platform for encouraging and developing such engagement. Playing may facilitate civic engagement by allowing players to practice and experience different civic competencies in the safe environment of the game. This chapter discusses the results of research in this up-and-coming field and critically assesses those results in light of the opportunities this form of play might offer citizens when negotiating contemporary forms of citizenship.

Keywords: Civic engagement, citizenship, media, play, serious games, persuasive gaming

This chapter explores whether playing political video games can facilitate civic engagement and, if so, how it encourages political participation. Over the last several decades, there has been an increasing academic focus on the diverse properties, characteristics, effects, and consequences of games and gaming. The research spans across a wide variety of topics that range from addiction and other negative effects of excessive gaming, to a focus on simulation from a design and educational perspective, to the beneficial effects of games in relation to health issues (e.g. revalidation and exergames). These topics have been scrutinized from different perspectives. Games have been analyzed from an economic perspective (focusing on the multimillion-dollar game industry), a psychological perspective (addressing

Glas, R., S. Lammes, M. de Lange, J. Raessens, and I. de Vries, eds. 2019. *The Playful Citizen. Civic Engagement in a Mediatized Culture.* Amsterdam: Amsterdam University Press.
DOI: 10.5117/9789462984523/CH02

a wide range of motivational questions), an educational perspective (where games are studied in the context of formal and informal learning), and a cultural perspective (where games are studied as cultural artifacts of play) (Raessens and Goldstein 2005; Ritterfeld, Cody, and Vorderer 2009). In other words, the field of game studies is maturing and is thus providing additional knowledge that contributes to a better understanding of the relationship between gaming and culture. We see, slowly but surely, the field moving away from the bad versus good debate and starting to ask the bigger questions: how and in what settings can games best be used to what end?

The immense global popularity of playing video games is one important instance of what Raessens has called "the ludification of culture" (2006, 2014). However, ludification is by no means confined to playing (entertainment) games as playfulness increasingly penetrates different cultural domains (Frissen et al. 2015, 9). For example, leisure time (fun shopping), work (presenting repetitive tasks in a playful manner), and school (edugames). In this chapter, we will focus on the political domain. We aim to investigate whether and, if so, how citizens might become engaged in politics by playing (political) video games. We will discuss both games that purposively communicate a political message, as well as games with more indirect political implications.

The chapter starts by exploring contemporary notions of citizenship and what that entails in today's (Western) democracies. Related to the shifting conceptualization of citizenship, or what it means to be a good citizen, the changing media landscape is briefly discussed, after which we zoom in on games. We then move to discuss the wider notion of play in relation to engagement and how there are indications slowly starting to emerge that games are an excellent tool to engage (young) people, also in more political matters, even though it also becomes clear that 'true' engagement, or extended and substantial change in political interest/engagement, is always the product of the dynamic between playing such a game (the game as first contact and instigator) and the player's discussion about the (contents of the) game with his/her peers. We argue that this might be explained by political socialization theory (see also Lin et al. 2010; Bourgonjon and Soetaert 2013), which leads to the conceptualization of games as one form of socializing agent.

The good citizen is an active citizen: Citizenship in the twenty-first century

It is a widely shared value in Western democracies that citizens should engage with political and social issues. This is deemed necessary in order to maintain a healthy functioning democracy, since democracies thrive when citizens are active agents and participate in public debate informing themselves about issues relevant to them in particular and society in general. It is often argued that this informational prerequisite is required in order for citizens to make well-informed decisions in more formal electoral processes and to be able to fully participate in society (Ekman and Amnå 2012). This full participation entails, among other things, voting in local and national elections, being able to identify that a neighbor might need help, and knowing where to go when there is a problem in one's community. In other words, it is expected that citizens know their rights and responsibilities and that they are able to act upon those when necessary. Therefore, being a 'good citizen' relates to the functioning of political and electoral processes (e.g. making an informed decision when voting) also on a societal level (e.g. being concerned with civic issues both on local and national level).

In other words, in order for a democracy to flourish it heavily depends on the civic virtues and the engagement of its citizens (Verba, Schlozman, and Brady 1995; Honohan 2002; Schols 2015). This civic engagement of the active citizenry can roughly be described as all actions that any individual citizen undertakes to change something for the better that affects not just him- or herself, but also the broader community he or she is part of. These actions can, for example, be described as, but are not limited to, volunteering to help out other people in need, taking part in a demonstration for equal rights or signing a petition to help free a fellow citizen from wrongful imprisonment. Citizens speaking up and being concerned with their communities and social surroundings benefits democracy overall. The formal institutes of power, like for example the government, are thus made accountable and, as such, are forced to listen to the people, which, in turn, guarantees quality of government and a healthy and thriving democracy.

What this means in practical terms has been, in particular in the last decades, reason for heated debates, both in- and outside of academia (Dahlgren 2006, 2009). For most Western democracies, active citizenship used to be described via participation in more formal institutions or volunteer work, but also membership in a political party. This tendency is also reflected in academic research that has measured the degree of good and active citizenship using the aforementioned characteristics. For over a decade, for example, the authoritative International Social Survey Program (ISSP) has used four categories of citizenship to assess what good citizenship should entail according to respondents: Participation (e.g. importance of voting and being active in politics); autonomy (e.g. being able to form one's own opinion); social order (e.g. obeying the law); and solidarity (e.g. supporting people who are worse off) (see also Dalton 2008). These surveys are used worldwide, both nationally (e.g. the General Social Survey in the United States) and internationally (e.g. the European Social Survey).

However, these questions mainly address the normative conceptualizations of the 'good citizen' according to citizens themselves. It describes, in other words, what a 'good citizen' should be doing and not what citizens actually do. And while there is a predictable discrepancy between citizens' civic values and their actual behavior, expressions of these values were seen to be rather stable. Up until about the start of the twenty-first century, in most Western democracies civic values relating to social order were valued to be more important to good citizenship than any others (Dalton 2008). This duty-based citizenship expresses itself in the acts citizens perform in relation to society (as the community of citizens). Among these social acts, political party membership was relatively high, as was union membership, as well as the self-evident duty to vote in elections.

Increasingly, however, there have been signs that citizens seem to be participating less, at least in these formal institutions (Kerr et al. 2009). A research study by Hoskins, Villalba, and Saisana (2012) shows that younger generations particularly lack the civic competences needed to be(come) successful active citizens and that these competences have been in decline over the past several decades among European youth. These results are in line with previous research that signals a steady decline in civic engagement in general and political participation in particular over the course of the last half century (e.g. Craig 1996; Levine and Lopez 2002; Lopez and Donovan 2002; Wattenberg 2002). Most known in this respect is perhaps Robert Putnam's work *Bowling alone*, in which he argues that "declining electoral participation is merely the most visible symptom of a broader disengagement from community life" (2000, 35), but he is surely not alone in this analysis (e.g. Kaase and Newton 1995; Norris 2002).

However, with the increase in main stream internet access in most Western democracies around the turn of the century, quite a few opposite readings of the state of democracy started to emerge. Rather than seeing a decline in engagement and participation, some scholars started to recognize a fundamental change in the way citizens engage and actively participate. In particular, online participatory practices were celebrated (e.g. Jenkins

2006; Jenkins and Carpentier 2013; Thorson et al. 2013; Kligler-Vilenchik and Shresthova 2014; Jenkins, Ito, and boyd 2016). It has been acknowledged that patterns of engagement and participation that are visible offline can also be seen online (e.g. Smith 2013; Gainous and Wagner 2014), so enthusiasts remain confident in their argument that democracy is thriving. They point out that young people increasingly show high levels of participation and engagement, but that they show this in different ways than before (e.g. Stolle and Hooghe 2005; Rainie et al. 2012; Schols 2015).

These different ways of participating and engaging with political and civic matters were for a long time not regarded as political practices. This might be one way to understand the contrasting readings of the state of democracy as outlined above. More recently, however, these different approaches are beginning to be reflected at the conceptual level with changes in the measurement of political participation and civic engagement. Joakim Ekman and Erik Amnå (2012), for example, propose a new typology for participation and engagement that makes a clear distinction between manifest (i.e. political participation including formal political behavior) and latent (i.e. civic engagement and social involvement) forms of participation. The idea of latent forms of participation is especially crucial in understanding these newer forms of political behavior.

A more fundamental explanation of the aforementioned contradictory results might be to take generational differences into account regarding the very notion of what citizenship entails. In other words, what it means for citizens to be a 'good citizen' changes and has been changing over the last several decades. This is best reflected in a shift in people's views concerning the importance of the different civic values discussed earlier. Rather than emphasizing the importance of contributing to and interacting with democracy's formal institutions (reflected in party memberships, for example, which translates into a dutiful form of citizenship), it has become increasingly important, especially but not only for younger generations to express their political and civic engagement in different ways (Bennett 2008; Bennett, Wells, and Freelon 2011). Dalton (2008) refers to this as the difference between dutiful and engaged citizenship, also referred to as allegiant and assertive citizens (Dalton and Welzel 2014). Interestingly, this is also reflected in a change in the importance of civic values. So-called allegiant citizens value social order more (e.g. obeying the law), while assertive citizens place more importance on autonomy (e.g. being able to form your own opinion in your own way) and solidarity (e.g. supporting those who are worse off) as markers of good citizenship (Hoskins, Villalba, and Saisana 2012).

Additionally, Chouliaraki (2010) argues that citizenship should be conceptualized as expressing oneself in public. This seems increasingly relevant with more opportunities to express oneself and engage online. Self-mediation in this sense might be at the core of engagement and participation and lead to new forms of playful citizenship. She states that:

> This mediated participation of ordinary people in public culture is being hailed as blurring traditional boundaries between media producers and consumers, and leading to new forms of playful citizenship, critical discourse and cosmopolitan solidarity. Drawing on a view of self-mediation as a new terrain of democratisation that is, however, embedded within the regulative regimes of the market or the state, [we should] critically explore the dynamics of mediated participation as an ambivalent discourse that is shifting the sensibilities and practices of citizenship. (Chouliaraki 2010, 227)

For Chouliaraki (2010, 3), the ability to express yourself in order to make yourself visible and audible is key here. Therefore, creating and sharing content online constitutes an act of citizenship and should be considered as a form of citizen performance and voicing. In this sense, the changing media landscape, particularly the rise of the gaming industry, most definitely plays a significant role in the further exploration of playful citizenship.

Media landscape: Games as socializing agents and informal contexts

Games have increasingly been the focus of academic research and the field of game studies has matured over the last two decades (Raessens 2016). Game studies as an interdisciplinary field examines games from a communicative, psychological, design, and Humanities perspective approaching games as simulations, representations, and cultural artifacts (e.g. Le Diberder and Le Diberder 1998; Aarseth 2001; Frasca 2003b; Raessens and Goldstein 2005; Bogost 2007). Games are and have been celebrated for the specific properties they bring to the table. These characteristics seem to be particularly beneficial in settings where a player wishes to explore and experiment while also being able to experience the consequences that his or her choices might have (Jansz 2005; Squire 2007; Neys and Jansz 2010).

Games offer "a set of experiences a player participates in from a particular perspective, namely the perspective of the character or characters the player controls" (Gee 2007, 23). Within a game, the player often has to achieve certain goals to progress further. Players can decide on their own how to achieve these goals by making their own choices (within a certain framework). There is also a system of immediate feedback in place that tells the player (in more or less clear terms) what the consequences of their actions are and how these might be improved. In this way, games in general encourage players to interpret their experiences in certain ways and to seek explanations for their errors and expectation failures. Additionally, the practice of gaming is often set in a social setting as well. It is not uncommon for players to seek each other out and to discuss strategies or to solve problems related to the game (sometimes referred to as 'augmented play,' see Ito et al. 2009). As a result, the social network around the game is equally important in the overall gaming experience as the game play itself (Squire and Jenkins 2003; Gee 2007). The medium of the game can, in this sense, be regarded as a socializing agent.

The positive effects of playing games have been established in many different domains. These include, for example, increasing students' motivation to learn in a school environment, the acquisition of more expert knowledge and digital skills, as well as improving the performance of surgeons (Lieberman 2006; Ritterfeld and Weber 2006; Gee 2007; Goris, Jalink, and Ten Cate Hoedemaker 2014). There are three reasons usually given for these effects. The first focuses on the entertaining properties of games: games are perceived as "possibly the most engaging pastime in the history of mankind" (Prensky 2005, 101). The second factor concerns the interactive nature of games: playing a digital game is impossible without the active involvement of the players (Cover 2006). Consequently, players must pay attention to what they are doing and what they see on their screens. Gonzalo Frasca (2003b) points out that this means games offer distinctly different rhetorical possibilities; games offer different tools for conveying opinions and feelings than do more traditional media that depend heavily on the mechanism of narrative representation. Games, in contrast, mostly rely on the mechanism of simulation. This also becomes clear when considering the third point. The truly unique properties of games arguably lie in their expressive power. According to Bogost (2007), digital games are an expressive medium. They visually represent how real and imagined systems work and invite their players to interact with those systems in a playful manner. The capacity of games to reveal complex situations (Mitgutsch 2011b) in a relatively simple and often fun way is what distinguishes this medium from other, more traditional, media forms (see also Corbeil 1999).

However, while there gradually seems to be an increasing academic interest in the uses and effects of games in different areas of people's lives, to date little attention has been given to the opportunities games might offer in relation to politics and citizenship. A notable exception is the research by Kahne, Middaugh, and Evans (2009), which explores the civic potential of video games in general. They argue that "gaming might foster civic engagement" (2009, 6). Since their focus is on the civic dimensions of video game play among young people, they have investigated what games have to offer youth regarding civic and political engagement compared to more traditional classroom settings. They find many parallels both in the structural form of the medium of the game (e.g. possibilities for some sort of simulation of part(s) of the political process and tools that facilitate collaboration and mentoring) as well as in the content of some games (e.g. learning how certain democratic processes work, learning about a particular event (war) or social issue (poverty), how to debate and share and form one's own opinion). Following Dewey's conceptualization of the democratic community, Kahne and his colleagues argue that games can be considered such places as well. This is particularly the case with the increase of participatory culture as described by Jenkins (2006) and Kligler-Vilenchik and Shresthova (2012). In this way, games can be seen as "places where diverse groups of individuals with shared interests join together, where groups must negotiate norms, where novices are mentored by more experienced community members, where teamwork enables all to benefit from the different skills of group members, and where collective problem-solving leads to collective intelligence" (Kahne, Middaugh, and Evans 2009, 6-7).

Moreover, there has also been research on the civic potential of Massive Multiplayer Online Role-Playing Games, or MMORPGs, such as Blizzard Entertainment's *World of Warcraft* (e.g. Steinkuehler 2005; Curry 2010), as a 'third place' for civic development. The results of these studies seem to confirm previous findings that playing such games may help develop collaboration and leadership skills in general (Whitton and Hollins 2008; Jang and Ryu 2011) and willingness to help (Peng, Lee, and Heeter 2010). Furthermore, Raphael et al. (2010) suggest in their study that the "most effective games for civic learning would be those that best integrate game play and content, that help players make connections between their individual actions and larger social structures, and that link ethical and expedient reasoning" (2010, 199) to spark ethical reflection among their players. In addition, they obtained similar results as Kahne, Middaugh, and Evans (2009), who focused on how different civic skills were practiced and learned through gameplay (Raphael, Bachen, and Hernández-Ramos 2012).

The playful environment and social structure that the medium of the game offers is particularly relevant in this respect. In line with political socialization theory, when considering the game as a socializing agent, this medium can be regarded as one of the most important influences on how young people learn civic skills and engage in civic activities beside family and school. These finding are also supported the research of Bourgonjon and Soetaert (2013) as well as Lin and her colleagues (2010). This is especially relevant when we take into consideration the aforementioned shift, especially among younger people, toward more engaged forms of citizenship that value expression, autonomy, and solidarity more highly as traits of good citizenship.

Of particular interest in light of this chapter are games that are specifically aimed at affecting some sort of social change, that is, some form of attitudinal or behavioral change with their players. While such games have been studied for some time, it is only recently that this subdomain has required significant academic attention. Usually referred to as serious games,[1] they can be defined as games that aim to do more than entertain only (Ritterfeld, Cody, and Vorderer 2009, 6; Bellotti et al. 2013). The creator of the game specifically intends the game to be more than just entertainment, he wants it to inform even more, or even persuade the player in a playful yet serious manner.

Political video games: Games with an impact[2]

Ian Bogost (2007) coined the term persuasive games as a response to the dichotomy (still commonly used) of entertainment games versus serious games. He argues that the aforementioned terminology wrongfully suggests that entertainment games are not suited to communicating serious messages (i.e. to be used for something other than just mere entertainment). Moreover, the term 'serious games' alludes to an almost exclusive focus on game content, rather than on the process of communication of the specific medium. This procedural aspect of gaming is what allows for the communication of serious information in such a unique way. The term 'persuasive gaming' reflects the centrality of this procedural rhetoric while at the same time focusing on those games that challenge given norms and worldviews. As

1 This specific delineation from entertainment games, particularly trying to define what these serious games are *not*, has left the field of game studies with a myriad of different terms that aim to capture this difference (e.g. games for change, social games, political games, etc.). For the purpose of this chapter, we will refer to such games as serious games or, when discussing the specific subfield of interest, political games.

2 Parts of this section have appeared, slightly altered, in an earlier publication, namely Neys (2014).

such, the intent of the creator of the game to persuade the player is also important in defining it as a persuasive game (De la Hera 2017).

There are many different forms of persuasive games addressing different topics and developed by different stakeholders. There are games that focus on health issues, e.g. *Re-Mission* (Realtime Associates 2006), which shows children undergoing cancer therapy the importance of adhering to their medical treatment programs; on social awareness or advocacy, e.g. *McDonald's Video Game* (MolleIndustria 2006), which is concerned with the meat industry and its negative impact on society; on humanitarian crises, e.g. *Darfur is Dying* (interFUEL 2006), which deals with the famine in Darfur and its effect on local families; or games that promote a particular company or organization, called 'advergames.' The military makes use of these types of games as well, both for recruiting and instruction. *America's Army* (2002) is probably the most successful and well-known example in this regard. The United States Army, developer of the game, claimed a significant increase in recruitment information requests due to this game alone (Huntemann and Payne 2010).

The political subgenre of these persuasive games specifically focuses on games that challenge certain political stances or worldviews or address political issues. In order to fully appreciate and understand the different games available within this subgenre, the different parties that can develop such games should be taken into account alongside the topic or issue they address. This differentiation mainly happens in three dimensions: political institutions (such as political parties), non-profit organizations (such as the United Nations or HopeLab), and individuals.

Now that we have defined political video games and the theoretical background is set, we can explore and situate the empirical findings in this field and try to understand whether or not this form of play might offer citizens new and different ways of engaging in politics.

Playing political video games: Civic engagement and political participation

While the subgenre of political video games is small, the field is diverse in terms of the type of games it has to offer. And while *The Cat and The Coup* (Brinson and ValaNejad 2011) and *Endgame: Syria* (GameTheNews 2013) are two of the few relatively recent examples, it is not surprising that, as most of these games are created in the West (primarily in the United States or Western Europe), so the little research that has been conducted in this field also stems from these regions.

At the turn of the century, the first political video games started to appear. Several games emerged particularly in the aftermath of the terror attacks in New York on 9/11 2001. A good example is *September 12th* by Gonzalo Frasca (2003a). The game shows a market square where citizens and terrorists can be seen walking around. The player has the choice to shoot rockets at the market to kill the terrorists. However, a shot, no matter how well aimed, always results in civilian casualties, which, in turn, leads to some of the grieving survivors turning into terrorists as well. The intent of the creator was to inform players of the importance of a political stance (such as, that violence will only generate more violence) and to make them reflect on this issue, much like political cartoons (Bogost 2006; Neys and Jansz 2010).

After 2004, political video games became a true, albeit small, subgenre. This mainly had to do with the emergence of political video games during the political campaigns for the United States general elections. In that year, *The Howard Dean for Iowa Game* (Persuasive Games 2003) was developed by the American Democratic Party; it was one of the first games commissioned for the United States general elections and, as such, added to the overall success of Howard Dean in harnessing the potential use of the internet for campaigning. Its aim was to help supporters of Howard Dean to understand grassroots outreach and to encourage them to participate in pre-caucus campaigning in Iowa.

Bogost (2006) advocates the analysis of the games themselves in order to scrutinize their use of procedural (rather than verbal) strategy to convey their messages. His work is important for the field of game studies in that it recognizes the subgenre of political video games as persuasive media. It is only after this work emerged that slowly the first exploratory studies started to appear that focus on citizens' responses to such games and have adopted the practice of gaming as the main focus of their research.

After just over a decade of research, the general tenure of these studies overall is positive. There is some evidence that suggests that playing political video games contributes to an increase in political participation and civic engagement (Neys and Jansz 2010; Waddington 2013). After playing political games, players indicate that they have become more engaged with the topic discussed in the game and have obtained more knowledge about the subject. They also indicate their intent to participate in more formal ways, for example by contacting an interest group (Neys and Jansz 2010). Jacobs (2016) studied *My Cotton Picking Life* (Rawlings 2012) about child labor in the cotton industry, comparing the effects of the game with those of a video clip covering the same issue. He found that playing the game had a stronger effect than watching the clip when experiencing the workload of the children. In their study about *Darfur is Dying*, Peng and her colleagues (2010) observed that people's willingness to help increased after playing. They compared video game play with text and video about the same topic, namely the famine in Darfur. They concluded that, when compared to the other two media formats, "playing [the game] resulted in greater willingness to help and greater role-taking" (Peng, Lee, and Heeter 2010, 735).

The effects on social behavior are especially evident when people talk with friends and family about the issues addressed in the game. This is also referred to as "social facilitation" (Neys and Jansz 2010) or "civic talk" (Klofstad 2011). This relates back to conceptualizing such games as socializing agents that play a role in the political socialization of their players. In other words, it shows that the effects and impact of playing these games should always be set in the context of everyday life, and not be regarded as isolated events. Raessens (2015) concurs with this point of view in his analysis of *Darfur is Dying* and *Food Force* (Deepend 2005). The focus of his analysis is conceptual rather than empirical. He argues that the game experience of being 'co-creator' results in a "forceful discursive space and practice, with real enough power to influence the terms in which people think, feel and act" (2015, 258).

This becomes even more apparent when looking at longer term effects, as illustrated by our own research (Neys et al. 2012) on *Poverty Is Not a Game* (iMinds 2010). This game was developed by the European Union in relation to the European year against poverty and social exclusion (see also Grove et al. 2012). The game aims to raise awareness and to discuss the complex mechanisms underlying poverty, especially among youth. The study questioned players immediately after playing the game and again three months later through self-report measures. As was expected, the intended political behavior measured immediately after playing scored higher than the actual political behavior after three months.

The results point toward the indirect effects of playing: the player's interest in and engagement with the topic in question (poverty) increased and, as such, had an indirect effect on participation. About one third of the players indicated that they had become more politically interested after the three months period. In fact, while these players indicated at the time of the first measurement that they were not politically interested, after three months they self-reported that they *had* become politically interested. Further investigation of this particular group showed that, again, social facilitation or civic talk was what appeared to be important for this process (Neys et al. 2012). While it is impossible to make any causal claims about what caused this positive change in political interest, research shows that it was this same group that indicated they had talked with their family and peers about the subject of poverty the most. Playing the game can then be regarded as the instigator, while talking might have, at least partly, facilitated an increase in political interest or at least facilitated a change in perception about whether or not players identify as politically interested. Playing the game arguably transformed players' understanding of their world in relation to the topic discussed in the game. Ruggiero (2015) observed a sleeper effect in her longitudinal study among players of *Spent* (McKinney, Urban Ministries of Durham 2011), a game about homelessness. The game did not have an effect immediately after playing, but when the participants were tested again three weeks later, the players held more favorable attitudes toward homelessness than those who did not play. Apparently, playing the game resulted in prolonged reflection on its subject matter.

This kind of transformative learning is exemplary for how games work. According to Konstantin Mitgutsch (2011a), this shows the distinctive power of games when compared to more traditional media. However, while academic research into game features, and the workings and mechanisms of (serious) games are increasing (e.g. Bellotti et al. 2013; Jacobs, Jansz and De la Hera 2017), the field is not currently able to make more authoritative claims about the way political video games do or do not engage their players in the long run.

Conclusion

This chapter has explored whether playing political video games can facilitate civic engagement and, if so, how it encourages political participation. While research is still scarce in this particular niche field of game studies, we can conclude in general that most, if not all, research generated positive results. Playing games in general, and political games in particular, does seem to facilitate some form of engagement and participation.

After discussing the first studies conducted on the issue of political games, we can carefully conclude that people do seem to become engaged with the topic or issue dealt with in the game after playing. It does seem to be the case, however, that these effects are of a transformational nature, meaning that "the perceived and achieved learning *in* the game and the contextualized and framed learning experience made *through* playing the game are transferred" (Mitgutsch 2011b, 51). The experiences in the game over time get applied to real life contexts and in this way, affect the player. The research so far suggests that the process of social facilitation is important in this respect, namely talking with friends and peers about the issue dealt with in the game (Neys and Jansz 2010). In this way, the game functions as an instigator where players reflect on the issue in terms of what it means to them personally. As such, games can be considered as socializing agents. This makes sense as, after all, games and gaming are part of everyday life.

It is evident, however, that more research is needed in this field. Longitudinal research should further investigate the long-term effects, while more comparative research is necessary to investigate the differences between games and other media. Representative and larger samples of players will also help in validating the first conclusions that were drawn here. It is also important to determine exactly who plays these games and if only people play such games that are already interested in politics. There are some promising indications that playing political games might also benefit those who do not think of themselves as politically interested. This challenging question is the topic of further investigation in this young and promising field which can shed light on contemporary forms and expressions of citizenship.

Acknowledgments

This research is part of the project *Persuasive gaming. From theory-based design to validation and back*, funded by the Netherlands Organisation for Scientific Research (NWO; 2013-2018; project number 314-99-106).

References

Aarseth, E. J. 2001. Computer game studies, year one. *Game Studies* 1 (1): 1-15.

Bellotti, F., B. Kapralos, K. Lee, P. Moreno-Ger, and R. Berta. 2013. Assessment in and of serious games: An overview. *Advances in Human-Computer Interaction* 2013:1-11.

Bennett, W. L. 2008. Changing citizenship in the digital age. In *Civic life online: Learning how digital media can engage youth*, ed. W. L. Bennett, 1-24. Cambridge, MA: The MIT Press.

Bennett, W. L., C. Wells, and D. Freelon. 2011. Communicating civic engagement: Contrasting models of citizenship in the youth web sphere. *Journal of Communication* 61 (5): 835-856.

Blizzard Entertainment. 2004. *World of Warcraft*. [Windows/OS X]. Blizzard Entertainment. Game.

Bogost, I. 2006. *Unit operations: An approach to videogame criticism*. Cambridge, MA: The MIT Press.

—. 2007. *Persuasive games: The expressive power of videogames*. Cambridge, MA: The MIT Press.

Bourgonjon, J., and R. Soetaert. 2013. Video games and citizenship. *CLCWeb: Comparative Literature and Culture* 15 (3). http://docs.lib.purdue.edu/clcweb/vol15/iss3/8.

Brinson, P., and K. ValaNejad. 2011. *The Cat and the Coup*. [Windows]. Game.

Chouliaraki, L. 2010. Self-mediation: New media and citizenship. *Critical Discourse Studies* 7 (4): 227-232.

Corbeil, P. 1999. Learning from the children: Practical and theoretical reflections on playing and learning. *Simulation and Gaming* 30 (2): 163-180.

Cover, R. 2006. Audience inter/active: Interactive media, narrative control and reconceiving audience history. *New Media and Society* 8 (1): 139-158.

Craig, S. 1996. *Broken contracts: Changing relationships between Americans and their government*. Boulder, CO: Westview Press.

Curry, K. 2010. Warcraft and civic education: MMORPGs as participatory cultures and how teachers can use them to improve civic education. *The Social Studies* 101 (6): 250-253.

Dahlgren, P. 2006. Doing citizenship: The cultural origins of civic agency in the public sphere. *The European Journal of Cultural Studies* 9 (3): 267-286.

—. 2009. *Media and political engagement: Citizens, communication and democracy*. New York: Cambridge University Press.

Dalton, R. J. 2008. *The good citizen: How a younger generation is reshaping American politics*. Washington, DC: Congressional Quarterly Press.

Dalton, R. J., and C. Welzel, eds. 2014. *The civic culture transformed: From allegiant to assertive citizens*. New York: Cambridge University Press.

De Grove, F., J. van Looy, J. Neys, and J. Jansz. 2012. Playing in school or at home? An exploration of the effects of context on educational game experience. *E-Journal of e-Learning* 10 (2): 199-208.

De la Hera, T. 2017. Persuasive gaming: Identifying the different types of persuasion through games. *International Journal of Serious Games* 4 (1): 31-39.

Deepend. 2005. *Food Force*. [browser]. United Nations World Food Programme. Game.

Ekman, J., and E. Amnå. 2012. Political participation and civic engagement: Towards a new typology. *Human Affairs* 22 (3): 283-300.

Frasca, G. 2003a. *September 12th*. [browser]. Newsgaming. Game.

—. 2003b. Simulation versus narrative. Introduction to ludology. In *The Video Game Theory Reader*, eds. M. Wolf and B. Perron, 221-236. New York: Routledge.

Frissen, V., S. Lammes, M. de Lange, J. de Mul, and J. Raessens, eds. 2015. *Playful identities: The ludification of digital media cultures*. Amsterdam: Amsterdam University Press.

Gainous, J., and K. M. Wagner. 2014. *Tweeting to power: The social media revolution in American politics*. London: Oxford University Press.

GameTheNews. 2013. *Endgame: Syria*. [browser/Android/iOS]. Game.

Gee, J. P. 2007. *Good video games, good learning: Collected essays on video games, learning, and literacy*. New York: Peter Lang Publishing Inc.

Goris, J., M. B. Jalink, and H. O. ten Cate Hoedemaker. 2014. Training basic laparoscopic skills using a custom-made video game. *Perspectives on Medical Education* 3:314-318.

Honohan I. 2002. *Civic republicanism*. London: Routledge.

Hoskins, B., E. Villalba, and M. Saisana. 2012. *The 2011 civic competence composite indicator (CCCI-2): Measuring young people's civic competence across Europe based on the IEA international citizenship and civic education study*. Luxembourg: Publication office of the European Union.

Huntemann, N. B., and M. T. Payne, eds. 2010. *Joystick soldiers: The politics of play in military video games*. New York: Routledge.

iMinds. 2010. *Poverty Is Not a Game*. [browser]. Game.

interFUEL. 2006. *Darfur is Dying*. [browser]. mtvU. Game.

Ito, M., J. Antin, M. Finn, A. Law, A. Manion, S. Mitnick, D. Schlossberg, S. Yardi, and H. A. Horst. 2009. *Hanging out, messing around, and geeking out: Living and learning with new media*. Cambridge, MA: The MIT Press.

Jacobs, R. S. 2016. Play to win over: Effects of persuasive games. *Psychology of Popular Media Culture*. http://psycnet.apa.org/doi/10.1037/ppm0000124.

Jacobs, R. S., J. Jansz, and T. de la Hera. 2017. The key features of persuasive games: A model and case analysis. In *New perspectives on the social aspects of digital gaming: Multiplayer 2*, eds. R. Kowert and T. Quandt, 153-171. New York: Routledge.

Jang, Y., and S. Ryu. 2011. Exploring game experiences and game leadership in massively multiplayer online role-playing games. *British Journal of Educational Technology* 42 (4): 616-623.

Jansz, J. 2005. The emotional appeal of violent video games for adolescent males. *Communication Theory* 15 (3): 219-241.

Jenkins, H. 2006. *Confronting the challenges of participatory culture: Media education for the twenty-first century (white paper)*. Chicago, IL: MacArthur Foundation Digital Media and Learning Program.

Jenkins, H., and N. Carpentier. 2013. Theorizing participatory intensities: A conversation about participation and politics. *Convergence: The International Journal of Research into New Media Technologies* 19 (3): 265-286.

Jenkins, H., M. Ito, and d. boyd. 2016. *Participatory culture in a networked era*. Malden, MA: Polity Press.

Kaase, M., and K. Newton, eds. 1995. *Beliefs in government.* Oxford: Oxford University Press.

Kahne, J., E. Middaugh, and C. Evans. 2009. *The civic potential of video games.* Cambridge, MA: The MIT Press.

Kerr, D., L. Sturman, W. Schulz, and B. Burge. 2009. *ICCS 2009 European report. Civic knowledge, attitudes, and engagement among lower-secondary students in 24 European countries.* Amsterdam: IEA.

Kligler-Vilenchik, N., and S. Shresthova. 2012. *Learning through practice: Participatory culture civics.* MacArthur Foundation. http://ypp.dmlcentral.net/sites/all/files/publications/Learning%20Through%20Practice_Kligler-Shresthova_Oct-2-2012.pdf.

—. 2014. "Feeling that you are doing something": Participatory culture civics. *Conjunctions. Transdisciplinary Journal of Cultural Participation* 1 (1). http://www.conjunctions-tjcp.com/article/view/18604.

Klofstad, C. A. 2011. *Civic talk: Peers, politics, and the future of democracy.* Philadelphia, PA: Temple University Press.

Le Diberder, A., and F. Le Diberder. 1998. *L'univers des jeux vidéo.* Paris: La Découverte.

Levine, P., and H. M. Lopez. 2002. *Youth voter turnout has declined, by any measure.* Center for Information and Research on Civic Learning and Engagement. http://civicyouth.org/research/products/Measuring_Youth_Voter_Turnout.pdf.

Lieberman, D. A. 2006. What can we learn from playing interactive games? In *Playing video games: Motives, responses, and consequences*, eds. P. Vorderer and J. Bryant, 379-395. Mahwah, NJ: Lawrence Erlbaum.

Lin, W. Y., P. H. Cheong, Y. C. Kim, and J. Y. Jung. 2010. Becoming citizens: Youths' civic uses of new media in five digital cities in East Asia. *Journal of Adolescent Research* 25 (6): 839-857.

Lopez, H. M., and C. Donovan. 2002. *Youth and adult voter turnout from 1972-2002.* Center for Information and Research on Civic Learning and Engagement. http://www.civicyouth.org/PopUps/FactSheets/FS_Youth%20turnout1972_2002.pdf.

McKinney, Urban Ministries of Durham 2011. *Spent.* Game.

Mitgutsch, K. 2011a. Playful learning experiences. Meaningful learning patterns in players' biographies. *International Journal of Gaming and Computer-Mediated Simulations* 3 (3): 54-68.

—. 2011b. Serious learning in serious games. Transformative learning in video games. In *Serious games and edutainment applications,* eds. M. Ma, A. Oikonomou, and L. C. Jain, 45-58. New York: Springer.

Molleindustria. 2006. *McDonald's Video Game.* [browser]. Molleindustria. Game.

Neys, J. 2014. *Social media political gaming.* In *Sage encyclopedia of social media and politics,* ed. K. Harvey, 1171-1173. London: Sage Publications.

Neys, J., F. de Grove, J. van Looy, and J. Jansz. 2012. Poverty is not a game: Behavioral changes and long-term effects after playing PING. In *Proceedings of the 62nd annual conference of the International Communication Association, Phoenix, May 24-28, 2012.*

Neys, J., and J. Jansz. 2010. Political internet games: Engaging an audience. *European Journal of Communication* 25 (3): 227-241.

Norris, P. 2002. *Democratic phoenix: Reinventing political activism.* New York: Cambridge University Press.

Peng, W., M. Lee, and C. Heeter. 2010. The effects of a serious fame on role-taking and willingness to help. *Journal of Communication* 60 (4): 723-742.

Persuasive Games. 2003. *The Howard Dean for Iowa Game.* [browser]. Game.

Prensky, M. 2005. Computer games and learning: Digital game-based learning. In *Handbook of computer game studies,* eds. J. Raessens and J. H. Goldstein, 97-122. Cambridge, MA: The MIT Press.

Putnam, R. D. 2000. *Bowling alone: The collapse and revival of American democracy.* New York: Simon and Schuster.

Raessens, J. 2006. Playful identities, or the ludification of culture. *Games and Culture* 1 (1): 52-57.

—. 2014. The ludification of culture. In *Rethinking gamification,* eds. M. Fuchs, S. Fizek, P. Ruffino, and N. Schrape, 91-114. Lüneburg: meson press.

—. 2015. Playful identity politics: How refugee games affect the player's identity. In *Playful identities: The ludification of digital media cultures,* eds. V. Frissen, S. Lammes, M. de Lange, J. de Mul, and J. Raessens, 245-260. Amsterdam: Amsterdam University Press.

—. 2016. Game studies. In *The international encyclopedia of communication theory and philosophy,* eds. K. B. Jensen, R. T. Craig, J. D. Pooley, and E. W. Rothenbuhler, 1-5. Hoboken, NJ: Wiley.

Raessens, J., and J. Goldstein, eds. 2005. *Handbook of computer game studies.* Cambridge, MA: The MIT Press.

Rainie, L., A. Smith, K. L. Schlozman, H. Brady, and S. Verba. 2012. *Social media and political engagement.* PEW Research Center. http://pewinternet.org/Reports/2012/Political-Engagement.aspx.

Raphael, C., C. Bachen, K. M. Lynn, J. Baldwin-Philippi, and K. A. McKee. 2010. Games for civic learning: A conceptual framework and agenda for research and design. *Games and Culture* 5 (2): 199-235.

Raphael, C., C. Bachen, and P. F. Hernández-Ramos. 2012. Flow and cooperative learning in civic game play. *New Media & Society* 14 (8): 1321-1338.

Rawlings, T. 2012. *My Cotton Picking Life.* [browser]. GameTheNews. Game.

Realtime Associates. 2006. *Re-Mission*. [Windows]. HopeLab. Game.

Ritterfeld, U., M. Cody, and P. Vorderer. 2009. Introduction. In *Serious games: Mechanisms and effects,* eds. U. Ritterfeld, M. Cody, and P. Vorderer, 3-10. New York: Routledge.

Ritterfeld, U., and R. Weber. 2006. Video games for entertainment and education. In *Playing video games: Motives, responses, and consequences,* eds. P. Vorderer and J. Bryant, 399-413. Mahwah, NJ: Lawrence Erlbaum.

Ruggiero, D. 2015. The effect of playing a persuasive game on attitude and affective learning. *Computers in Human Behavior* 45:213-221.

Schols, M. 2015. *Young, online and connected.* PhD thesis Erasmus University Rotterdam.

Smith, A. 2013. *Civic engagement in the digital age.* PEW Research Center: http://pewinternet.org/Reports/2013/Civic-Engagement.aspx.

Squire, K. 2007. Games, learning, and society: Building a field. *Education Technology* 47 (5): 514.

Squire, K., and H. Jenkins. 2003. Harnessing the power of games in education. *Insight* 3 (1): 5-33.

Steinkuehler, C. A. 2005. Cognition and learning in massively multiplayer online games: A critical approach (Doctoral dissertation). Available from ProQuest Dissertations and Theses database (UMI No. 982810331).

Stolle, D., and M. Hooghe. 2005. Inaccurate, exceptional, one-sided or irrelevant? The debate about the alleged decline of social capital and civic engagement in western societies. *British Journal of Political Science* 35 (1): 149-167.

Thorson, K., K. Driscoll, B. Ekdale, S. Edgerly, L. Gamber Thompson, A. Schrock, L. Swartz, E. K. Vraga, and C. Wells. 2013. YouTube, Twitter and the Occupy movement: Connecting content and circulation practices. *Information, Communication & Society* 16 (3): 421-451.

United States Army. 2002. *America's Army.* [Windows/PS4]. United States Army. Game.

Verba, S., K. Schlozman, and H. Brady. 1995. *Voice and equality: Civic voluntarism in American politics.* Cambridge, MA: Harvard University Press.

Waddington, D. I. 2013. A parallel world for the World Bank: A case study of *Urgent: Evoke,* an educational alternate reality game. *Revue Internationale des Technologies en Pédagogie Universitaire* 10:42-56.

Wattenberg, M. 2002. *Where have all the voters gone?* Cambridge, MA: Harvard University Press.

Whitton, N., and P. Hollins. 2008. Collaborative virtual gaming worlds in higher education. *ALT-J, Research in Learning Technology* 16 (3): 221-229.

About the authors

Jeroen Jansz holds the Chair of Communication and Media in the Department of Media & Communication at Erasmus University Rotterdam. He is a member of the Erasmus Research Centre for Media, Communication, and Culture. His research is about the reception of new media. The appeal of digital games is a long-standing research interest. He is co-founder of the Game Studies Division in the International Communication Association, a member of PEGI's expert group (Pan European Game Information) and President of NeFCA, the Netherlands Flanders Communication Association.

Joyce Neys is a PhD candidate at the Erasmus Research Centre for Media, Communication and Culture at Erasmus University Rotterdam. She is currently working on the research project *Empowered citizens: How new media facilitate civic engagement* under supervision of Prof. Jeroen Jansz. The project investigates how citizens use different forms of new media as a political tool. In particular, she is interested in citizens who create their own media content, such as online political video games, political remix videos, and political machinimas. Neys is also a lecturer in the International Bachelor Communication and Media program at Erasmus University Rotterdam where she teaches statistical analysis and new media and civic engagement.

3. Analytical game design: Game-making as a cultural technique in a gamified society

Stefan Werning

Abstract
This chapter aims to show how designing and modifying games is becoming a "cultural technique" (Kramer and McChesney 2003) similar to reading or writing, and an important requirement for active citizen engagement in an increasingly ludified society (Raessens 2006). For that purpose, "constructionist gaming" (Kafai and Burke 2015), i.e. game co-creation, is situated among other critical playing practices like theorycrafting. Numerous examples, from early Flash games created as commentary on the 2003 invasion of Iraq to game jams such as the 2013 *GeziJam*, demonstrate how grassroots game development can establish ephemeral public spheres for playful citizen intervention. Finally, the chapter outlines analytical game design as a conceptual framework for incorporating these principles into media studies research and educational practice.

Keywords: Analytical game design, constructionist gaming, playful citizenship, cultural techniques, game design literacy

Media technologies are connected to the concept of citizenship in manifold ways and the rapid changes in media technologies are one important reason why, analogously, the notion of citizenship is rapidly changing. One aspect of citizenship in this context is the capacity to express and discuss one's opinion. In that regard, media institutions like public service broadcasters have been interpreted as an "embodiment" of the notion of the public sphere, i.e. a physical, social or other kind of space for discourse among citizens, thereby becoming a "technology of citizenship" themselves (Nolan 2006, 226).

Glas, R., S. Lammes, M. de Lange, J. Raessens, and I. de Vries, eds. 2019. *The Playful Citizen. Civic Engagement in a Mediatized Culture.* Amsterdam: Amsterdam University Press.
DOI: 10.5117/9789462984523/CH03

This aspect is directly related to the notion of performativity or "performative publicness," which includes "affective and playful dimensions" of social interaction as well as, drawing on the notion of performative utterances, the constitution of "civil selves" (Chouliaraki 2012, 2-4).

A conceptualization of citizenship that is more specifically suited to the premise of this chapter is the notion of 'silly citizenship,' which foregrounds aspects of play, "struggle," (Hartley 2010, 233) and contested identities. Accordingly, citizenship as a concept, an abstraction, has had different connotations in various discourses since its emancipation from the confines of the city in the nineteenth century. Negotiating this "conceptual baggage" and reaffirming the validity of citizenship, according to Hartley, requires a playful attitude (Ibid., 234).

Social spaces that would afford the performance of citizenship are increasingly permeated by layers of software (Kitchin and Dodge 2011) that provide new opportunities, but also come with new types of requirements. Emergent political parties such as the *Piratenpartei* (pirate party) in Germany or the *Partido de la Red* (net party) in Argentina, which represent common citizen sentiments on the level of polity, not only practically draw on software tools like *Liquid Democracy* (Litvinenko 2012) and *DemocracyOS*, but also use programming as a conceptual model of active citizenship and software as a metaphor of how a modern society should function. Douglas Rushkoff aptly summarized this situation using the moniker "program or be programmed" (2010), a phrase that emphasizes the urgency of the situation and the (assumed) lack of a third option. The degree to which the logic (or at least the rhetoric) of program code is gradually becoming embedded into public discourse is reflected by the fact that software has become a metaphor for political organization and for the role of the citizen within it.

However, with the increasing adoption of gamification principles and mechanisms at all different levels of society—including education, corporate training and even tentatively in parts of the public sector (Wood 2013; Asquer 2014), being an independent citizen arguably requires not only basic knowledge of software and programming, but also of games and game design.

Already in the 1950s, sociologist Norton Long proposed that we understand the local community as an ecology of games (Long 1958), a concept that has been repeatedly used to investigate policies even until the present (e.g. Lubell 2013). From this perspective, the manifold dependencies between different sectors of society, including "banking, newspaper publishing, contracting [and] manufacturing" (Long 1958, 251), can be understood as players involved in multiple, partially overlapping games at the same time. While Long focuses on the rationales of the 'players' that, in some cases, have to negotiate different roles, his approach is also relevant from the perspective of the game designer, i.e. the policymaker, 'modeling' society as an assemblage of interlocking games.

From this angle, which has become only more plausible in light of the gamification debate, this chapter argues that citizens not only need to be able to assume the player's perspective, but the game designer's as well. They must strive not just to master a given game, but to understand it in terms of its contingencies and potential alternative 'design choices.' One example where this expanded perspective becomes particularly tangible is the ideology of startup ecosystems; software developers adopting the entrepreneural 'persona' by definition use digital technology to at least partially rewrite the rules of a particular social 'game' (e.g. Uber for urban mobility and Airbnb for accommodation) rather than playing the traditional game more effectively.

With reference to 'end users,' the notion of "retail hacking" (Schwartz 2010) already tentatively indicates how an applied understanding of game design helps to address socio-economic issues. The term refers to the fact that consumers (particularly from low-income families that would otherwise have problems affording the amenities of everyday life) gradually combine and exploit the manifold coupon and rebate schemes offered by large retailers (originally for their own economic benefit) to multiply their savings and to continue participating in society despite their financial troubles. While this situation is not explicitly game-like, the terminology and rhetoric used by retail hackers[1] indicates that they construct (or 'design') their consumption practices as a de-facto game with the goal of maximizing value-for-money. For instance, techniques like 'stacking' and 'rolling' are—both conceptually and terminologically—reminiscent of power gaming and 'combo' systems. By taking rules from different 'sub-games' (the individual rebate schemes), they build a new game that, according to their self-perception, maximizes their agency as citizens and economic subjects.

Thus, the goal of this chapter is to show how, similar to reading, writing, and communicating, designing and modifying games is becoming a 'cultural technique' (for an overview of the term and its connotations see Kramer and McChesney 2003) for active citizen engagement in an increasingly ludified society (Raessens 2006, 2014). In terms of citizenship, 'cultural techniques' constitute the required skills to participate in public spheres and in social negotiation processes. More broadly, the term refers to culturally

1 The term 'hacking', at least outside of criminal activities, already exhibits a conceptual link to a playfully irreverent disposition (Stober, Walz, and Holopainen 2013).

formative practices, which are practices that afford cultural production, exchange and archiving/remembrance in the first place, but also develop their own characteristic quasi-cultural contexts over time. For instance, even though he does not explicitly use the term, Jay Bolter shows how speech and, more broadly, even thought processes are significantly influenced by the materiality of writing and the "writing space" (2001). A similar argument can be made for digital games as well; that is, if written words serve as an interpretive filter for oral rhetoric, 'writing' games can be conceived of as a filter for playing and interpreting games, for not just thinking about games, but also thinking 'through games'.

The following section will prepare a more detailed understanding of game-making as a cultural technique by looking at how playing practices have turned games into cognitive tools and how game creation itself is becoming a playful activity.

From productive playing practices to playful game production

With the increasing abundance of games available and the increasing differentiation of player audiences, it comes as no surprise that, over time, playing practices have become much more diversified, going well beyond the initial aim of 'mastering' the game. More specifically, many of these practices can be understood as productive, even genuinely 'analytical.' Even in the early days of the field of game studies, the "demystification" (Friedman 1999) of the (digital) game as a system stood out as a central motivation. Ted Friedman furthermore usefully points out that—in opposition to film reception, one might add—players approach identification from a procedural perspective; in the case of *SimCity* (Maxis 1989), for instance, they switch between different identificatory positions (mayor, treasurer, head of police, etc.) to interpret the simulated system from different angles rather than build an 'empathetic' relationship with any of them.

More recently, theorycrafting has been investigated (e.g. Paul 2011) as an increasingly formalized set of playing practices aimed at understanding the rule system of a game, down to its variables and algorithms, by strategically testing and documenting the observable systemic behavior rather than simply 'playing to win.' It is important to note that this highly idiosyncratic and seemingly arbitrary behavior is intrinsically political, it represents a more or less conscious attempt at challenging (albeit not really altering) the political economy of the games industry. In that sense, i.e. in terms of its 'quasi-political' agenda, theorycrafting is comparable to spoiling (Jenkins

2006), a more well-studied, subversive practice of television reception. Moreover, the games that theorycrafters play are often 'virtual worlds' (usually MMORPGs or hybrid games like *Destiny* (Bungie 2014)), continuously changing systems that 'encourage' players to experiment with policies and more or less formalized patterns of social control.

Theorycrafting is not the only recent playing practice that can be considered intrinsically 'analytical,' though. For instance, in-game photography (e.g. Poremba 2007), the act of taking pictures (or, more precisely, screenshots) in digital games rather than playing by the rules, can be understood as analytical on several levels. First, it draws on the player's photographic gaze to produce a new understanding of the virtual environment according to the rationales of photography such as mise en scène and framing. Second, based on the types of 'photographs' taken, it appears that this practice allows for players to re-investigate established pictorial genres such as landscape photography, still life, and portraits, with regard to seemingly anachronistic notions like aura (Duttlinger 2008).[2] Finally, professional in-game photographers adopt an analytical stance in that they document the parameters in which a photo is taken, thus allowing others to reflect on the 'material' contingencies, develop a media-reflexive view, and re-produce or modify selected aesthetic strategies.

While playing practices thus become more 'productive' and analytical over time, inversely, game development can also increasingly be understood as a genuinely playful and simultaneously analytical, knowledge-producing practice. This play element obviously is most visible in independent game development, which is internally organized through game jams (Guevara-Villalobos 2011), competitions to create games within self-imposed constraints,[3] rather than hierarchy and technical specialization as well as standardization. However, professional game development also embraces aspects of playfulness. For example, Birdwell describes how the game *Half-Life* (Valve 1998) was created by taking apart the original prototype and, for instance, requiring designers to take an arbitrary set of parts and recombine them in novel, fun ways (1999). Moreover, Van der Graaf illustrates how Linden Lab, the developer of *Second Life* (2003), introduced a virtual currency called "love scores" (2012, 486) that employees could receive from

2 A prominent archive of highly sophisticated in-game photographs can be found in Harris (2018).

3 Apart from the set theme that every game jam participant has to follow, the Global Game Jam offers a selection of 'modifiers', additional thematic requirements that allow for contestants to choose their own 'difficulty level'.

other colleagues or award to their colleagues, thereby incentivizing them to help each other out; even though 'love' is paid out as a bonus each quarter, this is still a mostly tongue-in-cheek, highly idiosyncratic way of fostering group identity through 'playful' interaction. On that note, the following section will explore what kind of knowledge game-making can produce.

Between ludoliteracy and algorithmic literacy

One of the first steps toward game design becoming a 'cultural technique' is *Adobe Flash*, an authoring system that, while originally developed for designing interactive animations, has been among the first tools that opened up game creation to a broader, more mainstream audience. *Adobe Flash* has already been studied from a software studies perspective (e.g. Sorapure 2006), for example with regard to how it affects writing practices despite being originally intended primarily for multimodal composing. However, for the purpose of this argument, *Adobe Flash* is particularly relevant because it allowed for accelerating the creation of simple, digitally sharable applications.

Take, for instance, the Flash games created in response to the US invasion of Iraq in 2003, which journalist Clive Thompson described as the "newest form of social comment" (Thompson 2002). Many of the games Thompson describes convey a rather blatant (only in some cases "procedural") rhetoric (Bogost 2007, 52) or use pop-cultural and game-specific references and metaphors to connote the events of 9/11. However, a few outstanding examples such as *New York Defender* (Stef & Phil 2001) can even be described as positively "persuasive" (Ibid., 59ff.) and at least enable players to potentially reassess the subject matter using genuinely game-specific means.

Apart from easy-to-use functions for collision detection and player interaction via mouse, keyboard, and gamepad, the most notable affordance of *Adobe Flash* as a tool to promote game creation was the *Flash Player*, a browser plug-in that quickly became ubiquitous and facilitated the distribution of Flash-enabled games. In terms of game development as a 'cultural technique,' this is relevant for multiple reasons. The accumulation of Flash games on platforms like *Newgrounds* shifted the focus from the often still trivial individual games toward the sheer quantity of games and, thus, made the amateur game developer community 'visible' for the first time, both for a mainstream audience and its own members. Put differently, the Flash game websites act as platforms that employ a set of socio-technical mechanisms (Niederer and Van Dijck 2010) to foster group identity, to allow the community to grow organically, and to incentivize peer review in addition to learning from one another. For instance, the rating system on a site like *Newgrounds* allows newcomers to already earn some recognition without having to compete on 'equal ground' with more established developers and still constitutes an attention economy that motivates veterans to push the envelope and aim for ever higher scores.

The gradual 'demise' of Flash (Salter and Murray 2014) is an important event in software history and culture. However, for the purpose of this chapter, it is even more noteworthy because existing, more dedicated game-creation tools like *RPG Maker* (1988-), *Game Maker* (1999-), and entry-level 3D engines like *Unity 3D* (2005-) eventually became the first point of contact with algorithmic thinking and scripting for media users that grew up with video games, a fact that indicates the increasing convergence of ludoliteracy (Zagal 2010) and algorithmic literacy. As indicated above, creating games, both from an amateur and independent game perspective, is becoming intrinsically playful; at the same time, game design—conceptualizing a given subject matter by way of rule systems—becomes intrinsically technical, shaped by material affordances and constraints. The following section will elaborate on how these developments are relevant in terms of citizen engagement and politically mindful media use.

Analytical game design as playful citizen engagement

Experimental games already exhibit clearly observable tendencies to use digital games as a medium of socio-political expression. For example, *Twine* (2009-) is a freely available, highly accessible, and thus popular tool that allows for creating experimental text-based games. At the same time, it notably enhances the use of game design as a form of public expression because it increases the thematic and rhetorical diversity of digital games, allowing for the expression of otherwise marginalized viewpoints. Unsurprisingly, some of the most notable *Twine* games tackle issues like gender identity and subcultural sensibilities, which otherwise rarely have a place in either commercial or independent game design.

Furthermore, as amateur game developers become more confident in the use of tools as well as procedural rhetoric, contributions to game jams increasingly address socially relevant or even political themes. For example, the *Game of Politics* (Telnov et al. 2012), created for the Global Game Jam 2012, is a deck-based card game about political decision-making and the election process. Conceptually very similar, but developed three years later,

Vox Populi (Lewis and Henley-Roussel 2015) is also a game based on physical playing cards, in which, "[a]s your party's campaign organizer, you must forgo every principle, make any deal you can, and screw over everyone else in order to grasp the reins of power." In comparison, *Doctrine* (Mielczarek et al. 2014) tackles the broader issue of divergent political ideologies and employs less 'naturalistic' design mechanics, using colored filters worn as headgear and differently colored messages to indicate how ideologies can make a person 'blind' toward non-conformist opinions.

Smaller game jams are occasionally even 'designed' and leveraged as tools for political participation themselves. For instance, the *GeziJam* was held in June 2013 to support and raise awareness of the protesters trying to stall the destruction of the Taksim Gezi Park in Istanbul. The conceptually related *#JamForLeelah* reflected on the suicide of Leelah Alcorn in December 2014 and challenged participants to tackle the issue of transgender sensibilities through the creation of games. In some cases, game developers are trying to monetize this awareness and create games to raise funds for socio-political causes. For instance, the game *Kubba* was created by Ahmed Abdelsamea (2012), an Egyptian indie designer, to generate revenue benefiting the refugees of the Syrian civil war (Curley 2012). The game mimics the more or less iconic Western game franchise *Cooking Mama* (Office Create 2006), challenging players to prepare the eponymous Syrian dish, Kubba. The game is a variation of the earlier Flash game *Ta'mya* (2012); yet, while the original has English text and is available on *Kongregate*, a website hosted by United States games retailer *GameStop*, *Kubba* was only playable on the now-defunct Arabic equivalent *GameTako*.

Yet, most of these experimental games usually operate according to the logic (or, with Michel Foucault, the dispositif) of art rather than education. They all have a 'product form,' a defined beginning, middle, and end including some sort of menu system. The aforementioned game jams exhibit several structural similarities to the system of festivals and awards that constitutes an important infrastructure for art in its currently practiced sense and, in itself, is unmistakably game-like (English 2005). Games developed by scholars or 'reflective' industry practitioners are sometimes even commissioned 'as art,' i.e. they are ordered and paid for by institutions formally or informally related to the 'art world' (Becker 1982) or publishing industry. Ian Bogost's *Simony* (2012) and Jason Rohrer's *Game Design Sketchbook* experiments are but two prominent examples. Second, they are sometimes displayed 'as art' in the context of a thematically integrated exhibition; again, Bogost's *Simony* as well as many games by Tale of Tales clearly illustrate this principle. Third, they are often discussed and framed in terms of art discourse, focusing on common tropes such as the creator persona (e.g. Rohrer's *Gravitation* (2008)), the subversion of expectations, or a media-reflexive habitus (e.g. Bogost's *Cow Clicker* (2010)).

In comparison, the concept of *Analytical Game Design*, which is phenomenologically explored at the Utrecht Game Lab, defines a methodological framework to translate the notion of game-making to the educational domain and, as a potential second step, to political participation. The concept draws on the Kuleshov experiments, a series of film vignettes—often only a few seconds long—produced by directors like Kuleshov and Pudovkin in the 1920s, which systematically explore the expressive 'vocabulary' of film as a then-new medium (Prince and Hensley 1992). While these experiments are still acknowledged for their aesthetic values and originality, it is important to note that they originated in an experimental culture of film-making; thus, considering the Kuleshov experiments and the countless re-creations that have been created over time, both by film students and acclaimed directors, it appears that the individual experiment does not primarily create knowledge, but instead the process of creating and comparing multiple variations on the same theme and of sharing one's own interpretation by playfully remixing it.[4]

Adhering to these principles, 'analytical' game experiments as defined by the Analytical Game Design framework are:

- vignettes, not 'complete' games;
- built on existing media and cultural studies research;
- intended to test hypotheses and challenge user preconceptions;
- easily modifiable and remixable;
- an ongoing process by constituting a 'dialog' with the enabling technologies ascognitive tools;
- usually abstract in terms of audio-visual detail and semantics;
- published in a way that affords discussion and multiplicity;
- and (optionally) utilizing analytics for non-commercial purposes.[5]

Few existing games can be considered 'theory-driven'; for instance, while Dan Pinchbeck has implemented some of his academic inquiries into first-person gaming and "ludic manipulation" (2009) in games like *Amnesia: The Dark*

4 Looking up the Kuleshov experiment on YouTube provides an overview of the manifold ways in which the same experiment has been interpreted—by famous directors and film students alike—over the years.

5 For more detailed information, see the slides of a panel on the topic, organized at the 2016 DiGRA/FDG conference in Dundee (Werning 2016).

Descent (Frictional Games 2010), other games by the same author/company are only belatedly reflected upon, for instance in terms of environmental storytelling (Pinchbeck 2008). Will Wright's *SimEarth* (Maxis 1990), a later instalment in the franchise started by *SimCity*, is one of the few games based on a theory, the highly contested, but still influential Gaia hypothesis (Bogost 2006, 167) proposed by James Lovelock and co-developed by Lynn Margulis in 1972 and beyond. The hypothesis holds that organisms and inorganic matter on Earth organize to form a self-sustaining complex system; thus, it proposes a set of relationships between co-existing species and a number of system variables such as global temperature, the amount of oxygen in the air, or salt in the oceans. The model is conceptually ideally suited to formalize activities on a global scale for use in a video game, particularly given the technological constraints in the early 1990s. The game arguably not only presents an 'interpretation' of and commentary on the hypothesis, but it also uses it as part of a particular rhetoric, which is—with Bogost—a persuasive strategy.

The notion of Analytical Game Design aims for an even more direct relationship between theoretical background and ludic implementation. For example, Seymour Chatman famously analyzed different modes of narrative in literature and films with a close comparative reading of Guy de Maupassant's *Une partie de campagne* and Jean Renoir's 1936 film adaptation (Chatman 1980). Chatman proposes a set of categories for his analysis, including concepts such as description vs. assertion (128), ambiguity (132), and focalized narration as well as evoking the reader's perceived complicity with the morally dubious disposition of the narrator (133). While no games exist that systematically explore these categories,[6] designing game experiments would be a fruitful way to tackle these questions and to 'translate' Chatman's approach of close-reading to (digital) games. The inherently playful quality of this approach is acknowledged by Stephanie de Smale, who expands on the concept and reads analytical game experiments against Theodor W. Adorno's notion of the essay as form (2016, 4).

While the previous example pertains more to representations of individual perceptions, the same can be done on a broader scale, including representations of social and cultural phenomena. Simulation games like the aforementioned *SimCity* or *Civilization* (MPS Labs 1991) exhibit interesting cultural stereotypes through their attempts to express common perceptions given the

6 This statement might have to be relativized a bit, as games like *Gone Home* (The Fullbright Company 2013) for instance can be interpreted as playing with the 'mode' of description. However, no games do so in a truly systematic and iterative manner.

characteristic constraints of their rule systems. For example, while religious buildings have been implemented in *Civilization* as 'tools' to pacify discontent citizens, later instalments like *Civilization IV* and *V* (Firaxis Games 2005, 2010) systematically elaborate on the concept, repeatedly altering the intrinsic rule bias. In that sense, consecutive instalments in the same franchise and especially player-created modifications, which alter the game's procedural rhetoric and introduce multiplicity instead of one authoritative set of game rules (Werning 2017), can be understood as intrinsically 'experimental' in that they modify parameters and processes, thereby making them observable and accessible for discussion through the players.

To summarize, games and the playful wrestling with (often self-imposed) constraints have been used as a tool to overcome established patterns of thinking. In the context of artistic production, this approach has been formalized by collectives like *Oulipo* (Andrews 2012), but it can also be observed in the aesthetic principles of the Dada movement (Prager 2013), or in the work of composers like John Cage and John Zorn. Toy designer Shimpei Takahashi demonstrated the principle in a 2013 TEDxTokyo presentation using examples of his own. Ideally, using games as a conceptual reference point, the same approach can be applied in contemporary socio-political contexts, in which problems regularly arise from applying standardized thinking to new types of challenges (which is, as McLuhan argued, because "politics offers yesterday's answers to today's questions"; quoted from Genosko 2005, 235).

Conclusion

The goal of this chapter has been to demonstrate how, not least through novel production and distribution tools like *Unity 3D* and *itch.io*, game-making is gradually developing into a cultural technique and an opportunity for citizens to understand and shape their social environment. Thus, returning to Rushkoff (2010), the extension of 'program or be programmed' cannot just be 'play or be played'; instead, being able to (co-)create games oneself is an important next step to altering the power relations built into the contemporary gamification of society.

Since this chapter was designed to be exploratory, rather than focusing on just one particular case, many issues could only be touched upon and require further investigation. The role of game distribution websites constitutes only one fruitful opportunity for further research. For instance, while platforms like *Newgrounds* arguably do not constitute a proper 'public sphere' in the sense of Habermas, they can alternatively be understood as 'third places.'

The term, which Ray Oldenburg originally coined to describe hybrid spaces between home and work environments, such as cafés and community centers, has already been applied to online games themselves (Steinkuehler and Williams 2006), but the concept could also be brought to fruition to analyze the functions of game distribution platforms as sites of mediated citizen engagement and game-based public discourse.[7]

A second way to extend the perspective outlined above would be to go beyond actual game creation. For instance, research on war games on the corresponding online forums indicates that, even without the technical means to change them, players intrinsically interpret and discuss digital games in terms of their design contingencies, and therefore their potential alternatives. For instance, players of *America's Army* (United States Army 2002) request and discuss the inclusion of new weapons based on their experience with televised documentaries (Werning 2009, 318). From that angle, modding (the modification of commercial games, often using freely supplied tools) constitutes an interesting hybrid case. For instance, one *Civilization V* mod called *Emigration* includes 'emigration' as a new gameplay mechanic, which addresses the increasing mobility of citizens both within a country and across borders. The mod can be understood as a comment on the political bias of the original game because its rules incentivize players to 'use' emigration as an offensive strategy ("[d]evelop your empire and your rival's citizens will leave their homeland for your prosperous country").[8] Another mod for the same game called *FIFA World Cup Host Resolution* even delivers a more targeted 'message' by utilizing *Civilization V* to 'expose' FIFA's intrinsic system of power by introducing 'migrant workers' as new unit types. While the host game does not allow for a very naturalistic rendering of the FIFA context, particularly the effort and inevitable inconsistencies of trying to 'express' this system under the constraints of the game's modding tools spark controversy and necessitate a thorough, critical engagement with the subject matter at hand. For good reason, serious games like the *Democracy* series (Positech Games 2005-) have been developed with mod-ability in mind, both to keep the game relevant over a longer period of time and to alleviate the discrepancy between 'players' and 'designers'.

Finally, a culturally comparative perspective on game creation and the notion of 'cultural techniques' would be a useful extension of the argument presented in this chapter. For instance, the developer of the aforementioned

7 One need only look at the plethora of (still often mundane but increasingly reflective) games created as 'comments' on contemporary elections, see Newgrounds (2018).

8 See the 18 May 2013 update in the change notes of the mod (Valve 2018).

Flash game *Kabba* argues that "[p]olitical activism is common in Arab-made indie games" (Johnson 2012). This suggests that 'collective' or at least culturally formative experiences can have a profound impact on game creation, a hypothesis that would by definition substantiate the claim that game-making already constitutes a 'cultural' technique.

References

Abdelsamea, A. 2012. *Kubba*. [browser]. GameTako. Game.

Andrews, C. 2012. Constraints, poetry and play in Jacques Roubaud's Parc Sauvage. *Australian Journal of French Studies* 49 (2): 142-152.

Asquer, A. 2014. Not just videogames: Gamification and its potential application to public services. In *Digital public administration and e-government in developing nations*, ed. E. F. Halpin. 146-165. Hershey, PA: IGI Global.

Becker, H. S. 1982. *Art worlds*. Berkeley, CA: University of California Press.

Birdwell, K. 1999. The cabal: Valve's design process for creating half-life. *Gamasutra. The Art & Business of Making Games*. http://www.gamasutra.com/view/feature/3408/the_cabal_valves_design_process_.php.

Bogost, I. 2006. Videogames and ideological frames. *Popular Communication* 4 (3): 165-183.

—. 2007. *Persuasive games: The expressive power of videogames*. Cambridge, MA: The MIT Press.

—. 2010. *Cow Clicker*. [Facebook]. Ian Bogost. Game.

—. 2012. *Simony*. Museum of Contemporary Art, Jacksonville. Multimedia artwork.

Bolter, J. D. 2001. *Writing space: Computers, hypertext, and the remediation of print*. New York: Routledge.

Bungie. 2014. *Destiny*. [multiplatform]. Activision. Game.

Chatman, S. 1980. What novels can do that films can't (and vice versa). *Critical Inquiry* 7 (1): 121-140.

Chouliaraki, L., ed. 2012. *Self-mediation: New media, citizenship and civil selves*. London: Routledge.

Curley, N. 2012. GameTako launches online game to benefit Syrian refugees. *Wamda*. http://www.wamda.com/2012/07/gametako-launches-online-game-to-benefit-syrian-refugees.

De Smale, S. 2016. Game essays as critical media and research praxis. In *Proceedings of the first international joint conference of DiGRA and FDG, Dundee, August 1-6, 2016*. http://www.digra.org/wp-content/uploads/digital-library/paper_2351_revised.pdf.

Duttlinger, C. 2008. Imaginary encounters: Walter Benjamin and the aura of photography. *Poetics Today* 29 (1): 79-101.

English, J. F. 2005. *The economy of prestige: Prizes, awards, and the circulation of cultural value.* Cambridge, MA: Harvard University Press.

Firaxis Games. 2005. *Civilization IV.* [Windows/OS X]. 2K Games/Aspyr. Game.

—. 2010. *Civilization V.* [Windows/OS X/Linux]. 2K Games/Aspyr. Game.

Frictional Games. 2010. *Amnesia: The Dark Descent.* [multiplatform]. Frictional Games. Game.

Friedman, T. 1999. The semiotics of Sim City. *First Monday* 4 (4). http://firstmonday.org/htbin/cgiwrap/bin/ojs/index.php/fm/issue/view/104.

Genosko, G. 2005. *Marshall McLuhan: Renaissance for a wired world.* New York: Routledge.

Guevara-Villalobos, O. 2011. Cultures of independent game production: Examining the relationship between community and labour. In *Proceedings of Think Design Play: The fifth international conference of the Digital Game Research Association, Hilversum, September 14-17, 2011.* http://www.digra.org/dl/db/11307.08157.pdf.

Harris, D. 2018. DET. *Deadendthrills.* http://deadendthrills.com/game-index.

Hartley, J. 2010. Silly citizenship. *Critical Discourse Studies* 7 (4): 233-248.

Jenkins, H. 2006. *Convergence culture: Where old and new media collide.* New York: New York University Press.

Johnson, J. 2012. Can a Flash game improve the lives of Syrian refugees? *Kill Screen.* http://killscreen.com/articles/can-flash-game-improve-lives-syrian-refugees.

Kitchin, R., and M. Dodge. 2011. *Code/space: Software and everyday life.* Cambridge, MA: The MIT Press.

Kramer, S., and A. McChesney. 2003. Writing, notational iconicity, calculus: On writing as a cultural technique. *MLN* 118 (3): 518-537.

Lewis, D. J., and M. Henley-Roussel. 2015. *Vox Populi.* [Windows]. Global Game Jam. Game.

Litvinenko, A. 2012. Social media and perspectives of liquid democracy: The example of political communication in the Pirate Party in Germany. In *Proceedings of the 12th European conference on e-government, Barcelona, June 14-15, 2010,* 403-407. Reading: Academic Publishing International.

Long, N. E. 1958. The local community as an ecology of games. *American Journal of Sociology* 64 (3): 251-261.

Lubell, M. 2013. Governing institutional complexity: The ecology of games framework. *Policy Studies Journal* 41 (3): 537-559.

Maxis. 1989. *SimCity.* [multiplatform]. Maxis/Brøderbund/Infogrames. Game.

—. 1990. *SimEarth.* [multiplatform]. Maxis. Game.

MPS Labs. 1991. *Civilization.* [multiplatform]. MicroProse. Game.

Mielczarek, G. et al. 2014. *Doctrine.* [Windows]. Global Game Jam. Game.

Newgrounds. 2018. Searching the games portal for 'election'. *Newgrounds.* http://www.newgrounds.com/portal/search/games/election.

Niederer, S., and J. van Dijck. 2010. Wisdom of the crowd or technicity of content? Wikipedia as a sociotechnical system. *New Media & Society* 12 (8): 1368-1387.

Nolan, D. 2006. Media, citizenship and governmentality: Defining 'the public' of public service broadcasting. *Social Semiotics* 16 (2): 225-242.

Office Create. 2006. *Cooking Mama.* [iOS/Android]. Office Create Corp. Game.

Paul, C. A. 2011. Optimizing play: How theorycraft changes gameplay and design. *Game Studies* 11 (2). http://gamestudies.org/1102/articles/paul.

Pinchbeck, D. 2008. Dear Esther: An interactive ghost story built using the Source engine. In *Interactive storytelling*, eds. U. Spierling and N. Szilas, 51-54. Berlin, Heidelberg: Springer Berlin Heidelberg.

—. 2009. Shock, horror? First-person gaming, horror, and the art of ludic manipulation. In *Horror video games: Essays on the fusion of fear and play*, ed. B. Perron, 79-94. Jefferson: McFarland.

Poremba, C. 2007. Point and shoot. Remediating photography in gamespace. *Games and Culture* 2 (1): 49-58.

Positech Games. 2005. *Democracy* [Windows/OS X/Linux]. Positech Games/ Tri-Synergy. Game.

Prager, P. 2013. Play and the avant-garde: Aren't we all a little dada? *American Journal of Play* 5 (2): 239-256.

Prince, S., and W. E Hensley. 1992. The Kuleshov effect: Recreating the classic experiment. *Cinema Journal* 31 (2): 59-75.

Raessens, J. 2006. Playful identities, or the ludification of culture. *Games and Culture* 1 (1): 52-57.

—. 2014. The ludification of culture. In *Rethinking gamification*, eds. M. Fuchs, S. Fizek, P. Ruffino, and N. Schrape, 91-114. Lüneburg: meson press.

Rohrer, J. 2008. *Gravitatian.* [Windows/MacOS/Linux]. Jason Rohrer. Game.

Rushkoff, D. 2010. *Program or be programmed: Ten commands for a digital age.* New York: OR Books.

Salter, A., and J. Murray. 2014. Marking new ground: Flash, HTML5 and the future of the web arcade. In *Proceedings of the 9th international conference on the foundations of digital games, Liberty of the Seas, Caribbean, April 3-7, 2014.* http://www.fdg2014.org/papers/fdg2014_paper_27.pdf.

Schwartz, M. 2010. The coupon rebellion. *Wired Magazine* 18 (12): 188-193-224.

Sorapure, M. 2006. Text, image, code, comment: Writing in Flash. *Computers and Composition* 23 (4): 412-429.

Stef & Phil. 2001. *New York Defender.* [browser]. Game.

Steinkuehler, C. A., and D. Williams. 2006. Where everybody knows your (screen) name: Online games as 'third places'. *Journal of Computer-Mediated Communication* 11 (4): 885-909.

Stober, J., S. Walz, and J. Holopainen. 2013. Hacking as a playful strategy for designing artistic games. In *Context matters! Proceedings of the Vienna games conference 2013: Exploring and reframing games and play in context*, eds. K. Mitgutsch, S. Huber, J. Wimmer, M. G. Wagner, and H. Rosenstingl, 308-321. Vienna: New Academic Press.

Telnov, J. et al. 2012. *Game of Politics.* [Windows]. Global Game Jam. Game.

Thompson, C. 2002. Dot-columnist: Online video games are the newest form of social comment. *Slate*, August. http://www.slate.com/articles/technology/webhead/2002/08/dotcolumnist.html.

United States Army. 2002. *America's Army.* [Windows/PS4]. United States Army. Game.

Valve. 1998. *Half-Life.* [Windows/OS X/PS2]. Sierra Studios. Game.

—. 2018. Steam community: Emigration: Change notes. *Steam.* http://steamcommunity.com/sharedfiles/filedetails/changelog/115134695.

Van der Graaf, S. 2012. Get organized at work! A look inside the game design process of Valve and Linden Lab. *Bulletin of Science, Technology & Society* 32 (6): 480-488.

Werning, S. 2009. *Real wars on virtual battlefields: The convergence of programmable media at the military-civilian margin.* Bielefeld: transcript Verlag.

—. 2016. DigraFDG2016: From practice-based game research to game design as cultural technique. *Slideshare.* http://www.slideshare.net/stefanwerning/digrafdg2016-from-practicebased-game-research-to-game-design-as-cultural-technique.

—. 2017. Modding as a strategy to (de-)legitimize representations of religion in the civilization franchise. In *Participatory digital cultures and contemporary discourses of (de)legitimization*, eds. A. S. Ross and D. J. Rivers. London: Routledge.

Wood, C. 2013. Gamification: Governments use gaming principles to get citizens involved. *Government Technology.* http://www.govtech.com/local/Gamification-Governments-Use-Gaming-Principles-to-Get-Citizens-Involved.html.

Zagal, J. P. 2010. *Ludoliteracy: Defining, understanding, and supporting games education.* Pittsburgh, PA: ETC Press.

About the author

Stefan Werning is an Associate Professor for Digital Media and Game Studies at Utrecht University. He holds a degree in North-American Studies from Bonn University (Germany), a PhD (2010) in Media Studies from Bonn University and received his habilitation (2014) from Bayreuth University (Germany). Previously, he worked as an Assistant Professor in Bayreuth and Bonn. Stefan has been a visiting scholar (2005) and fellow (2006-2010) in the program in Comparative Media Studies at MIT. He worked in the digital games industry while completing his PhD research, most notably at Codemasters (2005) and Nintendo of Europe (2007-2009).

4. Re-thinking the social documentary

William Uricchio

Abstract

This chapter reflects on how people actively engage with interactive documentaries and how this constitutes a shift in audience participation. As a playful format, interactive documentaries invite viewers to also become creative participants. The author makes a convincing case for the civic potential of allowing viewers to play with the documentary film format, foregrounding the interactive documentary as a potent challenger to its traditional, linear, and author-driven counterpart. He speaks in this context of a 'producerly' audience that has an active input in the documentary textual interactive system. Uricchio speaks of interactive documentaries as a new media format, that does not so much replace existing, more hieratically structured media formats, but rather can exist alongside them as a participatory alternative.

Keywords: Interactive documentary, audience participation, producerly audience, playful media formats

It is happening again. The documentary, long underappreciated for its transformational impact on film form, is again offering new ways of representing and intervening in the world. Only this time, rather than simply using new techniques to represent social change, the documentary form is itself the subject of social and technological change. Documentary marks the place where our representational endeavors come face-to-face with reality. Little wonder that Vertov's attempts to position film as part of a social network remain so relevant, and that Direct Cinema and Cinema Verite's efforts to redefine the filmmaker-subject relationship had such a large impact (Singer 1987; Saunders 2007). Today, at a moment when location-aware mobile HD video cameras are nearly ubiquitous, where networked computers have broken the distribution bottleneck, and where game play,

Glas, R., S. Lammes, M. de Lange, J. Raessens, and I. de Vries, eds. 2019. *The Playful Citizen. Civic Engagement in a Mediatized Culture.* Amsterdam: Amsterdam University Press.
DOI: 10.5117/9789462984523/CH04

crowd-sourcing, and the social turn have redefined media practice and enabled widespread participation, documentary makers have been quick to respond. This chapter will explore the implications of these new voices, of the new, playful, interactive organizational logics and the new social and political enablement of the documentary form.

First, a few words about the stakes of change. As will be discussed, the ongoing transformation in documentary promises to empower new voices, encouraging 'the people formerly known as subjects'[1] to participate in their own representation and have a hand in shaping their texts (see Lessig 2015, 37). It engages its users in interactive environments, offering opportunities to interrogate, explore, and comment upon ideas. Moreover, it enables global access, is available anytime, and is actively pushed through social recommendation networks. Still too emergent to be 'hard-baked' into orthodox practice, fixed definition, or even a broadly agreed upon agenda, I shall refer to this direction as *interactive documentary*, including within it not just non-linear textual structures that must be navigated by the user, but location-based and crowd-sourced documentaries as well, since these, too, belie fundamental forms of interaction with text, place, and public.[2]

In the pages ahead, I would like to explore developments in this sector, describing some of their key attributes, locating the 'new' within the historical practices from which they have emerged, and considering their challenges to our inherited notions of narrative and engagement. Particularly in this last regard, the narrative potentials of play will loom large, offering useful ways to reconsider the operations—and implications—of interactive documentary.

The digital dynamics underlying the interactive documentary (Nichols 1991; Galloway, McAlpine and Harris 2007; Aston and Gaudenzi 2012) are familiar, for we have seen them ripple through the music industry, take form in phenomena such as Wikipedia, and re-shape the nature of political campaigns. Thanks to networked digital technologies, the old divides between producers and consumers, between experts and the crowd, between the center and the margins, have weakened, taking new and sometimes unfamiliar forms. At a moment when Moore's Law continues its geometric progression of ever more powerful (and even cheaper) processing capacities, consumers now have easier access to audio and video equipment that less than a decade ago was limited to professionals. In 2013, YouTube users

1 Title of a public conversation held by Kat Cizek and Gerry Flahive, 23 October 2012, at MIT's Open Documentary Lab.

2 Other terminology includes i-Docs and web docs.

were posting over 72 hours of video to the site *every minute*; and Facebook essentially required its over one billion active users to construct multimedia, autobiographical timelines on their pages, assembling their photos and video clips, geo-locative maps, links, and diary entries.[3] Both of these examples testify to active popular engagement with digital media production, and while non-fiction is amply evident on YouTube, Facebook has managed to draw its users into the production of something that might reasonably be termed autobiographical mini-documentaries. Profiles are shaped, updated with representations of recent activities, and even augmented by others through 'tagging' functions. While these carefully curated assertions of self may seem rather minimal as documentaries, that over one billion people have sorted out how to construct and navigate them, as they seek to present themselves and keep up with their friends, suggests that the move to participation in the interactive documentary may be far less radical than mainstream linear film and video-makers and scholars might assume.

These developments underscore just how widespread public embrace of digital audio-visual production tools and assembly processes have been. They also reveal considerable levels of social exchange and collaboration and they point to the emergence of new collectivities of social networks unfamiliar to our scholarly traditions. And yet, we inhabit a moment of 'disconnect.' From the perspective of the dominant film and television industries, these widespread activities seem largely peripheral… even insignificant. Box office and television viewing rates remain healthy, and the industry's biggest worries are about how to coordinate content and audiences across multiple media platforms, how to defend their market share against erosion from the game industry, and how to curb piracy. Generally, with the exception of fast-growing interest in the 'second screen,' they have not expressed much curiosity about these new forms of production. When they have, it has either focused on their marketing potential, or given voice to their fears regarding the disruptive potentials of interactive storytelling techniques.

And yet one might argue, as does Henry Jenkins and his colleagues (Jenkins, Ford, and Green 2013), that even in the domain of quotidian media consumption, we see signs not just of an active, but of a 'producerly' public—one that contributes to the textual ecosystem, and one that knows

3 Since then, these numbers have grown exponentially; in September 2016, Youtube statistics sites reported a 416 per cent increase to 300 hours of video uploaded per minute (Statistic Brain 2016). According to a 2011 Pew Internet & American Life Project study, "Fully 71% of online Americans use video-sharing sites such as YouTube and Vimeo, up from 66% a year earlier. The use of video-sharing sites on any given day also jumped five percentage points, from 23% of online Americans in May 2010 to 28% in May 2011" (Moore 2011).

how to pursue its interests across different media platforms and within interactive textual systems. Unlike the 'active' reader celebrated by a generation of literary theorists, where activity largely entailed creative textual engagements and interpretation, these readers take a hand in constructing their own texts from the building blocks and environments made available to them by what would normally be considered the 'producing' side of the equation. But the selection of which textual elements to include, their sequence and pacing, the ability in some cases to make external links or add comments, or in the case of games, to create new structures within a given environment, all transform the 'reader-producer' divide into something far more co-creative and collaborative on a *textual* level. The familiar interpretive level also comes into play, of course, arguably in a reconfigured form since it seems bound up in some of the processes that shape the text and in the condition of textual uniqueness (i.e. versions of texts specific to the individual navigator or player). This combination of textual assemblage and interpretation—required as we move across media platforms and channels—today seems just as routine as the activities of myriad Facebook and YouTube users, and, in its own way, just as productive.

What's happening

It is perhaps worth asserting that our history of the cinematic, in general, is rooted—in particular—in the documentary reflex. The first decade of filmmaking was dominated by *actualité*—phantom train rides, urban panoramas, parades, industrial processes, and the curiosities of the natural and man-made world—continuing a long fascination with the registration of visible evidence that can be found in photography, painting, and panoramic traditions (Uricchio 2011). But one might go on to argue, in terms that echo André Bazin, that the whole enterprise of photo-realist cinematography (as opposed to animation or abstraction), whether deployed for fictional or non-fictional purposes, derives its power from an assumed unproblematic relationship between the recording process and the real materialities of the pro-filmic event, even if, as is often the case with our dramatic fictional traditions, they are enveloped in the impossibility of magic. Much as media scholars can complicate and (rightly) undermine this view, our society's photo IDs and our justice system's reliance on surveillance footage and photographic evidence suggests how deeply rooted are these associations, and how much implication lies bound up within them. And these associations with the 'real,' in turn, help to fuel and support our engagement with fictional worlds. Like the young viewers of the Chinese magician in Vertov's *Man with a Movie Camera* (1929), we are fascinated by that-which-cannot-be-and-yet-seems-to-be. It remains to be seen, in an age of ever-intensifying digital effects, whether this cultural association will persist.[4]

Something transformative is taking place, and as usual in our media history, documentary is the canary in the coalmine. From its start, documentary has connected its audiences with the events of the world. It has offered a shifting metric of media's capacity to expose, represent, engage, and transform that world. And, if we take a broad view of documentary as a discursive mode that is not inherently bound to the motion picture, it has consistently been at the forefront of technological and stylistic change, using its tools to reveal the previously hidden, and to enable its viewers to see the familiar in new ways.[5] The history of photography, and its modulations through stereoscopy, the panorama, and color, returns repeatedly and almost compulsively to depictions of the real as a benchmark of the latest technological turn's ability to 'capture' and document some once-missed aspect of the world. In the case of cinema, as well, not only was the first decennium dominated by the documenting impulse, but filmmakers' earliest uses of innovations such as the moving camera (panoramas and tracking shots of cityscapes), color (Pathé and Gaumont's nature films), and sound (Ruttmann's *Melodie der Welt*, 1929, and Vertov's *Enthusiasm*, 1931) explored the representational capacities by engaging the world around them.

Today's interactive documentary represents the most significant change in documentary form, mode of address and public reach since Direct Cinema and Cinéma Vérité. In the early 1960s, 16mm cameras and portable sound equipment enabled a new relationship between the filmmaker and the subject, resulting in new and distinctive styles of filmmaking that, thanks to television, found new markets and mass audiences just as theatrical outlets for documentary shorts began to fade from sight. Similarly, the interactive documentary arises from the affordances of today's networked digital technologies, redefines the line between makers and publics by enabling creative collaboration, results in new styles and approaches to argument and storytelling, and has the internet at its marketplace. We

4 To be clear, I do not wish to argue for the indexicality of the photographic image, nor to suggest that it is under siege in the digital era; rather, I am making a far softer claim regarding the formation and malleability of cultural associations.

5 See MIT's Open Documentary Lab (2018) for an overview of documentary precedents and contemporary practices.

have seen exponential proliferation of these new documentaries in places like Canada's National Film Board and at the International Documentary Festival Amsterdam's DocLab; they have been pulling in impressive user numbers; they are showing signs of generating significant engagement and impact; and they are finding unexpected support and audiences in radio (Edmond 2015) and the online newspaper (The *New York Times* and Cizek's *Highrise* project, Cizek 2010).

For the record, fixed, linear filmmaking is neither dead, nor dying! It is alive, well, and wonderfully suited for many forms of argument and storytelling. However, its status and meaning are changing thanks to the interactive documentary's twofold impact. On one hand, as part of the larger 'user-generated' churn and breakdown of institutional filters represented by the internet, the rise of interactive documentaries re-contextualizes the status of institutionally produced linear stories. It renders linearity into a choice rather than the only option. On the other hand, it adds new perspective and technique to our expressive repertoire. It potentially maintains the complexity of issues that would be deformed by linearity; it enables new voices to be heard, to speak for themselves; and it enables users to find their own way and pursue their own interests in a story environment. The challenge is to know and be able to articulate which modes of documentation are most effective for a given task. And to the extent that communication is an underlying intent, it also means understanding the needs and tolerances of the audience. We inhabit a culture steeped in thousands of years of great 'linear' storytelling, and it is a tradition that will thrive. But a growing portion of the population also regularly uses interactive forms (games); they also routinely co-create (Facebook, YouTube); and for this population, interactive forms are also basic components of the culture.

As we look at contemporary culture, we can see that our old habits of sitting back and listening to a master storyteller can be complemented by collaborative efforts, as people navigate their way through interactive and location-based experiences, provide footage of *their* experiences and engage in more immediate ways than we have seen before. Notions of 'authorship,' the stable text, and familiar divisions of labor between makers and viewers appear contested and uncertain. The instant temporalities of a connected culture have brought their own challenges, blurring the line between journalism and documentary, precisely at the moment when the institutional traditions behind these practices—the press, the cinema, television—themselves struggle for redefinition. We inhabit a moment of accelerated change, with all of the challenges to the old certainties and inherited traditions that this brings.

Documentary, long identified with a *form*, with the 'linear' media of film and television, has been reborn as a *mission*, as a mode of engagement and interaction that is increasingly agnostic about form. The new documentary, with its challenges to established categories, practices, and behaviors, offers the tantalizing and terrifying possibilities of a *terra incognita*. At the same time, it offers a vantage point from which we can evaluate some of our assumptions and established practices. As it loosens its long association with cinematic and television exhibition (in part because of increasingly limited access to both screens), it increasingly appears on the web within multiple frameworks, including institutions not usually associated with documentary such as radio and press. This shift in locus encourages one to reconsider the taken-for-grantedness of those earlier venues, and to look for other documentary practices 'out there' that we have ignored or categorized out of existence. The changes that are increasingly evident in some sectors of documentary practice have challenged not only established notions of the text and authorship, they have also challenged the institutional assumptions behind documentary production and exhibition. As much as these moves offer promise and possibility, they also offer their share of challenges for the status quo, for our notions of use and impact, and for the very ways that we understand the meaning of the term 'documentary'.

Playing with narrative

Caspar Sonnen, director of Doclab—a festival program for new media within the International Documentary Festival Amsterdam (IDFA)—sometimes explains the difference between the traditional linear documentary and its interactive counterpart with the analogy of visiting a city. Nothing beats a great tour guide—someone knowledgeable about a location's history and meanings, someone who can direct our attention to the many things we would not have otherwise seen, and someone who can tell great stories. On the other hand, we have all had the experience of wandering through cities on our own, and when we do, whether armed with knowledge or not, we attend closely to our environment, keeping an eye on addresses and landmarks (in the hope we can find our way back!), following our interests and desires, making unexpected detours and discoveries, and creating our own stories. It is a useful analogy, as much because it makes clear that neither of these approaches is a threat or inherently superior to the other. They offer different affordances, suit different needs, require different stances. And, I would argue, they both offer narrative engagements.

In his many lectures, MIT's Scot Osterweil uses a different analogy to make a related point. He distinguishes between the experiences of listening to a great storyteller and playing. In the first case, like the guided tour, we are led through experiences we would otherwise not have been privy to, abandoning ourselves to the craft of the narrator who leads us through the carefully plotted structure of the story (Marsh et al. 2011). In the case of play,[6] something many of us abandoned relatively early in life, we imagine, and indeed, co-create a world and its rules, inhabit a character, and have a goal that we share with our playmates. But we have no idea, as we play, whether the good guys will win or not. We do not know what our fate will be. We simply improvise, inhabiting our characters and living the experience as it unfolds. Osterweil argues that this experience, like Sonnen's example of wandering, is profoundly narrative in character. The difference is that Osterweil's notion of play includes notions of character (such as invented, fictional notions), rules that we must adhere to, and an arbitrary goal. As the Creative Director of MIT's Education Arcade—a research lab that produces computer games for learning—Osterweil has a notion of play-as-narrative that unsurprisingly aligns with thinking in the game space, where story outcomes are unknown while the player navigates the diegetic world and its rules.[7]

This may seem an obvious point, but mainstream academic definitions of narrative draw a clear distinction between those events that, like the guided tour and told story, are 'narrated' versions of past or known events; and those that, like wandering on one's own or playing, are indeterminate and simply part of life's experiential flow. In a strict sense, no 'teller' of 'past events' means no narrative. And yet our experience while wandering or playing can seem as immersive, compelling, motivated, and coherent as any story; and in the case of play, it explicitly contains many of the same features (character, setting, rules, and an 'as if' fictional world). This latter point, of course, brings its share of complications to the documentary, but as I will suggest, it also offers important ways to rethink the place of

6 There are, of course, many varieties of play; Osterweil's reference is to character-based play.

7 The appearance of computer games around 1960, and particularly interactive fiction games such as *Zork* (Anderson, Blank, Lebling, and Daniels 1977), signaled a new turn in traditional narrative forms. Interactive literature, emblematized by the work of the Electronic Literature Organization founded in 1999, and interactive 'films', rooted, for example, in the work of MIT's Interactive Cinema Research Group in the late 1980s (or even earlier, in Radúz Činčera's *Kinoautomat* at Expo 67), both attest to the relatively recent emergence of systematic developments in new forms of narrativity. However, as Whitney Anne Trettien reminds us, one can find much earlier precedents, in Trettien's case, going back to the eighteenth century (Trettien 2009).

imagination in the domain of the non-fictional. But first, the problem of what constitutes a narrative.

The 1980s saw both the rise of computer games and the emergence of alternate views regarding narrative. Three broad strategies can be distinguished. The first more or less maintains the existing definition of narrative ('the retelling of past events'), but redefines the player's activity, with some narratologists arguing that the wanderer's or player's consciousness serves as an implicit internal voice and thus provides the 'teller' to just-experienced events, which are technically 'past' by the time they are cognitively processed. A variation on this approach takes such challenges as the 'just-experienced' problem and the indeterminate nature of conclusions, arguing that the narrative is what is constructed retrospectively, after the process is completed, as we remember and retell our experiences. A second strategy takes a more fine-grained approach, stepping back from a grand theory of narrative to focus instead on the micro-structures of narrative, the process by which questions are repeatedly posed and then answered in order to sustain viewer interest and move the overall narrative ahead. Rather than thinking of narrative as an overarching structure of the entire experience (whether Aristotle's or Freytag's 'beginning, middle, and end'), it can instead be understood as the building blocks of an experience, each with its own cycle of 'exposition, transformation, and resolution'.

Storytellers are quite adept at keeping us on the edge of our seats with this technique, interweaving mini-narratives as a means of establishing the characters, settings, and events that will constitute the overall narrative. From this perspective, certain forms of the interactive narrative—such as the interactive documentary or interactive literature—simply disaggregate these 'mini-narratives' from one another, allowing the viewer to reassemble them in a manner that suits her interest. The basic DNA of the narrative—the sequence—stays intact, while the larger assembly process is open to user modification. A third and more radical approach argues that narrative is part of our psychological armature, a way of seeing, rather than a character of the text. Best known as cognitive narratology, here, narrative describes a way of encountering the world, an organizing experience, an existential gestalt (Herman 2009). Created and experienced on the fly, it is situational and does not have to await *post facto* retelling or the aggregation of mini-narratives in order to constitute a narrative experience. Rather, it manifests itself in the perception of coherence and linkage among experienced events. The various claims to support the interactive documentary's narrative status can be found within this spectrum of arguments.

Of course, more than mere argument supports one or another of these approaches to narrative. Interactive documentaries come in many different forms, some of their textual structures adhering rather closely to long established narrative traditions; others, explicitly taking the form of mini-narratives that the user can move among and link; and still others offering rich if disaggregated possibilities to the motivated participant, who can connect the dots into a narrative experience. Some projects (*Alma: A Tale of Violence*, Dewever-Plana and Fougère 2012 is a strong case; *Bear 71*, Mendes and Allison 2012, a weaker one) are essentially retellings of past events and lead inexorably to certain fixed conclusions, despite the fact that users may navigate multiple routes to that end state. These forms share qualities of the traditional narrative (a definite story arc based on past events, a narrator), even as they encourage excurses and wandering. Others (*Planet Galata—A Bridge in Istanbul*, Thalhofer and Bas 2010; *Question Bridge: Black Males*, Johnson et al. 2012) require the user to wander and navigate at their own pace, exploring the spaces, characters, and issues that they find interesting. The makers have made choices about what to include and offer structures to help shape and lend coherence to the user experience, but there is no preordained conclusion or story arc other than that conjured up by the user. Another, perhaps more extreme example may be found with *18 Days in Egypt* (Mehta and Elayat 2011), which offers a database of crowd-sourced mini-documentaries, tagged with minimal metadata, so that users can follow a particular maker or topic. Although quite fragmented, coherence in this case emerges from the pro-filmic event (the 18-day long revolution whose symbolic center was Cairo in 2011 and its aftermath) and the interface design, enabling motivated users to move among the many differently authored shards of still and video documentation and emerge with a rich multi-perspectival view. Like *Question Bridge* and *Planet Galata*, the onus is on the user to make sense of what is encountered; unlike them, the dispersed nature of the event coupled with the very different voices and styles of representation it includes (and the minimal metadata and guidance) requires greater levels of user motivation to work through the database.

The space between Sonnen and Osterweil's analogies of 'wandering' and 'play' is a fruitful one as we consider the ongoing development of interactive forms. One of the reasons that some documentary makers—rather than fiction makers—have so quickly adopted these new techniques is that in many cases, users already know the neighborhood in which they will wander and play. Users' pre-existing familiarity with 'reality' provides ample context and motivation for them to explore interactive options and have them cohere as a unified and meaningful experience. In a fictional setting, by contrast, the diegetic frame must first be established before users can meaningfully wander around the story world—something we can see from game design. In either case, the structure of the textual environment bears heavily on the nature of the user experience; just as the perception of narrative depends heavily on the user's affect. Sonnen's sense of 'wandering' makes great sense for non-fiction: we, the wanderer, are oriented, have some sense of our setting, and go on to explore it. As stated, 'reality' provides a sufficient context and motive. By contrast, Osterweil's notion of 'play,' peopled with invented or assumed characters who are rule-bound by the conceits of the game, makes great sense for fiction. But it costs time and energy to establish these invented characters, to delineate the basic contours of the fictional world and its operating rules. The threshold for the 'player' would seem to be higher than for the 'wander.' And yet, to restrict the player to fictional worlds would be to impoverish non-fiction, denying it imaginative and invented entry points and characters (as if a purely objectivist stance were even possible!).

We have only to look back on the 'official history' of our documentary tradition, which begins in 'creative interpretation,' as John Grierson's 1926 review of Flaherty's *Moana* reminds us. Several generations of documentary historians jumped on the bandwagon, underscoring the point by simply dismissing as 'naïve' the hyper-realist renderings of cities, factory processes, and peoples that dominated non-fiction from 1895 until the early 1920s, and embracing Flaherty's story conventions. This is a troublesome view, not because of its acceptance of an expansive vocabulary and notion of imaginative engagement, but rather for its exclusion of a rich representational tradition rather akin to wandering, one, moreover, that stands as the culmination of several ways of seeing in the late nineteenth century. That said, *Moana*'s invented characters, like those of *Nanook of the North* (1922) before it and generations of documentaries after, remind us that the fiction / non-fiction divide is not quite as clean as some would like it to be. And Osterweil's notion of the player goes one step farther, reminding us that meaningful invention need not only manifest itself in on-screen fictions, but rather can infuse our way of seeing as we walk through—and play in—a world. That is, rather than (like Flaherty) fictionalizing elements of the pro-filmic world in order to sharpen insights into its operations, being 'in character' allows us to bring a new vantage point to the world that we are exploring, to see it with new eyes, to engage it with an assumed agenda. One of the great potentials of interactive documentary is the flexibility that it affords the user to find her way through a constructed environment. That one can do this 'in character' would seem to provide ways of discovering new aspects of the world, of engaging with it in fresh ways, rather than simply seeing the world through the eyes of the other in the form of the maker of a linear film. Instead, as in the act of playing (rather than listening to the story told), we have the opportunity to assume a set of instincts, to invent a viewing position, and to enact it, respond through it, and in the process, learn.

Today's interactive documentary caters to the wanderer, and with wonderful effect. But it has an as-yet-underutilized capacity to address the player. For this to happen will require more than the efforts of documentary makers: we also have to do our part, and re-learn the art of abandoning ourselves to imagined roles, to the assumed rules and goals of a narrative conceit, and to 'play' our way through documentary environments.

Engagement

Over the past decade or so, 'engagement' has become an oft used term in the worlds of marketing and audience metrics, indicating a shift in interest from the mere 'exposure' of audiences to texts, to the quality of the audience's experience. Although initially presented by qualitative researchers as a challenge to a media industry built upon counting eyeballs and clicks, it has gained traction, encouraged by the rapid state of media change and the evident need for new perspectives. The internet as well as computer games, e-readers, and digital television all share potentials for user interactivity as well as data tracking, offering a quantitative underpinning to qualitative concerns, and helping to drive an emerging paradigm shift in institutional notions of audience participation.

This broad shift serves as a backdrop for the operations of the interactive documentary, which seems to promise enhanced opportunities both for user engagement and—especially for the funders of social impact documentary—for measuring something that might be interpreted as such. Among such 'engagement-inducing' activities we can distinguish: crowd-sourced funding to support particular documentary initiatives; crowd-sourced footage and community co-design; user-determined routings through textual environments; and the 'after-life' of projects that remain as active platforms for ongoing community interaction. Of course, not all of these are unique to the digital domain: crowd-sourced funding and sourcing, co-design, and even the community-based 'afterlife' of projects all have analog precedents. But the digital domain greatly facilitates these practices, and has the added value of making their operations in some senses more visible.

There is much here that we do not know. For example, are contributors to crowdfunding initiatives (say, Kickstarter or JuntoBox, which offer ways to fund projects without promising the funder any ownership of the project or revenues from it) more likely to feel engaged? Since this is a self-selecting group, contributing resources on the basis of interest, the answer is presumably 'yes'—they were engaged as a condition of giving to the project. But how, beyond funding, might this manifest itself? Might they draw in their circle of friends? Promote the project and its cause in a personal way, encouraging others around them to share their interest? Might they, in other words, take a more active role in proselytizing the project, thereby having a social stake in its use, than a non-involved participant? The same might be asked of people who contribute footage to a crowd-sourced initiative, such as Perry Bard's 2007 and ongoing *Man with a Movie Camera: The Global Remake* project (which offers remixes of user-generated footage to remake Vertov's film every day), or Kevin Macdonald's 2011 *Life in a Day* (which drew from 80,000 YouTube submissions). While the act of submitting footage presumes a high level of engagement, does this, in turn, lead to ongoing efforts to engage a larger cohort of participants and viewers to the project? I am unaware of detailed evidence regarding these behaviors; but the amplification logics of social media are increasingly well studied, and may offer an appropriate analogy for these behaviors.

Collaborative documentaries also avail themselves to forms of co-design. This established practice, dating back at least to the 1970s, is related to user-centered design and participatory design (although it does not presume that any stakeholder is more relevant than another). It is process-oriented, blurring the roles of designer and author, much as some documentary projects blur the roles of author and user. Co-design developed with the notion that better designs emerge from directly involving stakeholders in the design process; so, it seems reasonable to draw on this tradition if we want to enhance engagement, involving stakeholders in the documentation process. An example of such an approach is the cross-platform project *Sandy Storyline* (Premo, Falcone, and Gottesdiener 2012), described by Tribeca's Ingrid Kopp as "a community-generated narrative of the storm that seeks to inspire a safe and more sustainable future. [...] It creates a living archive that shows the potential for sharing stories on a very human scale" (2012). Organized by members of the social justice movement, *Sandy Storyline*'s avowed goal is to foster civic dialog so communities can decide, from the ground up, their own futures. *Sandy Storyline*, like *Hollow: An Interactive Documentary* (McMillion 2013)—an initiative "for the community, by the community," is deeply embedded in the lives of those who are its co-producers. *Hollow* uses video portraits, user-generated content, photography, soundscapes, interactive data, and grassroots mapping not just to document a community's past, but to play an active role in building its future. Although both projects are, as of this writing, quite new, they have no 'end' in sight, serving as ongoing, growing, and dynamic resources for their participants, who continue to contribute imagery and comments. Less of an 'artifact' (in the sense that films tend to be once completed and shown) than an ongoing forum for documentation, reflection, and exchange, projects like *Sandy* and *Hollow* point to a new and largely unexplored dimension of the 'new' documentary to which we need to attend. Their civic character holds great potential, providing ways for communities to share knowledge and experience, and offering citizens incentives for sustained participation.

As noted, one can certainly find precedents in the analog past for these incentives to engagement, such as Britain's 1930s *Mass Observation Project* that involved thousands of citizens for its findings (Sheridan 1993). But the affordances of networked computers and digital cameras have greatly lowered the barriers to participation and enhanced a two-way dialog between project developers and the public. As alluded to in the previous section on narrative, the interactive character of these documentaries, their requirement that the user 'wander' or 'play,' adds a distinctive opportunity to engage by making participants co-constructors of the text itself, rather than 'mere' readers. The user's interests presumably direct the process of negotiation through the documentary environment. While we can surmise that the ensuing textual experience differs from encounters with ready-made texts, like storytelling differs from play in Osterweil's terms, the nature of that difference and its implications for user engagement—as in the other cases—remains under researched and unknown. We do know that in some digital environments, users leave traces, allowing designers to discern behavioral patterns. Traces may offer evidence of engaged behaviors; and perhaps more importantly, they may offer insights into barriers to participation, points that could be redesigned or tweaked in some way in order to encourage more sustained participation. Because there is no fixed text, but rather a textual environment ripe with narrative possibilities, producers can continually refine the project, responding to aggregated behaviors and user feedback. Like the long 'afterlife' of some projects, this ability to continually fine-tune an interactive documentary in response to user behaviors offers a potentially new and powerful dimension for exploration.

Looking ahead...

Mobile telephony did not initiate distant communication, but it certainly enabled us to redefine fundamentally our notion of being connected. Indeed, the mobile phone's potential to connect us anytime and anywhere seems to have acquired a new sense of urgency, at least for those of us who carry one, most evident in the panic that sets in with forgotten phones or dead batteries. Moreover 'connection,' in the age of the smart phone, has come to mean far more than the potential to reach others or be reached by them. It entails experiential forms and cultural logics once relegated to distinctive media practices. It means being always connected to one's favorite music, photos, and books; connected to geo-locative information and spatially oriented; connected to email and online social networks; connected to the world through an ability to share experience through live-streamed and recorded audio and video. This conflation of once separated media practices, both enabled by technology and embodied in our everyday enactments, is familiar from the computer and examples across nearly every other digital platform (cameras that can also send images, e-books that play music, etc.). And this remix of our media practices, sensibilities, and opportunities, is fundamental to the new turn in documentary.

As noted at the outset, conditions such as the widespread penetration of cell phones, many equipped with HD video cameras, and those that are not, still enabled to carry out the work of documentation thanks to software systems like Vojo and Vozmob or Mobile Voices/Voces Móviles,[8] have shifted the locus of representation. The ability to record and transmit image, sound, and data such as location, is now in the hands of that 102.2 per cent of the (in this case, American) public equipped with mobile phones. The intertwining of recording and transmitting systems, the ease of access to web-based aggregating systems (whether live streaming sites such as Qik and USTREAM or aggregators of recorded material like YouTube) and elegantly simple story assembly tools (such as Zeega, Cowbird, and Storyplanet), have all empowered that public to take the next step, and tell their own stories. And, in cases like *Sandy Storyline*, *18 Days in Egypt*, and the many stories aggregated on Cowbird, they have done so. At the same time, the more active *stance* encouraged by these new affordances (not to mention, the daily realities of negotiating the internet and portals such as YouTube or sites such as Facebook) has also encouraged people to navigate

8 Vozmob provides a platform for immigrant and/or low-wage workers to create stories about their lives and communities directly from simple cell phones.

their own way through the audio-visual environments provided by others, in the process creating their own experiences and stories. Here, too, the quotidian status of the smart phone has not only made trivial the process of textual construction, but has greatly expanded the space of reception. We can view and interact with this material virtually anywhere that we can receive a signal; and thanks to geo-location technologies, documentaries can potentially be viewed *in situ*, interacting with the spaces and places that they document.

The implications of these shifts from over a century of professionalized documentary production and institutionalized sponsorship, distribution, and exhibition, are just beginning to be felt. On one hand, some professionals and institutions have reached out to the public, embracing them as partners in the project of collaborative documentation, as can be seen in the work of the National Film Board of Canada with Kat Cizek's *Highrise* series (2010) or Hugues Sweeney's *A Journal of Insomnia* (Duverneix et al. 2013). And on the other, as noted with *Sandy Storyline* and the many projects enabled through Vozmob, activists and the public have found ways to make their voices heard largely outside the domain of professional and institutional practices. Add this to the changes already noted—the destabilization of the fixed text, the challenge to the authority of the author, and new roles of contributor and collaboration taken up by the public, and the contours of the situation seem both new... and familiar. This shift from a limited, centralized, institutional discourse to an open, decentralized, and participatory process is familiar in the network age. Similar transformations might be condensed into the 'Encyclopedia Britannica/Wikipedia' dynamic: one, carefully vetted, attributable, and stable; the other, open, more or less self-regulating, and dynamic. Each have important affordances, but the shift from an institutional monopoly to a pluriform and open environment requires a perceptual shift. Faith in institutional vetting and the cult of expertise is no longer sufficient grounds (as if it ever were!) to navigate the world. Instead, the onus is on users to develop a critical stance, to assess, compare, and be open to contingencies. At this moment of regime change in the domain of representation, rather than fixating on a notion of unassailable truth (or lamenting its passing), we need to demand transparency, and to bring our critical judgment to bear, rather than relying on faith in—or giving obeisance to—a higher authority.

Like Sonnen's reference to wandering in the city versus taking a guided tour, or Osterweil's notion of play versus listening to a great storyteller, participation and collaboration in the representation of reality will exist alongside our long reliance on hierarchies of expertise. This is not a situation of either/or, of the well-authored, carefully crafted, and institutionally endorsed documentary versus its user-negotiated, participatory, and grassroots counterpart. Rather, it is a tale of different affordances and, more importantly, of the emergence of a new and critical stance. The appearance of a new art of documentary, though still finding its way, has necessarily recontextualized the long (and still) dominant tradition. And with that recontextualization, we can expect the critical reception practices required in the participatory age to bleed into even the most vetted and institutionally endorsed of documentary productions. In this sense, Sonnen's and Osterweil's heuristic binary opposition might well be complicated by *unruly* tours and *playful* listeners, practices that, repositioned within the civil society, add up to responsible citizenship.

Acknowledgments

This chapter is based on a manuscript written in 2013.

References

Anderson, T., M. Blank, D. Lebling, and B. Daniels. 1977. *Zork.* [PDP-10]. Game.

Aston, J., and S. Gaudenzi. 2012. Interactive documentary: Setting the field. *Studies in Documentary Film* 6 (2): 125-139.

Bard, P. 2007. *Man with a Movie Camera: The Global Remake.* A Bigger Picture Commission Art. Film project.

Cizek, K. 2010. *Highrise/Out My Window.* NFB Interactive. Multimedia project.

Činčera, R., J. Lihny, and M. Hornícek (dir.). 1967. *Kinoautomat.* Film.

Dewever-Plana, M., and I. Fougère (dir.). 2012. *Alma: A Tale of Violence.* Upian.com. Film.

Duverneix, T., B. Choiniere, P. Lambert, and G. Braun (dir.). 2013. *A Journal of Insomnia.* National Board of Canada. Film.

Edmond, M. 2015. All platforms considered: Contemporary radio and transmedia engagement. *New Media & Society* 17 (9): 1566-1582.

Flaherty, R. J. (dir.). 1922. *Nanook of the North.* Pathé Exchange. Film.

—. 1926. *Moana.* Paramount Pictures. Film.

Galloway, D., K. B. McAlpine, and P. Harris. 2007. From Michael Moore to JFK Reloaded: Towards a working model of interactive documentary. *Journal of Media Practice* 8 (3): 325-339.

Grierson, J. Review: Moana. *The New York Sun.* 8 February 1926.

Herman, D. 2009. Cognitive narratology. *Handbook of narratology* 19:30.

Jenkins, H., S. Ford, and J. Green. 2013. *Spreadable media: Creating value and meaning in a networked culture*: New York: NYU Press.

Johnson, C., H. W. Thomas, B. R. Smith, and K. Sinclair (dir.). 2012. *Question Bridge: Black Males*. Bay Area Video Coalition. Film.

Kopp, I. 2012. Sandy Storyline. *Tribeca Film Festival film guide archive*. http://tribecafilm.com/filmguide/archive/51424e82c07f5db7a600000c-sandy-storyline.

Lessig, L. 2015. *Free culture*. Lulu.com.

Macdonald, K. (dir.). 2011. *Life in a Day*. National Geographic Film. Film.

Marsh, T., C. Xuejin, L. Nickole, S. Osterweil, E. Klopfer, and J. Haas. 2011. Fun and learning: The power of narrative. In *Proceedings of the 6th international conference on the foundations of digital games, Bordeaux, June 28 – July 1, 2011*, 23-29. New York: ACM.

McMillion, E. (dir.). 2013. *Hollow: An Interactive Documentary*. Multimedia.

Mendes, J., and L. Allison (dir.). 2012. *Bear 71*. National Film Board of Canada. Film.

Mehta, J., and Y. Elayat (dir.). 2011. *18 Days in Egypt*. GroupStre.am. Film.

MIT Open Documentary Lab. 2018. MIT: Moments of innovation. *MIT*. http://momentsofinnovation.mit.edu.

Moore, K. 2011. 71% of online adults now use video-sharing sites. *Pew Research Center*. http://www.pewinternet.org/Reports/2011/Video-sharing-sites.aspx.

Nichols, B. 1991. *Representing reality: Issues and concepts in documentary*. Bloomington, IN: Indiana University Press.

Premo, M., R. Falcone, and L. Gottesdiener (dir.). 2012. *Sandy Storyline*. Multimedia.

Ruttman, W. (dir.). 1929. *Melodie der Welt*. Tobis Filmkunst. Film.

Saunders, D. 2007. *Direct cinema: Observational documentary and the politics of the sixties*. London: Wallflower Press.

Sheridan, D. 1993. Writing to the archive: Mass-observation as autobiography. *Sociology* 27 (1): 27-40.

Singer, B. 1987. Connoiseurs of chaos: Whitman, Vertov, and the poetic survey. *Literature/Film Quarterly* 15 (4): 247.

Statistic Brain. 2016. STATS: Youtube company statistics. *Statistic Brain Research Institute*. http://www.statisticbrain.com/youtube-statistics.

Thalhofer, F., and B. Bas (dir.). 2010. *Planet Galata: A Bridge in Istanbul*. Kloos & Co. Film.

Trettien, W. A. 2009. Computers, cut-ups and combinatory volvelles: An archaeology of text-generating mechanisms. MA Thesis: Massachusetts Institute of Technology.

Uricchio, W. 2011. A 'proper point of view': The panorama and some of its early media iterations. *Early Popular Visual Culture* 9 (3): 225-238.
Vertov, D. (dir.). 1929. *Man with a Movie Camera*. VUFKU. Film.
—. 1931. *Enthusiasm*. Ukrainfilm. Film.

About the author

William Uricchio is Full Professor of Comparative Media History at Utrecht University as well as Full Professor of Comparative Media Studies at MIT. He was principal investigator of the Singapore-MIT GAMBIT Game Lab, and at MIT he is founder and principal investigator of the MIT Open Documentary Lab. He is (co-)author or (co-)editor of several books including *Reframing culture: The case of the Vitagraph quality films* (Princeton University Press 1993) and *We Europeans? Media, representations, identity* (University of Chicago Press 2009). Uricchio is series editor (along with Jesper Juul and Geoff Long) of the MIT Press *Playful Thinking Series* on game related topics. His scholarly research considers the interplay of media technologies and cultural practices in relation to the (re-)construction of representation, knowledge, and publics. His current research focuses on forms of augmented reality and the cultural use of algorithms.

5. *Collapsus*, or how to make players become ecological citizens

Joost Raessens

Abstract

Contemporary games are increasingly used to make a difference at an individual, community, and/or societal level. Ecological games are one kind of such 'games for change': they seek to contribute to ecological thought and turn players into ecological citizens. This chapter draws inspiration from the conceptual framework of psychologist Stoknes. He theorizes the 'psychological climate paradox': the fact that although climate science facts are becoming more solidly documented and disturbing every year, most people either do not believe in these facts or do not act upon them. This chapter discusses how *Collapsus – Energy Risk Conspiracy* (Palotta 2010) might contribute to solving the paradox by making people reflect on the global, political, and cultural implications of climate change and act accordingly.

Keywords: Climate communication, ecological citizenship, games for change, psychological climate paradox

> When I say, 'Optimism is a duty,' this means not only that the future is open but that we all help to decide it through what we do. We are all jointly responsible for what is to come. So we all have a duty, instead of predicting something bad, to support the things that may lead to a better future.
> Popper (1999, 143-144)

Contemporary digital games are increasingly used not only to entertain, but also to persuade people, raising their awareness and changing or reinforcing their attitudes and behavior for the good of society. Ecological games belong to this category of 'persuasive games' (Jacobs 2017; Jacobs, Jansz, and De

---

Glas, R., S. Lammes, M. de Lange, J. Raessens, and I. de Vries, eds. 2019. *The Playful Citizen. Civic Engagement in a Mediatized Culture.* Amsterdam: Amsterdam University Press.
DOI: 10.5117/9789462984523/CH05

la Hera 2017). They seek not only to contribute to ecological thought, but also "'to make' people become ecological citizens" (MacGregor 2014, 120). In the last few years, digital games have encouraged support, sympathy, and action for a variety of ecological issues.[1] In this chapter, I examine how *Collapsus – Energy Risk Conspiracy* (Pallotta 2010) frames the immanent energy transition from fossil fuels to alternative energy sources.[2] My analysis aims to offer a conceptual clarification of the rhetorical (textual) strategies that a 'gamelike' production such as *Collapsus* uses to raise awareness about the issue of energy transition. I use the word 'rhetorical' here in the sense of a persuasive discourse "adopted by members of a particular affiliation to persuade others of the veracity and worthwhileness of their beliefs" (Sutton-Smith 1997, 8). My investigation draws inspiration from the conceptual framework of psychologist and economist Per Espen Stoknes, who theorizes what I would call one of the most pressing issues within the field of climate change communication, the 'psychological climate paradox': the fact that "climate science facts are getting more solidly documented and disturbing every year," while "most people either don't believe in or do not act upon those facts" (2015, 3). Though Stoknes provides a productive framework for understanding and overcoming the obstacles of conventional climate communication strategies, his set of recommendations remains very general. By analysing the empirical building blocks of *Collapsus*, I will develop Stoknes' framework further in order to turn it into a strategic toolkit for civic action that can be used in the domain of playful ecological communication. In the first section, I will briefly introduce *Collapsus* and discuss how Stoknes defines the psychological climate paradox and how he envisions solving it. In the second section, I will further develop and theorize some of his strategies. In the third section, I will discuss in detail if, and if so how, *Collapsus* might contribute to solving the paradox by making people reflect on the global and political implications of the energy transition and act accordingly. I present my conclusions in the last section.

1 For an overview of recent examples of environmental games, see the Games for Change (G4C) website, where we find its mission statement to be "catalyzing social impact through digital games" (G4C 2018). Also see Raessens (2017, 2018).

2 *Collapsus* was commissioned by the Dutch broadcasting company VPRO and produced by Amsterdam-based company Submarine Channel. It can be played at collapsus.com. *Collapsus* is an important case to discuss because it succeeded—back in 2010—in imagining the social and political implications of global warming in an innovative way. It was aimed at a predominantly younger and connected generation. Statistics show that it is difficult for documentary films to reach young audiences; only 18-20 per cent is younger than 34 years old. *Collapsus* reached 41 per cent of that age category.

The psychological climate paradox and how to solve it

The 'psychological climate paradox' that Stoknes is referring to—the more climate science facts you hear, the less likely you are to take action—is only an apparent paradox. It might be solved once it becomes clear, for example, that strategies other than presenting 'facts only' might indeed convince people to change their behavior regarding ecological issues. The persuasive argument in a documentary like *An Inconvenient Truth* (Guggenheim 2006) is primarily based on factual evidence about global warming. Former United States vice president Al Gore sketches a doom scenario, as its title already indicates, suggesting only at the end of the film that the climate crisis might be solved and how this might be achieved. *This Changes Everything* (Lewis 2015), a documentary inspired by Naomi Klein's book of the same name, on the other hand, frames global warming as an opportunity to build a better world. It does so by presenting compelling stories of communities all around the world that are resisting our 'failed' economic system and supporting environmentalism.

Another example of such a compelling story is *Collapsus – Energy Risk Conspiracy* (Pallotta 2010). *Collapsus* is an online production that engages users with realistic future scenarios (2012-2025) about anticipated energy crises and the necessity of transitioning from fossil fuels to alternative energy sources. This interactive experience consists of three screens or panels contained on one web page (for the three-panel structure, see Figure 5.1): it merges a fictional storyline via live action and animated graphics, with minigames (both presented in the center panel), documentary clips (right panel) and simulation games (left panel).

Collapsus is usually presented as a game. The Games for Change website, for example, refers to *Collapsus* in their list of environmental games. Submarine Channel, the production studio behind *Collapsus*, also includes *Collapsus* under the category of 'games.' We can use the five shared characteristics of games—they are goal oriented; the player has to follow specific rules; the system provides some kind of feedback; often there is a competition element; and participation is voluntary (Jansz 2016)—to understand the 'gameness' of *Collapsus*. The overall goal of *Collapsus* is to play it until the end while unlocking all the information made available by the three panels. More specifically, you have to win the minigames to reveal specific information, and win the simulation games by producing enough sustainable energy to meet the rising demand. One important rule is that you have to unlock the information when it becomes available in the different panels. You can cheat by skipping the minigames, for example, but then you would fail to understand some important aspects of the story; the system provides the player with feedback during the minigames and sim games. You do not

5.1: *Collapsus* – Three-panel structure.

compete with other players, but you do compete with the game's system. And you decide yourself whether to play or not.

From the perspective of 'mediality,' *Collapsus* can be seen as multi-medial, because it combines multiple media forms, or transmedial, because the media forms are complementary. But I would prefer to identify it as an intermedial production because the media forms in the different panels interact with each other. As Chiel Kattenbelt points out, intermediality results "in a redefinition of the media that are influencing each other, which in turn leads to a refreshed perception" (2008, 25).

If we want to answer the question if, and if so how, *Collapsus* can be used to engage individual citizens in the issue of energy transition, we first need to improve our understanding of the reasons why conventional climate communication does not always work optimally, or, worse still, works counter-productively (erecting barriers). Moreover, we need to know what we should do to overcome these barriers (solutions) and what concrete strategies we should use to make communication work (strategies), see Table 1.[3]

Table 1: Barriers, solutions, and strategies

Barriers (first section of this chapter)	Solutions (first section of this chapter)	Strategies (second section of this chapter)
distant in space and time	close, human, personal, urgent	* moral ideas: progressive, optimistic
doom scenario	opportunities, hope	* persuasion: narratives, documentaries, games
not compatible with our values	in line with our values	* social networks: many-to-many communication * citizenship: post-liberal, global

3 For a summary of Stoknes' argument, see his chapter 'From barriers to solutions' (2015, 87-94). I present my own interpretation of his argument in Table 1.

Three barriers might cause conventional climate communication to lead to a state of denial. The first barrier arises when global warming is framed as being distant in space and time. For the majority of us living in the West, the impact of global warming is still relatively far away, both in time and space. That is why Rob Nixon refers to climate change as 'slow violence.' He writes it is "a violence that occurs gradually and out of sight, a violence of delayed destruction that is dispersed across time and space, an attritional violence that is typically not viewed as violence at all" (2011, 2).[4] For example, research shows that only a minority of the Dutch population believe that fossil fuels have a significant impact on the climate; and only a very small minority see energy transition as an urgent challenge, especially when compared with issues such as the economy and migration (SCP 2016). The second barrier arises when global warming is framed as a doom scenario, an apocalyptic-movie mode without any thinkable practical solutions, which is depressing and generates the desire to avoid the topic altogether. Energy transition is indeed not uppermost in the Dutch mind (Ibid.). The third barrier arises when global warming is framed in such a way that it is not compatible with our values or our sense of identity. Dutch citizens, for example, are interested in the transition to other energy sources, not so much because of climate change, but because they like the idea of being energy independent; they want the stable delivery of energy and support the potential economic growth that results from such a transition (Ibid.).

In order to make climate communication productive, we need to turn these three barriers into solutions. First, climate change must be framed as being close, human, personal, and urgent. One possible way of doing this—as *Collapsus* does—is to link the subject (energy transition) to violent events taking place in the here and now of the story world. As a result, the energy transition is experienced by the characters and, hopefully, the players as "immediate in time, explosive and spectacular in space, and as erupting into instant sensational visibility" (Nixon 2011, 2). Second, climate messages must be framed in a positive, hopeful way, providing opportunities for consistent and visible action. As we will see later, *Collapsus* combines an alarming message with a variety of hopeful opportunities through different scenarios of civic engagement. Third, climate change must be framed in such a way that the solutions are in line with our values. That is, as long

4 This is, of course, not the case for those communities that are directly threatened by global warming (Lewis 2015), "particularly (though not exclusively) across the so-called global South" (Nixon 2011, 4). The most visible impact of global warming in our everyday lives in the West is in extreme weather conditions, like heatwaves, hurricanes, droughts, wildfires, and floods.

as they are not conflicting with the notion of environmentalism, as I will discuss in the next section. As I have discussed elsewhere, people 'play' their identity: people play their values, they play on the basis of who they are, how they understand themselves, the values they want to live by, and who and what they want to become (Raessens 2015). *Collapsus* tries to persuade its audience by presenting a variety of role models with different beliefs, values, and behaviors that the audience can identify with. For example, it links the necessity of energy transition with the notion of the stable delivery of energy and economic independence.

Strategies for raising awareness

On the basis of these three barriers with their corresponding solutions, I propose four complementary strategies to make climate communication more effective. The discourse around climate must mobilize and reinforce progressive and positive moral ideas; it must be persuasive, changing attitudes and behavior by using narratives, documentary information, and games; it must stimulate social learning by using the power of social networks; and it must stimulate a post-liberal and global form of citizenship.

Moral ideas: Progressive and optimistic. In order to increase our understanding of how *Collapsus* frames energy transition, it is productive to use Lakoff's distinction between conservative and progressive moral systems (e.g. Flanagan and Nissenbaum 2014). The two systems represent contrasting ideas about environmentalism, which is defined by Lakoff as follows: "The natural world is being destroyed and it is a moral imperative to preserve and reconstitute as much of it as possible as soon as possible" (2010, 80). Whereas the conservative system includes a number of ideas that work against environmentalism—such as nature being there for human use and exploitation, a let-the-market-decide ideology, and the idea that making a profit and economic growth are goals in themselves (Ibid., 74-75)—the progressive system includes various ideas that support environmentalism, such as empathy linking us with other beings and other things, responsibility for taking care of yourself and others, and the ethic of excellence calling on us to improve the environment (Ibid., 76). This is in line with Stoknes' argument: "We ought to [...] protect and compassionately care for ourselves, current and future generations, and the other beings we share the planet with" (2015, 118). One important thing Stoknes is adding here is that we need to reframe the climate message in such a way that the message is supported with hope, positive emotions, and opportunities. *Collapsus*, for example, presents progressive strategies for improving the environment via the transition from fossil fuels to solar and wind power.

Persuasion: Narratives, documentaries, and games. Collapsus tries to raise awareness about the difficult choices we all have to make in relation to the impending energy crisis. A better understanding and use of persuasive technology "will significantly expand the toolbox for climate communication" (Stoknes, 130). Because *Collapsus* combines a fictional storyline with documentaries and games, we need to analyze the persuasive rhetoric of these different media, not only separately, but also in their interconnectedness. The problem is that while strategies of persuasive rhetoric have been studied, the research has mainly considered these media forms in isolation. Think, for example, of the analysis of written, text-based media (Killingsworth and Palmer 1992) and image-based media (Dobrin and Morey 2009). To understand how persuasiveness is embedded in *Collapsus*' design, I will focus on the narratives it portrays (or allows the player to develop), the documentary information it presents, and the system and rules of the games it allows the users to play.

Narratives. In his study of persuasive games, Ruud Jacobs (2017) refers to the importance of character-based narrative persuasion. Research done on screen-based media in general, such as film, television, or games, shows that users' attitudes are more likely to change—leading, for example, to civic engagement—when the users identify with role models or protagonists who go through the same stages of change (on screen) as the users are supposed to (e.g. Slater 2002; Green and Jenkins 2014; Jenkins, Ito, and boyd 2016). Or, as Michael Ryan and Douglas Kellner put it: "The slow transformation of ordinary people into informed opponents of the corporate system probably appealed more to audiences than if the characters had begun as radicals" (Ingram 2000, 169). As we will see in more detail later, this form of social learning is what *Collapsus* aims to do. It wants to offer players the opportunity to identify with characters such as Vera and the changes she goes through in the various stages. Stoknes identifies three extra characteristics that storytelling should have in order to be able to convince people of the necessity of environmentalism. First, narratives must foster creativity: "There must be room for humour, emotion, visualization, point of view, climax, surprise, plot, drama. Above all, make it personal and personified" (2014, 148). Second, there must be room for more than one narrative perspective: "I don't think there is just *one* right type of climate story to tell to get people to understand the urgency of the issue and move them to action. Rather, a plurality of stories is needed, each creating meaning and engagement for different groups of people" (Ibid., 132). Third, the stories must offer the possibility of some kind of feedback. Stoknes asks: "Can we really measure if we're changing in the right direction [...]?" (Ibid., 152). As we will see in more detail in the next section, this, again, is what *Collapsus* tries to do.

Documentaries. *Collapsus* not only provides accurate documentation of the imminent energy transition, but it is also a playful re-enactment of this event. To better understand the persuasive power of *Collapsus* as a whole, we can direct our attention to what documentary theorist Michael Renov calls "the four fundamental tendencies or rhetorical/aesthetic functions attributable to documentary practice," which are to express, to analyze or interrogate, to reveal, and to persuade or promote (1993, 21). These four discursive functions are indeed present in *Collapsus*' fictional storyline, news reports, minigames, and simulation games, albeit in different forms: the difficult choices we all have to make are expressed in the lives of the main characters within the fictional storyline; the geopolitical implications of the energy transition are analyzed and interrogated in the news reports; the complexity, the best solutions and a conspiracy are revealed in the minigames and simulation games. *Collapsus* uses these three functions—expression, analysis/interrogation, and revelation—in the end to promote a specific position in this debate, and to persuade users to adopt this point of view.[5]

Games. According to Ian Bogost (2007), persuasive games have the unique capability of employing what he calls 'procedural rhetoric' to address serious topics, such as global warming. The goal of a game—for example 'supporting environmentalism'—can be found in its formal system, more specifically in the properties of the rules. Players are presumed to surrender to the seduction of a game by interpreting the game as suggested and being guided by its rules. The idea that procedurality structures, helps facilitate, or has a (strong) impact on the game's interpretation seems to be a valid observation, but not to the extent that it 'determines' its meaning (Sicart 2011). Games, and this applies to *Collapsus* as a whole, are polysemic and therefore open to many readings. Players may activate three interpretative strategies as a reaction to what Sherry Turkle calls the "seduction of simulation" (1996, 71). They can either surrender to the seduction by interpreting it more or less according to the encoded ideological message (resignation); they may understand—and possibly oppose—a simulation by decoding the

5 For the argument that not only news reports but also fiction and games can be used as a documentary medium, see Raessens (2006).

assumptions that are built into a medium (understanding); or they can completely disavow the social and political importance of these kinds of media (denial). In the case of *Collapsus*, simulation resignation seems to be the dominant reaction.[6] Dutch film magazine *Skrien*, for example, calls *Collapsus*' combination of narratives, documentaries, and games a "trendsetter for the future [...] *Collapsus* takes place in the coming decades and confronts you with *realistic* [my italics] future scenarios about the expected global energy crisis" (De Crom 2010, 8-9; translation by the author).

Social networks: Many-to-many communication. Stoknes emphasizes the use of the power of social networks. This idea can help us to understand an important aspect of global warming communication. We should not only use one-to-many communication models (such as television documentaries), but also interactive many-to-many communication models (such as meetups, whether online or offline). This is because group behavior can be a powerful way to influence individual people's behavior: "Being part of an eco-network is one of the biggest determinants of pro-environmental behavior" (Stoknes 2014, 105). This is why, for example, Tegenlicht, a documentary series from the Dutch public broadcaster VPRO,[7] and the cultural organization Pakhuis de Zwijger have been organizing regular meetups since 2013 that take place a few days after a particular television documentary has been broadcast. In these meetups, the audience can participate in discussions with experts about the specific topics dealt with in these documentaries, and reflect together with others on their meaning. As research shows, this social aspect of media use—known as 'debriefing' or 'social facilitation,' either online via weblogs or offline in a physical setting—can enrich reflection on the topic and positively affect persuasion or learning (e.g. Raessens 2007; Neys and Jansz 2010; Jacobs 2017). Although *Collapsus* is a single-player game and meetups in a physical setting had not yet started in 2010, audiences and experts could still meet virtually and exchange ideas via VPRO's weblog, energy.vpro.nl.

Citizenship: Post-liberal and global. Stoknes emphasizes that we must "act as social citizens, not individuals" (2014, 91). Faced with worldwide problems like global warming, pollution, and energy transition, environmental change

6 *Collapsus* received a Digital Emmy Award for Best Digital Fiction, a People's Choice Award, and Interactive Award nominations at the Dutch Spin Awards, and a World Summit Award for its technical and aesthetic qualities, and its convincing message.

7 VPRO Tegenlicht is a series of informative programes that research new ideas and trends in the world of politics, economy, society, technology, and science.

can only be envisioned when four conditions are met. First, green citizens, post-liberal politics, and environmental social justice movements need to mutually reinforce each other on a local and global scale. Second, green citizens need to behave pro-environmentally and participate in public debate. Third, post-liberal politics need to regulate markets and industries across borders via more stringent environmental legislation. And fourth, environmental social justice movements need to carry out ecological change on a global scale through group action. Changes in personal attitudes and/or behavior (think of green lifestyles and ethical consumption) should strengthen socio-political solutions, not replace them (Barendregt and Jaffe 2014; Klein 2014). As we will see in the next section, these four ideas are embodied by *Collapsus*'s characters. Global ecological citizenship is understood as "including the right to a non-polluted environment and the responsibility both to refrain from harming the environment and to participate in its preservation and rehabilitation" (MacGregor 2014, 114).

Unpacking *Collapsus*

As I explained earlier, *Collapsus* consists of three screens or panels contained on one web page (see Figure 5.1). The main fictional storyline is presented in the center panel. In approximately 35 minutes of playing time, you can observe the consequences of the energy crisis in the everyday lives of ten people. The right and left panels light up at certain points in the story. This storyline is designed in such a way that users have to choose their own perspective as the storyline unfolds by participating in three different ways. If you click on the right-hand, documentary panel, you can get a broader perspective by watching CitizEnergy web vlogs—with an average length of two and a half minutes—presented by two characters, Elena and Esperanca. They include comments from other *Collapsus* characters and short docu-clips where scientific experts provide players with background information. If you click on the left-hand, game panel, you can play simulation games with the goal of avoiding future blackouts. As part of the storyline in the center panel, minigames can be played.

According to Henry Jenkins, "transmedia storytelling is the art of world making. To fully experience any fictional world, consumers must assume the role of hunters and gatherers, chasing down bits of the story across media channels" (2006, 14). To be able to reconstruct *Collapsus*' storyline, a time-consuming task, users indeed have to interactively find ways to move around and inside the game's different elements. Experiencing *Collapsus* is what Katie Salen, Eric Zimmerman, and Miguel Sicart might call a playful activity. To *play* with *Collapsus* is to interactively play “with all of these structures [...] finding ways of moving around and inside them” (Salen and Zimmerman 2004, 304). “Play is creative [...] play is the act of creatively engaging with the world [...] to play is to make a world [...] play is a creative, appropriative activity” (Sicart 2014, 17, 73). Depending on the perspective you take, playing *Collapsus* can thus not only be interpreted as ‘gamelike’ or ‘intermedial’—as I argued above—but also as a ‘playful’ experience.

On the landing page of the website collapsus.com we recognize the London Eye—the place where the story will start—and are given the possibility to click on the ‘enter collapsus’ link. When we do so, we see a short introductory clip that gives us a little taste of what is to come; it creates a context for the upcoming experience. We can read the following text: “All over the world energy resources are drying up and the world is blacking out.” The text is accompanied by frightening music and worrying images of a woman in the middle of a civil-war-like situation. Later, we will discover that she is the story’s main protagonist Vera, vlogging from Tehran, Iran. After the intro the title emerges—*Collapsus – Energy Risk Conspiracy*. I will present what happens next in four steps. First, I will summarize the thirteen episodes of the fictional storyline and introduce the main characters. I will then present the three ways in which this storyline is completed or annotated, starting with the fifteen documentary news items in the right panel, followed by the six minigames within the center panel; and finishing with the two simulation games to be played in the left panel.

Fictional storyline. Collapsus is a conspiracy thriller about ten, mostly young people, located all over the world and how the worldwide energy crisis affects them. To help us, a world map is shown in the left panel where we can obtain information about the characters and where we can constantly track their locations (see Figure 5.2). In the first episode (①London»2012; see Table 2) the nine main characters are introduced: Vera, a world citizen and the leading character, who likes to vlog; Marianne, Vera’s mother and a member of the European Parliament; Jack, an American oil trader; Elena and Esperanca, founders of the CitizEnergy.org vlog that informs people about the impact of the energy transition; Tony, an environmental activist who resists the economic elite that obstructs the development of new, cleaner forms of energy; Chen, a representative of Tiger NRG, a Chinese energy firm; and Ali and Amir, two Iranian brothers who discuss the energy situation in Iran. In episode ③, Vera gives birth to her daughter, Liana, the tenth main character. Jack is Liana’s father.

5.2: *Collapsus* – World map.

At the bottom of the screen we see the storyline, which starts in 2012 and runs, as we discover when the story unfolds, until 2025. The story events take place in six different years, and consist of thirteen main episodes that are explicitly mentioned in the center panel (see the upper two rows in Table 2).

Table 2: Structure of *Collapsus*

Year	2012	2013	2015	2016	2017	2025
Episode	①London » 2012 ②London » 3 weeks later	③St Thomas' Hospital » 8 months later	④Sofia, Bulgaria » 2 years later	⑤Strait of Hormuz » Middle East ⑥Tehran, Iran	⑦Angola, Africa » Months later ⑧Riyadh, Saudi Arabia » Middle East ⑨Washington DC » USA ⑩ Boulder, Colorado USA » One month later	⑪Years later Austin, Texas » USA / Beijing, China ⑫Austin, Texas » USA ⑬Amsterdam » The Netherlands
ONews item/ ΦSim	OOOO[ΦO] O	O	[ΦO]	OOO	OO	O
Mini-game	❶❷	❸	❹	❺	❻❼	

Following the adventures of the main characters, we are led into a world of failing energy supplies and political and economic powers trying to cope with the transition from fossil fuels to alternative energy sources, while dealing with political dissension, uprisings, and a population terrified by increasingly frequent blackouts. London, for example, is confronted with blackouts and power failures in its energy network①②③; a climate conference is organized in Sofia and the energy order discussed④; terrorists blow up ships in the Strait of Hormuz, a highly strategic location for the international oil trade⑤; there is civil war and dictatorship in Iran⑥; there are food riots in Angola, and space-based solar power (SBSP) is introduced⑦; ideas for a peaceful and productive Middle East are discussed⑧; the world is in chaos⑨; research is conducted into new energy technologies, such as SBSP⑩; we see the demise of the fossil fuel industries, i.e. oil, gas, and coal businesses⑪; Tiger NRG executives like Chen are arrested, accused of an energy conspiracy⑫; and, finally, there is a multiple screen with several characters reflecting outloud on what they have done up to that point and what their ideas are for the future⑬.

This portrayal of a worldwide energy crisis, with all kinds of economic, political, and social implications, is an important persuasive dimension of *Collapsus* and in line with Stoknes' argument that "[t]he solutions to curbing wasteful practices and overconsumption are systemic, large-scale, and societal" (2015, 91). But to get there, as Stoknes also points out, we "need many small-step solutions in the right direction" (Ibid.). The reactions of most of the nine characters to the energy crisis are these kinds of 'small-step solutions.' The positive values the storyline attaches to them (and the negative values attached to Chen, and Jack to a lesser degree), are crucial in understanding *Collapsus*'s persuasive argument.

The nine characters positions can be understood best based on the five major stages of the stages-of-change model (see Table 3) and the segmentation analysis of *Global warming's six Americas* (Yale 2016). Merging the models of Slater and Yale helps to analyze how *Collapsus* 'uses' characters for persuasive purposes.

The first, *precontemplation*, describes people who have no intention of changing and often no awareness that there may be reasons to consider a behavior change. In the second stage, *contemplation*, people have recognized that a problem exists and are considering taking action in the not-too-distant future, but have not yet committed themselves to taking action. *Preparation* is a transitional stage in which people have begun to experiment with or attempt the relevant action and are intending to try the action again, but have not yet successfully modified their own behavior. *Action* represents, then, successful behavior changes for some specified length of time. *Maintenance*, the final stage, is the ability to sustain the behavioral changes over time (Slater 1999, 337).

Table 3: Stages-of-change model applied to *Collapsus*

	Precontemplation	Contemplation	Preparation	Action	Maintenance
Vera	X →	X →	X →	X →	X
Jack	X →	X			
Tony					X
Elena & Esperanca					X [X] (Esperanca dies)
Chen	X				
Ali & Amir					XX
Marianne					[X] (Marianne retires)

This stages-of-change model can be complemented by the segmentation analysis of *Global warming's six Americas* (Yale 2016):

> The Alarmed are fully convinced of the reality and seriousness of climate change and are already taking individual, consumer, and political action to address it. The Concerned are also convinced that global warming is happening and a serious problem, but have not yet engaged the issue personally. Three other Americas—the Cautious, the Disengaged, and the Doubtful—represent different stages of understanding and acceptance of the problem, and none are actively involved. The final America—the Dismissive are very sure it is not happening and are actively involved as opponents of a national effort to reduce greenhouse emissions. (Yale 2016)

As we can see in Table 3, Vera is the character that passes through every stage. In her first vlog (episode②), Vera is reporting on the London blackouts. Like her friends from CitizEnergy, she has a list of dos and don'ts for the next blackout. When the power outage starts, she advises us: "You eat all the ice cream in the freezer, read a book by candlelight, go out on the roof and gaze at the stars, or do the one thing we all do very well in the dark: have sex. Well, that's about all I have to contribute." She is more focused on her own personal problems, in particular being pregnant while the baby's father Jack is not around. And when her mother Marianne tries to explain the energy crisis to her, she answers: "I do not even know what that means." She calls it leftish talk; the most important thing for her is being pregnant (precontemplation). In her second phase, Vera visits her mother in Bulgaria④, where she is attending a conference on climate change. Vera seems to accept her mother's political analysis, but without committing herself to action. Her contemplation is being interrupted by her crying child. A little later, she seems to realize the need to resist when her mother Marianne tries to convince her to join her friends at the CitizEnergy network: "Vera, join them, use your audience, do some real reporting" (contemplation). Vera's vlog about the civil war in Teheran, Iran⑥ is her first attempt to do some real reporting. But she is still in doubt about what to do. On the one hand, she wants to stay and join the peaceful protests of the people of Iran; on the other hand, she wants to seek a safe haven and leave the country via Tehran's airport: "I'm almost home, dear Liana" (preparation). Vera's successful behavioral transformation begins when she meets Tony, just as she is getting ready to go back home. Tony asks her to follow him to see the truth⑥, that China and the United States are supporting the Khameini regime by delivering weapons (action). Vera's last phase starts when she tries to persuade Jack to share her point of view⑥—"Look around you, Jack. Look deeper. Is this the world you wanna live in? Oil and coal, inefficient, dirty, both limited resources that are bad for the world, bad for people. Do you see where this leads to?"—and ends with her announcement that she will become the new administrative head of the European SBSP program and will stop vlogging⑬ (maintenance).

Whereas Vera only gradually becomes alarmed about the energy crisis and chooses—in the end—to go for a technological solution (SBSP), six other characters are alarmed from the beginning. They are Elena and Esperanca, Marianne, Tony, and Ali, and Amir. They represent three other strategies—media, political, and activist—for dealing with the energy crisis. Elena and Esperanca are reporting, for example, about the climate change conference in Bulgaria and explaining how the food riots in Angola are caused by the energy crisis. While Esperanca dies in Angola, Elena continues this important work. Their vlogs can be seen in the right-hand panel of *Collapsus*—I will return to this later. Marianne's political career is shown from the beginning (her election as a member of the EU parliament) up to the end when she retires. She visits a climate change conference and explains her position to Vera: "The UK is falling behind, the infrastructure is laughable. What will they do? Allow themselves to be held hostage by Russia? As if foreign fuel is any kind of solution. You can trust the wind, you cannot trust Russia." And when Vera answers that she does not understand this, Marianne continues: "It means: why don't they diversify their sources of electricity: wind, nuclear, solar. Why don't they build storage facilities?" Tony, an environmental activist, is the first character we meet; his first statement sets the tone: "Do not believe the lies. Whose lies? The lies of the corporations who manipulate prices, and the countries that oppose alternative energies so that their resources are getting exploited and their pockets get fat." Tony uses the metaphor of a game and play to explain the energy crisis. According to him, these corporations and countries are strategic players within a worldwide arena (Duyvendak and Jasper 2016). They "game the system," manipulating and exploiting the current energy crisis to their own advantage: "Everybody's a player, it's a big game for them and no one is innocent. The name of the game: the free energy suppression and ecological devastation." At first sight, as Tony admits himself, people often see him as a crazy conspiracy theorist. But what he basically wants is not so illogical. When he meets Vera, he says: "You [Vera] want the truth, like I do. That's why I am here. I want the world to see, to really see. Follow me and I will show you the truth." Three elements of the story show that he is right: the subtitle of *Collapsus*, 'Energy risk conspiracy'; his discovery that China is indeed delivering weapons to Iran; and his disclosure of secret documents—framed as an act of civil disobedience—(in the 'Unlock the vault' minigame) that proves that there is a conspiracy between individuals within the coal, gas, and oil industry. Ali and Amir are working toward a peaceful and productive Iran, or even the entire Middle East, avoiding two extreme positions, i.e. people representing the Iranian government and oil interests, and people who want to use violence against the government.

Chen and Jack represent the other end of the spectrum. Chen is the archetypal bad guy, he is *dismissive* and shows no intention of taking climate change seriously. He blackmails Jack to join him at Tiger Energy (NRG), and is exposed and arrested in the end. Initially, Jack also defends the oil business ("Oil is cheap, it's versatile, oil built the 20th century," in his conversation with Vera), but he is realistic enough to change his position from *dismissive* to *doubtful*: "The [oil, coal] business is gone to hell, Chen." Jack also suggests that Vera should meet the representative of SBSP, David Peng. However, Jack is not committed to taking action himself: in the last episode, he is at home, taking care of Liana.

Collapsus ends with a multiple screen showing competing voices and images, with Vera in the center screen (see Figure 5.3). This is in line with Stoknes' argument that a plurality of stories is needed. Vera reflects on the energy transition ("It will be a rough transition, with heavy costs on all sides; and who's to say it's a transition we can manage") and announces her new job and her decision to stop vlogging: "Others will still do the work,"

5.3: *Collapsus* – Multiple screens.

she recounts, "and you should listen to them. Elena and the others know that we are not out of the woods yet." Marianne retires from politics ("It's time to let others take my place. I did not see how complex the world was when I first began this"), Elena continues vlogging ("We must always have a voice"), Ali and Amir are on the run ("We know things. Things about our old masters that will shine a light in dark places. It will be dangerous, but we must strive to reveal the truth"), Tony continues with his activist work ("I have tried to make a difference, I think I did, but at what cost? I have to keep trying, I have to"), and Chen tries to arrange a deal with the police to get out of prison ("I will sell everybody off, I'll be safe, I'm always safe"). These reflections on what happened in *Collapsus* are forms of 'interpassive feedback' (Pfaller 1999). This last episode provides the player with possible interpretations of the actions of the main characters; this media production is designed in such a way that it provides for its own reception. Even so, ultimately, it is up to the individual players to come up with possible interpretations.

Documentary news items. The fictional storyline is complemented by fourteen CitizEnergy news reports that pop-up at certain points in the storyline (see Table 2, row 3: 'O'). The first one, for example, pops up right after Tony's initial statement: "Do not believe the lies" (see Figure 5.4). We see the CitizEnergy logo, a world map with—in red—the place where the vlog comes from (in this case, London), the name of the vlogger (in

5.4: *Collapsus* – CitizEnergy news report.

this case, Elena) and a short text: "London, June 2012. World Hit by Fuel Chaos. Global shortages and United States monopoly of Asia and Middle East energy resources call for dramatic, regional 'proto-blocking.' Rapid Russian-Chinese and Central Asian alliances required to decentralize control and consumption of renewable energy resources." There are comments from the main characters, in this case Tony, Jack, and Esperanca, and a link to the Tegenlicht website. In the bottom right, we see a short documentary video clip with highlights from the VPRO Tegenlicht documentaries on energy that were broadcast on television. In the first news report, for example, we hear about America's addiction to oil, the Iranian interest in destabilizing oil regions to keep prices high, China's strategic need for energy supplies, and the difficulties of initiating reform. The news reports provide a solid basis for the stories and the urgency of the *Collapsus* characters' changing their behavior. Some examples include Tony's claim that countries and companies manipulate prices and oppose sustainable technologies out of self-interest, and Vera's progression from unconcerned to alarmed.

Collapsus is part of a long-term VPRO Tegenlicht documentary project on the imminent energy transition and the geopolitical energy wars caused by this transition. The three-part project took off in 2006 with a weblog and two television programs: *Energy War, Part I. The New Owners of the World*, and *Part II. The Green Race*. These programs portray the West as addicted to oil and gas, which are often imported from unreliable petro-capitalist, authoritarian states with a questionable reputation with regard to democracy and human rights. Countries such as Russia, Iran, and Venezuela use their energy supplies as a political weapon to defend their strategic interests. Only by developing new green technologies or green power, such as solar power, wind power, and biofuels, can the West diminish its dependency on these countries and, at the same time, stop destroying our planet and improve our environment. In 2008, VPRO Tegenlicht made an update, *Energy War. Plenty of Energy.* In this second part of the project, our dependence on fossil fuels is characterized, again, as being highly problematic. The greenhouse effect, rogue oil states, the reduction of world oil production and simultaneous increase in the demand for energy, and uncontrollable, fluctuating prices contribute to a common feeling of crisis. Tegenlicht raises the question of whether we can manage to adopt a new, green energy regime in time using alternative energy sources such as solar power, or whether we will lose this race against the clock.

The last part of this trilogy consists of a television program, *Energy Risk*, and the game *Collapsus*, both made in 2010. In *Energy Risk* (broadcast on 22 March 2010), two alarming future scenarios are presented to a panel of foreign experts in order to assess what kind of geopolitical conflicts Europe might end up in. In the first scenario, Russia abruptly and completely cuts off the gas supply to Europe because of a gas boycott in Uzbekistan. It becomes clear that Europe is too dependent on Russian gas, and, because of that dependency, too reliant on Russia's foreign policy. In the second scenario, the oil supply from the Middle East to the West is stopped unexpectedly by Iranian movements in the Strait of Hormuz. Iran can raise oil prices by destabilizing the region. The West is confronted with enormous oil shortages and the United States therefore decides to intervene militarily, but meets with opposition from China and Russia. Both scenarios demonstrate how geopolitical conflicts about remaining fossil fuels can potentially affect Europe, Europe's increasing vulnerability, and the necessity to switch more rapidly to alternative sources of energy. *Collapsus* was officially launched at the end of the *Energy Risk* program with a presentation of its trailer.[8]

8 *Energy Risk* was watched by 214,000 viewers. In the first three months, Collapsus.com had 200,000 unique visitors, 25 per cent from the Netherlands, 20 per cent from the United States, 10 per cent each from France and Germany, and 5 per cent from the UK (these statistics date from June 2010; information from VPRO Tegenlicht and Submarine).

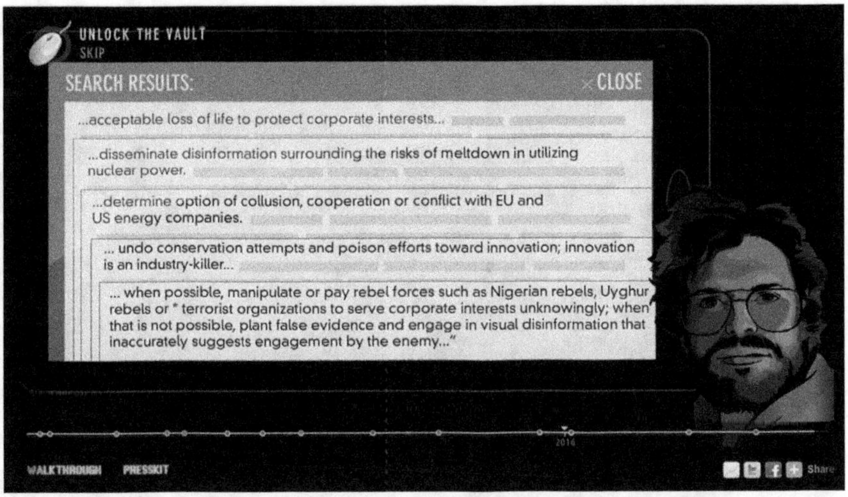

5.5: *Collapsus* – Tony unlocking the vault.

Minigames. The seven minigames play a small, yet important role in *Collapsus* (see Table 2, row 4). Three of them are related to Tony's effort to reveal some secret information. In the first minigame, the player has to move the cursor to reveal a message from Tony. If you fail or skip this game, you cannot read Tony's message: "I'm on the inside now [...] I trust you know what to do with this." In the sixth minigame, the player has to unlock the vault: "Head office filepad: Passkey protected. Slide to unlock," we can read on the screen. If you fail or skip this game, you cannot read the shocking documents Tony hands over to Vera later on, which will lead to the arrest of the Tiger NRG's representatives (see Figure 5.5).

In the seventh minigame, you have to move the cursor to reveal the following text: "We will use this info to destroy the puppet masters at any cost." If you fail or skip this minigame, you do not know that Tony is about to expose Tiger NRG's representatives. In two other minigames, the player has to tune into a conversation. If you fail or skip the fourth one, you miss a crucial point where Marianne convinces Vera to do some real reporting. If you fail or skip the fifth one, you cannot understand the relationship between the two brothers Amir and Ali. The second and third minigames do not play an important role.

Simulation games. In the second and fourth episodes, a binary choice pops up for the player (see Table 2, row 3) to see a news item (O) or to play a short-session sim game (Φ). Sim games are games that simulate aspects of reality relying on rule-based interactions as their core mode of signification.

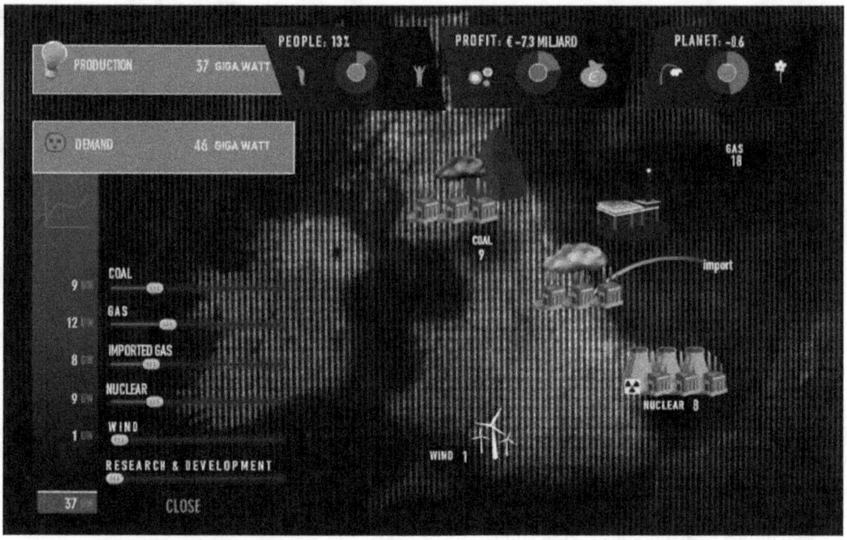

5.6: *Collapsus* – Playing field.

The player has to carry out two simple assignments.[9] The first time a binary choice pops up for the player, it is under the label 'Blackouts.' The news item in the right panel 'London: New Blackout Panic' deals with our energy dependency and how to deal with such a blackout. If you click on the left panel, you see a world map with Great Britain in red and London flickering. If you move your cursor to Britain, the following text pops up: "London—Avoid the blackouts. The UK has lowered its energy production using coal and nuclear energy by 30%. Demand has risen. Avoid the blackouts. Choose wisely!" If you click again, the playing field pops up (see Figure 5.6).[10]

You see that energy production (37 gigawatt) falls short of the demand for energy (46 gigawatt). The game has a simple goal: you have to produce more energy to meet the demand, making a choice between several energy sources (coal, gas, imported gas, nuclear, and wind) while keeping a harmonious balance between the three Ps: People, Profit, and Planet. The three Ps incorporate social, economic, and ecological dimensions that measure and

9 I will only analyze the first sim game. The second sim game deals with the gas crisis in Bulgaria, after Russia decided to cut the gas supplies. The goal of this sim game is to find alternative energy resources. The conclusion is that wood is better than coal, while oil is the worst choice.

10 As part of the British government's goal to improve the environment, they decided to generate less electricity from coal and nuclear fuel. Because of global warming, the use of air conditioning has exploded, which leads to an increase in demand (information from Submarine).

evaluate the impact of an organization's activities on the world—in this first game the impact of augmenting energy production in the UK.

The basic rule of the game—according to Bogost's procedural rhetoric, the most important element of a game's meaning—is an ideologically motivated one: players can win the game by choosing a specific energy source, or a combination of sources that meet the energy demand while keeping the impact on the Planet as low as possible. Coal turns out to be the worst choice, then gas, then nuclear, while wind is the best. I can demonstrate that this is the case by selecting five different actions and seeing what their impact is on the three Ps (Table 4).

Table 4: Impact of different energy sources

Source	Giga-watt	People	Impact on People	Profit	Impact on Profit	Planet	Impact on Planet
Coal	9	13 %	+27/6=+4.5	- 7.3 billion	+4.8/6=+0.8	- 0.6	-1.3/6=-0.22
	+6 (15)	40 %		- 2.5 billion		- 1.9	
Gas	12	13 %	+61/11=+5.55	- 7.3 billion	+8.2/11=+0.75	- 0.6	-1.4/11=-0.13
	+3 (15)	27 %		- 6.0 billion		- 1.0	
Im-ported gas	8	13 %		- 7.3 billion		- 0.6	
	+8 (16)	60 %		- 0.4 billion		- 1.6	
Nuclear	9	13 %	+33/6=+5.5	- 7.3 billion	+5.2/6=+0.87	- 0.6	-0.2/6=-0.03
	+6 (15)	46 %		- 2.1 billion		- 0.8	
Wind	1	13 %	+9/2=+4.5	- 7.3 billion	+1.2/2=+0.6	- 0.6	0.0/2=0.0
	+2 (3)	22 %		- 6.1 billion		- 0.6	

In the black cells, we see the initial state that was recorded. The People have a satisfaction rate of 13 per cent, the Profit is -7.3 billion euro and the Planet has a score of -0.6. Then, we increase the different energy sources to try to meet the demand: we increase coal from 9 to 15 (+6), gas from 12 to 15 (+3), imported gas from 8 to 16 (+8), nuclear from 9 to 15 (+6), and wind from 1 to 3 (+2). In each case, this is the most that you can do with one energy source in the short term. When you have reached the maximum for coal, imported gas, nuclear energy, and wind, a pop-up tells you: "To produce more, you need an extra plant. It takes two years to build one. Do you want to, yes or no?" With gas you get the message: "You can't produce more gas than you do." For every extra gigawatt of energy, Table 4 shows its impact on the three Ps:

- On the Planet: The impact of wind is 0.0 (0.0/2), nuclear is -0.03 (-0.2/6), gas is -0.13 (-1.4/11) and coal is -0.22 (-1.3/6). Conclusion: coal and gas have more of a negative impact than nuclear energy; wind is neutral. This supports the idea that electricity generated by *wind turbines* will not pollute the planet in the way that other energy sources do.
- On Profit: The impact of wind is +0.6 (+1.2/2), nuclear is +0.87 (+5.2/6), gas is +0.75 (+8.2/11), coal is +0.8 (+4.8/6). Conclusion: the positive impact of wind is only slightly less than that of coal, gas, and nuclear energy. This supports the idea that wind energy is not as expensive as it is assumed to be.
- On People: The impact of wind is = +4.5 (+9/2), nuclear is +5.5 (+33/6), gas is +5.55 (+61/11), coal is +4.5 (+27/6). Conclusion: the positive impact of wind is comparable to that of coal, nuclear energy and gas. This supports the idea that wind is indeed the best solution.

This conclusion also makes clear that a focus on *Collapsus*'s 'rule-based' procedural rhetoric alone is not enough to understand its meaning. In the Netherlands, for example, few environmentally minded people accept nuclear power as a serious alternative (SCP 2016) and they would probably oppose any positive reference to nuclear power if they were to play *Collapsus*.

A player can gain two important insights by playing this sim game. The first insight is a general one and in line with Marshall McLuhan's idea that the medium itself can persuade us, rather than the specific message it conveys (Dobrin and Morey 2009, 257-277). In playing the game, the user is actually experiencing the difficulty of harmoniously balancing the three Ps; the dilemmas and consequences of making choices become clear. The second insight is more precise and related to specific implicit or explicit environmental messages incorporated into the game design. As I showed in my analysis, this sim game privileges as an outcome investment in sustainable energy such as wind, rather than nuclear energy, gas, and coal—at least, if the player takes the impact on the Planet as the main criterion. Another player might privilege Profit, in which case nuclear energy, coal, and gas would still be a better choice than wind. We learn that diversification of energy resources—especially in the first two years—is necessary because it takes time to build new power stations and develop new, experimental solutions like space-based solar power. Wind energy only is not a solution.

Conclusion

In this chapter, I have analyzed how *Collapsus* uses a set of rhetorical strategies to engage individual citizens in climate issues. *Collapsus* is only one example (older, but still timely) of a growing number of ecological games that can serve as effective tools for promoting attitude change, pro-environmental behavior, and a better understanding of the complexity of the issues around climate change (Raessens 2017, 2018). Textual analyses like this chapter allow us to better understand individual productions like *Collapsus*, providing insight into its construction and socio-cultural relevance. According to many researchers, there is growing evidence on the effectiveness of games as a medium for persuasive communication (Neys and Jansz 2010; De Grove et al. 2012; Ruggiero 2015; Jacobs 2016, 2017; Jacobs, Jansz, and De la Hera 2017). This kind of validation research could help in the design of better games, and in determining the conditions that would help actualize the 'civic potential' from playing these games and help turn players into ecological citizens (Kahne et al. 2009).[11]

Research into the persuasiveness of media must allow for the fact that it is not always easy and straightforward to determine what exactly the intended message is. In relation to *Collapsus*, two kinds of limitations are of importance. First, the design process was characterized by pragmatic limitations. Because of financial and time restrictions, the designers of *Collapsus* needed to limit the number of variables in the sim game I discussed. To solve the problem of rising energy demands, the player can only try to increase energy production. Lowering the demand via energy-savings—a logical variable—is not an option. Second, realistic future scenarios had to be designed within the framework of existing generic conventions and the limitations of the narrative economy. The conventions of a conspiracy thriller for example, require that the complexities of a historical situation—such as energy transition—are simplified in a kind of morality play in which bad characters (such as Chen and, to a lesser degree, Jack) embody bad behavior, and good people (such as Tony and Vera, unraveling the conspiracy) defeat them in the end. And for reasons of narrative economy, Vera's politicization and personal growth from 'dismissive' to 'alarmed,' and from 'precontemplation' to 'maintenance' occur in short, simplified stages-of-change. The optimistic end she proclaims might also be misleading.

11 In our research project *Persuasive gaming. From theory-based design to validation and back*, we try to integrate these three research strands of analysis, design, and validation, see NWO (2018) and PGiC (2018).

She announces, "who can say what the future will bring? Well, me! I will be the new administrative head of the European SBSP programme." The intended message is that Vera will stop vlogging and start doing something more significant in the world. The game designers revealed to me in a conversation, that the technical solution Vera seems to embody (SBSP) is of minor importance for the storyline.

Environmental issues pose formidable imaginative and political difficulties for media producers. *Collapsus* tries to solve this by designing a story in which realistic energy transition scenarios are being described that are personal and urgent, having a direct impact on the characters from 2012 through to 2025. *Collapsus* shows different possible answers to the energy crisis, embodied in the beliefs, values, attitudes, and behavior of the different characters. By being in line with different sets of values and their possible stages-of-change, it can connect with, and possibly persuade, different groups of players. When we look at the strategies for raising awareness that I presented in section 2, we can conclude that *Collapsus* frames energy transition in a progressive and optimistic way so we can come up with solutions by developing empathy and responsibility, and that it uses different media (narratives, documentaries and games) and social networks to persuade its players to adopt a post-liberal and global form of citizenship. *Collapsus* is one possible answer to a question posed by Nixon: "How can we turn the long emergencies of slow violence into stories dramatic enough to rouse public sentiment and warrant political intervention?" (2011, 3). Because of its playful combination of a fictional storyline, documentary, and games, *Collapsus* was able to draw the attention of a large group of people, who were younger than the normal audience for documentaries, to the subject of climate change. *Collapsus* embodies what Henry Jenkins describes as 'civic imagination.' It shows the ability of a network of political agents (green citizens, politicians, activists, and vloggers) to imagine both a future world and how to turn this world into a better one (Jenkins et al. 2016, 152).

Acknowledgments

This research is part of the project *Persuasive gaming. From theory-based design to validation and back*, funded by the Netherlands Organisation for Scientific Research (NWO; 2013-2018; project number 314-99-106). I would like to thank Karel Brascamp and Christiaan de Rooij (Submarine), and Nina Huisman and William de Bruijn (VPRO Tegenlicht) for providing me with illustrations and background information on *Collapsus* and *Energy Risk*. I would also like to thank Jeroen Jansz, Teresa de la Hera, and Ruud Jacobs for their helpful and constructive comments on an earlier version of this chapter.

References

Barendregt, B., and R. Jaffe. 2014. *Green consumption. The global rise of eco-chic*. London: Bloomsbury.

Bogost, I. 2007. *Persuasive games. The expressive power of videogames*. Cambridge, MA: The MIT Press.

De Crom, A. 2010. Trendsetter van de toekomst. *Skrien* 3:8-13.

De Grove, F., J. van Looy, J. Neys, and J. Jansz. 2012. Playing in school or at home? An exploration of the effects of context on educational game experience. *Electronic Journal of E-Learning* 10 (2): 199-208.

Dobrin, S. I., and S. Morey, eds. 2009. *Ecosee: Image, rhetoric, nature*. Albany, NY: State University of New York Press.

Duyvendak, J. W., and J. M. Jasper. 2016. *Players and arenas: The interactive dynamics of protest*. Amsterdam: Amsterdam University Press.

Flanagan, M., and H. Nissenbaum. 2014. *Values at play in digital games*. Cambridge, MA: The MIT Press.

G4C. 2018. About us: Games for change. *Games for Change*. http://www.gamesforchange.org/about.

Green, M. C., and K. M. Jenkins. 2014. Interactive narratives: Processes and outcomes in user-directed stories. *Journal of Communication* 64 (3): 479-500.

Guggenheim, D. (dir.) 2006. *An Inconvenient Truth*. Paramount Pictures. Film.

Ingram, D. 2000. *Green screen: Environmentalism and Hollywood cinema*. Exeter: University of Exeter Press.

Jacobs, R. S. 2016. Play to win over: Effects of persuasive games. *Psychology of Popular Media Culture*. http://psycnet.apa.org/doi/10.1037/ppm0000124.

—. 2017. *Playing to win over: Validating persuasive games*. PhD thesis: Erasmus University Rotterdam.

Jacobs, R. S., J. Jansz, and T. de la Hera. 2017. The key features of persuasive games: A model and case analysis. In *New perspectives on the social aspects of digital gaming: Multiplayer 2*, eds. R. Kowert and T. Quandt, 153-171. New York: Routledge.

Jansz, J. 2016. *Serious gaming*. MOOC Erasmus University Rotterdam, Netherlands. http://www.coursera.org/learn/serious-gaming.

Jenkins, H. 2006. *Convergence culture. Where old and new media collide.* New York: New York University Press.

Jenkins, H., M. Ito, and d. boyd. 2016. *Participatory culture in a networked era.* Malden, MA: Polity Press.

Kahne, J., E. Middaugh, and C. Evans. 2009. *The civic potential of video games.* Cambridge, MA: The MIT Press.

Kattenbelt, C. 2008. Intermediality in theatre and performance: Definitions, perceptions, and medial relationships. *Cultural Studies Journal of Universitat Jaume I* 6:19-29.

Killingsworth, M. J., and J. S. Palmer. 1992. *Ecospeak: Rhetoric and environmental politics in America.* Carbondale, CO and Edwardsville, IL: Southern Illinois University Press.

Klein, N. 2014. *This changes everything: Capitalism vs. the climate.* New York: Simon & Schuster.

Lakoff, G. 2010. Why it matters how we frame the environment. *Environmental Communication* 4 (1): 70-81.

Lewis, A. (dir.) 2015. *This Changes Everything.* Bertha Foundation. Film.

MacGregor, S. 2014. Ecological citizenship. In *Handbook of political citizenship and social movements*, ed. H.-A. van der Heijden, 107-132. Cheltenham: Edward Elgar Publishing.

Neys, J., and J. Jansz. 2010. Political internet games: Engaging an audience. *European Journal of Communication* 25 (3): 227-241.

Nixon, R. 2011. *Slow violence and the environmentalism of the poor.* Cambridge, MA: Harvard University Press.

NWO. 2018. Persuasive gaming. From theory-based design to validation and back. *NWO.* http://www.nwo.nl/onderzoek-en-resultaten/onderzoeksprojecten/i/76/10476.html.

Pallotta, T. 2010. *Collapsus – Energy Risk Conspiracy* [browser]. Submarine Channel. Game.

Pfaller, R., ed. 1999. *Interpassivität: Studien über delegiertes Genießen.* Vienna: Springer.

PGiC. 2018. Persuasive gaming in context: From theory-based design to validation and back. *Persuasive Gaming in Context.* http://www.persuasivegaming.nl.

Popper, K. 1999. *All life is problem solving.* New York: Routledge.

Raessens, J. 2006. Reality play: Documentary computer games beyond fact and fiction. *Popular Communication* 4 (3): 213-224.

—. 2007. Playing history: Reflections on mobile and location-based learning. In *Didactics of microlearning. Concepts, discourses and examples*, ed. T. Hug, 200-217. Münster: Waxmann.

—. 2015. Playful identity politics: How refugee games affect the player's identity. In *Playful identities: The ludification of digital media cultures*, eds. V. Frissen, S. Lammes, M. de Lange, J. de Mul, and J. Raessens, 245-260. Amsterdam: Amsterdam University Press.

—. 2017. Gamen om de planeet te redden. *De Helling* 2:62-65.

—. 2018. Ecogames: Playing to save the planet. In *Cultural sustainability. Perspectives from the humanities and social sciences*, eds. T. Meireis, and G. Rippl, 232-245. London: Routledge.

Renov, M. 1993. Towards a poetics of documentary. In *Theorizing documentary*, ed. M. Renov, 12-36. New York: Routledge.

Ruggiero, D. 2015. The effect of playing a persuasive game on attitude and affective learning. *Computers in Human Behavior* 45:213-221.

Salen, K., and E. Zimmerman. 2004. *Rules of play: Game design fundamentals*. Cambridge, MA: The MIT Press.

SCP (The Netherlands Institute for Social Research). 2016. *Burgerperspectieven* 4. http://www.scp.nl/Publicaties/Alle_publicaties/Publicaties_2016/Burgerperspectieven_2016_4.

Sicart, M. 2011. Against procedurality. *Game Studies* 11 (3). http://gamestudies.org/1103/articles/sicart_ap.

—. 2014. *Play matters*. Cambridge, MA: The MIT Press.

Slater, M. D. 1999. Integrating application of media effects, persuasion, and behavior change theories to communication campaigns: A stages-of-change framework. *Health Communication* 11 (4): 335-354.

—. 2002. Entertainment education and the persuasive impact of narratives. In *Narrative impact. Social and cognitive foundations*, eds. M. C. Green, J. J. Strange, and T. C. Brock. 157-181. New York: Psychology Press.

Stoknes, P. E. 2015. *What we think about when we try not to think about global warming. Toward a new psychology of climate action*. White River Junction: Chelsea Green Publishing.

Sutton-Smith, B. 1997. *The ambiguity of play*. Cambridge, MA: Harvard University Press.

Turkle, S. 1996. *Life on the screen. Identity in the age of the internet*. London: Weidenfeld and Nicolson.

Yale Program on Climate Change Communication. 2016. *Global warming's six Americas*. climatecommunication.yale.edu/about/projects/global-warmings-six-americas.

About the author

Joost Raessens is chair and Full Professor of Media Theory at Utrecht University, and scientific director of the Utrecht Center for Game Research (gameresearch.nl). His research concerns the 'ludification of culture,' focusing on games for change in relation to global climate change and refugee and migration issues. Raessens was conference chair of the first DiGRA conference Level Up in Utrecht (digra2003.org) and leads the research project *Persuasive gaming. From theory-based design to validation and back* (persuasivegaming.nl). Among his book publications (see raessens.nl for a complete overview) are the *Handbook of computer game studies* (The MIT Press 2005), *Homo ludens 2.0: The ludic turn in media theory* (Utrecht University 2012), and *Playful identities: The ludification of digital media cultures* (Amsterdam University Press 2015).

6. The broken toy tactic: Clockwork worlds and activist games

Anne-Marie Schleiner

Abstract
The focus of this chapter is on 'activist simulation games,' which are motivated by an activist or political intention on the part of the game-maker, and which attempt to harness simulation and procedurality in the game to convey the maker's political critique or message to the playing public. Schleiner argues that that the 'toyness' of the world of such games, the miniature abstraction of the model that announces itself as game, not life, contributes to a nullification of the game's critical impact. To break away from this situation, she argues, requires a 'broken toy tactic' of interruption or sabotage that breaks the spell of games' procedural, operational logic.

Keywords: Activist games, serious games, procedurality, simulation, toy worlds, no play

Toy trains circle through a 1:25 scale model of traditional Dutch buildings and landmarks in the miniature city of Madurodam. Miniature cargo ships float along canals and toy delivery trucks loop around a peripheral freeway. These vehicle circulations have followed a reliable daily schedule ever since the tourist attraction was constructed in 1952 as a memorial to George Maduro, a young Jewish member of the Dutch Nazi resistance. On travel blogs, visitors remark on the punctuality of the miniature city's transportation, recalling their childhood fascination with the moving parts of Madurodam's toy vehicles. Despite the vacant artificiality of the setting, the frozen-in-place postures of Madurodam's doll-citizens, and the peculiar conglomeration

Glas, R., S. Lammes, M. de Lange, J. Raessens, and I. de Vries, eds. 2019. *The Playful Citizen. Civic Engagement in a Mediatized Culture.* Amsterdam: Amsterdam University Press.
DOI: 10.5117/9789462984523/CH06

of national landmarks in one Disney-like city, young and old still delight in the liveliness of the toy city.[1]

With similar interlocking, repetitious movements, like the hypnotic circuitous loops of a model train set, miniature computer game worlds draw the player into convincing abstractions of everyday operations. The hum of movement within a computer game, the automated circling of artificially alive 'non-player' characters, the scheduled passages of toy-like trains and vehicles and the movement of the sun and clouds, synchronize with outside-the-game spheres of operations, convincing the player of the parallel efficacy of the clockwork model. Bespelled by these motions, the player believes in the model regardless of whether game characters appear in photorealistic detail or are capable of a convincingly human, artificially intelligent conversation. Moving interlocking parts conform to a functional, rational diagram of a rhythmic clockwork universe where all is running as it should.

Similar to the application of simulation in the field of computer science, all manner of lively processes from the world are modeled into game worlds, from gardening to crowd fluxuations.[2] For instance, in the classic simulation genre game, designer Will Wright's *The Sims* (Maxis 2000), the domestic life of a suburban North American family is simulated in a doll-house-like game where vivacious Sims people eat, walk, urinate, socialize, and speak in 'Simlish,' a pseudo-language of emoticons. In this chapter, I will in particular draw on the investigations of Gonzalo Frasca (2001), Ian Bogost (2008), and Chaim Gingold (2003) into simulation and the 'procedural' logic of games, the lively processes and movements that unfold each time a game is played. Much of this theorization comes out of a post-graduate study program directed by Janet Murray, who initially proposed that a computer game is a cultural work produced by a "procedural author" (1997, 153).

Although my argument in this chapter will be informed by the substantial inroads that Bogost and others have wrought theorizing the dynamic

1 Last time I visited Madurodam, on a weekday in June of 2011, the aging toy city seemed somewhat forgotten by the Dutch, although it was still attended by busloads of Indian and Chinese tourists.

2 The term 'simulation' also invokes post-modern philosopher Jean Baudrillard's theories of simulation and 'simulacra', especially in reference to Disneyland and suburbia. Yet, Baudrillard's interest in simulation seems primarily bound up with describing the artificiality of a post-modern capitalist condition that has replaced authentic experience, a mourning for a loss of authenticity. Simulation in computer games, on the other hand, like in computer science, takes the artificiality of the model as a given without moral qualms—even as such models attempt to improve their fidelity to real life processes assumed to still be running outside the game.

procedural rhetoric of games, what has been somewhat overlooked, even by critics of 'procedurality' like Miguel Sicart (2011), is a closer consideration of procedurality itself. In particular, I am interested in the impact of these 'gamic' procedures on political or social critique in what are called 'serious games.' Serious games is a grab-bag appellation for diverse educational, training, and activist games, which I will for this chapter primarily limit to the analysis of 'activist simulation games,' games such as *Climate Defense* (Auroch Digital 2013) or *Sweatshop* (Littleloud 2011) with explicit political and/or persuasive ambitions on the part of their concerned citizen makers. A one- or two-person developer is often solely responsible for all aspects of the game-making in these independent small companies, including art direction, design, programming, and playtesting. The maker of an activist simulation game attempts to make use of mimetic algorithms in the game to present a persuasive argument in motion, to launch a social, environmental, or other activist critique, or to open a political question. As more ordinary citizens come of age among the 'ludoliterate' versed in the language and genres of gameplay, relatively easy to produce casual games are becoming an attractive vehicle for political action (Raessens 2010). Still, we are only beginning to forge an understanding of how such games both serve and fail as activist tools, as tactics, among others, available to the concerned citizen. Therefore, my definition in this chapter of an 'activist simulation game' is both: a. motivated by an activist or political intent on the part of the game-maker, and b. attempts to harness simulation and procedurality in the game to carry the maker's political critique or message to the playing public.[3]

A definition relying partially on the game-maker's intention does encounter inherent contradictions, as when, for example, games not explicitly intended to be politically persuasive, such as entertaining war games, can easily be read as propaganda. But the desire on the part of the game-maker to use a game as a form of political argumentation with a broader public, both when it succeeds and fails as it is countermanded by aspects of the game, is a primary tension that I will explore in this chapter. Referring to this difficulty in designing serious games Mary Flanagan writes: "These play spaces must retain all the elements that make a game enjoyable while effectively communicating their message" (2009, 249).

3 The activist simulation game contrasts to another common variant of serious games where a 'normal' entertaining game is interspersed with packets of 'serious' or pedagogic information that the player swallows like cans of vegetables in between courses of fun.

In an activist simulation game, a play move is not only an inconsequential act of fun, but also carries symbolic weight by referencing real issues and world problems, for instance signifying whether a member of a threatened species like the polar bear in *Polar Plunder* (AIMS Games Center 2013) can find enough food under the ice for her cubs despite Arctic climate change. And yet, in spite of this added worldly weight and consequentiality, it is often difficult to take serious games seriously. Although game-makers set out to shock players with a moving diagram of harmful and tragic operations, players conversely succumb to the enchantment of lively, toy-like, mechanical processes within the miniature, abstracted clockwork game world, no matter how damaging the actual operations in the exterior world, regardless of how many dolphins are killed or how many tracts of rainforest are destroyed. The game asks to be played and mastered, inviting the player to enter into its cause and effect mechanical loops, regardless of the consequences—it is only a game, after all.

The 'toyness' of the world of the game, the miniature abstraction of the model that announces itself as game, not life, contributes to this nullification of the game's critical impact, as I will discuss further on. Moreover, I will argue that the operational movements running inside the game induce a complacency akin to what Martin Heidegger referred to as "everyday sight," a way of "Being-in-the-World" already familiar to us from procedural interactions in the world outside the game (1927, 107). In order to better understand the effect of the procedurality of the game on the player, in this chapter I will draw on what may seem an unlikely and acontemporous source from outside the fields of game studies and computer science, where procedurality itself has often been accepted at face value as a positive rhetorical tool within games.[4] In *Being and time*, his primary work devoted to forwarding a temporal, embodied phenomenological understanding of human existence, Heidegger theorized a common, everyday mode of being (ontology) and a mental framework that he understood as a submersion within the everyday circulations and procedures of the work-a-day, social world (Ibid., 78). This practical view of the workings of the world is what he refers to alternately as "everyday sight" and "circumspection" (2003, 107). A railway line transports workers from the suburbs to the city; the

4 Heidegger is often considered an apolitical philosopher, or judged for his Nazi era actions as a university administrator in Freiburg, and therefore might seem distant from political critique or philosophy. Even so, his deconstructive philosophical method was highly influential for critical theory in the latter half of the twentieth century, and informed, for instance, the deconstructive methodology of Jaques Derrida. Also, Heidegger's phenomenological framework impacted political philosophers like Hannah Arendt and Georgio Agamben.

6.1: *September 12th* – Game screenshot.

suburban train stops to let a passenger off at an inner-city station guarded by a vigilant conductor who steps back and forth on the station platform. Such an interlocking set of functional workings, which we also see running compellingly in the toy city of Madurodam, is supplementary to Heidegger's "Dasein in the They," an immersed everyday orientation within the common world (1927, 167). We seldom question or "disclose" our place or the place of others in such work-a-day utilitarian operations, for to do so continuously would impede our ability to plug into the "equipmental workshops" we use to take care of daily business (Ibid., 105).

The dilemma that confronts the activist game-maker is that the very procedural logic of the simulation game that he or she hopes to harness for a provocative critique has a bewitching effect on the player, comparable to Heidegger's state of fascinated absorption in the practical workings of the world (1927, 107). Examples of equipment in *Being and time*, of clocks, hammers, planes, and needles, speak of a more rhythmic, mechanical, Industrial Age, but almost a century later, well into the Information Age, much of our world is still composed of functional, instrumental relations, on and off the screen (Ibid., 99). Circuitous operationality has found yet another abode in the weightless, abstract toy workings of computer games.

And yet there are exceptions to this rule of the genre, ways for concerned citizens to design games that snap the player out of the hypnotic circle of toy operationality, via what I will refer to as the broken toy tactic. A rupture in the game catapults the player outside the comforting and rewarding operational sphere of the clockwork game world and induces him or her to critical reflection, contestation, or action. While analyzing two popular activist games closely, I will argue that the player's shift from fascinated immersion in moving game world operations to a disturbed confrontation with a malfunction of play mirrors Heidegger's anxious illuminations of the operational clockwork loops of the world that might arise when a tool, like his oft invoked hammer, is broken or missing (1927, 102). A break in the smooth functionality of the game discloses its operational logic in greater "totality" (Ibid., 105). For Heidegger, a "clearing" of everyday sight uncovers the disquieting temporality of "the who's" existence, as well as illuminating his possibilities (Ibid., 167). Yet, in the hands of the concerned citizen game-maker, this unsettling existential pause or stop, this interruption of the game's workings, is also a moment ripe for critical reflection and evaluation that precedes the formation of a political stance and possible action, the intended transformation of 'games for change.'

Overseers of toy world operations

Let's enter into a closer comparison of toy world operations at work in two widely played pioneering activist simulation games. The player of Uruguayan Gonzalo Frasca's airstrike simulator game, *September 12th* (Frasca 2003a) assumes a 'god' or 'bird's-eye' position overlooking a Middle Eastern city from above (see Figure 6.1). This is similar to the perspective on Will Wright's classic *SimCity* (Maxis 1989) where the player as city planner constructs and manages a city from above. In fact, many simulation games, following the genre template set by *SimCity* and *The Sims* (Maxis 2000), position the player as a distant overseer of automated, minutely scaled, toy working worlds.

The goal at the outset of *September 12th*, similar to many commercial war games released after the terrorist attacks in the United States on September 11, 2001, appears to be to eliminate terrorists from the streets of a Middle Eastern city, identifiable by their gray robes and machine guns. But as the game proceeds, the player recognizes that the more frequently he launches missiles on the terrorists in the city, the more neighboring civilians, including women and children, are converted into terrorists. Forging a rational feedback loop between the player's actions and visible outcomes in the game environment, *September 12th* simulates an escalating cycle of conflict exasperated by the War on Terror. This interactive, escalation between player and game becomes a dynamic, interactive argument for "violence begets violence." Thus, the game procedurally makes a case for peace via the interactive simulation of strife between the terrorists and the player—who is cast in the role of an air force striker.

But here we may be slightly misled in applying Frasca's own belief in the rhetorical efficacy of simulation to the analysis of the game (2003b). The cycle of the escalation of violence largely becomes illuminated in a critical light because the game does not work properly as a game—the only way to 'win' the game would be to abstain from playing, from interacting with the game! On the flip side of the 'positive' simulation of a damaging cycle of the escalation of violence, lies a negative argument for non-intervention, for non-engagement, a 'no play imperative' in either war or games. Paradoxically, can the simulation of a harmful process only become visible (disclosed) to the player, and thereby leveraged as critique, if the game is made frustratingly unplayable, in effect rendered a broken toy? Before we continue with this question, let's take a few moments to consider how procedurality and simulation have been understood in game scholarship thus far.

Murray was one of the first to call attention to the procedurality of games and electronic media. According to Murray,

> [p]rocedural authorship means writing the rules by which the texts appear as well as writing the texts themselves. It means writing the rules for the interactor's involvement, that is, the conditions under which things will happen in response to the participant's actions. It means establishing the properties of the objects and potential objects in the virtual world and the formulas for how they will relate to one another. (1997, 152-153)

Bogost refers to the rhetorical impact of such gamic procedural mechanisms on the player as 'procedural rhetoric': "I suggest the name procedural rhetoric for the practices of using processes persuasively, just as verbal rhetoric is the practice of using oratory persuasively and visual rhetoric is the practice of using images persuasively" (2008, 125). As a rhetorical form, game procedurality appears to be an important new form of communication available in the public political sphere. Similarly emphasizing the communicative power of gamic procedures, according to Frasca, a game designer or 'Simauthor' (simulation author) communicates via the rules, logical processes, and algorithms in the game that model the trajectory of outside the game workings and outcomes:

> Whoever designs a strike simulator that is extremely hard to play is describing his beliefs regarding social mechanics through the game's rules rather than through events. [...] They are not only able to state if social change is possible or not, but they have the chance of expressing how likely they think it may be. (2003b, 228)

Activist game-makers such as Frasca therefore believe it is possible to harness the procedures of the game to mimic the probable outcome of a military assault, and to thereby communicate a particular belief about the workings of the world to the player-citizen, a citizen who may have voting rights and live in a nation with influence over the course of the war. Simulation games deliberately encourage the forging of correspondences from inside-the-game actions, procedures running within Johan Huizinga's "magic circle" of play (1950), to external spheres of action, so as to provoke a confusion that Bogost dubs as 'simulation fever': "But for the magic circle to couple with the world, it must not be hermetic; it must have a breach through which the game world and real-world spill over into one another" (2006, 136). Therefore, for the purposes of this discussion, what is important from Huizinga's much-cited and challenged magic circle is the relation between procedures running inside the game and those outside the game.

Worldly goings-on, when transposed via simulation to the game sphere or magic circle, become magically enchanting because they are miniature toy-like abstractions. My application of the magic circle to contemporary simulation games is not intended to imply that such digital games are magical, sorcerous rituals, as in Daniel Pargman and Peter Jakobsson's (2008) critique of the contemporary usage of Huizinga's term. The movement of causal loops within the game exerts the more mundane, everyday magic of the toy miniature, what Chaim Gingold (2003) refers to as a "miniature garden," a spatially reduced, abstracted world like a Japanese garden, model train set, or a doll house. Over the course of his Master's thesis, also conducted at Georgia Tech, Gingold expands on the term he encountered in an interview with Shigero Miyamoto, the influential Japanese game designer of Nintendo computer games. Gingold writes:

> [A] garden has an inner life of its own; it is a world in flux which grows and changes. A garden's internal behaviors, and how we understand those rules, help us to wrap our heads and hands around the garden. [...] Gardens, like games, are compact, self-sustained worlds we can immerse ourselves in. (2003, 7)

The reduction in scale and in complexity in a Japanese garden, the scaling down from forest to tree, from lake to pond, serve in a game as a cognitive aid for the player's apprehension of the systematic clockwork world, a miniature sphere of operations.

The simulation game's 'procedural argument' intentionally blurs the line between the miniature game world and the outside world, but there are important differences between the operations running on either side of this fence or *ludic border.* Although all games have dynamic, time-based procedures, not all of these play moves make much sense outside the game—in other words, to state the rather obvious, not all games are simulation games. For example, when a player makes a move in checkers, this does not correlate to a specific action undertaken in the world outside the game. In this way, the falling, colorful squares of *Tetris* (Pajitnov 1984) are just that, falling colorful squares. These primarily signify play moves. In such abstract games, actions procedurally advance the game forward toward a goal (or multiple goals) triggering wins and losses. By contrast, in the simulation game, actions and processes have a double signification as both gamic procedures and as metaphoric actions.

And yet this added layer of metaphoric significance does not mean that the player will reflect critically on the simulated operation in activist games, as will become apparent in the following example. By way of comparison to *September 12th*, let's now consider another widely played, free for download, activist simulation game that affords the player an overview of a miniature toy world. Similar to *September 12th*, Paulo Pedercini's farcical *McDonald's Video Game* (Molleindustria 2006), simulates a harmful operation, in this case, an environmentally destructive fast food corporate industry. *McDonald's Video Game* is structured as a managerial simulation game, and although designed and programmed entirely by Pedercini, the prolific creator behind Molleindustria, the game implements a slick graphical user interface button panel (see Figure 6.2) reminiscent of commercially produced *The Sims*. The *McDonald's Video Game* player alternates between managing four distinct production cycles: a. overseeing farm production; b. administering a cattle feedlot; c. managing a chain of hamburger-grill workers; and d. negotiating policies and marketing campaigns in 'corporate headquarters.' The challenge of the game is to effectively multitask, manage, and maintain the production routines in all four areas without letting one slip. As the player's skill improves, outcomes of actions in one sphere of operations have ramifications elsewhere in the game. For instance, if not enough cattle are raised, negative consequences arise further up the supply chain, ultimately effecting the McDonald's corporation bottom-line. Although *McDonald's Video Game* periodically discloses snippets of textual information about fast food industry practices, it is this simulation of lively processes that imparts a convincing overview of interlocking cycles of fast food bio-production, from deforestation to raising enough cattle for meat to fastfood public relations campaigns.

Despite recurrent dips into bankruptcy, *McDonald's Video Game* operates so well as managerial training software with the management of a miniature,

6.2: *McDonald's Video Game* – Game screenshot.

toy-like, cheerful cow and hamburger world that the ironic subtext of this being an unethical business practice is often missed by players. For instance, when my game design students in Singapore played *McDonald's Video Game*, they seemed largely unconcerned about the detrimental side effects of this type of production on workers, animals, consumers, or the environment. They were willing to undertake whatever was necessary to keep the game system alive and the McDonald's corporation above the bottom line, even adding diseased cows to the food chain.

The enchanting ordinariness of toy world equipment

Unlike the vehicles circulating in the toy model city of Madurodam, games like *September 12th* and *McDonald's Video Game* require interaction from the player via buttons or a graphical user interface (GUI), conventionally organized into an instrumental dashboard at the edge of the screen. *September 12th* presents the player with a weapon for targeting and shooting the terrorists; *McDonald's Video Game* offers the player a colorful toy-like button interface of slaughterhouse machinery to first convert the livestock into hamburgers, and then a different range of equipment for converting hamburgers into dollars. This observation on the equipment of the game interface may seem obvious, but it is this very ordinariness in game interaction that poses another challenge to critical and activist game design because 'equipmental' interactions with game procedures contribute to the player's 'everyday sight.' In a chapter of *Being and time* entitled 'The worldhood of the world,' Heidegger describes the equipment required for his everyday operational view of 'Being-in-the-World': "In our dealings we come across equipment for writing, sewing, working, transportation, measurement. [...] A totality of equipment is constituted by various ways of the 'in-order-to,' such as serviceability, conduciveness, usability, manipulability" (1927, 97).

When observable in the clockwork toy world, these equipmental operations impart everyday common sense. Referring to the simulation of a natural cycle in a clock, Heidegger writes: "In a clock, account is taken of some definite constellation in the world system" (2003, 72), and further on he writes: "When we make use of the clock-equipment, which is proximally and inconspicuously ready-to-hand, the environing Nature is ready-to-hand along with it" (Ibid., 101). In other words, those earthly relations that are simulated or incorporated in the equipment, such as the movement of the sun from day to night being replicated in the clock, are easily 'discovered' and naturalized in the 'clock-equipment'.

Equipment, or the "ready-to-hand" is easy to see, contrasting to Heidegger's "presence-at-hand," the term he uses to refer to the sounds and colors of perceived but not yet differentiated "reality," such as a rumble of noise that upon reaching the ear does not quite resolve into the screech of a passing motorbike (1927, 228). Unlike the confusion that an intrusion of "presence-at-hand" reality might occasion, the equipmental operations of the ready-to-hand world are easily apprehended, made sense of, or 'discovered.' The equipment's functionality seems obvious, running smoothly in plain sight, in the common-sense realm of 'the They.' Naturally, the player would want to use the available buttons to operate the farm machinery and produce hamburgers. Thus, simulation games simulate alleged processes from outside the game sphere in plain view, invoking the everyday perspective of how things work, the operations of fast food production, or of an efficient airstrike. If we apply an extended Heideggerian interpretation, 'equipment' refers not only to interface buttons, but also to the larger operations (in his terms 'workshops') that these buttons trigger or manipulate. For instance, *September 12th* presents the player with a weapon for targeting and shooting the terrorists; while *McDonald's Video Game* offers the player a colorful toy-like button-interface of slaughterhouse machinery to turn livestock into hamburgers, and then a different range of equipment for turning hamburgers into dollars.

Although ready-to-hand equipment is easily discoverable, it is also hidden, in another sense. The familiarity of everyday sight or circumspection, conceals "the totality" of a clockwork operation, the in-order-to relations that it is connected to, including objects and persons at a distance (Heidegger 1927, 105). Immersion in the clockwork world's operations is a state of "concernful" absorption that is to a certain extent blind and alienated, not only to its own existence, but to the larger repercussions of the operation (Ibid., 101). The game's movement compels the player to accept its operations as ordinary, as unquestionable cycles of everyday life, unfolding within plain view or, to be more precise, in relation to simulation genre games, within the elevated plain view of the great overseer of the toy world operations. The challenge that then confronts the concerned citizen game-maker is that no matter what these simulated operations are, as they run with the evocative mimicry within miniature toy worlds, they acquire everyday currency and uncritical acceptance among players via the motion of their interlocking, toy-like workings.

Player vs. game

But do the toy world's procedures really subsume the player to such an extent? Is the operational functionality of the game truly so bewitching? Furthermore, an allegation could be made that Bogost's rhetorical transmission of procedural game logic from the sender (the game-maker or 'Simauthor') to receiver (the player) is limited by a communications model of sending and receiving. The player in this analysis, even while interacting with the game, becomes a passive recipient of rhetoric in motion. In a similar vein, Sicart critiques the limited role that players are afforded in designer-weighted, instrumental 'proceduralist' game studies, writing that players "are important, but only as *activators* of the process that sets the meanings contained in the game in motion" (2011). Are game designers, then, the only ones afforded the role of agents of engaged ludic citizenship? In support of player agency, Frasca proposes that players, not only game designers, potentially impact the ultimate rhetorical "outcome" of a game by channeling the course of play into directions unimagined by the game-maker (2003b, 228). Frasca calls upon Brazilian theater director Augusto Boal's "Theater of the Oppressed" as a model for how a game can depart from Aristotlean narrative closure. Frasca writes "one of [Boal's] most popular techniques, re-enacts the same play several times by allowing different audience members to get into the stage and take the protagonist's role," resulting in unforeseen outcomes (Ibid.).

For instance, such player-directed outcomes are evident in the spectacular demise of artificial game life, of entire families and their pets, in a dark genre of the Sims known as 'Disaster Sims.' The player's influence on the game's rhetorical outcome in such cases amounts to a breaking of the original game designer's 'script' to breed a suburban American family. With these morbid, broken games, often ending in fire, we return via a different path, following the player's initiative rather than the game-maker's, to derailed and broken game equipment.

On the other hand, when the toy is *not* broken, when the system is running without interruption, as when the player engages with the productive fast food mechanizations of *McDonald's Video Game*, the player remains blind to its workings even as she plugs into its persuasive everyday perspective. Losing track of time, the player immerses herself in a sequence of game challenges that, if designed well, alternates rewards (points, bonuses, and additional tools) with escalating peaks of difficulty, oscillating within what psychologist Mihaly Csikszentmihalyi refers to as a pleasurable "flow state" between challenge and skill (1990, 74). Thus, the player's fascinated state of absorption during gameplay suggests a loss of agency to the game's mechanics, except for when the player willfully alters the course of the game's 'oppressive script'.

Similarly, again from the realm of phenomenological philosophy, Heidegger's student Hans-Georg Gadamer makes the inverse proposal that the game plays the player rather than the player the game (1975). Gadamer conducted an inquiry into aesthetics and art that brought him to the phenomenology of play. Gadamer's player gives up his will to the game while performing the reflexive moves demanded by a game: "The structure of play absorbs the player into itself, and thus frees him from the burden of taking the initiative, which constitutes the actual strain of existence" (1975, 105). The player merges with the game, entering into an ongoing interactive, reflexive feedback loop: "What happens to us in the experience of art, Gadamer suggests, is very much like what happens to us in play: we lose ourselves" (Weinsheimer 1985, 102). Unless the player is forced to reflect upon correspondences reaching beyond the game, the player's critical and reflective capacity, political or otherwise, is easily bewitched amid the movement of game actions. Reacting with neither doubt, nor, on the contrary, belief, the player flows with the game's operational allegations about how the world works.

Only when the model is broken or interrupted by a renegade player, such as the maker of a Disaster Sim, or a game cheater or breaker, or through some form of sabotage installed by the game-maker, does the toy world's algorithms and workings become visible. Frasca's *September 12th* catapults the player outside the cozy assumptions of the clockwork game world and the comfortable correlations between rewarding player proficiency with toy weapons and 'how things work.' The brokenness of *September 12th* manifests in that playing well delivers loss, subverting the expectation of the player to master a rewarding challenge of eliminating terrorists. In *McDonald's Video Game*, on the other hand, the very operationality of the model of fast food production cycles transmitted to the player overcomes the game's critical impact. Beautiful toys that run too well are always enchanting, no matter how ugly the outcome of their workings. The player is lost in the game.

Broken toys and the no play imperative

The operational logic of the game takes hold. A player's action inspires a resulting reaction on the part of the game. The game, in turn, compels the player to further reflexive play moves and if the game is designed well, the player loses herself, losing even a sense of the passage of hours and days, within the game, absorbed into the game's workings, immersed in a feedback loop, Gadamer's aesthetic union of player and game. The player performs a role among other processes running within the clockwork world through interaction with the game machine and the management of its simulated processes. Like the imprint of a popular tune that demands to be liked through its repeated exposure to the ears, players unreflectively absorb the logic of military operations, internalize the production cycle of hamburgers, and flow with the hum of tractors. How satisfying when at least the toy world is operating as it should.

In the rational, operational spheres of games, as in the instrumental spheres of life, one's everyday perspective turns away from suffering and the consequences of damaging human operations. Most feel powerless to disengage from, halt, or redirect harmful goings-on that are naturalized. Players flee their own mortality to the artificial circulations of ageless clockwork, toy worlds. In this sense, Madurodam's endless ship and train circulations are a soothing and forgetful memorial to the untimely demise of young George Maduro.

A tactical recipe for the activist simulation game consists then of two steps, first a positive, then a negative; first to constructively program a simulation of a harmful operation from the world into the game, followed up by either a game-maker, or player instigated interruption, or sabotage that breaks the spell of the game's movement and procedurality, thereby illuminating its operationality in a critical light. Absorption in the everyday world of 'equipmental' dealings and transactions are broken at this rift of 'in-order-to' relations among entities, things, and persons. Induced to a discomforting re-evaluation and analysis of the games' operational logic, the player performs a critical diagnosis of the wrongness or rightness of the broken play equipment. After being subjected to the broken toy tactic, a worldly operation's common sense, the everyday claim on existence comes into dispute, becoming a matter of critical concern for the citizen-player.

What is paradoxical with the broken toy tactic is that the game and activist critique remain in the last instance incompatible—only by interrupting or ejecting the player from the game, the no play imperative, is a critique illuminated and a political questioning made possible. Moreover, the intended effect of such games is not just a break in the game, but also the possibility of putting a stop to the destructive worldly procedure that is being simulated. The no play imperative extends beyond the game to the refusal to be a 'player' in the harmful processes of the world, a refusal to play at war, a refusal to play at the exploitation of the environment in the production and consumption of fast food. Thus, the most earnest mixture of politics and games seems to be delivered in games that do not believe in playing per se, but in the impossibility of separating the world and game, of separating procedurality in one realm or the other on either side of the ludic border. The activist game attempts to catapult the player from absorption in the clockwork toy world, to a realm of politics that he or she is otherwise quite busy avoiding.

Acknowledgments

This chapter is a rewritten version of the chapter 'Clockwork worlds: Activist games, harrowing missions, and broken toys' from A. M. Schleiner. 2012. *Ludic mutation: The player's power to change the game*. PhD thesis University of Amsterdam. See also Schleiner (2017).

References

AIMS Games Center at Miami University. 2013. *Polar Plunder.* [Android]. Miami, FL: Miami University. Game.

Auroch Digital. 2013. *Climate Defense.* [Android]. Bristol: Auroch Digital. Game.

Bogost, I. 2006. *Unit operations: An approach to videogame criticism*. Cambridge, MA: The MIT Press.
—. 2008. The rhetoric of video games. In *The ecology of games: Connecting youth, games, and learning*, ed. K. Salen, 117-140. Cambridge, MA: The MIT Press.
Csikszentmihalyi, M. 1990. *Flow: The psychology of optimal experience*. New York: Harper & Row.
Flanagan, M. 2009. *Critical play: Radical game design*. Cambridge, MA: The MIT Press.
Frasca, G. 2001. Videogames of the oppressed. MA thesis: Georgia Tech University. http://www.ludology.org/articles/thesis.
—. 2003a. *September 12th*. [browser]. Newsgaming. Game.
—. 2003b. Simulation versus narrative. Introduction to ludology. In *The video game theory reader*, eds. M. Wolf and B. Perron, 221-236. New York: Routledge.
Gadamer, H. G. 1975. *Truth and method*. London: Sheed and Ward Ltd.
Gingold, C. 2003. *Miniature gardens and magic crayons*. MA thesis: Georgia Tech University. http://slackworks.com/~cog/writing/thesis/aesthetics.php#2.1.
Heidegger, M. 1927/1962. *Being and time*. New York: Harper & Row.
—. 2003. *Political and philosophical writings*, ed. M. Stassen. New York: Continuum International Publishing Group.
Huizinga, J. 1950. *Homo ludens: A study of the play-element in culture*. Boston, MA: Beacon Press.
Littleloud. 2011. *Sweatshop*. [browser]. Brighton: Littleloud. Game.
Maxis. 1989. *SimCity*. [multiplatform]. Maxis/Brøderbund/Infogrames. Game.
—. 2000. *The Sims*. [multiplatform]. Electronic Arts. Game.
Molleindustria. 2006. *McDonald's Video Game*. [browser]. Molleindustria. Game.
Murray, J. 1997. *Hamlet on the holodeck: The future of narrative in cyberspace*. New York: The Free Press.
Pajitnov, A. 1984. *Tetris*. [multiplatform]. Game.
Pargman, D., and P. Jakobsson. 2008. Do you believe in magic? Computer games in everyday life. *European Journal of Cultural Studies* 11 (2): 225-244.
Raessens, J. 2010. *Homo ludens 2.0: The ludic turn in media theory*, inaugural address. Faculty of Humanities, Utrecht University, the Netherlands.
Schleiner, A. 2012. *Ludic mutation: The player's power to change the game*. PhD thesis University of Amsterdam.
—. 2017. *The player's power to change the game: Ludic mutation*. Amsterdam: Amsterdam University Press.

Sicart, M. 2011. Against procedurality. *Game Studies* 11 (3). http://gamestudies.org/1103/articles/sicart_ap.
Weinsheimer, Joel C. 1985. *Gadamer's hermeneutics: A reading of truth and method.* New Haven, CT: Yale University Press.

About the author

Anne-Marie Schleiner is engaged in gaming and media culture in a variety of roles as a critic, curator, activist, artist, and designer. She has participated in art residencies and given workshops in Germany, Belgium, Spain, and Mexico. She has exhibited in international galleries, museums, and festivals. Documentation of her performative culture work is available in the Video Data Bank. She holds a doctorate in Cultural Analysis from the University of Amsterdam, and her book *The player's power to change the game* (Amsterdam University Press 2017) explores media art, activism, and game rhetoric. She has taught game design and digital art at universities in the United States, Mexico, and Singapore, and is a Lecturer in Design at the University of California, Davis.

7. Video games and the engaged citizen: On the ambiguity of digital play

Ingrid Hoofd

Abstract
This chapter questions how video games may aid civic engagement by youths. It does so by critically examining recent empirical findings on this topic, noting that such findings are often couched in a too optimistic view of the possibilities for civic engagement through games. It backs up this claim by connecting digital play with informational capitalism, proposing that this analytical connection should be complemented by foregrounding the subversive origins of play as a 'challenge' or 'duel'. The chapter ultimately suggests that play carries radical potential in terms of a transgression of oppressive social structures, but that this potential can only be tapped by pushing playful engagement beyond the logic of the cybernetic control mechanisms on which it is currently predicated.

Keywords: Serious games, civic engagement, Baudrillard, informational capitalism, cybernetics

> Modern repression is carried out in the name of play.
> – Baudrillard (2001, 66)

The mission to keep young people interested and engaged in a variety of forms of civic participation certainly seems to be a laudable enterprise for any self-respecting progressive and democratic society. Hard-won democratic rewards and virtues like voting, volunteering, and giving to charity, would appear to be rights and responsibilities that need to be inculcated in the young as soon as their proper socialization sets in. Especially when in the 1970s and 1980s it seemed that young people's participation in civic behavior

Glas, R., S. Lammes, M. de Lange, J. Raessens, and I. de Vries, eds. 2019. *The Playful Citizen. Civic Engagement in a Mediatized Culture.* Amsterdam: Amsterdam University Press.
DOI: 10.5117/9789462984523/CH07

was declining in many Western countries—leading to perhaps overwrought claims of supposed youthful political apathy (Ghosh 2011)—this led educators and politicians to start to look at alternative ways to re-engage youth to ensure the continuation of democratic institutions and behaviors and, by extension, of society. With the rise of the internet and social media, many research studies have been conducted concerning the potential benefits and shortcomings of e-democracy, online government services, and online civic engagement, and policy changes have been adopted. Indeed, a plethora of sociological studies emerged in the 1980s and 1990s around the potential of the internet for civic activism and online social movements (OSMs), as well as their impact, however limited, on real social and political change (see for instance Donk et al. 2004, as well as McCaughey and Ayers 2003). Simultaneously, the rise of video-gaming in those decades has led to a barrage of studies on serious gaming for educational purposes that range from computer-assisted chemical modeling to games that simulate ethical decision-making (Michael and Chen 2006).

This chapter will engage the question of how video games may—or especially also, may *not*—aide morally upright civic engagement by young people. It will do so by critically examining the empirical findings on this topic discussed in Joseph Kahne, Ellen Middaugh, and Chris Evans' landmark study *The civic potential of video games* (2009), arguing that the writers of this otherwise helpful study eventually adopt a too optimistic view of the possibilities of civic engagement through video games. This chapter will support this assessment by discussing literature that spells out the connection between digital play and informational capitalism, in particular building on Stephen Kline, Nick Dyer-Witheford, and Greig de Peuter's excellent study of the connections between video games and 'the military-industrial complex' in *Digital play* (2003). However, this chapter suggests that the latter study, however insightful, should be complemented by looking closer at the subversive origins of play as 'challenge' or 'duel' in order to analyze the potential of digital play in more depth. The chapter, in turn, suggests by way of an examination of some of the work of Jean Baudrillard that the foundation of play does carry a certain radical or subversive aspect in terms of a potential transgression of oppressive social structures and boundaries. This radical potential can however only be tapped by pushing playful engagement beyond the safety of their existence as foremost cybernetic control mechanisms; in other words, the contemporary 'civic' potential of video games lies in the ways it may *exacerbate* informational capitalistic risk. Hence, this chapter eventually seeks to raise the stakes of what true civic engagement, when dealt with from a politico-ethical angle that questions the relationship between cybernetic play and contemporary forms of gendered, raced, and classed disenfranchisement, may really entail. In order to arrive at this point, it will start off by drawing out the assumptions that emanate from the empirical research in *The civic potential of video games*, after which it will propose a perspective that re-theorizes the relationship between contemporary cybernetic play and civic socialization within an unequal economic landscape marked by simulation and risk.

Promoting civic engagement: To what or whose ends?

Interestingly, as Kahne, Middaugh, and Evans in *The civic potential of video games* point out, large-scale empirical research studies into how video games in particular may specifically aide or hinder civic engagement among the youth have been rather scarce. Moreover, most research conducted on video games and citizenry have instead speculated that playing video games simply takes time away from the exigencies of democratic citizenship or have assumed that the violent or individualistic content of video games will lead to anti-civic behavior (2009, 3). Given that a large segment of young people admits to playing video games more or less regularly, researching the ways in which gaming concretely relates to civic behavior like voting, volunteering, or helping the less fortunate, then certainly appears to make political, moral, and societal sense. In *The civic potential of video games* therefore, Kahne, Middaugh, and Evans set out to report on one of the first truly empirical investigations into the ways in which video games provide the grounds for potentially engaging young people in democratic processes in the United States. As they themselves confirm, their research, funded by the Chicago-based MacArthur Foundation, endeavored to collect empirical evidence for Henry Jenkins' famous claim in *Confronting the challenges of participatory culture* that new digital and networked tools bring about "participatory cultures" with "relatively low barriers to artistic expression and civic engagement" (2009, 5). In order to operationalize their research, Kahne, Middaugh, and Evans aimed at finding possible links between video-gaming and democratic behavior. They set out to collect survey data pertaining to self-reported forms of civic behavior, racial, and gender identification, as well as people's age and income bracket, together with time spent playing and the relative popularity of video games among the various groups. They also collected data about actual civic behavior and participation that the data-subjects undertook during the course of the survey. Perhaps not surprisingly, the authors conclude in their report that youth's civic engagement can be increased if done in a proper context—for instance, together with a classroom debate or with parental follow-up—with serious games that specifically simulate civic or moral behavior. Examples of such games are *Real Lives* (Educational Simulations 2001), *Democracy* (Positech Games 2005), *Zora* (Bers 2001), *SimCity* (Maxis 1989), and *Civilization* (MPS Labs 1991), and the researchers encourage parents and teachers to actively stimulate the playing of such games among teens, although they do note that the level of experienced civic engagement appears to be lower for girls than for boys (2009, 47). Of course, the researchers agree that the relationships between gaming and civic behavior are mere correlations; they did not for instance "control for respondents prior [civic] commitments," nor did they delve deeper into the problem around the method of self-reporting such 'civic experience' (2009, 41). Nonetheless, the research study appears to support the idea, however judiciously, that video games can be harnessed for inculcating democratic values into youngsters.

Besides the more obvious problems (lack of proof of causal links, biases in self-reporting) with the empirical survey method however, there are a range of other issues and assumptions that riddle this well-intended and otherwise well-conducted research project. This range of issues primarily emanates from the fact that the authors do not consider the general role of gaming technologies in the wider United States and global social environment that is shaped by a fundamentally uneven political economy. In other words, the correlations may simply stem from the equivalences between the unequal amounts of cultural capital of various socio-economic backgrounds, and levels of civic engagement in general. But more specifically, the researchers do not take into account the fact that Jenkins' astute observation about new technologies allowing for a more 'participatory' culture points toward the non-neutral emergence and imbrication of video-gaming (as well as other cybernetic technologies) in an updated form of global capitalism with its own new forms of disenfranchisement. Various scholars prefer to call this updated form 'informational capitalism' with an eye on the ways in which the apparently laudable attempt to spread digital media and media content in, for instance, schools in fact paradoxically exacerbates inequalities (Morris-Suzuki 1986; Van Dijk 2005; Fuchs 2007). Informational capitalism in turn for the most part thrives, as, for instance, Tiziana Terranova famously argues in 'Free Labor: Producing Culture for the Digital Economy,' on various forms of 'free labor' that internet users and online gamers provide, thereby facilitating an enmeshment of what seems to be leisure time with new forms of production (2000, 33). This imbrication of play with industry interests, as Julian Kücklich has subsequently pointed out, leads to forms of 'precarious playbour' in which, for instance, 'modders' provide crucial in-game innovations by putting in large amounts of pleasurable, yet unpaid time on the off-chance of perhaps getting a temporary job for a video game company (2005, n.p.). Therefore, what is lauded as 'user agency,' 'volunteering,' and 'active participation' is actually a novel type of value extraction from new media 'prosumers.' And while this, in and of itself, may arguably not be that problematic as long as these prosumers at least willingly or voluntarily give their time to provide free labor for new media companies, Kahne, Middaugh, and Evans write in a discursive register that mistakes the individual exercise of democracy, freedom, and the bringing about of actual social change with a sneaky *socialization* of gaming youth via new media technologies that eventually helps them comply with the workings of this uneven and immoral global capitalist order.

The problem, then, is that the harnessing of video games to boost democratic behavior may irresponsibly pre-empt the possibility to challenge the profoundly *undemocratic* configuration of the global information society. In other words, Kahne, Middaugh, and Evans mobilize a too-simplified and optimistic understanding of the promising connection between video games and civic society. What is therefore required beyond this empirical study, is to instead elaborate on the wider connection between video games and responsibility in order to propose another route for civic engagement proper. In order to do so, I suggest that a better understanding of the imbrication of video games and capitalism should first engage with the various deep-seated and problematic assumptions and aims that underlie such a simplified analysis like the one proposed in *The civic potential of video games*. Allow me, then, to elaborate how the researchers sneak such youth normalization efforts in via an arguably outdated register of democratic and civic effects emanating from what on the surface appear to be 'bottom-up' democratic gaming activities. According to the authors, the *playful* acquaintance with issues of political import via games simply allows young people to start caring for civic problems in a manner different from unhelpful *top-down* educational and parenting techniques. Youths after all, they proclaim, "prefer to talk with friends [...] rather than with their parents" and "prefer action that is informal and grass-roots" (2009, 50-51). Moreover, the authors argue that "traditional instruction in a civics curriculum has frequently been cited as a major reason civics courses in general have little impact" (2009, 52). Hence, the authors propose that digital gaming allows for the dissipation of such top-down approaches to the inculcation of civic virtues among the young. By especially immersing young players into games like *SimCity* or *Democracy* that simulate civic or democratic activities, these games supposedly allow for creating an environment that, for instance, John Dewey claimed is crucially centered on the democratic ideals of "dialogue and active experimentation that reflects social concerns" (2009, 4). Seen in this light, play in general and hence digital play in particular, with its implied association to forms of improvisation and behavioral freedom, would certainly appear to have the potential of a liberatory and democratizing politics that caters to the desires and interests of its user rather than to systemically oppressive entities. New technologies that provide an essentially playful environment may therefore on the surface aide in for instance allowing citizen-users of all ages with a 'freer,' more interested and less directed engagement with their social and civic surroundings. The fact that adolescents play video games a lot is according to the authors fortuitous, since it allows for the "nurturing [of civic behavior via video games] to begin [at] a time when youths are thinking about and trying to anticipate their lives as adults" (2009, 5).

Despite the implication of a 'freer' and less directed engagement however, the authors' aim actually turns out to be quite directed indeed. The ways in which these social researchers tend to be unwittingly implicated in social and economic normalization procedures becomes apparent in how the report seeks to hide its government-managerial socialization agenda with a veneer of positive words and recommendations, as if collaborative and simulatory games can simply be harnessed in the 'right familial or educational context' for the creation of a more egalitarian United States and global society. In light of this, it is telling that their research is sponsored by the MacArthur Foundation, which in its online 'About Us' says it concerns itself with the effects of new technologies on youth in order to "improve U.S. public policy" while claiming that such studies will in fact bring about a "more just, verdant and peaceful world" (MacArthur Foundation, n.d.). The term 'verdant' (also meaning 'lush') is significant here, as its usage in this context may not only point toward the ideal of a 'greener' world, but also of a more commercially 'thriving' society. This usage therefore suggests an imbrication of this private foundation with potential commercial interests—some of which may obviously lie with those media industries who want to capitalize on the 'civic potential of gaming.' Moreover, we can notice this imbrication with commercial interests also in the argumentation for and research background of *The civic potential of video games* itself, as it nowhere questions the non-neutral terms and conditions of civic techniques. This can for instance be gleaned from its assumption that "raising money for charity" (2009, 5) is a democratizing act, even if various scholars have pointed out that financial philanthropy as a virtue only makes sense in a starkly unequal economic environment (see e.g. Gomberg 2002). It furthermore talks about simply teaching students "the dynamics of economic, political, and legal systems" (2009, 18), thereby discursively normalizing such systems. And finally, the argument for the more effective 'marketing' of games for youth ultimately betrays an at least partially commercial mindset (2009, 50). The research presented in *The civic potential of video games* therefore arguably has a stake in the United States' social and political economy not only via its ideological register around active participation, 'freedom,' and democracy, but also regarding the ensuring that any critique or analysis of video-gaming does not potentially hurt the United States' media industry.

But, I would argue that the general problem with studying the influences of video-gaming without regard to its imbrication in a novel political economy that primarily enriches affluent media owners in the United States and abroad, does not stop there. The real problem lies instead in the ways in which the emergence of digital play is symptomatic of the more insidious shift toward a consumer culture in which games and play, despite their basic radical potential in society, have been denigrated to become mere *functional* elements in this global economy. This denigration can be noticed in the subtle ways in which the authors of *The civic potential of video games* make problematic slippages and confusions between a gamer's or game character's actual political, economic, and social environment, and the simulation that is the video game they are playing. This slippage emerges when they, for instance, discuss the moral and political virtues of games like *Halo: Combat Evolved* (Bungie 2001), *SimCity*, and *Real Lives*, in which youths subsequently report that they experience collaboration, how to manage a city, and how to empathize with another youth in an impoverished country. But pre-programmed in-game experience is always fundamentally different from real-world ambiguities that cannot be computed or simplified in advance. As I have argued previously in 'The neoliberal consolidation of play and speed: Ethical issues in serious gaming' (2007) via an analysis of *Real Lives* and *Global Warming: CO2FX* (Global Warming Interactive 2010), such experiences of managerial control or empathy with the underprivileged should crucially be analyzed as *simulatory* experiences that first and foremost bolster the fantasy of cybernetic control while dangerously removing its user from the actual messy reality of cities and poverty. Moreover, such games dangerously *obscure* the extent to which global cybernetic systems of control and prediction are in fact the motor behind the aggravation of local and global inequalities, thereby leading to what I call a "double objectification"—a stereotyping on top of a distancing effect—of the other (2007, 14). It does not help that the *The civic potential of video games* authors also obscure the ways in which cybernetic technologies hide their complicity with, for instance, growing income gaps by arguing for the potentially leveling effects of games as "equalizing civic learning opportunities" with regards to *age* differences, while completely dodging the much more pernicious issue of *class* disparities in their report (2009, 47). As I conclude in 'The neoliberal consolidation' (2007), the aggravation of contemporary oppression is, paradoxically, a direct result of the well-intended and novel forms of empowerment that gaming technologies allow. This is because these gaming technologies, as accelerated cybernetic infrastructures, are at the same time tools of an intensified surveillance and disenfranchisement (2007, 13).

Video games and the cybernetic quest to eliminate risk

While one may argue that drawing out such complicities is beyond the scope of *The civic potential of video games*' explorative research, the resulting silence from the authors about the ways in which video games are thoroughly implicated in the novel form of capitalism and its various forms of inequalities along lines of gender and class, warrants a closer look at this imbrication if we really want to take their laudable call for a more democratic and egalitarian society seriously. I therefore now turn to Kline, Nick Dyer-Witheford, and De Peuter's illuminating study on this imbrication of games with the reproduction of power in *Digital play: The interaction of technology, culture and marketing* (2003). This book claims, following the neo-Marxist interpretation of David Harvey in *The condition of postmodernity* (1990), that the emergence of video-gaming exactly marks the moment of "significant 'sea change' in which capitalist societies operate" (2003, 60). This change has to do with the need for capitalism to constantly open up new markets in a situation in which the market of material goods started to be largely saturated from the 1960s onwards. This, in turn, led to the emergence of new areas for consumption in the form of 'experiential commodities,' in which leisure and pleasure are sold as if they were true human needs. It is also important to note that these kinds of commodities emerged out of Cold War research and development, and therefore integrate the consumer more intimately within a cybernetic logic of command, control, communication, and information, or in military parlance: 'C3I' (2003, 88). Therefore, Kline, Dyer-Witheford, and De Peuter argue that digital play in particular constitutes the exemplary consumer good of what they call 'post-Fordist/postmodern/promotional' capitalist societies and their strong ties to especially military research and development (2003, 60). This is because the commodification of leisure and pleasure via cybernetic technologies allows for the continuous involvement of the user in ongoing capitalist production across time and space, as these new commodities are ephemeral, portable, networked, and interactive, and allow for the continuous creative expression of the user's simulated identity via playful lifestyle choices. Due to the cybernetic logic and aesthetics of video games, according to Kline, Dyer-Witheford, and De Peuter, digital play tends to open up specific 'subject positions' that amount to 'masculine and militarized' positions that "mobilize fantasies of instrumental domination and annihilation" (2003, 255). This is a result of the historically intimate connection between the military and game design industries, which larger logic in certain games re-emerges in the remediation of spectacular and violent media content that we also see returning in televised news and in blockbuster Hollywood movies. Digital play as a simulation therefore crucially parallels and feeds the hyper-real simulation that is highly mediated global capitalism—in short, video games' simulated content points to the fact that it is our reality that is a very intricate simulation (2003, 69). Exploring this critique of digital play further, Dyer-Witheford and De Peuter in their follow-up *Games of Empire* assert that video games provide 'machines' that lock subjects firmly into the workings of the 'military-industrial complex' by being a particular manifestation of 'cognitive capitalism' (Dyer-Witheford and De Peuter 2009). Hypothesizing that "videogames are a paradigmatic media of Empire [...] and some of the forces that presently challenge it," (2009, xv) they finally argue that virtual gaming is "ambivalent" insofar that "game virtualities remove us from, but also prepare us for, these actual subject positions [...] simulat[ing] the normalized subjectivities of a global capitalist order" (2009, 192 and 312). Importantly, they do suggest, following the work of Gilles Deleuze and Félix Guattari, that such machinic forms of subjective control can never be total and will inevitably lead to aggravated tensions in society at large. I will return to this alternative 'potential' of games later.

Moreover, such intricate simulations have the effect of what Elizabeth Losh in 'The desert of the unreal' warningly calls "the efficiencies of learning and other forms of psychic integration" of the player into a setting geared toward military goals that may be beyond the player's purview (2009, 109). Following this point, as well as the general analysis in *Digital play*, I again argue that to have citizens engage via these digital tools with issues of national and political import—regardless of whether this is done via *Halo*, *SimCity*, or *Civilization*—therefore also potentially carries the implied aim of indoctrinating and implicating these users into a normalization of a more intricate and subtle capitalistic and militaristic social environment, depending on to what extent these games obscure such relations and connections.

This environment, then, is only 'post-capitalist' insofar as the system of labor and consumption no longer relies on the alienation of the user-consumer, but in the merging of the 'prosumer' with the cybernetic feedback system that modern capitalism has become. Crucially, what then superficially appears as forms of empowerment or emancipation via these tools is paradoxically also exactly its opposite: the near-total immersion of the citizen-consumer in a web of pre-shaped 'points of cybernetic play' in which all outcomes have been predicted, pre-structured, or pre-empted as much as possible within the generalized attempt of such machinery to 'eliminate risk' (Beck 1992, 47). Understood in this way, youths' civic and moral responsibility is captured and displaced into a media network in which they can no longer *truly* make a difference for the United States or global society, except perhaps by fatally exacerbating the possibility of a true event.

This understanding of games as having been depreciated as normalization and indoctrination mechanisms mirrors the ways in which our society conceptually denigrates play as a mere developmental stage in children. What I claim is at issue, therefore, is finally the way in which two definitions or versions of play and games are operable in a report like *The civic potential of video games* as well as in the more optimistic theories around video games and the 'ludification' of culture as such. These two definitions of play are firstly, the dominant and erroneous *psychological* definition of play (like in children's play) as a way to experiment with and even push social rules and boundaries, and secondly, the *cybernetic* definition and function of play, in which play and gaming consists of the manipulation of a system of control toward its optimal performance. The problem, I contend, is that these two definitions often mesh into one another when debating the positive aspects and effects of digital play. This is because, while the former definition sees video games as a return to a childlike 'freedom' away from or in denial of the demands and responsibilities of society, the latter definition in fact creates a correspondence between the gaming subject and the objective demands of a capitalist and technocratic system that, for instance, Dyer-Witheford and De Peuter call "ludocapitalism" (2009, xiv), whereby the gamer obliquely becomes the eventual object of an insidious form of manipulation. It is for this reason, I suggest, that Jean Baudrillard's work on play and games, for instance his 'Police and play,' tends to make the point that playing games—and not just digital games, but also games as mere leisure in general—in our highly mediated society primarily consists of a "trap" of "symbolic counter-dependence which forms part of our cultural mechanisms" where "generalized repression [...] becomes part of an intense participation" (2001, 61). The pleasure of playing games, according to Baudrillard, stems from the artificial production of needs and desires, leading to a "complicit euphoria" when engaging in the generalized game that cybernetic society on the whole has become (2001, 61). In other words, Baudrillard suggests that our entire modern society consists of a capitalist seduction of the masses to engage in playing, as well as the accumulation of pleasure and experience as not only a new form of production, but also as a way to divert libidinal energy away from an *actual* challenge to or transgression of this seductive system. The ludification of society, then, far from being a true revolutionary or freeing transformation for the subject, instead ensures that that subject is "harmoniously integrated into the dynamics of production" by providing the illusion that play and gaming allows her or him to guiltily give in to his own childlike desires (2001, 65). Gaming is thus presented in the popular imaginary as a return to a freer and infantile state, whereas actually it is engaging in the highest-order demands of cybernetic capitalism. Moreover, the 'guilty pleasure' of playing games is "above all socially orchestrated like any other cultural trait of behavior or clothing," ensuring that the consumption of culpability itself allows for the *mis*understanding of the mere "signs of play" as a true playing with the actual stakes of life and the social order (2001, 66). Actual transgression or radical social change, then, seems near-impossible, and can only be found in what he calls the "unpredictable transgressions and convulsions in the system of values." One may think here of events that *seemingly* have little to do with video games, like the never-explained flash crash of 2001, terrorist suicide attacks, or the ongoing increase in high-school shootings in the United States. At the same time, however, video games may have contributed to such accidental events by raising the stakes of informational capitalism in much more obscure ways, which I will address next.

Play as challenge to neoliberal socialization

After taking the important caveat by Kline, Dyer-Witheford, and De Peuter as well as the assessment by Jean Baudrillard in 'Police and play' seriously, the possibilities and impossibilities for citizen-directed liberatory and democratizing play via digital tools like video games and other forms of digital play should be understood as paradoxically oppressive *because* they are seemingly emancipatory. It is, namely, the very same computational and infrastructural mechanism that allows for student empowerment, which at the same time re-distributes social and economic hierarchies in exceedingly unequal ways. But here, too, is an oblique relation to be found between the excessive events mentioned just now and video games: the flash crash resulted from 'playing' the stock market, and the shootings simulate the simulations that are shooter games. I would therefore also suggest that a totalizing theory of capitalism as a system that can *completely* predict and pre-empt outcomes—and ultimately eliminate all risk—via games and play in the ways Kline and his colleagues sketch, forgets that capitalism today actually relies on extremely *unstable illusions*, which get illustrated via such excessive and surprising events. Therefore, I propose that one can always imagine upping the stakes via a challenge to the rules of leisure and pleasure as such; in other words, any system can be 'gamed' beyond its limits. In order to grasp this potential of video-gaming on a more extra-structural level, I propose that the seemingly pessimistic and totalizing assessment Baudrillard makes in 'Police and play' nevertheless should be complemented with his more intricate analysis of the symbolic logic of rules and games in his earlier work *Seduction* (1990). In this work, he seeks to comprehend 'prosumerist' seduction as the potential *thwarter* of the pervasive order of production, which he jokingly calls the "Great Neutral Aleatorium" (1990, 143). Here, too, Baudrillard argues that play today is the "ambience or playful eroticization of a universe without stakes," but that games in their original agonistic character of the 'duel' actually form a superior form of social ordering vis-à-vis a society based on the production and assuaging of supposedly essential human needs and desires (1990, 156). This is because in cultures where the gods (or any large powers) are invited—for instance, by ways of ritual sacrificial offering—to show their powers, humans actually play for *real* and there are potentially *lethal stakes* that may completely change a community, a society or the course of history. This means that societies that truly acknowledge seduction as the flip-side of production are able to 'place bets' that are truly radical in the face of the law or of authority. So, while in our modern society games are co-constitutive of a "demand [which] is prompted by the model, and the model's precession is absolute, [so that] challenges are impossible," still games and rule-based play can be seen as a remnant of a "yearning to be free of the contract and the social relation, the longing for a crueller if more fascinating destiny for exchange," in short, "a yearning for a more adventurous world, where one plays with value more recklessly" (1990, 152-157).

What I take from Baudrillard's assessment is that, even if our society is one where seduction in Baudrillard's words has become "cool" or "cold" since it no longer raises any stakes (1990, 162)—and therefore does nothing to really change society toward a more egalitarian or democratic state—the incessant pushing of production via the seduction of video gamers into leisurely 'prosumerism' nonetheless carries with it an equally increasing unpredictable or risky element. This is because 'cold' seduction via 'prosumption' is centered on the individual satisfaction of desires and pleasures that eventually appear unreal in the face of *truly* giving oneself away for a larger cause, whether this cause be moral, civic, democratic, or otherwise. Altruistic self-satisfaction via digital engagement is, therefore, always ultimately unfulfilling because the performance and experience of empathy or leadership is, ultimately, indeed only a simulatory illusion that will forever stand in tension with actual moral and material global effects that is in part caused by the machinery of 'cold' seduction. Moreover, it is quite possible that young people, due to their underdeveloped socialization, may at some level be more sensitive to the tensions around such 'altruism' than well-adjusted social researchers. The much-lamented youthful political and moral "disaffection" that I noted at the onset of this chapter, is hence, I suggest, best interpreted as a symptomatic effect of the "fake game without stakes" that modern living has become (Baudrillard 1990, 163). Since the acknowledgement of the power of seduction is, according to Baudrillard, historically gendered in Western societies, this may also explain why in the United States "girls experience lower civic gaming opportunities" as the authors of *The civic potential of video games* bewilderedly note (2009, 47); they may not be as easily seduced into video games' 'militarized masculinity.' After all, not only are in-game representations frequently sexist (Kline, Dyer-Witheford, and De Peuter 2003, 265), but girls are possibly more sensitive to the fact that gaming relies on an illusion that is at some level complicit with a highly gendered and patriarchal social order. This also means that games are, or at least can be, much more serious than the regular psychological definition of play as a supposed recursion to a childlike phase gives it credit for, and that it is finally on the level of the theatrical function of the media industry, which obscures that industry's imbrication in the productive and predictive function, that the real challenge to the inequalities of contemporary capitalism should be played out. Or, as Baudrillard puts it rather obliquely at the end of 'Police and play': "only subversion of an instinctual order can constitute a point external to the system" (2001, 68).

Conclusion: Raising the stakes of civic subversion?

The final question, then, becomes what might accomplish such a subversion? In light of this question, I would like to briefly discuss two promising ways in which software programmers and designers have tried to up the stakes in video-gaming by pointing toward a beyond of its pervasive, yet never totalizing grasp on play's potential radicalism. The first way entails introducing an explicit element of self-reflexivity in a game, such that the in-game representation no longer obscures its relation to an unequal global economy, but instead critically re-stages this relation. There are a number of interesting attempts made in this area, like for instance the games *Necessary Evil* (Gualeni 2013a) and *You Have to Burn the Rope* (Bashiri 2008), which both seek to frustrate the player's usual sense of smooth control over the game-world, or thwart the escapist disconnection with the context in which video games are played. As Stefano Gualeni, one of the makers of *Necessary Evil*, nonetheless admits in 'Self-reflexive video games as playable critical thought,' such games often encompass a kind of "uncouth gameplay" that might lead to an unpleasant or indifferent gaming experience, which may aim for some kind of player awareness but will not fundamentally alter the rules of the larger game that is post-Fordism (2013b, n.p.). The reach of self-reflexive video games will therefore—also seeing that it will still have to operate entirely within the contemporary economy of 'seductive prosumerism'—eventually remain limited to the uneventful stakes of contemporary informational capitalism. The second way would encompass a more serious transgression of the rules of digital communication via various forms of malicious hacking. However, while challenging the status quo via malicious hacking obviously transgresses some moral or legal boundaries, informational capitalism, with its emphasis on the constant harnessing of ephemerality and creativity via the seduction of also a player's more obscure impulses, may simply incorporate and produce such transgressive activities as part of what Stephen Flowers has called "outlaw innovation" (2008, 178). So, even self-reflexivity as well as hacking may ultimately not lead to the subversion of the ways in which our social order relies on the production of subversive instincts and pleasures via video games. Nonetheless, I suggest that they point in the right direction, and would urge critical social scientists and game designers to further ponder its 'uncouth' potentials. And while Kahne, Middaugh, and Evans also seek to point toward such potentials, the overall argument in *The civic potential of video games* nonetheless remains stuck in a moralism about proper civic behavior that does not lead to any of the necessary 'uncouthness' at all.

To sum up, this chapter has argued that much contemporary digital play—whether done via more obviously militarised games like the *Halo* series or more blatantly 'civic' games like *Democracy*—is wholly wrapped up in the logic of cybernetic prediction, oppression, and the reproduction of the inequalities of global capitalism. As such, the seduction of digital gaming is a 'cold' one in which there is nothing really at stake. The chapter has proposed that such a digital environment in which stakes and risks have been pre-empted at least to a larger extent than in a pre-cybernetic media environment, can never allow for true ethical engagement and radical democratic change implied on the level of certain video games' 'civic' content. Hence, the chapter concludes that, following especially Baudrillard's assessment of the ambiguity of play while also paying attention to the warnings of Kline, Dyer-Witheford, and De Peuter, eventually only play that engages on the structural, formal, or functional level of its digital tool may open up the possibility of a liberatory politics. Games like *SimCity* or *Zora*, as *The civic potential of video games* report claims, therefore, certainly generate a particular experience of moral and civic learning, but such an experience primarily involves the practice of playing *within* the general ambience of the optimization of "self-control" technologies geared toward the management of risk (Beck 1992, 234). It therefore does not translate into the nurturing of a more democratic and ethically just society, but instead socializes youths into a contemporary technocracy fraught with multiple forms of inequality. This is because the in-game spatial or social representation, while seemingly full of 'freedom' of movement and choice, only serves to hide the way in which such 'freedom' reproduces an essentially oppressive functionality within contemporary global informational capitalist society. In their place, the chapter has pointed out that certain forms of playful self-reflexivity and hacking offer promising routes to subversion that nonetheless still need to be pushed way beyond the system's breaking point so as to potentially accomplish play's essential radicality. This chapter therefore has positioned itself initially in-between, but finally beyond the debates of Kahne, Middaugh, and Evans as well as Kline, Dyer-Witheford, and De Peuter, as it holds that the former fail to sufficiently address how video games are also microcosms of larger, socially oppressive, and unequal arrangements, while the latter in *Digital play* forget how structural play with 'dubious' technologies is always possible on the level of the tool's rule-based grammar. It concurs with the latter that the stakes for a liberatory politics indeed have been partially compromised and complicated, as truly subversive, radical, or civically engaged play is rendered increasingly difficult to discern and carry out in our informational capitalist societies due to the near-total enmeshment of emancipatory desires and new media. But it also suggests that one can always 'up the game' and its unjust and finally arbitrary rules by exposing these rules as simulations. Dyer-Witheford and De Peuter do try to investigate the possibility of raising such stakes by looking at a variety of promising games in the chapter 'Games of multitude' in *Games of Empire*, like tactical games, polity games, hacktivism, and other forms of counterplay. Eventually, however, this investigation still leads them to conclude that the "play of multitude still remains locked inside games of Empire" (2009, 213). This is because all these games still fundamentally rely on extracting surplus value by locking users into preprogrammed interactive subject positions. Dyer-Witheford and De Peuter therefore propose that perhaps "gaming alternatives that open onto truly 'new universes of references' come mainly from outside the play factory" (2009, 212). I suggest that if we really want our youth to grow up with a sense of democratic purpose in which they can bring about a world in which we can all lead meaningful lives, we should perhaps understand that, paradoxically, youth's seemingly irrational and 'passive' civic behavior, borne out of a logical disaffection with zero-stakes technocracy, is not so much the problem, but the key to a more just society. This is not to say that indulging in passivity constitutes the opposite of the problems of interactivity, but that youth, as the *The civic potential of video games* report correctly showed at the start, find themselves on the threshold of what it *really* could mean to become a responsible adult. And their instincts may tell them that deep down, not all is well in the sphere of civic simulation.

References

Bashiri, K. 2008. *You have to burn the rope.* [browser]. Game.

Baudrillard, J. 1990. *Seduction.* Trans. B. Singer. New York: St. Martin's Press.

—. 2001. Police and play. *The uncollected Baudrillard*, ed. G. Genosko, 61-69. London: Sage Publications.

Beck, U. 1992. *Risk society: Towards a new modernity.* London: Sage Publications.

Bers, M. 2001. *Zora.* [Windows]. Massachusetts Institute of Technology. Game.

Bungie. 2001. *Halo: Combat Evolved.* [Xbox/Windows/OS X]. Microsoft Game Studios. Game.

Dyer-Witheford, N., and G. de Peuter. 2009. *Games of Empire: Global capitalism and videogames.* Minneapolis, MN: Minnesota University Press.

Educational Simulations. 2001. *Real Lives.* [Windows]. Educational Simulations. Game.

Flowers, S. 2008. Harnessing the hackers: The emergence and exploitation of Outlaw Innovation. *Research Policy* 37 (2): 177-193.

Fuchs, C. 2007. *Internet and society: Social theory in the information age.* New York: Routledge.

Ghosh, P. 2011. Why is there so much voter apathy in U.S. elections? *International Business Times*, 19 September 2011. http://www.ibtimes.com/why-there-so-much-voter-apathy-us-elections-315494.

Global Warming Interactive. 2010. *CO2FX*. [Web]. Global Warming Interactive. Game.

Gomberg, P. 2002. The fallacy of philanthropy. *Canadian Journal of Philosophy* 32 (1): 29-65.

Gualeni, S. 2013a. *Necessary Evil*. [browser]. Game.

—. 2013b. Self-reflexive video games as playable critical thought. *Gamasutra*. http://www.gamasutra.com/blogs/StefanoGualeni/20131029/202847/selfreflexive_video_games_as_playable_critical_thought.php.

Harvey, D. 1992. *The condition of postmodernity: An enquiry into the origins of cultural change*. New York: Wiley and Sons.

Hoofd, I. M. 2007. The neoliberal consolidation of play and speed: Ethical issues in serious gaming. *Critical Literacy: Theories and Practices* 1 (2): 6-15.

Jenkins, H. 2009. *Confronting the challenges of participatory culture: Media education for the 21st century*. Cambridge, MA: The MIT Press.

Kahne, J., E. Middaugh, and C. Evans. 2009. *The civic potential of video games*. Cambridge, MA: The MIT Press.

Kline, S., N. Dyer-Witheford, and G. de Peuter. 2003. *Digital play: The interaction of technology, culture, and marketing*. Montreal: McGill-Queen's University Press.

Kücklich, J. 2005. Precarious playbour: Modders and the digital games industry. *The Fibreculture Journal* 5. http://five.fibreculturejournal.org/fcj-025-precarious-playbour-modders-and-the-digital-games-industry.

Losh, E. 2009. The desert of the unreal: Democracy and military-funded videogames and simulations. In *Virtualpolitik: An electronic history of government media-making in a time of war, scandal, disaster, miscommunication, and mistakes*, ed. E. Josh, 97-136. Cambridge, MA: The MIT Press.

MacArthur Foundation. n.d. About us. *MacArthur Foundation*. http://www.macfound.org/about.

Maxis. 1989. *SimCity*. [multiplatform]. Maxis/Brøderbund/Infogrames. Game.

McCaughey, M., and M. D. Ayers. 2003. *Cyberactivisms: Online activism in theory and practice*. New York: Routledge.

Michael, D. R., and S. Chen. 2006. *Serious games: Games that educate, train and inform*. Boston, MA: Thomson Course Technology.

Morris-Suzuki, T. 1986. Capitalism in the computer age. *New Left Review* 160:81-92.

MPS Labs. 1991. *Civilization*. [multiplatform]. MicroProse. Game.

Positech Games. 2005. *Democracy* [Windows/OS X/Linux]. Positech Games/Tri-Synergy. Game.
Terranova, T. 2000. Free labor: Producing culture for the digital economy. *Social Text* 18 (2): 33-58.
Van Dijk, J. 2005. *The deepening divide: Inequality in the information society*. Thousand Oaks, CA: Sage Publications.
Van de Donk, W., B. Loader, P. Nixon, and D. Rucht. 2004. *Cyberprotest: New media, citizens, and social movements*. New York: Routledge.

About the author

Ingrid M. Hoofd is an Assistant Professor in the Department of Media and Culture at the Humanities Faculty of Utrecht University, the Netherlands. Her research interests are issues of representation, feminist and critical theories, philosophy of technology, game studies, and information ethics. She is the author of *Higher education and technological acceleration: The disintegration of university teaching and research* (Palgrave 2016), and *Ambiguities of activism: Alter-globalism and the imperatives of speed* (Routledge 2012). Her research analyzes the ways in which alter-globalist activists, as well as left-wing academics, mobilize what she calls 'speed-elitist' discourses and divisions in an attempt to overcome gendered, raced, and classed oppressions worldwide. These analyses outline the accelerated tensions and relationships between various new technologies (electronic games, e-learning platforms, and social media) and activist-academic moral imperatives from a critical-cultural and deconstructionist perspective.

Part II

Ludo-epistemologies

Introduction to Part II

René Glas, Sybille Lammes, Michiel de Lange, Joost Raessens, and Imar de Vries

Part II of the book is concerned with how play, civic engagement, and knowledge can be understood as intimately related. It counters the assumption that play and science are incompatible concepts and instead seeks to identify a productive interconnectedness between them. What we wish to discuss here is best described by what René Glas and Sybille Lammes call ludo-epistemologies in their contribution to this book. Building on philosopher of science Paul Feyerabend's concept of anarcho-epistemology, they use this term to make a case for forging productive relations between play, civic participation, and knowledge production.

Hailing from different fields and backgrounds, the authors in this section share a keen interest in finding ludic ways to overcome the asymmetry between the 'bastions' where knowledge is produced and daily life. All too often, we seem to live with these techno-scientific artefacts thrown at us like a *deus ex machina* or an external fate. The contributions in this section probe the use of play as a means to overcome this asymmetry and develop a critical academic stance as to how play can be a meaningful method, design, or tactic for accomplishing this.

Jessica Breen, Shannon Dosemagen, Don Blair, and Liz Barry take a very hands-on approach to this in their collective contribution *Public laboratory: Play and civic engagement*. Here, the authors talk about play as a means of civic engagement. They see play as a tactic to bring about social change, in particular by giving citizens the possibility to map pollution and other social issues. Their Public Lab, based in the USA, offers a wide range of playful tools as everyday items—such as kites and balloons—and also organizes playful gatherings to encourage citizens to take civic action. Their work is a testimony to how civic action and scientific practices can be shaped through play and shows that this can lead to the production of alternative knowledge that can empower citizens.

In her chapter *Sensing the air and experimenting with environmental citizenship*, sociologist Jennifer Gabrys also speaks about the potential of civic engagement through playful approaches. However, she reflects on site-specific citizen-sensing projects where creative means are used to engage citizens with technologies for measuring air pollution. Gabrys argues that such local and material initiatives should be approached as material processes in which new ways of data retrieval and democratic engagement are developed that can potentially give rise to new power relations in knowledge production. Play and creativity, according to Gabrys, are important parts of such experimental processes and allow us to come to more symmetrical ways of living and *doing* knowledge.

In *Biohacking: Playing with technology*, new media scholar Stephanie de Smale takes a similar approach to the lab as an experimental site. She reflects on how quotidian experimental sites (urban communities, a building) can be turned into laboratories. De Smale shows that bastions of techno-scientific production can literally be moved elsewhere by creating alternative labs outside their traditional boundaries. The Public Lab mentioned above is an interesting example of an attempt to embed labs in daily life through DIY practices. De Smale discusses another strong case, the production of microscopic images outside the traditional laboratory, and shows how hacking as play can be an important method for the production of alternative knowledge.

The final chapters in this part could be read as a trialogue, or perhaps as a mini-debate, about how playful citizen science can be envisaged, critically examined, and understood, especially in relation to citizen science games. Although the authors do not speak directly to each other, they take positions in a highly timely debate, and their views resonate with and complement each other. The first contribution is the aforementioned text by Glas and Lammes, *Ludo-epistemology: Playing with the rules in citizen science games*. Drawing on the fields of game studies as well as science and technology studies (STS), the authors want to push the envelope with a discussion of how citizen science games are conceptualized and designed. They propose a radical move in which citizen science games become more than just top-down instruments for teaching science or feeding data back to scientists, and call instead for a reconceptualization of what people think science is and can become, what citizenship is and what play is. Taking up Paul Feyerabend's challenge that scientists are also citizens and that we need to break down boundaries in order to adopt a more democratic kind of knowledge production, they argue that this should also prompt us to rethink the potential of citizen science games. They argue that by making games that give players agency to bend or break established rules, we can bring play *into* knowledge practices.

This contribution is followed by two more chapters about the interconnectedness between play and knowledge production in games. In *The playful scientist: Stimulating playful communities for science practice*, game scholars and designers Ben Schouten, Erik van der Spek, Daniël Harmsen, and Ellis

Bartholomeus take a similar stance to Glas and Lammes. From a more designer-informed perspective, they call for citizen science games that are less one-directional and engage citizens more directly with what knowledge production is about. To accomplish this, so they maintain, games have to be designed in such a way that they hold the interest of players for a longer time span and they have to trigger players' intrinsic motivation.

In their chapter *Laborious playgrounds: Citizen science games as new modes of work/play in the digital age*, game scholar Sonia Fizek and anthropologist Anne Dippel take a critical look at the promises and pitfalls of citizen science games and how they can put citizens in the role of 'playborers,' doing work for scientists by playing and unwittingly providing free labor. The asymmetries that we mentioned in the first paragraphs of this introduction are thus reiterated instead of being destabilized or weakened, so they warn.

In summary, the contributions in this section all engage with how play and knowledge can be combined in productive ways to stimulate creativity and empower citizens. Yet, as many authors also point out, we should look at this potential in a highly critical (and maybe even skeptical) way, as play can also enforce the asymmetries between where techno-science flourishes and where it is produced when used in a non-reflective, one-directional, and unengaged way.

8. Public laboratory: Play and civic engagement

Jessica Breen, Shannon Dosemagen, Don Blair, and Liz Barry

Abstract

This chapter explores the potential of play in relation to community-based civic science research using DIY scientific tools made possible by the Public Laboratory for Open Technology and Science (Public Lab). It discusses projects and approaches that the Public Lab has developed since its launch in 2010 to facilitate meaningful civic science collaboration. This includes a focus on narrative forms to connect participants to science research, relying on a spontaneous, playful emergence of collaborative activity rather than pre-developed forms of gamification to allow the incentives for participation to be intrinsic to the nature of the activity. This transforms the practice of scientific research and civic engagement into something that is both effective and ultimately enjoyable and productive, for all of those involved.

Keywords: Public Lab, civic science, playful participation, civic engagement, DIY, community

Right before we reach the end of LA-23, a long stretch of road through Plaquemines Parish, Louisiana, we turn off into the parking lot of a marina. The drive from New Orleans to Venice took us through a landscape of rural agriculture, refineries, and tight-knit communities and into one of the epicenters of the oil spill cleanup. We'd spent the drive cutting up two-liter soda bottles, installing the Canon Hack Development Kit (CHDK) on a Canon camera and guessing what it would be like when we got to our final destination, the Chandeleur Islands. It had only been a few days since we had listened to the news of the Deepwater Horizon rig explosion. Now, it was 9 May, and after endless days of navigating work,

Glas, R., S. Lammes, M. de Lange, J. Raessens, and I. de Vries, eds. 2019. *The Playful Citizen. Civic Engagement in a Mediatized Culture.* Amsterdam: Amsterdam University Press.
DOI: 10.5117/9789462984523/CH08

> confusion, and media, we heard that the first signs of oil were headed toward the Chandeleur Islands. We were meeting a charter boat captain who had volunteered to take the three of us—equipped with a weather balloon, helium tank, duct tape, and other miscellaneous parts—to one of his favorite sport fishing spots out there. He wanted to see the oil's impact, too.
>
> We motored slowly down the long canal that would lead us into the Gulf of Mexico. We passed trawlers converted into oil skimming vessels, the remnants of pipeline structures, and the quickly disappearing Breton Sound, finally making our way into the relatively calm waters within the Chandeleur Island chain. Over the side of the boat, coagulated red objects floated past, swimming among the oily sheen. A foul smell hung in the air, leaving us all with aching eyes and heads by the time we returned to shore later in the day. We spent the afternoon navigating the coastline, considering wading to shore (but not feeling comfortable getting into the alien-looking water), and playing with the balloon mapping materials we brought along. With a toolkit that consisted of one large balloon, a newly constructed soda bottle rig, kite reel, a camera and gloves, we experimented with different tie-off techniques on the balloon, duct taped shut a hole that formed in the rubber of the balloon, and finally launched it into the perfectly calm afternoon. Floating 1,500 feet above us, well below the official 3,000 foot floor that had been imposed on flyovers that week, we swapped stories, watched pelicans and helicopters flying on and off the island and captured images that would later illustrate a story of the surreally beautiful devastation that was unfolding around us.

Play is an activity that is positively viewed by the player, self-motivated, freely chosen, and actively engaging (Garvey 1990). This concept of play extends back to what play meant to us in an educational context when we were young children, i.e. exploration and experimentation and figuring out how to engage with the space you occupy in new ways. We construct this chapter based on two central questions: how do we bring play into civic engagement? And how do we come to engage as a community of civic science practitioners in a space that requires us to constantly re-imagine play through exploration?

A brief history of the Public Laboratory for Open Technology and Science

In the spring of 2010, NGOs, Gulf Coast residents, and members of Grassroots-Mapping.org, coalesced to collect over 100,000 aerial images of the Deepwater Horizon disaster. Access to the coast was restricted in the aftermath of the oil spill, with local residents and journalists alike prevented from witnessing affected areas. There was much frustration due to the lack of volunteer opportunities to assist in oil clean-up, the media blackout, and difficulties accessing information vital to assessing ecological and public health risks. In response, the Public Laboratory for Open Technology and Science (Public Lab) formed to pilot a Do-It-Yourself method of collecting aerial imagery utilizing a helium-filled weather balloon and kites equipped with refurbished digital cameras housed in repurposed soda bottles to prevent them from fluttering in the wind. By flying these improvised rigs between 500 and 2,000 feet off the ground, we were able to capture high-resolution photos of the spill's effects and provide an inexpensive mechanism for grassroots community engagement and for monitoring both corporate and government response to the spill.

Since that time, Public Lab has expanded its toolset to include the development of DIY scientific tools to address a broad swath of environmental and social justice issues. These tools include a spectrometer, available as a kit on the Public Lab website, which was developed with the aim of identifying polyaromatic hydrocarbons in soil and sediment, but has been explored within the community for a variety of other further uses. The Public Lab community has also developed a 'thermal flashlight' for detecting thermal leaks, modified Roombas that paint with light to map indoor air pollutants like formaldehyde, devised hydrogen sulfide detectors that make novel use of photographic paper to sense emissions near hydro-fracking sites, and designed near-infrared cameras that produce images of plant health. We continually work to expand our articulation of community-based participatory models of science-based environmental engagement, adapting and refining our DIY research tools within a socially and politically aware context (Dosemagen, Warren, and Wylie 2011).

Why so serious? Intersections of play and civic engagement

Within Public Lab the intersection of play and civic engagement takes different forms. It can be found in our engagement with the broader citizen science community as we choose to relate our work in both narrative and visual formats, including the research notes and videos on the community website and the illustrated guide to balloon mapping included in our balloon kits. It is also to be found in the very tools we use and the means through which they are created. Science is, at its heart, a creative, collaborative process. It is advanced as individuals question their world, design experiments to challenge assumptions, and share their results with a community of other thinkers, who, in turn, question, experiment, and share their findings. Employing multiple modes of learning helps to engage a broader transect of people and expands the Public Lab community by rendering complex information accessible to many different types of researchers and learners. Likewise, the creative repurposing of everyday items as scientific tools, along with the collaborative nature of tool creation, helps return the scientific process to its roots as a collaborative community endeavor (Latour and Woolgar 1979).

Bringing play back into science: Narrative forms of scientific research and engagement

The purpose of the Public Lab process and tools is, fundamentally, to tell stories (de Certeau 1984). We believe that narrative forms of scientific research and engagement allow individuals to better connect to their topic and each other, thus the toolkit of civic science should, in the ethos of Public Lab, create an opening for people to develop a narrative process around an exploration that they are undertaking. The Public Lab community embeds technologies themselves in a narrative— a set of possible uses, which enable specific inversions of power in communities with environmental concerns. This is not just 'balloon mapping,' but 'grassroots satellite photography'— it matters who does it and why. For example, Public Lab created a DIY spectrometer that has been distributed to over 3,000 people around the world. The process of engaging with the tool has become one of creating a community that experiments, explores, and learns together in all stages of the process. Extending the range of your vision by sending cameras up thousands of feet on a balloon, connected to you by a tenuous 'optic nerve' of kite string (which lets you hear and feel the wind itself through its vibrations), and exploring an area from a new perspective is just one way Public Lab members playfully reconfigure technology to suit their needs. Tools created for civic science practices are ones that, at the root, require us to question both our social and physical boundaries. Maps created by the community with these images allow for a joint process of transcribing new narratives into the images. Questions can be developed about preconceived ideas of state instituted boundaries such as language, composition of ethnic populations, ideas of urbanity, and physically segregating markers.

Creating narrative layers in the process of civic science tool development and use can also help to connect us to the longer running, potentially generational narrative of engagement within our neighborhoods. The collaborative art of using tools that allow a community to investigate, connects us to the past while serving to help us formulate future means of engagement and management with our environment. An example of this type of engagement with civic science tools can be demonstrated by community members working around the Gowanus Canal in Brooklyn, New York. They have used aerial mapping tools to link the past use of a site, through a narrative format, to future management and preservation efforts as a part of a larger community effort of remembrance and reconstituting ownership. As written in a research note on the Public Lab website:

> The key reasons for interest in the site was that this particular lot had been identified as the sole remaining remnant of 'Marylander Hill,' described by historians as a grave site for early colonial settlers, slaves and War of Independence soldiers [...] Based on historical maps and recorded evidence [...] the 'Over My Dead Body' Mapping Team launched their 56" diameter red weather balloon from the nearby Gowanus Canal Conservancy's high tech Mission Control Center, home of GLAM (Gowanus Low Altitude Mapping) at 2nd Avenue and the Gowanus Canal [...] Looking at the photographs a couple of minutes later [...] a curious fact was uncovered by scrutinizing the high-resolution images: the cracks in the concrete—the 'grassroots'—were telling a story. (Diegel 2012, n.p.)

The above case demonstrates that in civic science there is the potential to create engaging narrative to form a compelling story about the environment that gives a call to action. The 'Over My Dead Body' Mapping Team were able to support their argument that there was in fact a Revolutionary War cemetery located on Marylander Hill by using simple tools showing that the cracks in the concrete line up with the kind of soil settling one would expect to see in a cemetery. By incorporating problem identification, tool development, data collection and analysis, the Public Lab model can facilitate a feeling of involvement in one's space and environment through the transformative narrative of engagement (Blair et al. 2013). This process outlines key points relating to play in the form of questioning and creating new ideas and interpretations, but also holds formal engagement methods, such as the open source licensing that Public Lab uses as key to ensuring an exploratory environment that prides itself on allowing and encouraging reinterpretation and new discoveries. In detailing a process that asks people to think about how they can once again become engaged in the management and use decisions of their environment, the process provides a critical means for engaging at every step of the process.

In moving away from the classic model of citizen science, wherein individuals assist professional research scientists by submitting data points as part of a larger research project, some of the steps in the Public Lab process that allow deeper engagement include:

1) Engage people as fellow researchers, not subjects; the community is involved in all aspects of the project from question development, research design, and data collection to analysis;
2) Taking seemingly complex consumer technologies and with simple hacks, re-imagining them as instruments for data collection;
3) Build in social engagement and accountability as part of the process of play in civic science. For instance, aerial mapping, through a balloon attached to a kite string, links the process of data collection to the person holding the string, making that person visible and accessible;
4) Create collaborative workflows allowing people to continue working together after the balloon mapping is complete. Open source platforms such as Public Lab's MapKnitter.org allow people to work together to create a community-based map of their neighborhood;
5) Use open source to encourage the adaptation and reuse of Public Lab tools and methods and, in essence, ensure a safe space for people to collaboratively create and build locally modified tools which can then be adopted for grassroots investigations in diverse communities.[1]

"Easy on the eyes": The role of the visual in civic science participation

Public Lab embraces legibility and chooses to rely on people's intuitive visual fluency. This helps avoid jargon. Stylistically, engaging visual communication in Public Lab so far has ranged from sketched cartoons to pixelated, low-resolution graphics, with new genres cropping up all the time. Public Lab finds that there are several advantages to emphasizing informal

1 These points were first developed by Mathew Lippincott, Shannon Dosemagen, and Sara Wylie for a keynote at Rensselaer Polytechnic Institute's Triple Helix Technoscience as Activism conference on 28 June 2012.

visualizations in our work. These advantages are found primarily in two realms: tool development processes and data structure design.

While many people would say the reimagining of science tools using reusable, recycled material is playful, an equal number of people may find that while it may be a fun form of play for the technologists, it is difficult for average people to participate. Part of the way Public Lab connects the knowledge of people with technological expertise to people with a place-based expertise is the use of illustrated instructional materials.

Public Lab is re-orientating the space of design, engineering, and collaboration (back) into a more legible and accessible place: a piece of paper. We have observed that open source software groups and scientists often erect barriers through prerequisite software/tools that they take for granted. Sketches can readily be posted to the Public Lab website via an emailed digital photo, allowing immediate community information sharing and feedback, and a continuous stream of documentation. Often the drawings and sketches assembled during the process of tool development find their way into an illustrated guide for the tool's use—Public Lab's preferred type of instruction manual.

Designing tools goes hand in hand with designing the data structures used for recording environmental information. Since most people find image-based data easier to directly understand with less interpretation (in contrast to a spreadsheet of numbers), drawings and raster images are central to how Public Lab communicates its research. Examples of image data include aerial photographs, aerial maps, video of a spectrum emitted by a chemical, time-lapse photo that captures thermal flashlight 'heat painting,' and videos of experimental setups and techniques. Therefore, Public Lab's model for tool development prioritizes users' ability to immediately produce visual output from their tool; Public Lab is less interested in sensors that are unable to be assembled without extended training and that create data which require a complicated series of steps between data acquisition and visualization. Public Lab prefers to start visual and stay visual.

Research tool use: Play as a mode of interaction 'in the field'

Engaging in research activities outside, in public places, can enable chance encounters with neighbors, business owners, workers, local authorities, school children—in short, a full cross section of the citizenry. Public Lab seeks to enable and encourage such serendipitous engagements with the way in which its tools are employed in the field. Public Lab's work invokes a sense of play in the very tools we employ in our mapping techniques—including outsized helium balloons and brightly colored kites with fuzzy tails. These objects radiate an aura of playfulness that facilitates engagement across boundaries of age, education, and politics. For these reasons, the Public Lab community prefers, for example, to use kites and balloons instead of the practice of using drones for aerial imaging, in which the operator is not easily apparent. In-person accountability and opportunities for building a coalition around the issues at hand are some of the most salient benefits of the socially grounded environmental research that Public Lab carries out.

That our aerial cameras are both launched from, and returned to, the group of people holding the string seems like an obvious point, however it has wonderful consequences—candid group shots of people young and old looking up, smiling and pointing at every mapping excursion. Taking field research to the next level, balloons and kites can even be launched from a boat, which invokes the spirit of intrepid and adventurous activities in the pursuit of science.

Once a year, the online Public Lab community meet at an event referred to as a Barnraising—a gathering of community members from across the country (and beyond) focused on the creation of a new tool. This is somewhat like a conference, but with an emphasis on 'doing stuff together' rather than just presenting papers and discussion. In the spirit of bringing a community together to collectively raise a structure such as a barn, Public Lab gather to develop tools, toolkits, supporting materials, such as guides and tutorials, to test the tools and to develop new research directions and projects. Participants represent a wide range of interests from technologists and designers to social scientists and community organizers. We hold these events at a 'field research station' out in the Louisiana Delta and we make sure to leave enough time every day to go outside and play.

Fieldwork respects the expertise of residents and workers who have a long-standing lived experience of the environment in question. Fieldwork enhances embodied knowledge, and builds a deeper connection with the environment and environmental issues. Fieldwork equips people to speak from a place of authenticity through personal experience. Building the equipment to capture a dataset that vouches for one's site observations adds a level of personal investment and this personal investment can add fuel to resulting advocacy campaigns.

Reinventing the citizen science toolkit

In the Public Lab community, sometimes the genesis of a new grassroots science technique is the identification of a specific need—the requirement for an airborne device that will capture certain frequencies of light, for example, or a DIY method for identifying contaminants in water—which inspires researchers to then begin brainstorming about designs for a new device. This is a creative and collaborative process, guided always by the constraints of producing a tool that is effective, inexpensive, and accessible. Often the most useful ideas emerge after initially taking design constraints lightly and proposing whimsical concepts that are later seen to contain the kernel of a more solid design.

Just as significant, however, is a tool design dynamic that follows a sort of reverse trajectory: researchers discover, or are presented with, a new tool, and after some thought realize that this existing tool might, with modification, be used to address an outstanding research problem. At Public Lab, we have witnessed this dynamic occur many times: people with an interest in the environment are shown a balloon mapping kit—the simple, but novel combination of a digital camera attached to a balloon—and ideas immediately begin to materialize ways in which the kit might be used to answer questions they already have. Most people do not realize that they would have any use for a DIY spectrometer until they see a demonstration of its ability to distinguish between different brands of olive oil or vintages of wine; their eyes light up, and they begin to imagine new uses for the device. At an event called LEAFFEST, parallel discussions of an airborne webcam device and the uses of aerial near-infrared (NIR) imagery playfully merged into a solid design for a new device: a near infrared webcam device capable of creating composite images on the fly.

Who sets the rules of the game? Gamification vs. playful participation

In describing the sort of interactions that Public Lab aims to facilitate in civic science, it is important to make a subtle, but significant distinction between a 'playful' approach to engagement, and the relatively recent trend toward the gamification of science (Deterding et al. 2011; Prestopnik and Crowston 2012). We find the gamification approach problematic. Akin to the manner in which crowd-sourcing is employed, gamification is typically carried out by experts invested in a particular research or behavior modification outcome; this outcome is often communicated to game participants, if at all, as an afterthought, resulting in game-players whose energies are being spent in service of an agenda which they are not fully aware of. Further, the incentive structure embedded in most games assumes that 'racking up points' will sustain enough interest and be sufficient incentive to induce participation; anyone who has played such a game more than a few times knows that these games can become tiresome (Iacovides et al. 2013; Mekler et al. 2013). Most importantly, because game players are typically not co-creators of the rules of the game and the associated assignment of points as rewards to various behaviors, they do not have an opportunity to embed their own values in the game's incentive structure. We find the potential distance between the values and goals of the game's designers, and the values and goals of game participants, to be a troubling aspect of typical gamification approaches.

In contrast, the playful approach embodied in Public Lab's activities seeks engagement through a spontaneous emergence of collaborative activity, in which the incentives for participation are intrinsic to the nature of the activity ("I am building a kite mapping kit so that I can see my neighborhood from 1000 feet up"); the result is a set of practices and tools that reflect precisely the priorities, interests, and values of each participant.

Conclusion

From launching a balloon over the Gulf of Mexico to sitting in front of a computer as a rainbow-like sample from a spectroscopy experiment appears, civic science creates a space for diverse groups of people to engage, collaborate, share and create. An oft-repeated mantra in the Public Lab community when encouraging people to post their first research note is "things going wrong are just as important as things succeeding." This notion stands in direct contrast with traditional practice in science and in education which does not usually publish failed results.[2] Nevertheless, this is emblematic of Public Lab's approach. Accepting that mishaps and failures are important events for learning, empowers participants to be more open, free, playful, and creative in their scientific explorations, recognizing the point at which a change of direction is necessary, and making space for new research directions to emerge.

The open source, collaborative set of practices that Public Lab uses allows for a continually growing space—one that is not typical of more traditional scientific institutions. Our agendas, research questions, and methods follow an open, grassroots, bottom-up approach, in opposition to

2 With the possible exception of the *International Journal of Negative & Null Results*, established in 2012 to publish scientific work deemed unpublishable by other scientific journals because it was unsuccessful.

traditional top-down, hierarchical dynamics. This is evidenced in the way in which changes to tool designs are valued in the community, where even the slightest contributions—such as a community user-suggested change from using cardboard to plastic stabilizers to fly a camera rig, based on experience in the field—ultimately develop into an improved, widely used research tool design.

Further, and most importantly, these collaborative practices ensure that the research activities in which Public Laboratory engages—practices which emerge from the myriad small and large contributions of a diverse community—always reflect the values, priorities, and preferred modes of interaction of the people that constitute its research community. This transforms the practice of scientific research and civic engagement into something that is both effective, and ultimately enjoyable and productive, for all of those involved.

References

Blair, D., J. Breen, S. Dosemagen, M. Lippincott, and L. Barry. 2013. Civic, citizen, and grassroots science: Towards a transformative scientific research model. In *Accountability technologies: Tools for asking hard questions*, eds. D. Offenhuber and K. Schechtner, 23-31. Vienna: Ambra Verlag.

de Certeau, M. 1984. *The practice of everyday life*. Berkeley, CA: University of California Press.

Deterding, S., D. Dixon, R. Khaled, and L. Nacke. 2011. From game design elements to gamefulness: Defining "gamification". In *Proceedings of the 15th international academic MindTrek conference: Envisioning future media environments, Tampere, September 28-30, 2011*, 9-15. New York: ACM.

Diegel. E. Raising the dead: Grassroots mappers help look for America's first veterans' cemetery. *Public Lab*. http://publiclab.org/notes/eymund-diegel/11-9-2012/raising-dead-grassroots-mapping-helps-look-america-s-first-veteran-s-c.

Dosemagen, S., J. Warren, and S. Wylie. 2011. Grassroots mapping: Creating a participatory map-making process centered on discourse. *Journal of Aesthetics and Protest* 8, 217-228. http://joaap.org/issue8/GrassrootsMapping.htm.

Garvey, C. 1990. *Play: Enlarged edition*. Boston, MA: Harvard University Press.

Iacovides, I., C. Jennett, C. Cornish-Trestrail, and A. L. Cox. 2013. Do games attract or sustain engagement in citizen science? A study of volunteer motivations. *CHI'13 Extended Abstracts on Human Factors in Computing Systems*, 1101-1106. New York: ACM.

Latour, B., and S. Woolgar. 1979. *Laboratory life: The construction of scientific facts*. Princeton, NJ: Princeton University Press.

Mekler, E. D., F. Brühlmann, K. Opwis, and A. N. Tuch. 2013. Disassembling gamification: The effects of points and meaning on user motivation and performance. *CHI'13 Extended Abstracts on Human Factors in Computing Systems*, 1137-1142. New York: ACM.

Prestopnik, N., and K. Crowston. 2012. Purposeful gaming & socio-computational systems: A citizen science design case. In *Proceedings of the 17th ACM international conference on supporting group work, Sanibel Island, FL, October 27-31, 2012*, 75-84. New York: ACM.

About the authors

Liz Barry is a founding member of the Public Laboratory for Open Technology and Science and is on the staff as Director of Community Development, guiding the group's unique combination of place-based organizing and online peer production. She teaches in Columbia University's graduate urban design department and speaks internationally on collaboration and urban environmental management. In 2015, the City of New York scaled *TreeKIT*—a project that Barry co-developed with Philip Silva to measure, map, and monitor street trees—up into a city-wide initiative called *TreesCount!* Barry was a Fellow at the Design Trust for Public Space on Five Borough Farm Phases II & III (2012-14), and was named a Sunlight Foundation OpenGov Champion (2012).

Don Blair's work focuses on cooperative approaches to scientific research, development, and governance of technology in the areas of agroecology, regenerative agriculture, food and water security, and climate-related risk mitigation. He is currently a Research Associate at Edge Collective, where he is working to develop 'open infrastructure' for researchers and farmers contending with extreme or resource-constrained environments. He also co-organizes BARN, the Boston Agroecology Research Network. Don has recently served as Open Water Fellow at Public Lab; Research Affiliate at the Center for Civic Media at the MIT Media Lab; researcher and strategist at Food+Future; Citizen Science Liaison with FarmHack; and as an organizer for the Gathering for Open Agriculture Technology (GOAT). He holds a BA in Ancient Philosophy and an MSc in Physics from the University of Massachusetts Amherst.

Jessica Breen is a fellow with the New Mappings Collaboratory, where her research uses social media and collaborative mapping techniques to understand the role of art and creativity in urban place-making. Jessica is an organizer with Public Lab, as well as being active in the OpenStreetMap and MapTime communities. Jessica is currently a Research Assistant with Mapshop, where she works with students, faculty, and community groups in the production of geographic representations and raising the critical mapping capacities. She holds an MSc in Environmental Studies and is pursuing a doctorate in Geography at the University of Kentucky. She can be found on Twitter @jessibreen.

Shannon Dosemagen is a founder and Executive Director of the Public Lab non-profit organization. In her current work with Public Lab, Shannon is interested in thinking through the use of community-collected data for the purpose of influencing policy around the environment and public health. She has an MSc in Anthropology and Nonprofit Management and is an Ashoka Fellow, a 2015-16 Harvard Berkman Center for Internet and Society Fellow, and a senior fellow of the Environmental Leadership Program. Shannon has contributed to articles in *The Information Society* (Special Forum, March 2014), *Journal of Aesthetics and Protest* (Issue 8, 2011) and *Accountability Technologies: Tools for Asking Hard Questions* (Springer 2013). She can be found on Twitter @sdosemagen.

9. Sensing the air and experimenting with environmental citizenship

Jennifer Gabrys

Abstract

This chapter analyzes community-led citizen sensing projects as a new form of environmental citizenship. Sensing and monitoring air quality can be playful forms of civic engagement with public issues. In these site-specific citizen sensing projects, creative means are being used to engage citizens in measuring air pollution with the aid of technology. The chapter argues that such experimental initiatives should be approached as material processes in which new forms of data retrieval and democratic engagement are developed that can potentially give rise to new and more just power relations in knowledge production.

Keywords: Environmental citizenship, citizen sensing, data, air quality, citizen science

If you should find yourself standing outside the Hobgoblin Pub on New Cross Road in the Borough of Lewisham, London, you might notice a grayish-white box approximately two-and-a-half meters high scrawled with a faded and cascading line of graffiti. Wedged in a space between the buildings and facing out toward the road, the air vent and monitoring equipment at the top of this structure may be one of the few details that betray the purpose of this object, which is to measure air quality at this fixed spot in London. One of the stations in the London Air Quality Network (LAQN) that covers 33 boroughs, this monitoring station contributes to the hourly indexes of air quality and news of episodes of high pollution risk in London. Detecting sulfur dioxide (SO_2), particulate matter 10 and 2.5 (PM 10, PM 2.5), as well as nitrogen oxide (NO) and nitrogen dioxide (NO_2), the station generates data that indicate whether the UK is meeting EU air quality objectives for

Glas, R., S. Lammes, M. de Lange, J. Raessens, and I. de Vries, eds. 2019. *The Playful Citizen. Civic Engagement in a Mediatized Culture.* Amsterdam: Amsterdam University Press.
DOI: 10.5117/9789462984523/CH09

both the short- and long-term emission of pollutants. The data also inform environmental science research and are managed and made available by the Environmental Research Group (ERG) at King's College London where this network is managed and run (London Air Quality Network n.d.).

Passersby may experience in a potentially fleeting way the connection between this station, the local air quality, and the data it generates, which typically circulate in spaces of environmental science and policy. The data that is generated at this fixed site could be seen to be black-boxed, and located in spaces somewhat remote from everyday experiences of air quality on the street. In order to bring air pollution data gathered at this station and the approximately 100 other stations in the LAQN, ERG have designed a 'London Air App' to allow people to observe emissions levels at key monitoring sites, and to make inferences about their own personal exposure when passing through these sites. While this strategy makes the data of fixed sites more accessible through an air quality app, the modes of pollution that individuals experience in their everyday trajectories may be quite different than the types of pollution that are captured through fixed monitoring sites generating data that is averaged over set monitoring periods. For instance, the fixed point at the New Cross Road station typically records an annual exceedance of NO_2, which is a pollutant formed in the combustion of fuel and is largely the result of high levels of automobile use in the city. In fact, this site exceeds the EU air quality objectives which is no more than 40 $\mu m/m^3$ of NO_2 per year. Yet, all along New Cross Road individual moments and locations of exposure may generate a far different set of 'pollution episodes,' with different consequences for urban dwellers in these areas.

Inevitably, the question emerges of how individuals may map their own exposure to air pollution, which is likely to differ from the sites of the official monitoring stations. One response that attempts to monitor air quality beyond fixed sites includes community deployments of diffusion tubes which are a low-cost analog method for gauging air pollution, but require many week-long deployments of tubes that are then sent off to labs for analysis and data production. In this case, the process of gathering air pollution data may be more egalitarian, but the generation and analysis of meaningful data is something that takes place in a remote laboratory setting. Beyond this approach, environmental monitoring is now proliferating from a project undertaken by environmental scientists and governmental agencies to a practice in which DIY groups and creative practitioners are engaged, often as a form of citizen or grassroots science. Many of these monitoring projects might be called 'citizen sensing,' since they typically deploy smart phones and portable sensors with the intention of democratizing the collection and use of sensor data. The general ethos of these projects is that by enabling the monitoring of local environments, it may also be possible to achieve increased engagement with environmental concerns.

One primary way such citizen-sensing projects have sprung up is through direct engagement with sites of contamination or pollution. Air, noise, and water pollution are local environmental disturbances, even if distributed, that most urban dwellers experience on a regular basis. Yet, even then, some urban residents experience more than others since sites of pollution are often concentrated in lower-income urban areas. Citizen sensing of pollution is a strategy that attempts to bring pollution data from the spaces of expert and governmental oversight to an experience that is available to citizens equipped with mobile phones and portable sensors. A proliferation of creative practice, creative computing, and DIY projects have emerged in the area of sensing environmental pollution. Some citizen-sensing projects use the itinerant aspects of individual exposure to air pollution as a site for unique and mobile monitoring experiments, which cannot be compared to fixed sites of detection. For example, Preemptive Media's *Area's Immediate Reading* consists of a mobile and individual air monitoring device for gauging individual exposure to air pollutants (Preemptive Media 2006). Other projects suggest that by focusing on environmental disturbances new questions about the health of individual bodies in relation to environmental health can emerge. For instance, Natalie Jeremijenko's *Environmental Health Clinic* tests pollutants in river water samples to raise discussions about individual health and exposure to environmental pollutants (Jeremijenko n.d.-a). Whether displaying pollution levels or developing platforms to make pollution information more accessible to help facilitate sound decision making, the majority of citizen-sensing pollution projects attempt to make the details of environmental pollution more immediate and actionable.

These projects test, experiment with, and mobilize alternative modes of environmental citizenship in order to address environmental concerns. Yet, in what ways do practices of environmental monitoring with sensing devices give rise not just to experimental modes of participation and civic engagement, but also to different modalities for experiencing environmental pollution?[1] Within these projects, how does the experience and

1 This discussion on the experience and experiment of sensing air pollution draws and builds on my previous work on environmental sensors, which I develop in the context of Isabelle Stengers' analysis of the shared (French) etymology of experiment and experience (in relation to Whitehead). See Whitehead 1929; Stengers 2008; Gabrys 2012.

experiment of air pollution become a site of political as well as potentially playful engagement? In this chapter, I consider how creative practices that sense air pollution, also experiment with the tactics and arrangements of environmental citizenship in order to open up the possibility for new experiences, engagements, and political encounters with environmental matters of concern. These experiments and experiences, however, are not just a matter of enabling citizens to use technology to act on their environments. Rather, as I suggest here and in the larger *Citizen Sense* project that this work draws from, computational sensing technologies are bound up with the generation of new relations, entities, occasions, and interpretive registers of sensing. Sensor-based engagements with environments do not simply detect external phenomena to be reported, rather they bring together experiencing entities to make possible new arrangements of environmental sensing and data.

While citizen-sensing practices attempt to generate new modes of civic and actionable environmental data, at the same time I consider in what ways it might be possible to develop an analysis of these environmental practices that does not necessarily fix them as objects of study, but rather creates generative approaches by considering the data practices that emerge through these projects, which might further spur new experiments with additional data practices. With an examination of citizen-sensing projects that develop experimental and creative approaches to monitoring air quality, including *Feral Robotic Dogs*, *Pigeon Blog*, and *Air Quality Egg*, I consider how these technological modes of sensing generate distinct practices of environmental citizenship in and through engagement with data.

While these environmental sensing projects are ostensibly focused on creating opportunities for citizen scientists (of sorts) to generate their own data, these projects also create additional data in and around the practices they set in motion. This is another way of saying that rather than consider environmental citizenship as something that inheres within a particular subject position, I am instead interested in considering how practices distributed across human and more-than-human registers might emerge through distinct performances or enactments of environmental citizenship. Environmental citizenship is by no means a new concept, and has been discussed at length across a range of literatures too vast to summarize here. But I take as a cue, from Rebecca Ellis and Claire Waterton, the notion of "environmental citizenship in the making" (Ellis and Waterton 2004), or as I would further suggest, a processual and relational approach to environmental citizenship based on Whitehead's conception of citizenship (Whitehead 1929), as a way to think through the emergent practices of monitoring and sensing urban air quality as a distinct performance and articulation of environmental citizenship (Gabrys 2013).

In considering the types of practices that emerge, I examine environmental citizenship as a distributed process rather than as something that is situated at the site of a fixed human subject. Distributed and more-than-human modes of participation contribute to air pollution and its monitoring. From computational sensors to moving air masses, manufacturing and transport, vegetation and animal bodies, temperature gradients and topography, economic inequality and real estate, as well as policy and modeling, a number of factors converge in the project of experiencing and experimenting with sensing air pollution. Which of these processual entities are more or less evident in monitoring the air? What does the air (and 'the environment') become through monitoring devices, and what are its materializations and experiences? What are the relationships, political engagements, and ways of mobilizing data that make for the most a/effective environmental practices? And if monitoring and citizen sensing are emerging as new modes of environmental participation, in what ways do these experiments further enable practices for engaging with and addressing air pollution, and for speculating with environmental objects and environmental politics?

Citizen science, citizen sensing, and doing science differently

The current range of citizen-sensing projects can be perceived to draw on a longer history of environmental practice in the form of citizen science. Amateurs' monitoring of their environment, for instance, have in the past contributed to the emergence of natural history, while more contemporary attempts have informed the rise of popular environmentalist movements and the public's current engagement in environmental matters of scientific and political controversy. Science and technology studies (STS) focused on citizen science—environmental and otherwise—have, in many cases, analyzed how public engagement with science is variously organized to influence the ways in which the public can be constituted as entities able to participate in environmental politics (Irwin and Michael 2003). Amateur natural histories, biodiversity monitoring projects and toxic waste events have been among the citizen-science and public engagements studied by STS researchers (Wynne 1996). In these studies, citizen science and public engagement with science emerge not as easy fixes to making science more democratic, but rather as particular expressions of environmental politics, citizenship, and matters of concern.

Citizen science—and sensing—can be seen as both an augmentation to science, as well as an expanded way of practicing science in relation to pedagogical and political aims (Jasanoff 2003). Many current scientific initiatives suggest that the observation and monitoring of earth processes remains one of the core areas for advancing scientific understanding of environmental change. At the same time, environmental monitoring projects often seek to find ways to broaden the scope of environmental observation beyond the sciences exclusively, and to make ecological observation more accessible and engaging to a diverse range of participants. The process of gathering and making these observations more participatory is often seen as a way to overcome the relative crisis of environmental engagement in political and cultural spheres: by making environmental change more evident and distributed across sensing subjects, environmental action may also be facilitated.

There is extensive literature discussing citizen engagement in monitoring air pollution, although often at the level of how the public responds to or engages with scientific findings, and not as practitioners of science themselves (e.g. Bickerstaff and Walker 2003; Whitehead 2009). Yet, at the same time, analyses of participatory and environmental-justice-focused engagement with air pollution have discussed the many and even non-computational ways in which air samples may be collected in order to inform environmental science and politics. The *Louisiana Bucket Brigade* is an environmental activist group that Gwen Ottinger discusses as engaging in a DIY-bucket collection method of monitoring air quality in a neighborhood adjacent to oil and gas refineries located in a region referred to as "Cancer Alley" in a part of the United States with particularly high rates of cancer (Ottinger 2010). While the bucket becomes a device for collecting air samples in a more democratic and local way, the analysis of the air samples must still take place in laboratories (similar to the diffusion tube air analysis) that are not sites of citizen engagement. The project presents a low-tech way of conducting a version of citizen science, which is largely focused on environmental activism and justice.

From citizen science to participatory sensing, crowd-sourcing, civic science, DIY media, and citizen sensing, a number of terms have emerged to describe these widespread practices of environmental monitoring and data gathering that work in various ways to democratize technoscientific tools and our understanding of the environment. While these terms are used in different ways to stress the scientific, big data, or civic aspects of these practices, in this chapter I work with the term citizen sensing in order to draw explicit attention to the ways in which computational and mobile practices of environmental monitoring might be discussed as modes of citizen *sensing*, specifically. Citizen-science projects, I suggest, are increasingly transforming into citizen-sensing projects, where digital devices equipped with sensors are used to monitor environments and gather data.

Practices of monitoring and sensing environments that were once the focus of scientific disciplines have migrated to a number of everyday participatory applications, where users of smart phones and networked devices are able to track, study, and report on their environments. Citizen sensing, as I am defining the practice here, encompasses or refers to those sensing activities that often use computational sensing technologies in the form of smart phones, mobile and low-cost electronic devices such as Arduino, Nanode and Raspberry Pi, and platforms to report and potentially act on environmental events.[2] Such distribution of sensing capabilities across sensor networks and multiple mobile and individualized platforms, have arguably become a focused site for environmental and technological engagement. Citizen-sensing projects are closely related to citizen-science studies, but differ in how they seek to enable environmental practice through direct engagement with environmental monitoring technologies, rather than as necessarily filtered through engagement with experts. The citizen-sensing applications that strongly resemble citizen science projects most often are based on similar practices of individuals voluntarily tracking and monitoring environmental data related to everything from pollution to biodiversity counts. Citizen-sensing practices have been described at times as making inventive contributions to both the research and development of technological tools and to the varing methods of environmental monitoring (Burke et al. 2006). These practices range from undertakings that address the ways in which microsensor data may complement other environmental observations, including remote sensing in order to provide more complete pictures of environmental issues, as well as ubiquitous-computing approaches that often focus on the capacities and practices of sensor technologies. These

2 The most commonly referenced platform for environmental data is one that has been in continual transformation. First taking the form of *Pachube*, as developed by Usman Haque, this platform was subsequently developed as a quasi-open yet commercially based structure in the form of *Cosm*, as has now become a more commercial and subscription-led platform rebranded as *Xively*. The development and migration of this platform from an open community to a commercial enterprise is a topic that could be researched and analyzed at length. However there is no room in this paper to deal with this parallel development in how environmental sense data may actually be aggregated, presented, and made accessible in an online format.

practices can also include social or civic media projects that emphasize the ways in which social networking can mobilize collected data in new ways to effect policy and mobilization.

Sometimes mobile sensor technologies have enabled more thorough practices of environmental monitoring and observation than those already being conducted by citizen-science initiatives, as in counting and tagging biological activities. In other cases, the capacities of mobile sensor technologies have enabled more distributed and potentially more accurate collection of data, such as urban air or noise pollution. Some applications extend the scope of citizen sensing to encompass not just microsensor data and the use of smart phones, but also draw on remote sensing and mapping to enable the tracking of deforestation or animal movements. In still other instances, these mobile sensor applications have enabled new forms of democratic organization and communication about environmental issues by effectively crowd-sourcing environmental observations in order to inform environmental policy and action. What emerges in this diverse set of practices that are in many ways connected to citizen science is a set of proposals for democratizing environmental engagement and developing other ways of doing environmental science and politics.

Many of the claims for citizen sensing are arguably still in the realm of proposals and experiments, where the hope is that distributed capacities of computational sensors *will* enable increased civic engagement with environmental issues. But in what ways do citizen-sensing engagements influence the modes of environmental participation that emerge? And what does it mean to 'sense' or experience air pollution with computational sensors? While the impacts of air pollution on human health are one of the key motivators for establishing quality standards, often the means of monitoring and enforcing these standards misses the more localized pollution experienced by people who actually live in urban areas affected by these events. Environmental health and individual health are bound up in articulations of what does and does not count as a 'pollution episode.' Strategies for monitoring pollution at the citizen or individual level are seen as a way to counter or redress the possible gaps in data, but there is more to these projects than this, since in mobilizing sensors to bring environmental monitoring into a more democratic set of engagements new material-political actors, engagements, and experiments emerge—along with new political possibilities and controversies.

Sensing technologies are entangled with and mobilize new environmental monitoring practices and new ways of gathering data. But, the other more primary reason for engaging with these practices as citizen *sensing* practices, is to draw out the ways in which computational devices are at once sensing and actuating technologies, as well as modes for sensing and experiencing environments. In this sense, citizen science and citizen sensing may have similar objectives in observing and monitoring environments, but they unfold through very different material entanglements and relationalities, ways of practicing and generating data, and in their articulation of what counts as environmental politics. The modes of engagement and spaces through which data is gathered, analyzed, and communicated are key aspects to the emergence of these environmental modes of practice. Citizen-sensing projects are frequently described as data campaigns, or as identifying an issue about which more data may be needed in order to effect policy changes. As numerous STS researchers have noted, however, data are always embedded within political practices, structures and institutions that inform everything from how data are delineated and collected, to how they are joined up, communicated and acted upon (e.g. Bowker 2005). It is these practices of data gathering as characteristic of environmental monitoring and engagement that I will focus on for the remainder of this chapter by looking at three projects that engage specifically with computational modes of sensing environments in order to gather data and inform environmental action. I am interested in finding out what relations, practices, and political possibilities emerge from these distinct mobilizations of environmental data.

Dogs, pigeons, and eggs: Creaturing data

In many ways, pollution monitoring has been a key initiator for creative practice and creative computing projects engaged in gathering environmental data. *Area's Immediate Reading, Pigeon Blog, Common Sense, Street Sweepers, Feral Robotic Dogs, Air Quality Egg,* and others, are various scientific and environmental monitoring projects that have different actors, arrangements, tools, and spaces where the readings are conducted. At the same time, in pollution monitoring projects, the gathering of sense data is often closely tied to affecting and effecting political action and environmental change, by addressing how data is collected, generated, and acted upon. Yet, in each of these projects environmental sense data emerges not as a universal category or form, but as a concrete entity that is a part of the process of participating in environments. "The actual world is a process," as Whitehead writes, and this "process is the becoming of actual entities.

Thus actual entities are creatures; they are also termed 'actual occasions'" (1929, 22). Actual occasions are living creatures, or lively meetings of entities that concretize routes in and through events. In this sense, the gathering of data might be identified as more than a static fact that documents air quality at any given time or place, and instead be approached as a practice that gives rise to particular entities that further generate concrete worlds. These entities are "creatures" that form and are formed by processes—here through practices of gathering environmental data.

Working with this Whitehead-inspired analysis of how the specific entities of environmental data emerge through sensing, I suggest that environmental sensing projects are *creaturing* processes, where the entities that emerge are continuous with specific situations and modalities of participation. The projects I discuss below engage in the creaturing of data in a double sense, however, since they also deploy more-than-human participants, including robotic dogs, homing pigeons, and plastic eggs, as concrete entities for drawing together citizen-sensing practices. Data, in this sense, are not an abstract store of information or something to be coherently visualized, but rather are bound up with the making of actual occasions and material processes. Data may typically appear to be the primary objective of environmental sensing projects, which focus on obtaining data in order to influence environmental policy and practices, but along the way the relations and material arrangements that data gathering sets in place begin to *creature* (and in the process, materialize) new entities and societies of objects that emerge through these practices. By turning to the creaturing and materializing of data, I consider in the projects that follow how data mobilize or underwrite environmental practices, while at the same time often failing to materialize in the ways anticipated which generates participatory arrangements that are different than those intended. The failure of environmental sense data to perform as an easy spur to environmental action, it turns out, can even be a key way in which the *creaturely* aspects of data emerge. Data unfold less through instrumental or even epistemic registers, arguably, and more as affective and materialized attractors for experimenting with environmental citizenship.

Dogs

One of the earliest creative practice projects to engage with environmental sensing, *Feral Robotic Dogs*, was originally developed by Natalie Jeremijenko in 2002 and advanced with additional versions and deployments through 2006. The project adapted existing Sony Aibo toy dogs by upgrading them with all-terrain bodies, and environmental-sensing brains and noses. Ready-made robotic toy dogs with pre-programmed tasks were identified as having more interesting potential use: these are creatures that so to speak await further instructions. The first generation 'gamma dog' was designed to store and transmit environmental data from any radioactive source that exceeds EPA thresholds. It was anticipated that the deployment of these dogs in multiples could "provide informational spectacle and conclusive on-data convergence in a given local area" (Bureau of Inverse Technology n.d.). During its development, these semi-autonomous gadgets were rerouted to 'sniffer' dog mode by fitting them with environmental sensors capable of detecting environmental pollutants including volatile organic compounds, carbon monoxide and methane, while at the same time providing general indications of air quality.

A number of deployments for the dogs were then arranged at sites likely to be polluted, including a former gas plant at East 173rd Street Works at the Bronx River in New York, where the dogs scouted for volatile organic solvents and polycyclic aromatic hydrocarbons; and at Baldwin Park in Orlando, Florida, where the robot dogs were deployed to search for volatile organic compounds at 'sites of community interest,' including a former landfill site that was a proposed site for a new middle school. This Florida deployment specifically sought to:

> provide an opportunity for evidence driven discussion of the environmental issues facing the community, and the opportunity to coordinate diverse opinions and interpretations of the phenomena at hand. Because the dog's space-filling logic emulates a familiar behavior, i.e. "sniffing something out," anyone can participate and try to make sense of this data in real time without necessarily having the technical or scientific training usually required to interpret data from other sources on the same phenomena. It has the potential to raise the standards of evidence involved, promote diverse valid interpretations involved in complex environmental and political processes. (Jeremijenko n.d.-b)

Environmental data was to be obtained by the dog's movements since they were designed to map pollutants by moving toward them and sniffing them out. This is one way of rendering environmental data more perceptible, and more spectacular, while also changing the possibilities of who can generate and access data, as well as who has the evidence necessary and means for contributing to environmental and political debates. Inevitably, the process of monitoring pollutants here and in the projects discussed below is bound up with available sensors that are able to measure specific gases. Such versions of data-led environmental citizenship become tied to prior investments in developing sensors with specific technical capacities, often for industrial or scientific uses.

While discussing this project, the group of artists and technologists that came together to work on the project suggested that robotics, environmental sensing, and mapping could propel activism in new ways to different types of engagements, where both gathering data and creative exploration with environmental monitoring might generate renewed engagements with local environments (Lane et al. 2006). Here is a sensing project that is speculating about the possibility for participatory and even citizen-based data collection that intends to create what Benjamin Bratton and Natalie Jeremijenko have elsewhere called "shorter circuits" between environmental information and the observers of that information (Bratton and Jeremijenko 2008). With the collection of environmental data, it is expected that a more immediate and accountable mode of environmental action may also be possible.

Yet, this direct connection between data and action is not necessarily automatic, and in many ways draws on a presupposed efficacy that scientific data are assumed to have in the world. The ways in which climate change data, for instance, fails to have an immediate effect on political action may give rise to speculation about whether data necessarily constitute incontrovertible evidence which can be used to inform and change environmental politics. The failure of data to lead to environmental action may, on one level, have to do with the assumed force of a scientifically evidenced and 'rational' argument, where decisions made in relation to environmental matters of concern are suffused with competing political interests. Yet, on another level, the ways in which data in and of themselves are meant to be—and yet may also fail to be—compelling may raise questions about the affective registers of data. Is a robotic dog a more affective and effective data-creature than a spreadsheet or bar chart? The point here is not to set up a false dichotomy between these data forms, but rather to ask about the ways in which the creaturing and materializing of data may be one way to experiment with the modes and practices of environmental citizenship. In these creaturely arrangements of dogs, pigeons, and eggs, new distributions of participation environmental data and political action may even emerge, but the ways in which this participation informs environmental debate remains an open question that continues to be explored and taken up in subsequent environmental and citizen-sensing projects.

Pigeons

If the *Feral Robotic Dogs* project deployed air-sensing technologies through a robotic toy to make new technical modalities of environmental monitoring more widely available, the *Pigeon Blog* project raises the question of how air quality sensing shifts even further when pigeons are the reporters and carriers of sensing equipment. *Pigeon Blog*, developed by Beatriz da Costa with Cina Hazegh and Kevin Ponto in 2006, is a project that used sensor backpacks fitted to homing pigeons to collect low-attitude air quality readings while the pigeons flew through the frequently polluted skies of Southern California. The sensor backpacks consisted of a combined GPS receiver that provided latitude, longitude, and altitude readings, a dual automotive carbon monoxide and nitrogen oxide sensor, a temperature sensor, and a purpose-built mobile phone for transmitting text messages. The backpack kit was developed as a miniature unit small enough to be carried by the pigeons, so that real-time air quality data could be transmitted and visualized as pollution levels on the *Pigeon Blog* and within a Google Map visualization (da Costa 2006, 2008).

Situated in Southern California and initially developed in Los Angeles, the project addressed the ongoing problem of air pollution and environmental justice by developing an open-source sensing kit that could be used for "grassroots scientific data gathering" (da Costa 2006). The *Pigeon Blog* project specifically responded to the limited number of fixed air monitoring stations that are focused on generating long-term average data about air quality, and which may not necessarily be located in areas of the highest pollution episodes. By increasing the number of local measurements and data about local exposures, the *Pigeon Blog* project sought to complement, if not challenge, existing data on air pollution by looking at the distribution of pollution at a finer and more inhabited level. This approach was shared with *Area's Immediate Reading*, or *A.I.R.*, a 2006 Preemptive Media project (briefly mentioned in the introduction to this chapter), in which da Costa collaborated along with Brooke Singer and Jamie Schulte. Consisting of portable air monitors, *A.I.R.* enabled urban dwellers to complement coarser and fixed air-quality data by collecting local data through individual journeys (Preemptive Media 2006). Equipped with GPS and coordinated to a database of known pollution sources, the air monitor senses carbon monoxide (CO), Nitrogen Oxides (NOx), and ground level Ozone (O3) at distinct locations, and provides real-time visualizations of air pollution levels in relation to an (EPA) air quality index. By making individual maps of urban air pollution exposure, urban dwellers could become more aware and engaged in discussing environmental issues through everyday exposure, individual risk, and neighborhood-level mapping.

In both *Pigeon Blog* and *A.I.R.*, citizen sensing is presented as an activist project of sorts, yet this is not the usual approach to environmental politics that most often develops in relation to issues such as urban air quality. By specifically enrolling pigeons into the project of sensing air, the *Pigeon Blog* project questions how to develop a mode of "interspecies co-production in the pursuit of resistant action" (da Costa 2008, 377). The pigeons were sent out as 'reporters' to draw attention to the issue of air pollution, while at the same time providing inventive and more accessible ways of gathering data in order to provoke new possibilities of political action. Pigeons participated in this project in multiple ways. Pigeons are not only creatures with particular navigational abilities that often fly according to major landscape features such as highways, but they are also a pervasive bird (if often reviled) in urban areas. Moreover, most pigeons have a close proximity to polluted urban areas, and may provide a specific view of low-altitude air pollution in areas of high traffic. Further, pigeons can act as biosensors making distinct urban experiences available through proxy modes of sensing so we can obtain more insight into our environment.

Pigeons can also be seen to be key contributors to creaturing data and environmental participation in ways that move beyond the usual space of environmental activism. Da Costa makes the point that projects such as *Pigeon Blog* generate new capacities for engaging with environmental information and for mobilizing participation that are not exclusively focused on "how bad things are" (2008, 379). While the project initially set out to provide alternative datasets that might be more widely gathered to add to the expert approaches to environmental monitoring, in many ways this objective was not achieved. Long-term or even complementary datasets were not generated from the project, and this anticipated outcome even became somewhat incompatible with the project's attempt to experiment with new modes of environmental practice and participation. Instead, the most enduring contribution made by *Pigeon Blog* was its method of experimenting with urban, technological, and more-than-human entities that were to become part of the project of sensing, experiencing, and reporting on air quality. It may be that, while this approach began with a focus on data about air quality, it arrives with a wider approach to environmental practice that is less exclusively data-driven, and is more attentive to the expanded, even ecological, modalities of citizenship that might emerge with such a distributed approach to sensing environments (Braidotti 2006; Gabrys 2012).

Eggs

As early experiments into environmental sensing, *Feral Robotic Dogs* and *Pigeon Blog* test ways in which new and distributed modes of participation among human and more-than-human modalities can shift the possibilities for political engagement in air quality. These projects continue to inform current citizen-sensing projects, which have only proliferated in the past few years because of the increasing availability and affordability of sensor technologies. *Air Quality Egg* is another project in this area that seeks to connect maker communities developing digital devices that will enable citizen sensing of air quality (Wicked Device n.d.). Developed as a 'community-led' project, where the community is largely comprised of creative technologists located in New York, London, and Amsterdam, the egg project consists of a Nanode sensing platform that detects carbon monoxide and nitrogen dioxide that the project participants identify as key air pollutants. The air-sensing apparatus is housed in a rapid-prototyped egg-shaped shell that was first tested at the second Citizen Cyberscience Summit in London in 2012. The project has subsequently earned considerable backing on Kickstarter. The project website indicates that the eggs are primarily located in the United States, Europe, Australia, and Japan, and gather various measurements that are uploaded to a Xively data platform.

While the *Air Quality Egg* project is ostensibly focused on air quality monitoring, its origin stems from technical communities that are highly motivated to experiment with the kit of sensing devices, or to engage in what has been referred to as 'participatory sensing' experiments by bringing the functionalities of sensors to more explicit points of encounter (DiSalvo et al. 2012). At the same time, there are many questions that arise as to how these devices perform, and the extent to which the data they generate are accurate. Concerns about the *Air Quality Egg* project have led to a heated debate about how viable it is to monitor air quality accurately given the scale and coarse instrumentation of these technologies, and whether the sensors were even accurately calibrated. To what extent are egg-gathered data useful and accurate? And what if the egg fails to even function in the first place (as was the case in several of the prototyping workshops)?

In a project video, however, commentators on the project suggest that accuracy of data was not the primary concern, since sense data may provoke environmental concerns that could always be followed up with more thoroughly scientific studies. Here, they argue, the focus was on the community of egg users and developers inclined toward testing devices that may create further calls to action, even if the links between the local, sporadic, and somewhat momentary datasets and informing environmental science, policy, and behavior were not always clear. At one point in the project video, which captured the testing of the egg during the London Cyberscience event in spring 2012, a participant remarked, "the chicken is not ready," referring to the back-and-forth attempts to have the egg set-up, calibrated and ready to gather measurements.

In the context of creaturely data, this project seems to be an entity in formation where a sensor-led technical kit is the egg-like impetus for galvanizing and drawing together environmental issues and action. The environments that emerge here are highly informed by computational modes of sensing and acting. Data gathered through electronic sensing is seen to be the force that propels perceived possibilities for activism, but here the force of data depends less on the accuracy of data and more on the process of making a device that can draw attention to data practices as materialized and potentially political engagements. Data is creatured in the *Air Quality Egg* as a data-generating device ready to hatch and give rise to new modalities of data-driven activism. Yet, it can be argued that the modes of participating in making devices and generating data are very different entities and occasions than modes of participating in environmental activism, which in the case of the egg may be a legitimating subtext, but which is not the primary focus in this tech-led approach to participation.

Conclusion: Experimenting with environmental citizenship

The three projects discussed here share a similar approach to environmental sensing by pursuing more democratic engagements of data gathering in order to inform environmental politics. Yet beyond these similarities, very different entities and modalities of citizenship come together in these projects. The *Feral Robotic Dogs* project tests specific deployments in landfills and the proposed site of a new middle school, making the point that from these specific sites, new communities of interest might emerge to influence environmental debate. Dealing with data is rendered as a more haptic and materialized experience, something demonstrated through a fleet of sniffing robotic dogs. The *Pigeon Blog* seeks to make urban air quality visible through a more-than-human engagement, which at once redistributes environmental participation while adopting a more experimental approach to sensing urban environments. And the *Air Quality Egg* focuses on developing an Internet of Things approach to creating a worldwide sensor network, where new devices and the data they generate are seen to lead to new possibilities for participation and the formation of communities.

Yet with each of these projects, the transition from environmental sensing experiment to citizen-based engagement in environmental issues remains unclear. There are multiple issues that emerge with more grassroots modes of environmental monitoring. As the London Air Quality Network points out, monitoring air quality on a DIY-level may not be as easy as it first appears due to the expense of precisely instrumented sensors, and the questions of accuracy that pertain to sensing projects that use less refined sensing equipment, or that are not set-up in a systematic way to study environments over time. The dogs, pigeons, and eggs of these projects are not gathering data with the required rigor of a scientific study, but they are making a case for the development of complementary data sets that influence what is monitored and how it is brought to our attention in order to be acted upon.

At this level of action, additional questions emerge as to how environmental sense data may inform environmental politics and actions. In an earlier human-computer interaction research project, *Common Sense*, which tested the deployment of sensors for measuring air quality on street sweepers, the project participants concluded that environmental community organization is actually the most critical factor in order for data generated through sensor deployments to be relevant, meaningful and actionable (Aoki et al. 2008). In some cases, community environmental organizations have been shown to be rather skeptical about the extent in which more data from computational sensors will necessarily facilitate more effective action. In this way, some researchers question whether more localized and data-led processes of environmental observation and monitoring actually do enable greater environmental participation.

While environmental sense data gathered without a clear link to community projects may not have the anticipated a/effects of facilitating greater participation in environmental matters of concern, these projects do experiment with the methods, techniques, communities, modes of participation, sites of monitoring, and evidential modes of activism and politics that might emerge as new entities and processes for engaging with environments and environmental issues. These experiments with affectivity, effectiveness and practice make space—as well as contribute to further controversies—regarding different approaches to environmental politics and participation that might be investigated further. Data as typically conceived may not be the critical unit for mobilizing environmental citizenship and action, and a gadget-led process for engaging with politics may not be the most definitive answer to developing new modes of environmental engagement. However, these citizen-sensing projects raise the question of what other experiments might emerge that open up the possibility for new types of environmental politics, and new modes of collective participation (Gabrys and Yusoff 2012). Within this space, the modes and practices of data—the creaturely entities in and through which data manifest and give rise to worlds—are arguably an area yet to be fully explored, since data are so frequently presented as the dematerialized evidence of environmental fact. But the modalities, materialities, and *creatures* of data may be one way of experimenting with the ways in which monitoring practices might establish new sites of environmental engagement, where affectivity might be one way to reconsider the effectiveness of data.

Acknowledgments

This chapter is based on a manuscript written in 2013, which since then has also been published (in a revised version) as 'Sensing air and creaturing data' in *Program earth: Environmental sensing technology and the making of a computational planet* (Gabrys 2016, 157-181). The research leading to these results has received funding from the European Research Council under the European Union's Seventh Framework Programme (FP/2007-2013) / ERC Grant Agreement n. 313347, *Citizen sensing and environmental practice: Assessing participatory engagements with environments through sensor technologies.*

References

Aoki, P. M., R. J. Honicky, A. Mainwaring, C. Myers, E. Paulos, S. Subramanian, and A. Woodruff. 2008. Common sense: Mobile environmental sensing platforms to support community action and citizen science (demonstration). In *Proceedings of the 10th international conference on ubiquitous computing (adjunct programs), Seoul, September 21-24, 2008*, 59-60. http://www.ubicomp.org/ubicomp2008/ubicomp08adjunct.pdf.

Bickerstaff, K., and G. Walker. 2003. The place(s) of matter: Matter out of place – Public understandings of air pollution. *Progress in Human Geography* 27 (1): 45-67.

Bowker, G. 2005. *Memory practices in the sciences.* Cambridge, MA: The MIT Press.

Braidotti, R. 2006. *Transpositions: On nomadic ethics.* Malden, MA: Polity Press.

Bratton, B., and N. Jeremijenko. 2008. Suspicious images, latent interfaces. *Situated Technologies Pamphlets* 3. New York: The Architectural League of New York.

Bureau of Inverse Technology. n.d. Feral robotic dog development squad 1.1 codename sniffer. *BIT.* http://www.bureauit.org/feral.

Burke, J., D. Estrin, M. Hansen, A. Parker, N. Ramanathan, S. Reddy, and M. B. Srivastava. 2006. Participatory sensing. In *Proceedings of ACM Sensys World Sensor Web Workshop, Boulder, CO, October 31, 2006.* New York: ACM.

da Costa, B. 2006. Pigeonblog 2006-08. *Beatriz da Costa's Blog and Project Hub.* http://web.archive.org/web/20130527223456/http://beatrizdacosta.net:80/Pigeonblog

—. 2008. Reaching the limits. In *Tactical biopolitics: Art, activism, and technoscience,* eds. B. da Costa, and K. Philip, 365-385. Cambridge, MA: The MIT Press.

DiSalvo, C., M. Louw, D. Holstius, I. Nourbakhsh, and A. Akin. 2012. Towards a public rhetoric through participatory design: Critical engagements and creative expression in the Neighborhood Networks Project. *Design Issues* 28 (3): 48-61.

Ellis, R., and C. Waterton. 2004. Environmental citizenship in the making: The participation of volunteer naturalists in UK biological recording and biodiversity policy. *Science and Public Policy* 31 (2): 95-101.

Gabrys, J. 2012. Sensing an experimental forest: Processing environments and distributing relations. *Computational Culture* 2. http://computationalculture.net/article/sensing-an-experimental-forest-processing-environments-and-distributing-relations.

—. 2013. Ecological observatories: Fluctuating sites and sensing subjects. In *Field_Notes: Field and laboratory as sites for art & science practices,* eds. L. Beloff, E. Berger, and T. Haapoja, 178-187. Helsinki: Finnish Society of Bioart.

—. 2016. *Program earth: Environmental sensing technology and the making of a computational planet.* Minneapolis, MN: University of Minnesota Press.

Gabrys, J., and K. Yusoff. 2012. Arts, sciences and climate change: Practices and politics at the threshold. *Science as Culture* 21 (1): 1-24.

Irwin, A., and M. Michael. 2003. *Science, social theory and public knowledge.* Maidenhead, UK: Open University Press/McGraw-Hill.

Jasanoff, S. 2003. Technologies of humility: Citizen participation in governing science. *Minerva* 41:223-244.

Jeremijenko, N. n.d.-a. Environmental Health Clinic. *Facebook.* http://www.facebook.com/xclinic.

—. n.d.-b. Feral Robotic Dogs. *New York University.* http://www.nyu.edu/projects/xdesign/feralrobots.

Lane, G., C. Brueton, G. Roussos, N. Jeremijenko, G. Papamarkos, D. Diall, D. Airantzis, and K. Martin. 2006. Public authoring & Feral robotics. *Cultural Snapshot* 11. http://proboscis.org.uk/publications/SNAPSHOTS_feralrobots.pdf.

London Air Quality Network. n.d. London air. *King's College London.* http://www.londonair.org.uk/LondonAir/Default.aspx.

Ottinger, G. 2010. Buckets of resistance: Standards and the effectiveness of citizen science. *Science, Technology & Human Values* 35 (2): 244-270.

Preemptive Media. 2006. AIR: Area's Immediate Reading. *Air Preemptive Media Project.* http://www.pm-air.net.

Stengers, I. 2008. A constructivist reading of process and reality. *Theory, Culture & Society* 25 (4): 91-110.

Whitehead, A. N. 1929. *Process and reality: An essay in cosmology.* New York: The Free Press.

Whitehead, M. 2009. *State science and the skies: Governmentalities of the British atmosphere.* Malden, MA: Wiley-Blackwell.

Wicked Device. n.d. Air Quality Egg. *Wicked Device.* http://www.airqualityegg.com.

Wynne, B. 1996. May the sheep graze safely? A reflexive view of the expert-lay knowledge divide. In *Risk, environment and modernity: Towards a new ecology,* eds. S. Lash, B. Szerszynski, and B. Wynne, 44-83. London: Sage Publications.

About the author

Jennifer Gabrys is Chair in Media, Culture and Environment in the Department of Sociology at the University of Cambridge, and Visiting Professor in the Department of Sociology at Goldsmiths, University of London. She is principal investigator in *Citizen Sense* and *AirKit,* two projects funded by the European Research Council. Her research investigates environments, digital technologies, and citizen participation through theoretical and practice-based work. Her books include a techno-geographical investigation of environmental sensing, *Program earth: Environmental sensing technology and the making of a computational planet* (University of Minnesota Press 2016); and a material-political analysis of electronic waste, *Digital rubbish: A natural history of electronics* (University of Michigan Press 2011). Together with Gay Hawkins and Mike Michael, she has co-edited an interdisciplinary collection on plastics, *Accumulation: The material politics of plastic* (Routledge 2013). Her work can be found at citizensense.net and jennifergabrys.net.

10. Biohacking: Playing with technology

Stephanie de Smale

Abstract

This chapter examines the process of image production by open-source microscopes from the perspective of play. The question what happens to images when microscopes move from the lab to open-source hacker spaces is probed by deconstructing the material layers of its production. Politically motivated to democratize science, open-source translations transform the use and function of biotechnology. And while the process of translation may compromise microscopes' scientific capability, they gain in value from experimentation by artists and citizens. As a result, playing with biotechnology is an educative and creative exploration of the use and construction of scientific instruments, where the multi-layered process of making an image becomes observable to the naked eye.

Keywords: Hacking, biotechnology, citizen science, open source, materiality, objectivity

On 8 October 2013, a group of artists, activists, and scientists gathered at the Waag Society in Amsterdam to discuss the relationship between biotechnology, the life sciences, art, and hacking (G-netwerk 2013). A central topic of this evening was biohacking, an emerging term that is used to describe activities that aid in the democratization of science, such as hacking laboratory equipment to create open source equivalents. Biohacking tries to take science out of the lab (Delfanti 2012, 163). It is practiced in garages, open hacker spaces, or 'open wet labs,' and is facilitated through the production of low cost laboratory equipment based on open source hardware (OSHW). From a biohacker's perspective, these technologies emancipate science by enabling the production of data and knowledge by non-professionals in the public realm (Delfanti 2012; Kera and Dusseiller 2012). A prominent example of this is the open source do-it-yourself (DIY) microscope developed by

Glas, R., S. Lammes, M. de Lange, J. Raessens, and I. de Vries, eds. 2019. *The Playful Citizen. Civic Engagement in a Mediatized Culture.* Amsterdam: Amsterdam University Press.
DOI: 10.5117/9789462984523/CH10

platform Hackteria.org. Users are free to create and adapt the design of these microscopes, and to produce data by creating images in any way they see fit. The appropriation of the microscope and the claim that biohacking is a counter-practice in the production of knowledge, makes it necessary to take a closer look at the production process of scientific images. Many scholars have written extensively about the role of microscopic images in scientific research (Knorr-Cetina and Amann 1990; Wise 2006; Daston and Galison 2007). Underlying their work is an oscillation between objectivity and subjectivity in scientific knowledge production, which has changed with the introduction of digital technology in (microscopic) image production. Digital scientific images are interactive and can be used, cropped, cut, and colored. The image is not fixed, but a result of the complex interrelation between producer, technology, and context.

Science historians Lorraine Daston and Peter Galison (2007, 382) recognize the introduction of digital image production as a shift from representation to presentation, "[i]mages in which the making is the seeing." Historian Norton Wise expresses a similar idea that visualization in science is not an illustration, but an argument (2006, 81). The microscope has been around for a while, but what does the appropriation of this device in different contexts, such as an open wetlab, do to scientific image production? Changing environments and settings can leave room for other, more playful encounters with (bio)technologies. This is also strongly associated with practices in citizen science projects that stimulate citizens to collect large amounts data for research projects. One example is the game *Binary Fission* (Verigames 2015), a puzzle game where users aid in testing the validity of algorithms. Using a microscopic perspective as a scientific backdrop for the game, the player works toward the formation of parts by moving them around. Both projects aim to involve citizens in knowledge production, but how do citizen science and biohacking relate to each other? Zooming in at biohacking in particular raises interesting questions about the cultural value vis-à-vis the scientific value of hacked lab equipment.

This chapter examines the process of image production in the DIY microscope from the perspective of play. Play is not tied to a particular activity, such as a game, but is brought out by a complex interrelation between people and their interactions with an object. It is an expression of creativity, which can be rebellious, political, and often goes against the grain. Indeed, as some scholars argue, play appropriates, distorts, and performs (Sicart 2014). Through the lens of play, I address the question of what happens to the production and appropriation of images when microscopes move from the lab to open source hacker spaces. The playful production and appropriation of Hackteria's DIY microscope serves as my main case study. Framing digitally distributed scientific images as objects in their own right brings attention to how they are made. Central to this argument is the text *Objectivity* (2007) by Daston and Galison, where scientific images are presented as tools that are interrelated with the producer and practice. Digital art and software scholar Ann-Sophie Lehmann asserts something similar by arguing that shaping the digital image is a craft with multiple layers of materiality (2012, 169). By materiality, I refer to both the physical materials, and social processes that shape the image. Using a similar approach as Lehmann, I conduct a material object analysis to uncover the material layers in the production of a DIY microscope. These layers constitute the process of encoding and decoding the microscope, such as the creation of prototypes, or digital schemata. Studying the translation of the microscope into the DIY microscope, I focus on the relationship between hacking as a playful practice and a process of creating knowledge.

First, by placing microscopic image production in the context of digital manipulation, I will analyze the relationship between microscopic image production and the notion of objectivity. Although this concept is highly contestable, it remains one of the pillars of modern science. Furthermore, by addressing how the producer, image, and practice are interrelated, I argue that this also creates space for a diversion of scientific practices. In the second section, I examine biohacking and the production of DIY microscopes to address the type of knowledge production afforded through the process of hacking and making. A citizen science game and biohacking are two different playful appropriations of science. The former is a game where the player collects data for the game's producers, the latter is an example of knowledge production through play as an iterative explorative process. Analyzing the production of the DIY microscope highlights how it is framed as an epistemic tool, where every translation or layer of materiality affects its message. In turn, the playful appropriation of the microscope shifts its epistemic message. Indeed, as the production process becomes an important part of the DIY microscope, the images tend to gain in cultural and educational value what they might lose in scientific appropriation. Furthermore, the context of play affords a specific form of knowledge production. This allows me to illustrate how play is firmly connected to hacker practices, and that biohacking is a critical product of playful experiments to liberate science.

Bringing science out of the lab

Dividing this section into three parts, I focus first on the function of scientific images and microscopic image production in providing objective knowledge. This allows me to highlight the paradox of modern microscopic image production as both a symbolic function of objectivity, and a tool for digital manipulation in the second part. The ability to capture and manipulate images digitally invites scientists to play around with the aesthetics of their images, extending the function of these images to the cultural realm. As I will discuss in the third part, this extension also works the other way around, as citizen science games contribute to knowledge production through play.

Function and manipulation of scientific images

How does contemporary image practice affect the notion of objectivity in science? This question draws attention toward the function of image production in scientific research. Throughout scientific history, instruments have been considered an objective tool in visualizing nature. The invention of the microscope not only opened up a whole world of biology once hidden from the eye, but was used as a tool to observe nature on a micro scale through an objective lens. Its function is both constitutive and symbolic, as instruments like microscopy served as "a means to and a symbol of mechanical objectivity" (Daston and Galison 2007, 139). With the microscope as an objective mediator, scientists tried to eliminate the subject. The epistemic message of the microscope is a tool for creating objective knowledge. Today, more involvement and subjectivity of scientists in microscopic image production is common practice. Using software programs to correct, to crop, or to alter images is a commonplace. For instance, color is often added in order to highlight specific elements of an image. Objectivity can be defined as "the suppression of some aspect of the self, the countering of subjectivity" (Ibid., 36). Throughout history different instruments require a different level of suppression and attitude toward suppressing the self.

In modern science such as nanotechnology, scientists can manipulate their sample on a micro scale. Nanotechnology is the manipulation of matter on the scale of atoms and molecules. The microscope becomes the hammer where the scientist sculpts the image into form: "With clicks and keystrokes, these digital images are meant to be *used*, cut, correlated, rotated, colored" (Ibid., 383, emphasis added). The image can be altered at multiple levels. Daston and Galison separate the practice of manipulation into virtual images and haptic images. Virtual images are a presentation of nature that are stored as a data set in image galleries and can be modeled after creation. Haptic images are a presentation of nature that is modified before the image is taken. Tools that afford the creation of both virtual and haptic images are microscopes like the scanning tunneling microscope (STM), or the scanning electron microscope (SEM). These microscopes can change the specimen under the microscope at an atomic and molecular level: "[T]he same device was used at one and the same time to image and to alter" (Ibid., 402). The STM captures atoms by tunneling signals in high vacuums, such as water. For a sample to be analyzed by the SEM, it needs to be plated in specific types of metal, for instance gold. This limits the type of specimens that can be analyzed, but does afford the scientist the ability of manipulation on a nano scale. As illustrated in the previous section, the affordance of the microscope is both influencing in, and influenced by scientific practice. The function and use of the microscope allow for manipulation of the image beforehand and after. Here, we see how the notion of objectivity is problematized, as data are manipulated on multiple levels. How can it still be classified as 'objective' when specimens are manipulated? A partial explanation lies in the materialization of microscopic images in different (scientific) contexts.

Materialization of the image

The subjectivity of digital scientific images is hidden under the cloak of mechanical objectivity. Sociologists Karin Knorr-Cetina and Klaus Amann dissect the constructed nature of images in scientific research, and argue "images are not just taken, they are designed and made" (1990, 259). Different environments play a role in knowledge creation, namely "the domain of laboratory practice; the context of invisible physical reactions; the future image as it will appear in publication; and the domain of case precedents and reference" (Ibid.). The image can be both an object of knowledge creation, and an object used to illustrate an argument. Voicing a similar argument, media scholars Mirko Tobias Schäfer and Frank Kessler show that the notion of mechanical objectivity is also present in the computational power of the computer (2013, 14). Computational processes that create digital images are ambivalent, because these images can change in context and be turned into different arguments. The universality of the computer and its software materializes scientific images in variable contexts. Physical, mechanical, and electronic techniques in the creation and manipulation of images are translated into software programs that can edit images with the click of a mouse. These types of software share the same environment and start to interact, mutate, and create hybrids. Lev Manovich refers to this as media hybridization. As he points out, "the unique properties and techniques of different media have become software elements that can be combined together in previously impossible ways" (Manovich 2013, 176). Considering the different techniques working together to create a scientific image, it becomes a hybrid product between the producer, their knowledge and intent, as well as the different materials with which it is made. For example, a scientist can use software programs—such as Photoshop—to alter images pixel for pixel, in the same way a designer does.[1] When analyzing microscopic images, it becomes clear that media hybridization also influences identity expressions of the scientist.

Analyzing the oscillation of objectivity and subjectivity in microscopic image production, Galison recognizes the scientist's self diverging into other expressions such as those of an artist (2010, 29). One example of this crossover is the Dutch microscopist Frans Holthuysen, who works as a researcher at Philips and makes images with a SEM-microscope for his research projects at the MiPlaza's Technology Laboratories Group. The images produced by Holthuysen not only have their scientific purpose, they also have aesthetic value. For instance, he won second prize at the MNE micro and nano-graph contest. This contest selects the best micrography images submitted by not only scientists, but also artists. The microscopic images Holthuysen makes have often been published and displayed at different museums, such as the 'design and the elastic mind' exposition, held at the Museum of Modern Art in New York in 2008 (Museum of Modern Art 2008). Holthuysen combines the ethos of a scientist and artist, playing around with his images in different contexts. The relationship between digital practice, microscopic image technology, and the producer's intent creates room for a playful appropriation of images. Photoshop or other programs, invite scientists to play with their data and appropriate images. While the extent of manipulation differs depending on the context, it cannot be denied that the availability to alter and enhance the image changes the epistemic message of the image itself. The boundary between science and culture is blurred as images meant for scientific research travel outside the lab and find their way in to museums. This cultural appropriation also works the other way around, as citizens are increasingly invited to participate in scientific research.

1 Manipulating images for publications is a grey area in scientific research. An ongoing debate in scientific journals and magazines such as *PLoS One* or *Nature*, is concerned with the fine line between what is considered as fraud, or the 'beautification' of scientific images (Gilbert 2009). In response, many of these journals have created guidelines for editing images.

Rise of citizen science games

Digital technologies and the internet infrastructure stimulated the involvement of amateurs and non-professionals in scientific research. Mobile and wireless technology has aided in the increase of non-professionals in the collection of data. This is stimulated by openness and collaboration, where interactions between users produce new insights about larger sets of scientific data. Henry Jenkins has dubbed this concept 'participatory culture': a culture with the presence of "artistic expression and civic engagement, strong support for creating and sharing one's creations, and some type of informal mentorship" (Jenkins et al. 2006, 3). Citizen science is the practice of research by amateurs and non-professionals, who use decentralized communication and media to collect scientific data and produce new knowledge. Crowd-sourcing and open research seem to be central ideas to this development.

Play as an epistemological tool can be used to better understand the development of citizen science and its role in the scientific community. Play is both an activity and an attitude. As an activity, play is an expression, "a mode of being in the world" (Sicart 2014, 2). We play board games and digital games, but we also play with technologies such as a smartphone. Indeed, we also play with software and hardware. However, why do we play around with some objects and not with others? I argue that it has to do with the design of the object and conditions of its use. Play happens in contexts that afford that activity, and this is created not only through rules, but also through objects, situations, and spaces. In other words, "[p]lay is contextual" (Sicart 2014, 6). Citizen science, seen from the perspective of play, redefines what it means to do science. The traditional rules of engagement in scientific knowledge production are very closed, as only trained scholars are deemed suitable to collect and interpret data. However, in citizen science projects, which are based on data collection by non-professionals and amateurs, everybody can participate in the creation of knowledge. As illustrated below, there are different forms in which this takes place.

Within the boundaries set by the producers of the project, citizen scientists are able to aid in the production of knowledge. This context lends itself to play, as the player is able to move around within a closed system. More recently, collecting scientific data has been transformed into games. One example of an organization avidly developing games is the Defense Advanced Research Projects Agency (DARPA) Crowd Sourced Formal Verification (CSFV) program, which has established VeriGames, a project to develop several citizen science games where players aid in collecting data by playing games. One example is *Binary Fission*, a puzzle game where players are Fission Initiative Network (FIN) agents and have to separate blue particles from orange particles to create sets for further processing. Binary fission is a biological process of division. For instance, the division of a cell into two cells, which can be analyzed under a microscope. Interestingly, although the representation of this microscopic process is visually presented to the player, it serves as mere decoration. For the game's producers, the valuable knowledge lies in mining the player's actions in the game. Behind this playful layer, algorithms are being tested for their correctness and the value of this application is the formal verification of software.

Binary Fission illustrates two critical issues concerning the role of citizens in citizen science projects. First, player agency and intent may provide different outcomes in the game. For instance, as a player in *Binary Fission*, I can decide that I want to play with different objectives. Instead of trying to separate the blue and yellow atoms, I can decide that I will try to pack as many atoms together, consequently changing the outcome. This agency of the user to play with the rules, problematizes data collection in the sense that it raises questions about the concept of validity. In the game, the player is not anonymous, since playing involves registration and the player has to sign in to play. As a consequence, the registered player/data collector could hypothetically be excluded from the study if he or she does not follow the rules. Although in some projects the collective wisdom of the crowd might eliminate the deviation of some data collectors, this process is not so easily traceable in other citizen science projects. Similar issues are raised by Glas and Lammes in Chapter 11 of this volume. Are citizen science projects only successful if the result can be quantified, measured, and validated? If so, then the future of this type of informal knowledge production will lead to homogenous projects for the 'hard' sciences. Therefore, we may need to come up with other types of data collection instead.

The second issue in citizen science projects like these is the political question of who benefits from the knowledge produced. In this particular example, the beneficiaries of the game are Verigames and DARPA, since the player is not actually aware of the results of his or her effort. It seems that the status quo of traditional scientific practice is not really disrupted. Instead, the player is used as a data-mining machine to generate small pieces of information. Just as we play around with toys, we play around with media. But toys, just as media, can be appropriated in different ways, and even be destroyed. Play is an appropriation of objects such as *Binary Fission*, or microscopes. As a result, play can be destructive, political, and serious. This is what scholar Mary Flanagan (2009) calls "critical play," or

Miguel Sicart (2014) defines as "carnivalesque play." This form of play "takes control of the world and gives it to the players for them to explore, challenge, or subvert. It exists; it is part of the world it turns upside down" (Sicart 2014, 4). As I will illustrate later in this chapter, biohacking is a perfect example of this appropriation.

Citizen science projects and biohacking activities are both activities performed by non-professionals, artists, or citizens, but with a different mode of appropriation. While the intent of citizen science projects is to contribute to research experiments and contributors are expected to 'follow the rules,' biohacking is a bottom-up movement that is based upon subverting existing knowledge structures. When historian Johan Huizinga theorized the role of play in everyday life, he discerned between four different types of "players" (Raessens 2014, 106). These four types of users have different attitudes toward objects or events. First, there is the regular user who does not question the rules of the system and follows them blindly. Second, there is the cheater, who only "pretends to be playing the game" (Huizinga 1955, 11). This is a player who does not play by the rules of the game and cheats in order to advance. This user is aware of the implicit and explicit rules. Third, there is the spoilsport, or the modder in modern terms, who modifies the rules of the game if the system will afford it. Open source products afford this modularity, since users are able to remix and alter the work. Finally, there is the "outlaw, the revolutionary" (Ibid., 12). These users transcend the system by inserting new ideas and functions in the game, consequently altering the entire system. For a citizen science project to succeed, the game needs *regular* players that behave and play the game as it was intended. While games such as *Binary Fission* rely on players to follow the rules and try to discourage cheating, in biohacking, the user is invited to be an outlaw by hacking and modifying the system.

In summary, I have shown from a broader perspective the dual function of scientific images as a source of knowledge and of evidence. The examination of microscopic image production revealed that digital images can be shaped in any form or according to any illustrative argument. Even though manipulation is becoming more common in pre- and postproduction of the image, dissecting this image reveals the symbolic and functional role of objectivity. Play as both an activity and an attitude is instrumental in citizen science projects. However, different levels of playability illustrate that concepts like objectivity need to be redefined. Furthermore, the extent to which these projects emancipate science is questionable. In a way, biohacking is a response to this. In the next section, I will unpack where and how this play takes place to illustrate how hacking lab equipment is a critical and playful appropriation of science.

Playfulness of hacking

In this section, I trace the process of decoding and encoding the microscope from the lab to the open hacker space and the attempt of biohacking to emancipate science from its institutional form. First, I trace the relationship between biohacking ideology and scientific knowledge production, which is illustrated by the act of hacking lab equipment. Then, I explore how hacking as a playful practice can be seen as a playful form of knowledge production. In the subsequent sub-sections, I trace hacking as a playful practice by closely analyzing Hackteria's DIY microscope. Lastly, I illustrate how the player and the microscope's design inform the type of knowledge produced.

Political message of biohacking

What kind of knowledge is produced in biohacking, and how does this relate to science? We have seen the function, manipulation, and regulation of knowledge production in science, and how citizen science complicates notions of validity and objectivity. In order to place practices of the DIY microscope in this context, both the images produced and the microscope will be analyzed. The environment and personal background of the producer influence the use of the microscope as an instrument and therefore a closer analysis of biohacker ideology is needed.

Biohacking brings biotechnology and lab instruments to a context that affords play. Biohacking is an expression that describes emerging movements of amateurs conducting life sciences outside traditional settings such as the lab or universities (Delfanti 2012, 163). Very often low-cost equipment is made in order to experiment outside the lab. One creation is the DIY microscope, developed in 2009 by micro- and nanoscholar Marc Dusseiller. The DIY microscope is made with open source ideology in mind, which means the microscope's design for everyone. In this context, it means "'free speech' not free beer" (Weber 2004, 5). Open source software (OSS) is computer software which is design to be released non-commercially. According to the Open Source Initiative (OSI), the main characteristics of OSS are its modifiable nature, public availability, and open distribution (Open Source Initiative n.d.). Open source hardware is based on the same principles. The ideology of open source is based on open distribution and modification and availability for everyone. Biohacking can be seen as a hybrid of open source ideology and hacker practices in the scientific realm of biology, life science, and biotechnology. Moving biotechnology from the context of a formal lab environment to a hacker space introduces these tools, technologies, and processes to non-professionals and amateurs. This results in the introduction of different approaches and appropriations of biotechnology and equipment. Hacking can be seen as this sort of appropriation, which is defined as an activity that appropriates material objects such as computers, or immaterial objects such as software in an attempt to redefine the existing system and subvert its affordances. Hacking as a form of play is "a contextual appropriation of a situation with the purpose of creating new values, expressions, or knowledge" (Sicart 2014, 67). Although play is formally bound to specific rules in a specific space, hacking as a playful practice renegotiates the existing status quo, or game, if you will. The intent is to purposefully create new ideas, knowledge, generate different values and to go against the grain. A biohacker space is the ideal ground for re-appropriating existing technologies and generating different scientific values. One such an example is Hackteria, an online platform, which advocates the open sharing of knowledge, open source technology and art in biology, life science and biotechnology (2013a; 2013b). Founded in 2009 by artist Andy Gracie, nano-scientist Marc Dusseiller, and artist Yashas Shetty, Hackteria publishes open source designs online and organizes workshops where they collaborate together with scientists, artists, educators, engineers, and hackers to create knowledge and share ideas. One central activity is hacking lab equipment together in order to share this technology with a wider public. The foundation is based on temporal spaces, and the emphasis is on mobility. This less formal context explicitly tries to be break open scientific knowledge production, which is reminiscent of the level of playability mentioned in the previous section.

The modder and hacker tries to divert the system by making up his/her own rules. The ethos of biohackers to deinstitutionalize science manifests itself in the practice of hacking lab equipment, and sharing those designs with the use of open web tools for collaboration such as wikis. Sociologist Allesandro Delfanti observes the development of biohacking as an ethos of activism, entrepreneurship, and artistic expression. According to this perspective, the practice "can be interpreted as an example of a direct transposition of free software and hacking practices into the realm of cells, genes, and labs" (Delfanti 2012, 163). What is clear is that biohackers are changing the rules of the system by bringing commercial lab equipment outside the traditional lab environment, and creating open source models based on these technological principles.

According to Delfanti, hacking lab equipment can be seen as an "active approach in the shaping of the institutional environment in which biological research takes place and in the questioning of the proprietary structure of scientific information" (2012, 164). Arguing for the relevance of biohacker spaces like Hackteria, Kera and Dusseiller point out these spaces are "becoming important sites of translation between scientific knowledge and technological innovation produced in the traditional and official labs and the everyday interests, practices and problems of ordinary people around the world" (2012, 3). As part of their argument, the authors illustrate their desire for hacker practices to liberate scientific knowledge. However, the question can be raised whether the practice of biohacking actually contributes to scientific research not just in the traditional sense. To evaluate if this is actually the case, we will need to take a closer look at the practice of making the DIY microscope. As Wise points out, when "the subject of making visible in science leaves the domain of mere illustration or mere technology and becomes a matter of making knowledge, then the making acquires much higher status" (2006, 79). By analyzing materiality, I aim to provide more clarity about the epistemic message of biohacker practices.

Materiality of playing

Figure 10.1 is an example of a DIY microscope that citizen scientists can create and use to analyze specimens. Since the instrument is also produced by the user, biohacking practices like the DIY microscope make hybridity of image and producer even more complex. There are multiple layers of materiality that affect image production. Just as Ann-Sophie Lehmann argues, the process of making an image has multiple layers of materiality, "from the making that leads to its encoding, to the material reality of the code itself, the CG [computer graphic] object being in-material, the simulation of diverse material qualities and therefore being all-materials, and finally, its re-translation into the analogue" (2012, 183). The process of interacting with different layers of material creates a deeper understanding of the thing itself.

How does this biohacker context materialize itself in an environment for playful knowledge production? The availability of open source software and hardware designs invites open-ended play. Playing, or tinkering affords knowledge of the object at hand. Tinkering, which is closely related to playing, is an iterative style of learning, where users learn about a technology through open-ended interaction (Resnick and Rosenbaum 2013). The relationship

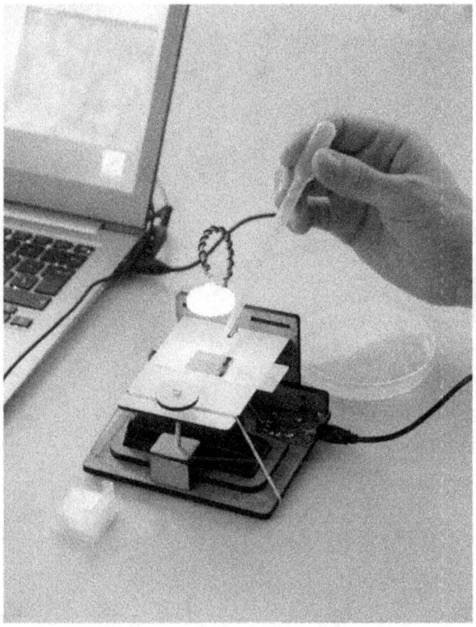

10.1: The DIY microscopy stage kit (Hackteria.org).

with tinkering highlights the material aspects of playing. This approach is often seen in do-it-yourself (DIY) and maker cultures. The rapid development of the consumer 3D printer is one example of the playful engagement with materials, as users literally have to put their own device together. As I noted elsewhere, playing around with technology enables a deeper understanding and stimulates creativity (de Smale 2014). In the case of the 3D printer, this has led to innovations in software and hardware that would not have been developed elsewhere. Due to the subjective nature of experience it is not possible to create experience, however, it is possible to design for a specific experience (Arrasvuori et al. 2011, 3). This suggests that there are specific design principles that afford the context of play. Play scholars Mitchel Resnick and Eric Rosenbaum (2013, 174) identify design principles that afford playful knowledge production: fluid experimentation, immediate feedback, and open exploration. The extent to which these design principles are found in the material layers of the DIY microscope will be explored below.

Fluid experimentation

The first layer of materiality is the process of making and encoding the DIY microscope. The inspiration for the DIY microscope with laser cut Z-stage is a regular optical microscope. Figure 10.2 shows the design for the Z-stage—drawn by Marc Dusseiller. In 2009, Dusseiller first wrote about hacking a digital microscope he called the DIY microscope. The DIY

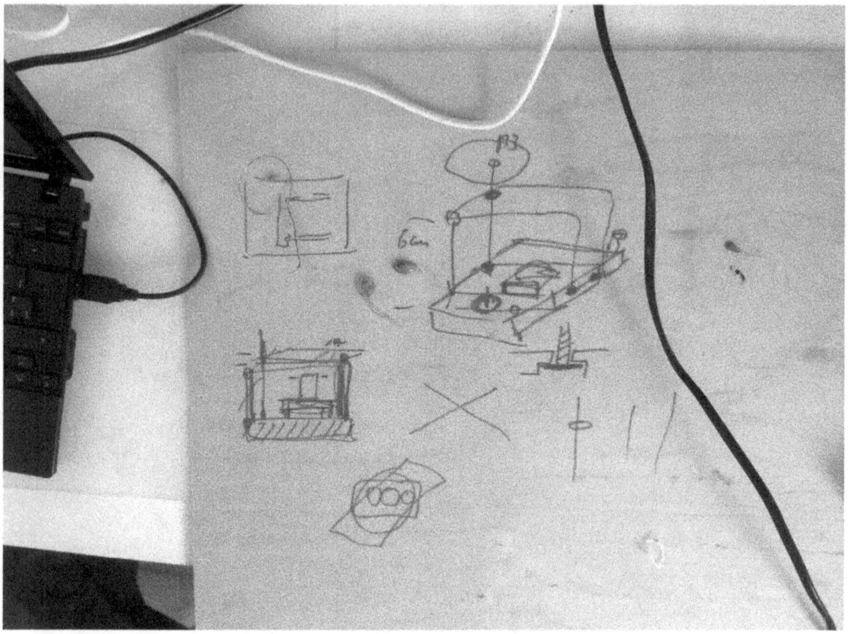

10.2: Designing the DIY microscope (Hackteria.org).

microscope has many different forms and designs, but the basic principle is hacking a digital camera, for instance a webcam. The camera is attached to a microscopic lens, and mounted on a Z-stage that can be made of plywood, plastic, glass, or any other hard material available. Practices like hacking lab equipment are as much an epistemic statement, as a tool for the production of images.

The open source nature of the DIY microscope allows for fluid experimentation, stimulating a context of play: "Tinkerers start by exploring and experimenting, then revising and refining their goals, plans, and creations" (Resnick and Rosenbaum 2013, 176). Prototyping is a technique for fluid experimentation that allows for fast results and a quick iteration. Figure 10.2 shows how the microscope as a scientific tool is being broken down into parts. The black box of the regular optical microscope is opened up, and translated into a new design. While the affordance of the traditional microscope is most often hidden because of its design, all the parts are visible with the open source design. This serves as an important instrumental function, since it allows for open exploration of the technologies. It is up to the user to assemble the microscope. The process of putting it together is very modular which allows for an iterative style of learning. This design is easily produced in open hacker spaces like Fablab with the help of a laser cutter. The original design of the microscope is changed to fit the epistemic virtue of biohackers, namely open source design, availability of biotechnology for the public, and the desire to share knowledge. This is evident in the design choices made by Dusseiller. Materials that are easily ready at hand can be used for this kit. Plexiglas, plywood, glass, or any other material that is hard enough can be used. After the analog drawing, the first prototype is made. The closed objective structure of the microscope is hacked and appropriated into a modular microscope that can be built outside the factory. In this process, the system, technology, and material of the microscope have been altered, affording a high level of playability.

Immediate feedback

The materiality of code is easily forgotten, but it plays a central role in the playful production of knowledge. After the prototype, the design was drawn in Adobe Illustrator (see Figure 10.3) as a Computer-Aided-Design (CAD). CAD drawings can be seen as a technical blueprint. The user chooses to design in Illustrator because it creates designs that are vector-based. Vectors can be blown up and cropped without losing shape or form. This means the microscope can be as big or as small as desired. The original CAT file is downloadable via wiki. This example illustrates the willingness of biohackers like Dusseiller to share knowledge and designs of the DIY microscope. Even though Illustrator is not open source, the open source ethics of open access for everyone, open distribution, and modularity are present. However, the modularity of shape and size might potentially be a problem with the production of scientific images, since the quality of the photos and the ability of the microscope to zoom may differ which would result in different types of images.

When translating the microscope into open source hardware and software processes, traditional lab space is transgressed. According to Kitchin and Dodge (2011, 61-63), software plays a significant role in the conceptualization of space. Coding the microscope into a machine-readable open source design means it can be distributed freely. Instead of a closed environment that is only accessible for scientists and researchers, hypothetically everyone with an internet connection has access to the design of a microscope. All the information about how to design a DIY microscope was placed on a wiki page. Wiki is a tool for collaboration, and users can also become authors by adding knowledge. The software environment is based on open collaboration, where the process of building a microscope also becomes a means of participation, through the openness and modularity of the software. The malleability of software and the ability to contribute allows for quick results

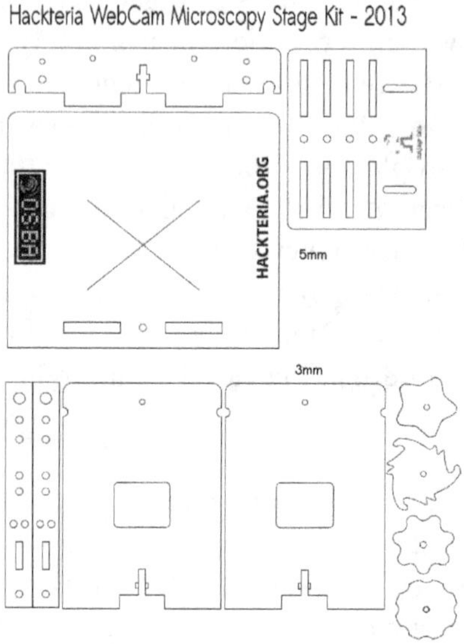

10.3: Encoding the microscope (Hackteria.org).

and feedback. Users are functioning in a context that allows immediate feedback and an environment that stimulates appropriation of existing technologies. By designing the digital environment to encourage tinkering with the design, a playful context is stimulated.

Open exploration

The ability for users to change the design, size, and materials of their microscope creates a context that allows for open exploration and user agency. As visible in Figure 10.4, its meaning has become modular. The design is flexible and open for the creation and re-creation of different practices. The last material translation is the re-translation from the design into an analog material, the DIY microscope. The materiality of the DIY microscope shows how the scientific image is broken down, and changed with every layer. The re-materialization of the microscope can come in different shapes, sizes and forms. This primarily depends on the choices the user makes in the material design, the type of webcam, and the type of (open source) software that is used. This means all the microscopes will be different, there is not one DIY microscope, but there is the idea of a DIY microscope that is expressed through the user. Offering this type of flexibility enables user agency and stimulates creativity. This creates a setting, a stage that invites players to interact, explore, play, and change the rules.

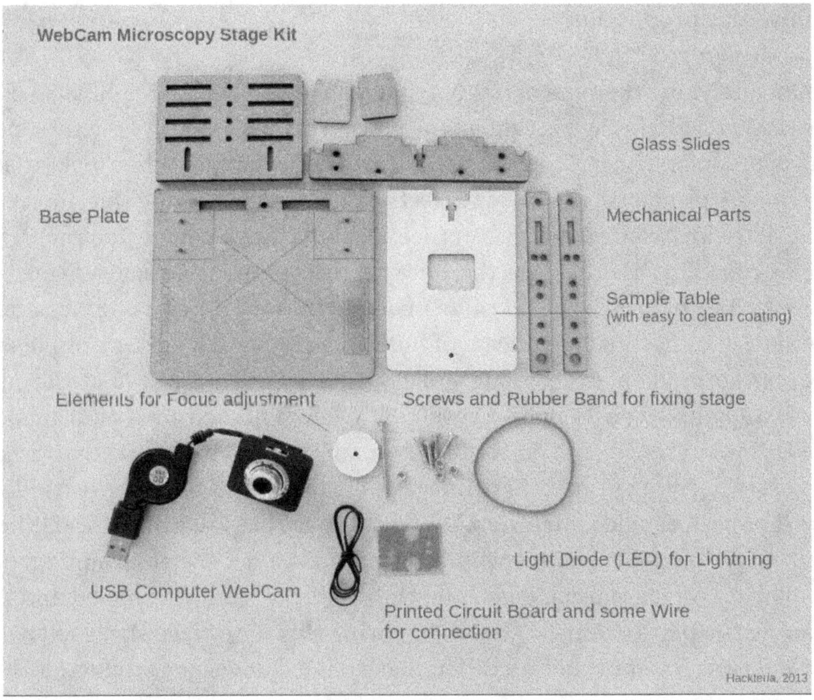

10.4: Materials needed for the DIY Microscope (Hackteria.org).

The analog version of the DIY microscope could not have existed without its digital form and the ability to create the microscope oneself changes the relationship between the producer, image, and microscope. The DIY microscope can be seen as an epistemic image, because it incorporates knowledge about how a microscope works.

This helps to "understand that the medium is not a black box, but an active instance translating, and thus interpreting and shaping, data input into the image we see" (Schäfer and Kessler 2013, 14). The process of building a microscope is equally—if not more—important than creating microscopic images. The value of the knowledge produced is not as much about what is seen under the microscope, but what it is made of. A microscope in science is used to analyze specimens and collect data. The microscope is a tool to achieve this goal. However, in the example of the DIY microscope it seems that the value lies more in the process itself and knowledge produced for the user.

Knowledge production

When analyzing the type of images that were produced and published on the Hackeria platform, it is evident the process of building a DIY microscope and of producing microscopic images cannot be separated. When looking at the images produced, there are two sets of images. On the one side, images that share knowledge about the process of building a device like the DIY microscope. On the other side, there are microscopic images that were made with the DIY microscope. But these images represent the end product, and are shown as part of the process of building. Figure 10.5 is an example of the appropriation of microscopic images with the use of a DIY microscope. Here, students at the Bauhaus-Universität Weimar hacked a webcam, made the DIY microscope, and created microscopic images to use in an artistic project. Analyzing its use, these images were used in creative contexts like an art project, or video projection. While the image has lost a direct scientific purpose, it has gained cultural and educational value. The environment of shaping an image is broadened, and the producer has both shaped and is shaping the production process. Comparing this with the citizen science game *Binary Fission*, there is a different output in knowledge production. In the game, the output is the data produced by the player. The player actively participates in knowledge production, but is left to wonder what the purpose of their participation is. With biohacking and the DIY-microscope, the value is much more process-oriented and dependent on the user's intent. The output of knowledge is not about the end product, such as the collection of data. Rather, it is about knowledge of technological processes and systems. Its value lies in understanding the technology and how it is made, and the pleasure is not in playing a game, but understanding the rules of the system and choosing to comply or ignore them. This changes the context of knowledge production. The DIY microscope is no longer a tool for analyzing data, but a process. Although this means that this knowledge is valuable for the player, the output is not necessarily valuable for scientific research. In this sense, hacking the microscope is a fruitful experiment of learning by tinkering, but it leaves the desire of Hackteria to liberate science—as of yet—unfulfilled.

In summary, by analyzing the process of making a DIY microscope, I have exposed the material layers that form the context of knowledge production from a tool for data analysis to a process of the playful production of knowledge. The material layers of the microscope interact to create an environment favorable for play. Fluid experimentation through prototyping, immediate feedback in playing with digital designs, and open exploration

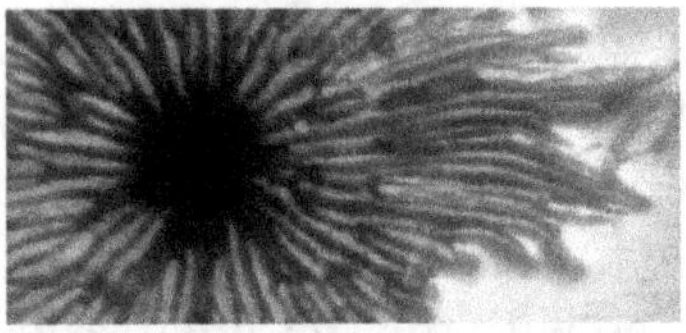

10.5: Appropriation of microscopic images in education (Neupert 2013).

in the form and function of physically making the DIY microscope set the stage for playful learning. As we have seen, the central goal for Hackteria is the practice, creation, and distribution of knowledge in biology, life sciences, and biotechnology. Although, with the case of the DIY microscope, the process of building it is more interesting than the images it creates. Play as epistemology illustrates how the practice of hacking is a context that affords the playful appropriation of science.

Conclusion: Image production from the lab to playful hacker spaces

The DIY microscope is a critical product of playful experiments to democratize science. In this form, it is not so much about the knowledge produced with the device, as about the valuable knowledge produced in hacking the microscope and creating open source variants. Citizen science projects like *Binary Fission* use those who play science games as data-collecting machines, where the design of the game allows little agency for the player. This formal environment of data collection does not emancipate science, but instead re-enforces a hierarchical, institutional form of science. An extension of that development—and in some parts a reaction to—is biohacking. The political message behind hacking lab equipment is the attempt to deinstitutionalize science.

Biohacking practices like the DIY microscope are still in an experimental stage, and the lens of play can help to explain how transporting the microscope from the lab to open hacker spaces alters its context. There is a specific form of play in biohacking since it creates a context for tinkering. Play is materialized in the design principles of fluid experimentation, immediate feedback, and open exploration. First, fluid experimentation is seen in the rapid iteration of building prototypes, of hacking the microscope and translating it into an open source microscope. From a user perspective, building a microscope creates the opportunity to learn how it works, and what the technological limits are. Second, immediate feedback is afforded through the adaptability of software. Third, open exploration is seen in the agency of the user to build the DIY microscope with any material and in any size he/she desires. Subsequently, there is a strong educational value in learning to understand how the microscope works. Yet the microscopic images that are produced with the DIY microscope are often used in an artistic or cultural context, where the artistic value is more important than the images possible scientific value. These images are part of the material process of creating a microscope, not of creating objective images.

On a broader level, digitizing the microscope "modulates the conditions under which sociospatial processes operate" (Kitchin and Dodge 2011, 64). This is visible in the translation of the microscope from the lab to the open hacker space. When image production moves from a closed centralized scientific environment to an open decentralized hacker environment, production becomes more complex. More layers of materiality affect shaping of the image, and the producer is intimately connected with the microscope. As a result, the process of production creates valuable knowledge for the user about technology and the system of the DIY microscope. It is too early to tell if the open source lab equipment is suitable for scientific data collection, but for me this is not the point of hacking lab equipment. Perhaps liberating science is found in educating a wider public about scientific instruments and how they can be made and used. While the motivation of translating the microscope may be political, the means through which this is achieved is play.

References

Arrasvuori, J, M. Boberg, J. Holopainen, H. Korhonen, A. Lucero, and M. Montola, 2011. Applying the PLEX framework in designing for playfulness. In *Proceedings of the 2011 conference on designing pleasurable products and interfaces, Milan, June 22-25, 2011.* New York: ACM.

Daston, L., and P. Galison. 2007. *Objectivity.* Cambridge, MA: The MIT Press.

Delfanti, A. 2012. Tweaking genes in your garage: Biohacking between activism and entrepreneurship. In *Activist media and biopolitics critical media interventions in the age of biopower*, eds. W. Sützl and T. Hug, 163-178. Innsbruck: Innsbruck University Press.

De Smale, S. 2014. Building material: Exploring playfulness of 3d printers. *Transactions of the Digital Games Research Association* 1 (3): 1-31. http://todigra.org/index.php/todigra/article/view/21/74.

Flanagan, M. 2009. *Critical play: Radical game design*. Cambridge, MA: The MIT Press.

Galison, P. 2010. *The objective image*. Inaugural Address. Faculty of Humanities: Utrecht University.

G-netwerk. 2013. Day 2 Denisa Kera the future of art & science collaborations. *Amsterdam: G-netwerk*. Video. http://www.youtube.com/watch?v=__qkr7tAGwc&feature=c4-overview&list=UUq-ZlKq8aZL_7Y-orBGtoxw.

Gilbert, N. Science journals crack down on image manipulation. *Nature*. http://www.nature.com/news/2009/091009/full/news.2009.991.html.

Hackteria. 2013a. DIY Microscopy. *Hackteria*. http://wlu18www30.webland.ch/wiki/index.php?title=DIY_microscopy.

—. 2013b. Laser cut microscopy stages. *Hackteria*. http://wlu18www30.webland.ch/wiki/index.php?title=Laser-cut_microscopy_stages.

Huizinga, J. 1955. *Homo ludens: A study of the play-element in culture*. Boston, MA: Beacon Press.

Jenkins, H., K. Clinton, R. Purushotma, A. J. Robinson, and M. Weigel. 2006. *Confronting the challenges of participatory culture: Media education for the 21st century*. Chicago, IL: MacArthur Foundation. http://www.macfound.org/media/article_pdfs/JENKINS_WHITE_PAPER.PDF.

Kera, D., and M. R. Dusseiller. 2012. Position statement: Hackteria.org – Nomadic science and democratized labs. *Sead: White papers*. http://www.academia.edu/2420045/Position_statement_Hackteria.org_-_nomadic_science_and_democratized_labs.

Kitchin, R., and M. Dodge. 2011. *Code/space: Software and everyday life*. Cambridge, MA: The MIT Press.

Knorr-Cetina, K., and K. Amann. 1990. Image dissection in natural scientific inquiry. In *Science, Technology, & Human Values* 15 (3): 259-283.

Lehmann, A. 2012. Taking the lid off the Utah-teapot: The materials of computer graphics. *Zeitschrift für Medien und Kulturforschung*, 1: 157-172.

Manovich, L. 2013. *Software takes command*. New York: Bloomsbury.

Museum of Modern Art. 2008. Design and the elastic mind. *New York: Museum of Modern Art*. http://www.moma.org/interactives/exhibitions/2008/elasticmind.

Neupert, M. 2013. A rewarding challenge: DIY-microscopy. *Hackteria*. http://hackteria.org/?p=2674.

Open Source Initiative. n.d. Open source definition. *Open Source Initiative*. http://opensource.org/osd.

Raessens, J. 2014. The ludification of culture. In *Rethinking gamification*, eds. M. Fuchs, S. Fizek, P. Ruffino, and N. Schrape, 91-114. Lüneburg: meson press.

Resnick, M., and E. Rosenbaum. 2013. Designing for tinkerability. In *Design, make, play: Growing the next generation of stem innovators*, eds. M. Honey and D. E. Kanter, 163-181. New York: Routledge.
Schäfer, M. T., and F. Kessler. 2013. Trust in technical images. *Mtschaefer.net* http://mtschaefer.net/entry/trust-technical-images.
Sicart, M. 2014. *Play matters*. Cambridge, MA: The MIT Press.
Verigames. 2015. *Binary Fission*. [browser]. Verigames. Game.
Weber, S. 2004. *The success of open source*. Cambridge, MA: Harvard University Press.
Wise, M. N. 2006. Making visible. *Isis*, 97 (1): 75-82.

About the author

Stephanie de Smale is a new media researcher at the department of Media and Culture Studies at Utrecht University, and is affiliated with the Centre for the Study of Digital Games and Play and the Centre for Conflict Studies. Her background is in communication and new media studies, specializing in games and play, design, politics, and violent conflict. Currently pursuing a doctoral degree, her NWO-funded research is a computer science/humanities collaboration that combines approaches from software studies, game studies, and conflict studies to analyze how wartime suffering is imagined and remembered in translocal digital culture communities and what its potential is for peacebuilding and postwar reconciliation in divided societies.

11. Ludo-epistemology: Playing with the rules in citizen science games

René Glas and Sybille Lammes

Abstract

In their chapter, Glas and Lammes critically investigate the limitations of citizen science game design when it comes to having amateurs playfully participate in the production of scientific knowledge. Moving away from the traditional distance between the scientist as expert and the citizen as layperson, and between science as serious and play as trivial, they argue for a recognition of play as fundamental to the scientific endeavor and see rule breaking and bending as an essential part of this process. From this perspective, they consider an approach to citizen science game design that includes playing with the rules as a more critical way of having citizens think about and participate in science.

Keywords: Citizen science games, production of knowledge, cheating, rules of play, theorycrafting, ludo-epistemology

Industry terms like 'serious games' and 'gamification' convey, or at least suggest, that games and other forms of playful media can be designed and implemented in such a way that users are not just entertained, but also educated, persuaded, or trained by engaging them in playful conduct. Citizen science games take this one step further, as such games implicitly or explicitly invite non-professionals to contribute to scientific research and knowledge production through play. Yet, as we will argue in this chapter, we need to reconsider what the concept of citizen science games can mean. Although we appreciate that existing citizen science games are highly valuable tools for (meta)data gathering, fact checking, and problem solving, we think that there is need for a different type, or understanding, of citizen science games. Moving away from a classical model based on the distinction

Glas, R., S. Lammes, M. de Lange, J. Raessens, and I. de Vries, eds. 2019. *The Playful Citizen. Civic Engagement in a Mediatized Culture.* Amsterdam: Amsterdam University Press.
DOI: 10.5117/9789462984523/CH11

between the scientist as expert and citizen as layperson, we call for a new kind of citizen science game that goes beyond such strict boundaries and truly merges the two positions by recognizing the play *in* science and the potential of citizens to critically reflect upon and engage with science *through* play.

To do so, we investigate how play can be a means of critical intervention and how citizen science games can provide players agency in bending or breaking established rules, as processes inextricably linked to both play *and* knowledge production. Using both game studies as well as a philosophy of science perspective, we argue that not just play, but also playing with rules offers new venues of critical engagement for the production of knowledge. Play can be a powerful means for opening up scientific endeavors to 'amateurs,' and the directly related activities of rule breaking/bending opens up new perspectives for designing alternative citizen science games.

In its classical form, citizen science is often defined as "a form of research collaboration involving members of the public in scientific projects to address real-world problems" (Wiggins and Crowston 2011, 1). As Bonney et al. (2009, 978) have pointed out in relation to biology, the notion of voluntary public participation in scientific research has a long history, with early examples in biological research going back to the late nineteenth century. The contemporary concept of citizen science, with "its integration of explicit and tested protocols for collecting data, vetting of data by professional [scientists], and inclusion of specific and measurable goals for public education," they argue, only evolved over the past few decades (2009, 978). Digital games, being rule-based *systems*, are a good fit for this *systematic* collection and analysis of data and, being an increasingly popular medium, are often considered to be a good platform for educational purposes of knowledge advancement as well (see Squire 2011). A host of citizen science games have appeared over the past several years, including *Foldit* (University of Washington Center for Game Science/Department of Biochemistry 2008), *Phylo* (McGill Centre for Bioinformatics 2010), *EteRNA* (Carnegie Mellon University and Stanford University 2010), *Quantum Moves* (UA Ideas CODER 2012), *Fraxinus* (The Sainsbury Laboratory 2013), and *Stall Catchers* (EyesOnALZ 2016), which are based on such principles. Many of these games can be seen as a form of human-computer interaction, where human activity is crowd-sourced to help computer systems solve problems by, for instance, interpreting data it cannot manage by itself. Yet, games relying on human-based computation via crowd-sourcing, like "games with a purpose" or GWAPs (Von Ahn 2006) or the games created through the Metadata Games platform (Flanagan et al. 2013), are not necessarily all citizen science games.[1] Dickinson and Bonney, argue for instance, that scientific interests, and the aim to publish results based on project data, should be part of a citizen science project from the outset, adding that "if researchers have no interest in the project, or in analyzing its data, then we would consider a project unsuccessful" (2012, 2).[2] Citizen science games like the ones mentioned above were initiated by the scientific community, and have indeed yielded publications in high-ranking journals (Hand 2010; Cossins 2013). One such study published in *Nature* dealing with the player-created scientific breakthroughs concerning protein-folding puzzle game *Foldit* even mentions the players (as 'Foldit Contenders Group' and 'Foldit Void Crushers Group') as co-authors (Khatib et al. 2011). Such publications show the potential of using games to engender new productive links between citizen science and play.

Foldit is often mentioned as an example of a citizen science game (see also Chapters 12 and 13 in this volume), yet it represents in our view just one pathway for this 'genre.' To be sure, we do not deny that games like *Foldit* can yield interesting crowd-sourced data and analyses, but at the same time we should be aware of the ideological, pragmatic, and missionary underpinning of such games: that 'science should be brought to the people,' so then, why not through play. As a provocative experiment, we ask ourselves: what happens if we embrace the notion that 'real' scientists are citizens as well, the latter being pivotal to how philosopher Feyerabend understood citizen science (1978). By breaking away from an assumed asymmetry between scientists and citizens, we want to explore the idea that doing science through play can be fruitful not only to enroll 'citizen-laymen,' but that it also can encourage citizens to more critically scrutinize scientific processes. In other words, we have to change our assumptions of what citizens are and can do in relation to science. Such a re-evaluation enables us to rethink the potential of citizen science games as critical and creative tools for engagement.

1 An interesting discussion is whether or not most citizen science games can actually be considered traditional games according to formal definitions (see Juul 2005) or should be seen as gamified media, in which gamification stands for "the use of game elements in a non-game contexts" (Deterding, Dixon, Khaled, and Nacke 2011, 2). While the distinction is relevant for formal analysis and design-related questions, as both elicit active engagement from users through playful interaction, which is the main goal of citizen science games, we do not engage with this distinction here, since we are primarily interested in the relation between play and knowledge production.

2 The game *Citizen Science* (Filament Games and Squire 2013), which aims to teach scientific literacy through play (see Gaydos and Squire 2010) would not adhere to this definition. While this educational goal is also part of the citizen science movement, this game does not invite the public to directly engage or collaborate in scientific research.

Scientists play too

Our reconsideration of the relation between, citizens, science, and play, also includes a recognition that scientist are citizens, which means 'real' scientific practices can be playful. To some it may be obvious and to others it may sound far-fetched, but scientists also play and they actually love it. Play may indeed seem, at first glance, the very antipode to science; as a popular kind of fictional entertainment, play seems irrational, infantile, and unsophisticated, all qualifications that scientists would rather avoid than be associated with. Yet, play is a major driving force of knowledge production and not necessarily opposed to seriousness (see Ehrmann, Lewis, and Lewis 1968). As play theorist Sutton-Smith argued in 'The playful modes of knowing' (1970), play is a fundamental way of obtaining knowledge. He maintained that play is an intelligent practice that helps us to explore, test, and evaluate situations. According to Sutton-Smith, "all forms of play are transformations of one or other of four basic modes by which we know the world," and the modes he recognized are: "copying," "analyze and seek causes," "predicting," and "synthesis" (1970, 2). It does not require much imagination to translate these leading principles of knowing through play to scientific practices, such as scientific exploration, testing, and reproduction. Similarly, philosopher of science David Hull maintains that play is an important characteristic of scientists' practices and describes this innate quality as "play behavior carried to adulthood" (1988, 305). In economic models of scientific communities, scientists are even seen as reward-driven gamers and the research they conduct as "a kind of game, a puzzle-solving operation in which the solution of the puzzle is its own reward" (Hagstrom 1965, quoted in Stephan, 1996, 1203). Although we are wary about drawing a direct connection between economical systems, science, and games, such observations do show that play and science are not or do not need to be in contention with each other. Play is actually key to processes of exploration and is therefore also an important part of techno-scientific change. Play may thus be crucial for developing the frame of mind that is needed for 'serious' social practices such as knowledge production (Csíkszentmihályi 2009; Mainemelis 2010).

Yet, play is also often viewed as infantile, trivial, serendipitous and at times even insane. These qualities seem rather far removed from how we want to perceive good and ethical scientific practices. This may be an important reason why scientists shy away from showing their playful sides in public. Or, as chemist Pierre Laszlo writes in a personal note in *American Scientist*:

> Play in scientific research is seldom discussed in print. Perhaps we scientists take it for granted. Or maybe we are a little self-conscious and try to hide it from others. After all, we don't want taxpayers to think they are subsidizing adults who are acting like a bunch of kids, thereby squandering hefty amounts of public money. Play in science is thus an elusive and difficult topic. (Laszlo 2004, 389)

There is a great difference between how science and artefacts are presented to the 'outer world,' and how they are actually produced in workplaces such as laboratories. This is important to acknowledge if we want to open new potential for citizen science games. Play is crucial to processes that precede the formation of scientific artefacts, but we, as 'normal' citizens, are not supposed to see this. Playing is an intrinsic part of scientific knowledge production, yet it is mostly covered up, or 'black-boxed' for outsiders, for the reasons sketched above. It is, however, important to acknowledge the asymmetry between the insider and the outsider when we want to understand what citizen science games are about and how they could be designed in different and innovative ways. If we want to make games that engage citizens critically, we have to acknowledge that play is not antipodal to science and that scientists are actually *civium ludens* as well. Then, citizen science games are no longer a contradiction in terms, but actually lay bare what science really is about. Moreover, it suggests that games can have the potential to become powerful tools for engaging citizens critically, encouraging them to reflect upon and to transform scientific processes through play.

As anthropologists of science Latour and Woolgar already showed in their seminal study *Laboratory life: The construction of scientific facts* (1979), production centers of techno-scientific artefacts are by no means the clean, tidy, and rational places they seem from the outside. Artefacts are social outcomes of complex processes in which actors form ever-changing alliances that are at times messy, 'warm,' and trivial. Sometimes we, as outsiders of such bastions of knowledge production, catch a glimpse of this side of science, albeit often in the shape of myths. A myriad of anecdotes spring to mind of stories of scientists' imagination or "mind-play" (Sutton-Smith 2001). To name just a few, one includes Nobel laureate and play theorist John Nash (Nasar 1998), who allegedly suffered from 'insane' genius, or other stories of 'incubator' dreams like Kekul apparently dreaming about snakes, which helped him find the ring-shaped molecular structure of Benzene (Tweney 1996). Such narratives are passed to the 'normal' citizen as acts of visionary or even religious genius (Noble 2013) in which a "new force takes hold of the soul and directs it, toward theoretical insight" (Feyerabend, 1987a, 701).

Although relying heavily on the romantic ideal of individual instead of collective creativity (Theodore 2010), these stories allow people outside the centers of knowledge production to at least catch a whiff of the less orderly and serious parts of laboratory lives and the (mind) play that is part and parcel of scientific endeavors.

If we accept that scientific practices can be playful ventures, we can instantly recognize instances when the rules were bent or broken. In its extreme form this becomes deviance, which is most often considered unruly, unethical, and unwanted behavior that, when detected, can lead to the subsequent end of play, and when applied to the 'real' world, the end of actual academic careers. From pseudo-science to hoaxes, from plagiarism to fraud—where scientists play, they also break or transgress rules. Far more than with games, deviance in science easily clashes with our notion that outsiders should be able to trust scientists. For instance, cheating in scientific practices is rightly seen as an indication of unethical, 'bad' scientific conduct, and it comes in many different shades and forms. As sociologist Bridgstock points out, there are many reasons for fraud, or cheating in science, such as strong beliefs in developed theories, but they can also include "career motivations and political views" (Bridgstock 1982, 364). Lesser forms of deviance, showing that fair play in academia is not always tenable, are highly common practices of (sexist) nepotism in peer-review systems in which we can recognize the (albeit sometimes unconscious) bending of rules in order to promote particular scientific schools, ideas, or gender relations (Wennerås and Wold 1997; Langfeldt 2001).

Looking through the cracks

As examples of cheating in science show, playing with the rules of scientific practices is not uncommon and varies in form and gravity. Judging from the sensational press coverages of floundering scientific projects, one could conclude that citizens love to see scientists cheat. This cultural fascination with failing and unethical science is related to the asymmetry that we described earlier. Similar to the myth of the insane and genius scientist, it brings to the surface what we deep down knew all along: scientists are human beings and citizens too. It points us to cracks in the plaster of the scientific bastions through which we can catch, albeit distorted, a glimpse of the game of science including its duplicitous, tricky, and deceitful sides. It reveals that scientific knowledge production is not at all aloof to deviance or playing with rules. Outside the closed fortresses of knowledge production, we are simultaneously fascinated, confused by, and estranged from what scientific practices entail.

We mention these examples to show how closed most techno-scientific strongholds are and how intrigued and scandalized we become when we witness the other "Janus face" (Latour 1993) of scientific practices in their less orderly forms. We also point this out because it is one of the rare moments we realize that scientists can play with rules to the extreme of cheating and being duplicitous. Yet, play can also be a highly ethical and productive element of techno-scientific change and acknowledging this may open new ways of overcoming the asymmetrical relationship between scientists and other citizens that is particularly important for developing innovative citizen science games. That bending the rules can be an important and positive element of knowledge production has been stressed by both philosopher of science Feyerabend, as well as by his less radical peer Thomas Kuhn (Bailin 1990). Feyerabend took a very uncompromising stance on how science could be revolutionized by calling for an anarchic epistemology in which rules were no longer a pre-given. Although probably both too radical and relativistic, his stance does provoke us to think differently about ingrained rules in science and how they can hinder new knowledge production as well as the development and design of true citizen science games. Or, as Feyerabend wrote himself in *Farewell to reason* (1987b) about his previous works (1975, 1978):

> In *Against Method* (AM) I argued that the customary accounts of scientific knowledge and scientific method are faulty and that scientists do not proceed 'rationally' in the sense of rationalist philosophers. In *Science in a Free Society* (SFS) I argued that the sciences are particular ways of gaining information and of interfering with the world, that there are other such ways and that these 'other' ways are satisfactory in the sense that they meet the material and spiritual needs of those who use them. I added that, like all institutions in a free society, the sciences should be subjected to a democratic control. (Feyerabend, 1987b, v)

Going beyond rationality and changing rules were important aims in Feyerabend's democratic project. He believed that bending or negotiating rules should be a crucial part of innovative scientific practices and could improve the quality and democratic value of science. In her article about science education entitled 'Creativity, discovery, and science education: Kuhn and Feyerabend revisited' (1990), Bailin points out that both Feyerabend and the influential philosopher of science Thomas Kuhn related the improvement of science (in Kuhn's case rational and 'progressive') to rule bending and rule breaking during creative processes. Through deviant ways of using rules in method and theory or even discarding them all together, paradigm shifts can occur:

> Revolutionary science [...] is characterized by a radical departure from the prevailing paradigm and the creation of a completely new one. It involves the overthrow of the presuppositions underlying the old paradigm and the establishment of a radically new framework. This new paradigm is not a logical continuation of the previous one, but involves a new way of viewing phenomena and is, thus, incommensurable with the old paradigm. The postulation and acceptance of the heliocentric view of planetary organization, would be an example of this kind of revolutionary science, upsetting the presupposition that centrality and fixity were necessary properties of the earth, and establishing a whole new framework for astronomical observation and theory. (Bailin, 1990, 35)

So, play is an important element of knowledge production in scientific workplaces, and negotiating or bending rules is also part of such processes and not necessarily a bad or unethical practice either. According to Feyerabend, it can even lead to innovative theories and methods that can be more democratic. If we want to come to a better and more symmetrical approach and understanding of citizen science games, such insights about the relation between play and the making of science are highly valuable. Playing—including playing with the rules of the game—and doing science have more in common than we may think at first glance, and the term citizen science games no longer seems to contain an internal contradiction when we take this perspective on board. Looking at existing citizen science games, which we will turn to next, paints a very particular picture of the freedom play is allowed.

The dangers of the cheater

Serious games generally have a very specific goal in mind. With citizen science games this is generating usable scientific data. Deviating from the preferred form of play might endanger such goals. It is for this reason that Sicart sees such forms of instrumental play as play "subordinated to the goals and rules and systems of the game" and "subordinate to reason, to the logic of achievement and progression externally determined by the player" (2011). For Sicart, this undercuts the more free-flowing, experimental nature of play, but within citizen science games limiting player freedom this is deliberate.

In order to understand how citizen science game design approaches the limits of play, we can first look at how it approaches cheating. In Clark Aldrich's *The complete guide to simulations and serious games*, for instance, we find a definition of cheating which reads: "to cheat is to purposefully subvert the intent and design of the experience," adding that it "reduces the effectiveness" of a game (2009, 262). This, as one could image, is problematic and needs to be prevented by design. This can be achieved in a gentle way by reminding players of the way a game is supposed to be played. In *Eyewire*, a game with the aim to map the human brain, players early on in the game receive a reminder not to initially worry about their mistakes: "[D]on't worry—even if you're wrong, you won't hurt science" (Wired Differently 2012). In literature on the design of citizen science games, the potential harm of cheating or other deviant play behavior concerns the quality of the data gathered and is discussed more directly. In an evaluation of the design process of *Happy Match!* (Syracuse University School of Information Studies & Arts 2012), a citizen science game concerning animal classification, Crowston and Prestopnik note that they are unsure of the effects of adding game elements to citizen science, as "creating too strong an incentive to get a high score might lead to participants attempting to cheat or 'game' the system, diminishing rather than increasing data quality" (2013, 4). In another similar study of the design of *Verbosity* (Carnegie Mellon University 2006), a game using human-computation to collect common-knowledge facts, Speer, Havasi, and Surana show they are very aware of deviant behavior, stating that "we need to detect the patterns that indicate cheating, frustration, or 'bending the rules,' and remove or alter those assertions so that what remains is reasonable common sense knowledge" (2010, 106). The creators of *Foldit* mention cheating as part of the Gameplay Guidelines in their Community Rules overview on the game's website, stating that:

> Any method of copying data from other players or external sources in order to increase your solo score is cheating. If you'd like to collaborate or expand upon another person's work, you must do so as an evolver. Cheating circumvents the intention of Foldit and jeopardizes its scientific goals. (Foldit Community Rules 2015)

The concerns mentioned above are understandable, and we do not want to trivialize efforts to curtail cheating or other potentially destructive forms of deviance. The whole point of citizen science games is to draw the public in to participate in research, not to cause potential havoc through unethical practices.

From a broader game design, but also from a cultural perspective, going beyond simply playing by the rules is not just common, the notion of rules themselves are also negotiable. It is important to remember there is a difference between the rules determined by a game's design (and thus the creators) and the rules that exist a priori to a game and/or are the result of social negotiation between players. The latter can be seen as 'implicit rules,' which concern "etiquette, good sportsmanship and other implied rules of proper game behavior" (Salen and Zimmerman 2004, 130). The rules can also be game specific or genre specific social codes of practice, like the "tenets laid down by individuals within the game who have no design power or automatically conferred authority" (MacCallum-Stewart 2011, 45). Therefore, whether or not something is considered deviant play or cheating is not always reliable from the perspectives of players. As Mia Consalvo points out in her book *Cheating: Gaining advantage in videogames*, a fixed definition of cheating is hard to provide, but on the whole, the overarching definition used by players is that cheating gives cheaters an unfair advantage (2007, 87). This advantage usually presides over others, but the notion of having an unfair advantage works in single-player games as well. Here, we find purist players for whom cheating simply means anything other than a solo effort in completing a game (Ibid., 88). In single-player games, a player can for instance use cheat codes or a walkthrough guide to get ahead in a game. As game scholar Julian Kücklich puts it:

> The pleasure of any game depends on a balance between its rules and the freedom these rules leave the player for unconstrained interaction. Cheats can solve this dilemma by decreasing the perceived level of constraint in the game, thus setting the playing process in motion again. (2004, 5)

In sum, what is considered as impermissible behavior with or within a game is not, or not merely, up to a game's designer—at least not from a player's perspective. What is considered unfair in the unfair advantage Consalvo mentions is an interpretation usually made by players concerning what they consider to be fair play.

With their emphasis on instrumental forms of play and relatively tight control on players' freedom to play otherwise, citizen science games might work well with the structured approach of scientific research. At the same time, to return to Sicart, they turn "the act of playing a game into a labor-like action, into work toward an externally decided, predetermined, and rational outcome designed by others than the players" (2011). While this might be the goal of citizen science games, for Sicart this contradicts the act of play:

> Play, for being productive, should be a free, flexible, and negotiated activity, framed by rules but not determined by them. The meaning of a game, its essence, is not determined by the rules, but by the way players engage with those rules, by the way players play. (Ibid.)

Part of this freedom, this flexibility, and process of negotiation, is not just following the rules, but playing with them, and at times deviating *from* them. Again, we do not wish to argue that serious game design, or citizen science game design, is misguided for being overly instrumental. The point here is that examining different views on playful science can help to broaden the scope of citizen science games, as we will argue next.

Another play on citizen science

We are not arguing that existing types of citizen science games should be open to rule-breaking forms of play since these could potentially negatively impact the data generated by the players; what we are arguing is that the notion of citizen science games needs to be extended beyond the more narrow definition of primarily being human computation-based games. This would allow forms of citizen science that do more justice to the inherently playful nature of science discussed above. To do this, we want to look at practices within the genre of the massively multiplayer online role-playing game (MMORPG), in which we recognize exactly this notion of citizen science.

Successful games from this genre like *World of Warcraft* (Blizzard Entertainment 2004) have spawned massive communities of players who actively engage in participatory practices, like the creation of fan art, user-interface modifications, information databases, and so on. While some of these practices are expressive in nature, others are more instrumental, resulting in enhancing knowledge about and skill within the game. Among expert players, a specific type of investigative activity aims to obtain a better understanding of the inner workings of the game itself. This process, which has become known as theorycrafting, gives players a sense of access into and insight over the black box that is the game software, which is subsequently used to enhance tactical knowledge and skill for the most challenging gameplay situations the game has on offer. Among the tools for such investigations are user-interface modifications, also known as AddOns, which collect and visualize data generated by player actions within the game. Such AddOns are also created and distributed by the player community. Game scholar Torill Elvira Mortensen (2008, 208) distinguishes between two types, one is a deviant form of playing with the intended game design that is not counterproductive ("that which hinders personal progress") and the other is destructive ("that which ruins the progress of others"). But rather, it seems this is a form of productive deviation that excels or surpasses normal progress, resulting in what Glas calls "hyperproductive demystification" of a game: "instrumental progress going above and beyond the game's own challenges and fiction, both of which are deconstructed in the process" (2012, 90-100). Such forms of play notably change the experience and meaning of a game, creating new forms of, and norms for, playing the game.[3]

The reason for relating theorycrafting to citizen science is that the practice of theorycrafting brings to light a convergence of play with scientific habits of mind, with players displaying forms of scientific argumentation, model-based reasoning, and theory-evidence coordination (Steinkuehler and Chmiel 2006; Steinkuehler and Duncan 2008). For game scholar Karin Wenz, theorycrafting can, in fact, be seen as the "scientification" of gameplay, referring to a positivist approach to science using quantitative methods (2013, 181). Like the participants in the citizens science games discussed earlier, the player's theorycrafting practices here show "an engagement with data not primarily as part of research but as part of a leisure activity" (2013, 181). One could argue that theorycrafting does not involve a team of professional researchers who initiate the research process, analyze the data, and publish the results, primarily with public education in mind. The distinction between citizens and scientists, however, collapses here: the players instigate research through scientific means themselves. And they publish their results also, since reports of their findings are transferred to the public (i.e. the game community) in the form of discussions, formulas, tools, guides, and tutorials through various websites and knowledge databases dedicated to theorycrafting. From a game design perspective, we can say that, when a game like *World of Warcraft* allows players to collect and analyze

3 It should be noted that theorycrafting is not merely seen as beneficial to a game's community, as it also invites discussion on elitism between players (one well-known website for the theorycrafting community is even jokingly called 'Elitist Jerks') and can leads to social control and other disciplinary effects as players judge each other's play performance based on collected data rather than social skill or experience (Paul 2011; Glas 2012; Wenz 2013). For Wenz, "theorycrafting as a form as scientification of gameplay thus legitimizes both control mechanisms: control over the game and control over those who play it" (2013, 191).

data about (parts of) its inner workings, we can see that scientific discursive practices can and often do emerge among the player base.

Probing the rules in games, then, can be productive for players. Within the field of game studies, it has also been recognized as productive for research purposes. While play as a dedicated method to investigate games is considered an essential part of digital game research (Aarseth 2003; Mäyrä 2008), Julian Kücklich emphasizes the advantages of using *cheating* as a methodological tool:

> [It] allows us to reflect upon the presuppositions that we bring to games, no matter from which perspective we are studying them. It also enables us to identify blind spots in our research perspectives and thus discover new avenues of inquiry with regard to the phenomena we study. Perhaps even more importantly, taking into account unorthodox forms of play can help us recognize flaws in our theoretical models, which are so often built upon the experience of playing by the rules, rather than breaking them. (2007, 357)

Researchers might, of course, already be prone to take such a position toward their research material. For people being asked to become citizen scientists, being confronted with few options to actually pursue such acts of reasoning and reflection as a result of experimentation within games, the benefits Kücklich mentions remain limited.

Conclusion

What we want to maintain in this chapter is that acknowledging the existing close relationship between more open forms of play (including potentially deviant ones) and science may be fruitful for broadening the scope of what we envisage as citizen science games, or citizen science play. This encourages or allows players to be reflexive about what the rules are and, by doing so, come to a better understanding what science is about—going beyond the presumed paradox of play and science. Play is not only a common practice in traditional centers of knowledge production, but is also *productive* in such settings. As such, it is not only a kind of preparation for the "real thing," as Sutton-Smith (1970) would have it, but also for being able to think 'out of the box'.

To make players productive rule-benders *may* sound like too radical a step to take, but it is after all a crucial intrinsic 'quality' of both playing and doing science. So why not use that potential to the full? It may be used in games as a way to make players into critical citizens who rise above the voyeurism of looking through the cracks that we described earlier in this chapter. Players can thus understand what scientific knowledge production is or could be and can also become more reflexive about how scientists as citizens operate, as well as becoming critical about the limitations of scientific engagement. It may also be used to create awareness that some kinds of rule bending are crucial to knowledge production, as Feyerabend claimed. Probing what is conceived as unbendable often leads to new insights. Feyerabend calls in this context for epistemological anarchism (1975) or, as Staley puts it, "abandoning any attempt to separate the good from the bad in science according to a fixed view of rationality" (1999, 603). We call for games that take ludo-epistemologies to heart, games that invite scientist to view themselves as citizens, and citizens to engage with the playful act of doing science.

References

Aarseth, E. J. 2003. Playing research: Methodological approaches to game analysis. Paper presented at *The 5th international digital arts and culture conference, Melbourne, May 19, 2003.*

Aldrich, C. 2009. *The complete guide to simulations and serious games: How the most valuable content will be created in the age beyond Gutenberg to Google*. San Francisco, CA: Pfeiffer.

Bailin, S. 1990. Creativity, discovery, and science education: Kuhn and Feyerabend revisited. *Interchange* 21 (3): 34-44.

Blizzard Entertainment. 2004. *World of Warcraft*. [Windows/OS X]. Blizzard Entertainment. Game.

Bonney, R., C. B. Cooper, J. Dickinson, S. Kelling, T. Phillips, K. V. Rosenberg, and J. Shirk. 2009. Citizen science: A developing tool for expanding knowledge and scientific literacy. *BioScience* 59 (11): 977-984.

Bridgstock, M. 1982. A sociological approach to fraud in science. *Journal of Sociology* 18 (3): 364-383.

Carnegie Mellon University. 2006. *Verbosity*. [browser]. Carnegie Mellon University. Game.

Carnegie Mellon University and Stanford University. 2010. *EteRNA* [browser]. Carnegie Mellon University/Stanford University. Game.

Consalvo, M. 2007. *Cheating: Gaining advantage in videogames*. Cambridge, MA: The MIT Press.

Cossins, D. 2013. Games for science: Playing scientist. *The Scientist.* http://www.the-scientist.com/?articles.view/articleNo/33715/title/Games-for-Science.

Crowston, K., and N. R. Prestopnik. 2013. Motivation and data quality in a citizen science game: A design science evaluation. In *Proceedings of the 46th Hawaii international conference on system sciences, Wailea, HI, January 7-10, 2013*. Washington, DC: IEEE.

Csikszentmihalyi, M. 2009. *Creativity: Flow and the psychology of discovery and invention.* New York: HarperCollins.

Deterding, S., D. Dixon, R. Khaled, and L. Nacke. 2011. From game design elements to gamefulness: Defining "gamification". In *Proceedings of the 15th international academic MindTrek conference: Envisioning future media environments, Tampere, September 28-30, 2011*, 9-15. New York: ACM.

Dickinson, J. L., and R. Bonney. 2012. Introduction: Why citizen science? In *Citizen science: Public participation in environmental research*, eds. J. L. Dickinson and R. Bonney, 1-14. New York: Cornell University Press.

Ehrmann, J., C. Lewis, and P. Lewis. 1968. Homo ludens revisited. *Yale French Studies* 41: 31-57.

EyesOnALZ. 2016. *Stall Catchers.* [browser]. Human Computation Institute. Game.

Feyerabend, P. 1975. *Against method.* London: Verso Books.

—. 1978. *Science in a free society.* London: New Left Books.

—. 1987a. Creativity: A dangerous myth. *Critical Inquiry* 13 (4): 700-711.

—. 1987b. *Farewell to reason.* London: Verso Books.

Filament Games and K. Squire. 2013. *Citizen Science.* [browser]. Filament Games. Game.

Flanagan, M., S. Punjasthitkul, M. Seidman, and G. Kaufman. 2013. Citizen archivists at play: Game design for gathering metadata for cultural heritage institutions. In *Proceedings of the 2013 DiGRA international conference: DeFragging game studies, Atlanta, GA, August 26-29, 2013*. http://www.tiltfactor.org/wp-content/uploads2/tiltfactor_citizenArchivistsAtPlay_digra2013.pdf.

Foldit Community Rules. *Foldit.* http://fold.it/portal/communityrules.

Gaydos, M., and K. Squire. 2010. Citizen science: Designing a game for the 21st century. In *Interdisciplinary models and tools for serious games: Emerging concepts and future directions*, ed. R. van Eck, 289-304. Hershey: Information Science Reference.

Glas, R. 2012. *Battlefields of negotiation: Control, agency, and ownership in World of Warcraft.* Amsterdam: Amsterdam University Press.

Hagstrom, W. O. 1965. *The scientific community.* New York: Basic Books.

Hand, E. 2010. People power. *Nature* 466:685-687.
Hull, D. L. 1988. *Science as a process: An evolutionary account of the social and conceptual development of science*. Chicago, IL: University of Chicago Press.
Juul, J. 2005. *Half-real: Video games between real rules and fictional worlds*. Cambridge, MA: The MIT Press.
Khatib, F., F. DiMaio, Foldit Contenders Group, Foldit Void Crushers Group, S. Cooper, M. Kazmierczyk, M. Gilski, et al. 2011. Crystal structure of a monomeric retroviral protease solved by protein folding game players. *Nature Structural & Molecular Biology* 18:1175-1177.
Kücklich, J. 2004. Other playings: Cheating in computer games. Paper presented at *The other players conference, Copenhagen, December 6-8, 2004*.
—. 2007. Homo Deludens: Cheating as a methodological tool in digital games research. *Convergence* 13 (4): 255-367.
Langfeldt, L. 2001. The decision-making constraints and processes of grant peer review, and their effects on the review outcome. *Social Studies of Science* 31 (6): 820-841.
Laszlo, P. 2004. Science as play. *American Scientist* 92 (5): 398.
Latour, B. 1993. *We have never been modern*. London: Harvester Wheatsheaf.
Latour, B., and S. Woolgar. 1979. *Laboratory life: The construction of scientific facts*. Princeton, NJ: Princeton University Press.
MacCallum-Stewart, E. 2011. Conflict, thought communities and textual appropriation in MMORPGs. In *Online gaming in context: the social and cultural significance of online games*, eds. G. Crawford, V. K. Gosling, and B. Light, 40-59. London: Routledge.
Mainemelis, C. 2010. Stealing fire: Creative deviance in the evolution of new ideas. *Academy of Management Review* 35 (4): 558-578.
Mäyrä, F. 2008. *An introduction to game studies: Games in culture*. London: Sage Publications.
McGill Centre for Bioinformatics. 2010. *Phylo*. [browser/Android]. Montreal: McGill University. Game.
Mortensen, T. E. 2008. Humans playing *World of Warcraft*: or deviant strategies? In *Digital culture, play, and identity: A World of Warcraft reader*, eds. H. G. Corneliussen and J. W. Rettberg. 203-224. Cambridge, MA: The MIT Press.
Nasar, S. 1998. *A beautiful mind: A biography of John Forbes Nash, Jr.* New York: Simon and Schuster.
Noble, D. F. 2013. *The religion of technology: The divinity of man and the spirit of invention*. New York: Random House.
Paul, C. A. 2011. Optimizing play: How theorycraft changes gameplay and design. *Game Studies* 11 (2). http://gamestudies.org/1102/articles/paul.

Salen, K., and E. Zimmerman. 2004. *Rules of play: Game design fundamentals.* Cambridge, MA: The MIT Press.

Sicart, M. 2011. Against procedurality. *Game Studies* 11 (3). http://gamestudies.org/1103/articles/sicart_ap.

Speer, R., C. Havasi, and H. Surana. 2010. Using *Verbosity*: Common sense data from games with a purpose. Paper presented at *The 23rd international Florida artificial intelligence research society conference, Daytona Beach, FL, May 19-21, 2010.*

Squire, K. 2011. *Video games and learning: Teaching and participatory culture in the digital age.* New York: Teachers College Press.

Staley, K. W. 1999. Logic, liberty, and anarchy: Mill and Feyerabend on scientific method. *The Social Science Journal* 36 (4): 603-614.

Steinkuehler, C. A., and M. Chmiel. 2006. Fostering scientific habits of mind in the context of online play. In *Proceedings of the 7th international conference on learning sciences, Bloomington, IN, June 27-July 1, 2006*, 723-729. New York: ACM.

Steinkuehler, C. A., and S. Duncan. 2008. Scientific habits of mind in virtual worlds. *Journal of Science Education and Technology* 17 (6): 530-543.

Stephan, P. E. 1996. The economics of science. *Journal of Economic Literature* 34 (3): 1199-1235.

Sutton-Smith, B. 1970. The playful modes of knowing. *ERIC Institute of Education Sciences.* http://eric.ed.gov/?id=ED050806.

—. 2001. *The ambiguity of play.* Cambridge, MA: Harvard University Press.

Syracuse University School of Information Studies & Arts. 2012. *Happy Match!* [browser]. Syracuse: Citizen Sort/Syracuse University. Game.

The Sainsbury Laboratory. 2013. *Fraxinus.* [Facebook]. The Sainsbury Laboratory. Game.

Theodore, D. 2010. Was Kekule's mind brainbound? The historiography of chemistry and the philosophy of extended cognition. *Spontaneous Generations: A Journal for the History and Philosophy of Science* 3 (1): 158-177.

Tweney, R. D. 1996. Presymbolic processes in scientific creativity. *Creativity Research Journal* 9 (2-3): 163-172.

UA Ideas CODER. 2012. *Quantum Moves.* [multi-platform]. University of Aarhus. Game.

University of Washington Center for Game Science/Department of Biochemistry. 2008. *Foldit.* [browser]. University of Washington. Game.

Von Ahn, L. 2006. Games with a purpose. *IEEE Computer Magazine* (June): 96-98.

Wennerås, C., and Wold, A. 1997. Nepotism and sexism in peer-review. *Nature* 387 (6631): 341-343.

Wenz, K. 2013. Theorycrafting. *Information, Communication & Society* 16 (2): 178-193.
Wiggins, A., and Crowston, K. 2011. From conservation to crowdsourcing: A typology of citizen science. In *Proceedings of the 44th Hawaii international conference on system sciences, Kauai, HI, January 4-7, 2011*, 1-10. New York: ACM.
Wired Differently. 2012. *Eyewire.* [browser]. MIT. Game.

About the authors

René Glas is Assistant Professor of New Media and Digital Culture in the Department of Media and Culture Studies at Utrecht University. With a background in film and new media studies, his primary field is game studies, in which he teaches and writes about a variety of topics, including game history and culture, fan and participatory culture, cheating and other forms of deviant play, serious and pervasive games, and media comparison. Glas is a founding member of Utrecht University's Center for the Study of Digital Games and Play. His book *Battlefields of negotiation: Control, agency, and ownership in World of Warcraft* (2012) was published by Amsterdam University Press.

Sybille Lammes is Full Professor of New Media and Digital Culture at The Centre for the Arts in Society (LUCAS) at Leiden University. She has been a visiting Senior Research Fellow at The University of Manchester, and has worked as a researcher at the Centre for Interdisciplinary Methodologies at the University of Warwick, as well as the media studies departments of Utrecht University and the University of Amsterdam. Her background is in media studies and play studies, which she has always approached from an interdisciplinary angle, including cultural studies, science and technology studies, postcolonial studies, and critical geography. She is co-editor of *Playful identities: The ludification of digital media cultures* (Amsterdam University Press 2015), *Mapping time* (Manchester University Press 2018) and *The Routledge handbook of interdisciplinary research methods* (Routledge 2018). She is an ERC laureate and has been the principal investigator of numerous research projects.

12. The playful scientist: Stimulating playful communities for science practice

Ben Schouten, Erik van der Spek, Daniël Harmsen, and Ellis Bartholomeus

Abstract

In this chapter, the authors elaborate on serious games and playful interactions in modern scientific practices, and on the way they can engender mutual scientific growth. They use a research-through-design approach, in which three possible scenarios and prototypes are studied to envisage the new role of the public library in practicing science in a changing society. Their conclusion is that the public library of the future should employ citizen science projects that are fun, accessible, malleable, and participatory, so that its new role can focus on offering meaningful information at the right time in the right place, contextualizing information using playful solutions, bringing together communities to share information, and enabling new scientific practices in unexplored fields.

Keywords: Citizen science games, playful, research through design, public library

Traditional methods for practicing science rely mainly on experts. However, newer forms of science practice have started to allow for non-experts to participate as well, a trend mirrored in societal change toward more participatory cultures. Citizen science projects exist in various forms and offer many ways for the public to participate. What most of these projects have in common is that participants contribute to scientific activities made available by experts through apps and desktop applications. What these projects often lack is the community building that allows the science projects

Glas, R., S. Lammes, M. de Lange, J. Raessens, and I. de Vries, eds. 2019. *The Playful Citizen. Civic Engagement in a Mediatized Culture.* Amsterdam: Amsterdam University Press.
DOI: 10.5117/9789462984523/CH12

to be meaningful for the citizen participating. In this chapter, we want to elaborate on serious games and playful interactions in these modern science practices, and look at the way they can engender mutual scientific benefit. We used a research through design approach; more specifically, we have designed three possible scenarios and prototypes to envisage the new role of the public library in science practice in a changing society.

Our starting point in this chapter is the current state of the art in what can be called citizen science. Citizen science (also known as crowd science, crowd-sourced science, civic science, or networked science) is scientific research conducted, in its entirety or in part, by amateur or non-professional scientists, often by crowd-sourcing and crowdfunding. In this chapter, we would like to address the practice of citizen science as part of the changing role of scientific institutions such as the public library. Funded by a research grant from the city of Eindhoven (the Netherlands), we studied several alternative roles for the library as an institute designed to cultivate knowledge and scientific literacy among the city's citizens.

We challenged a group of students at the Department of Industrial Design at the Eindhoven University of Technology to design a series of (playful) citizen science scenarios in which there is a clear role for the public library. In addition we invited an industrial partner, IJsfontein from Amsterdam, to join the consortium as a designer in residence. In this way, we want to bolster the ecosystem of the creative industries in the Netherlands, especially in bringing together the different stakeholders to co-create applications for social innovation.

The methodology that we used is that of research through design. Research through design is about creating knowledge through action-reflection with prototypes in a design process (Jonas 2007). Insights from these intermediate results (prototypes) are used to create more general conclusions (Sein et al. 2011). To reflect on the possible role of the library and citizens we (iteratively) designed prototypes followed by reflection, analysis, and synthesis. We wanted to focus on the process of experiential learning by citizens themselves within a participatory setting, as opposed to a more classical approach of consulting an expert or knowledge base made available by the public library. In this chapter, we would like to elaborate on how playful citizen science can impact the *process* of knowledge gathering, the configuration of knowledge itself, and the way knowledge is applied and shared.

State of the art in science practice

The World Wide Web has gradually grown as a source of information; much of the knowledge taught in schools can be found readily and on-demand on the internet, through online encyclopedias such as Wikipedia, social networks and internet forums. This socially distributed, collective intelligence (Lévy 1997) afforded by the internet may obviate the need for a large active knowledge base. However, it also has its downside. For one, it requires a new way of thinking about (and the education required to cope with) this hyper-connected world, often encapsulated in what is called twenty-first century skills and new media literacy (Jenkins 2009). Among these twenty-first century skills, problem-based learning is often employed and emphasis is placed on sense-making in authentic contexts (Lombardi 2007). In addition, as young people grow up constructing knowledge from various (often highly-pleasing sensorial) trans-medial sources, traditional instruction can be considered boring from their perspective.

Members of the millennial generation increasingly show a lack of motivation to learn with classical skill and drill practices (Ryan and Deci 2000; Deen and Schouten 2011) and prefer a more experiential and social approach to learning (Oblinger and Oblinger 2005). They generally spend more time using screen media, distracting them from their studies (Jenkins 2009). To encourage more autonomy-supportive educational practice is generally accepted as the best way to create more intrinsically motivated students (Deen and Schouten 2014).

As young people find things that intrinsically motivate them, they often join online communities, also called affinity spaces (Gee 2005; Schouten 2015), where they can share knowledge and skills pertaining to their interests with other people from across the globe. People share and learn from 'life-hacks' on YouTube and exchange elaborate co-constructed architectures and virtual landscapes in *Minecraft* (Mojang 2011). This participatory culture, in turn, shapes the worldview, or epistemic frame, of its community members (Shaffer 2006).

However, the internet as a knowledge base is fragmented and data are not always provided in a clear context. Moreover, while democratized cultures of participation can lead to creativity, it is well known that learning without proper guidance (there are typically no experts in grassroots movements who can provide guidance) can send people down "garden paths" (Gee 2004), meaning the epistemic frames that are formed may be skewed. Furthermore, in the last decennium, we see another development where interaction has

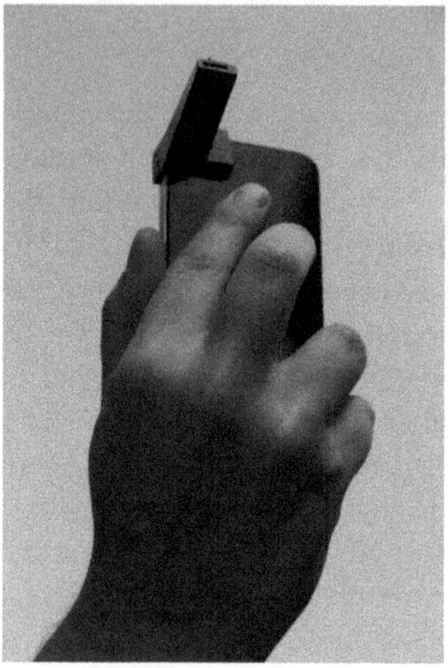

12.1: A smartphone with the *Ispex* add-on.

contributed to processing information, for instance in computer games and apps. Or, to put it differently, in addition to the vast amounts of data made available by the use of sensors installed on run-of-the-mill smartphones, now everybody can become a scientist. For instance, in *Ispex* (Figure 12.1), a simple smartphone is used in combination with an add-on device to measure air pollution in the atmosphere. The resulting data is aggregated over thousands of devices in order to draw maps and identify the most polluted areas that can pose potential risks to the health of individuals.

In these applications, there is a clear shift from just gathering data to processing the data into meaningful information that can empower citizens. One thing became clear in our research effort, citizen science makes it more fun for people to contribute to science and the main reason why citizens want to participate with applications such as *Ispex*, besides curiosity, is that they feel they can add (personal) value to society by contributing in some way.

In summary, a number of trends can be discerned. We see 1) that the World Wide Web seems to obviate the need for a knowledge base and classical information institutions such as libraries; 2) a shift to a participatory culture where citizens want to contribute within affinity spaces where groups of people are drawn together because of a shared commitment to a common activity; and 3) citizens of the millennial generation need expert guidance in acquiring a proper epistemic frame pertaining to their affinity space.

In the next section, we contend that cultivating and nurturing these cultures of science participation within affinity spaces can be a valuable new role for the public library, and that games and playful design offer ways to achieve this.

A symbiotic relationship through playful science

Games can play an important role, both as a means to motivate the citizen to engage in citizen science projects, but also to create real value for the citizen scientist through the engendering of complex learning, scientific skill acquisition, and empowerment. Games are so engaging because they satisfy the basic psychological needs of competence, autonomy, and relatedness (Przybylski, Rigby, and Ryan 2010). Through a process of encountering problems and autonomously finding ways to overcome them, the game player feels that they become more competent and is more likely to engage subsequently in the activity (Van der Spek 2012). What is more, the persuasive nature of games (Bogost 2007) has been shown to be a powerful tool for inducing attitude change (Wouters, Van der Spek, and Van Oostendorp 2009). Being engaged in collaborative science games can not only increase a person's knowledge about the subject, it can also improve his or her disposition toward science and learning. Related to this, science games can let players experience being a scientist, thereby acquiring the epistemic frame of a scientist and learning how to think scientifically (Shaffer 2006). Apart from being fun, games are experiential sense-making tools, where players immersed in the game learn about complex systems, at their own pace and volition, thereby acquiring the necessary cognitive skills to deal with increasing complexity (Squire 2003).

These aforementioned affordances are important for the concept of citizen science and in our case, the new role of the public library, for two main reasons. One is data, because as the possibilities of capturing data increase, so too do the complexities of dealing with it. With the internet, the Internet of Things, and big data as key concepts in the new information age, the necessity of having a large set of declarative knowledge decreases; however, the need for relevant cognitive skills and attitudes in order to deal with the ubiquitous complexity increases. Games are ideal ways to train for these skills and attitudes (Zimmerman 2007). While participating as individual players in a pervasive game of crowd-sourced information at different places, they also learn about the pervasiveness of individual information bits constituting a complex system. The feedback provided by the overarching game can then be used to comprehend the compound system and train for the skill of systems thinking. In addition, playing with these systems stimulates an improvisational and creative attitude necessary to operate in a world with ill-defined complex problems (Lombardi 2007; Zimmerman 2007).

For this reason, the new library can most accurately be envisioned as an institute, which focuses on (playful digital) interactions; predominantly digital, occasionally traditional, often serious, sometimes fun. The new library creates and curates affinity spaces where citizens can come together and contribute to science, and where games are used to make the process engaging, playful and more meaningful for these citizen scientists. This relates to the twenty-first century skills with which citizens self-organize social practices and learning, based on civic-driven change that 1) supports bottom-up approaches instead of top down decision making; 2) enables co-creation, allowing a large audience of users and experts to participate; 3) incorporates wisdom of the crowd and agent technology where information and decisions can come from many sources; and 4) provides a more dynamical and balanced way of research, less restricted by fixed rules or regulations.

Game design to improve citizen science uptake

While there is great potential for the many uses of citizen science, its efficacy is often hampered by the one-directedness of its value proposition. Clearly the scientist benefits from contributions (such as large data sets) freely provided by the general public, but what does the citizen stand to gain? Citizen science projects try to make contributing (to science) more fun and create a longer lasting appeal by adding playful elements for the participants. The game *Foldit* (University of Washington Center for Game Science/Department of Biochemistry 2008), for instance, is described in Wikipedia as

> an online puzzle video game about protein folding. The objective of the game is to fold the structure of selected proteins to the best of the player's ability, using various tools provided within the game. The highest scoring solutions are analyzed by researchers, who determine whether or not there is a native structural configuration (or native state) that can be applied to the relevant proteins. Scientists can then use such solutions to solve 'real-world' problems, by targeting and eradicating diseases, and creating biological innovations. (Wikipedia 2015, n.p.)

Some citizen science projects have incorporated additional game elements. These elements are often basic and are usually an added feature instead of a focus point. In most projects, these elements are achievement-based, where participants need to perform an action a certain number of times to gain points or proceed to more advanced levels. An example of this can be found in Cornell Lab of Ornithology's *CamClickr* project,[1] which

> uses basic gaming technology to provide a friendly spirit of competition. In level 1, the participant receives one point for each image sorted into an album (e.g., eggs, nestlings, or adults). After participants sort 99 images, they can move on to level 2 and earn four points for every tagged image. The challenge in level 2 is to classify each image with behavioral tags such as feeding young, preening mates, and incubating or rotating eggs. (Cornell Lab of Ornithology 2008)

While *Foldit* contains puzzles that can be intrinsically and cognitively interesting, most of the other citizen science projects primarily rely on isolated, superficial gamification principles such as competitive scoring mechanisms to keep the player engaged. This 'pointsification' (the scoring of points as the sole motivation to play) as an extrinsic reward can stimulate perseverance to complete an arduous task, but is only partially what games are about (Robertson 2010). There is little in the way of stimulating the player's fantasy (Malone 1981) or of providing moment-to-moment 'game feel' in the interaction (Isbister 2011). This means that a player already has to be motivated to start playing the game, the game itself does not provide a lot of meaning to the player. The community is sustained, but does not rise above itself.

Projects such as *CamClickr*, *Foldit*, and *EyeWire* (Wired Differently 2012) all claim to be games, but because their game elements (such as pointsification) do not add much fun or playfulness, we find it difficult to call these applications games. Moreover, these applications are what we call expert systems, meaning that results contribute to the knowledge base of the initiator and cannot be freely interpreted by users. Citizen science projects that are intrinsically fun because they contain game elements (such as storytelling) are rare. However, this does not mean that citizen science projects are not fun. Other aspects can make the projects attractive to people such as having a personal interest in the subject or providing a sense of accomplishment and making a larger contribution, as well as being part of a community or creating the opportunity for exploration.

1 *CamClickr* was launched in 2008. This project catalogues nesting behavior of birds captured in over 600,000 images. The resulting imagery led to the publication of one scientific article and *CamClickr* was featured in a biology curriculum (Vos and Cooper 2010), using a free online citizen science project to teach observation and quantification of animal behavior.

A future role for citizen science

In this section, we want to discuss a design research project entitled KLOS developed at the Eindhoven University of Technology to elaborate on more advanced functionalities and future scenarios for citizen science projects, using applied gaming and playful interactions.[2] The idea is to build (digital) playful labs for science practice, with the purpose of acquiring skills which in turn are organized and synthesized by the public library.

KLOS is a Citizen Science in Urban Gaming research project set up with cooperation by the Eindhoven University of Technology, the city council of Eindhoven, the public library of Eindhoven, and finally IJsfontein (Amsterdam), an industrial partner interested in participating in playful interaction design and research. As part of the Dutch government's new policies to cultivate collaborative relationships between industry, research, and government (known as the triple helix), this initiative resulted in the appointment of a designer-in-residence from the industry to Eindhoven University, for half a year. The starting point of the project was the following research question: How can citizen science and urban gaming contribute to the collaborative creation and dissemination of experiences to educate and obtain skills in several domains and how can the public library Eindhoven contribute to this new role?

Our students approached the research question by adopting a methodology of Reflective Transformative Design in order to obtain disruptive innovative systems (Hummels and Frens 2011). By imagining a different world, they try to break free of current constraints and try to come up with unique new products and services. We challenged around 25 students from Eindhoven University and Fontys University of Applied Sciences to design prototypes for the 'Library of the Future.' Over the course of thirteen weeks, the students worked in teams under the supervision of a professional expert. Together with supervisors and staff of the university, the students' design processes were observed and their concepts and questions were discussed. In the next section we will elaborate on some of the design cases.

2 KLOS refers to the Dutch expression 'Kennis Ligt Op Straat,' which roughly translates to 'Knowledge can be found everywhere'.

12.2: During our design process, we envisioned the new role of the library, using the metaphor of a tree bearing fruits that can be harvested, re-seeded, and consumed, in reference to the different roles of the library: dissemination, education, and utilization.

The library of the future

As part of our efforts to contribute to the triple helix policy, strengthening the collaboration between research institutes, industries, and governmental bodies, we invited a designer in residence from the renowned industrial partner IJsfontein. The role of the designer was to reflect on the newly proposed concepts delivered at the later stages and develop a final proposition for the public library to be realized after the initial research projects.

We envisaged the Library of the Future as a new type of institute designed to address the needs of a new type of citizen. In a future, when knowledge is just a finger tap away, this new institute will help develop twenty-first century skills, such as connected collaboration, critical thinking, and creativity. So, what is it precisely? The Library of the Future can most accurately be described as an institute focusing on skills and attitudes. Its services change constantly as people interact with it, much like the boundaries of science constantly change as we explore new fields. In traditional learning and skill and drill exercises with books, knowledge is transmitted to those willing to learn. In most of these cases there is a lack of interaction during the transfer of knowledge. The student simply 'consumes'.

The Library of the Future is different. Using the metaphor of a tree, it behaves like a fruit-bearing tree, with fruits of knowledge, skills, and attitudes (see Figure 12.2). Citizens can pick the fruits, harvest the seeds, and then plant trees of their own, feeding back into the system. The citizen will create the actual structure of this knowledge base and the library acts as the community gardener, introducing relevant playful activities and providing ties to pertinent experts.

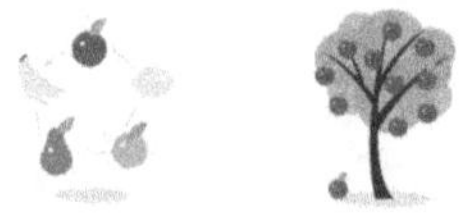

12.3: Different kinds of fruit, with one corresponding tree.

12.4: Fruit out of context.

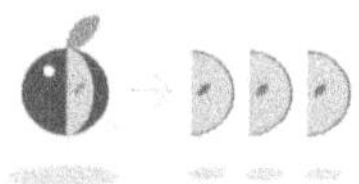

12.5: Connecting sections of fruit.

12.6: Tree that bears alternative produce.

Another key shift of the Library of the Future is one of teaching skills for learning by oneself as opposed to offering knowledge. Citizens of the future might only need to learn where information can be found when they need it, and they should be focused on learning practical skills and working on new ways to access knowledge. To be more precise, the new services of the library will help facilitate 1) how meaningful information can be retrieved; 2) how data can be processed, used, and contextualized; 3) how information can be shared and thus contribute to science; and 4) how education and exploring new areas of research can be encouraged. We see the library as a dynamic system with several features, namely excellence, wisdom, conjunctive and connected, and contemporary.

Excellence

The primary function of the library is to create meaning and context for citizens and offer them twenty-first century skills such as critical thinking, creativity, and the ability to solve problems. The constant 'hunger' for information will be put in context. The role of the library is to bring quality to the process. Knowledge is levered, giving a sense of what you want to know or should want to know. The library offers suggestions on where to go next in your quest for information. It is important where the right 'knowledge' tree can be found (see Figure 12.3). As an example, in the future, this could be the latest augmented reality apps that enable a user to simple scan an object, a building, a word, and find useful information about it.

Wisdom

If you know where to look, you have a very good chance of finding the answer online. But this 'quick fix' answer lacks any context (see Figure 12.4). You can google 'how long to boil corn?' and find the precise number of minutes. But it teaches you nothing more about cooking, nor does it suggest where to go from there. Knowledge has become common with the help of the internet and mobile handheld devices. There is almost too much now. Sometimes it is hard to assess the quality of it, or to form an opinion on a subject. The Library of the Future will be focused on providing expertise and helping to process information.

Conjunctive and connected

The library tries to connect citizens by finding other people who have similar interests (see Figure 12.5). It also allows experts who are knowledgeable to find interested civilians and vice versa. The process can work both ways. An expert might be in need of fresh ideas, reviews, or just a lot of data. A citizen might have a brilliant idea but needs help to develop it. The Library of the Future will be a knowledge broker, facilitating the connection between citizens and experts alike. In many ways, everyone will be able to become an expert.

Contemporary

The Library of the Future will provide new ways to practice science, as it wants to support bottom-up approaches of research (starting with the user) instead of top-down research. This will allow entirely new and alternative bodies of knowledge to be developed (see Figure 12.6). New experts, no matter how insignificant they might feel, can add new insights and knowledge to the library and can be found by anyone within the system.

The future will hold entirely new products not yet designed. Each product will be tailored to transfer specific expertise in the best and most efficient way possible. Increasingly, more devices will be connected to other devices, allowing for even more exciting capabilities and for a much greater focus on making knowledge accessible, more interactive, and fun. In the next section, we will examine three example projects that the Library can host in the future.

Examples of playful science practice

In this section, we will show how the requirements discussed above resulted in various design projects. We studied three of the projects, based on differing expertise: 1) Music experience (*Rhytmos*); 2) the art of debating (*Battle of Wits*); and 3) science education (*Blob*). We analyzed them according to seven different factors (see Table 1).

Table 1: Projects and analytical factors

	Rhytmos	*Battle of Wits*	*Blob*
Fun factor	++	++	+
Playful learning and critical thinking	++	++	++
Empowerment and bottom-up approach	++	+	++
Attitude change toward science	+-	?	++
Motivational aspects: Autonomy	+	++	++
Motivational aspects: Competence	++	++	++
Motivational aspects: Relatedness	+	+	++

Design case 1: Rhytmos by Milan Knust Graichen

Objectives: The first project was targeted at understanding rhythm in playing music. The library can serve as a public music instrument where people/citizens can learn about rhythm and the interaction between tones and tunes. It is anticipated that by playing music together in a public environment, getting connected, and experiencing the process of mutual learning, users should become more interested in playing music. The library could take an active role in contributing to peoples' music skills and their experiences of making music, instead of just simply lending music CD-ROMs and literature. In this way, the library's focus is on enabling citizens to develop and create music and obtain new skills instead of just consuming.

Description of design: *Rhytmos* helps people to develop rhythmic skills in a playful way. It is an LED floor on a city square with a moving line on the floor (see Figure 12.7). Depending on where you position yourself, the rhythm will change, and the player/user will understand the consequence of that position and explore its relation to other players. While some people have a natural ear for music and a sense of rhythm, not everyone is born with these skills. This urban sculpture is designed to trigger people's curiosity and invite people living in urban spaces to explore and investigate rhythm together.

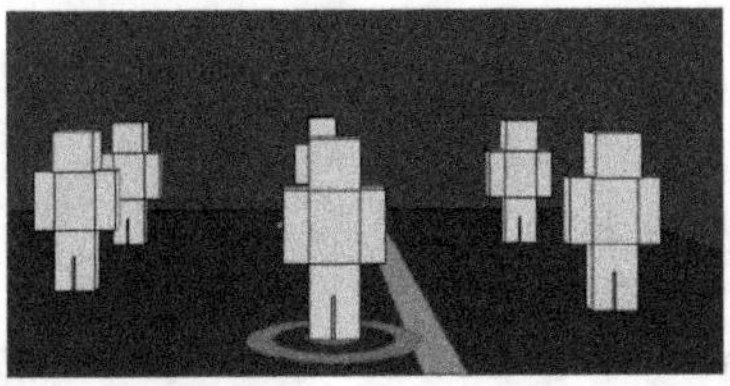

12.7: *Rhytmos* is a LED floor on a city square with a moving line for music experiences. The rhythm changes according to your position relative to the line and the other users.

Analysis: Providing and enabling citizens to co-create and experience music in a public space creates an engaging and collective environment in which they can explore and learn. Intrinsic motivation is triggered by curiosity. The threshold to communicate with a stranger or your neighbor is lowered. Music can elicit engagement and curiosity in itself; in this concept, people are free to participate or just be a spectator of other people who play and explore. The curiosity to understand sound interaction is engaging and playful, there are no other rules and no interaction can be wrong. Users can learn from their experience. For instance, one person who does not understand their influence in the playful interaction can have it explained so they can then be invited to explore it further.

Design case 2: Battle of Wits by Doenja Oogjes

Objectives: This project promotes the skill of debating. The library will not only provide knowledge, but the Library of the Future will enable people to build and develop their resources and play around with ideas and perspectives as parts of furthering citizen science. Critical thinking and debating exercised in a playful way can elicit creativity and perspectives or counter arguments that can be examined, since the game provides a safe environment in which no argument is ever right or wrong. But for the sake of the game, the citizen scientist/player is triggered to explore a certain mindset.

Description of design: *Battle of Wits* is a game meant to stimulate an open approach to gaining knowledge. The game consists of two sets of chalkboard hexagons, chalk markers, a deck of playing cards containing statement cards (with statements about current subjects or ongoing issues), and chance (see Figure 12.8). By coming up with as many original arguments as possible, players have to consider the topic from all different points of view, or at least experiment with various perspectives and lenses. The game is won when one player/team locks in the other team with arguments.

12.8: *Battle of Wits* is a game about debating. Your argument can be locked by arguments from the other team configured on the table.

Analysis: In this app for the Library of the Future, we focused on open access to information, citizens' skill development, relationships with peers, and critical thinking. The playful context of a game enables/allows higher contrast and freedom and more creativity to view a topic from new, different, and even extreme perspectives. It includes listening well and acknowledging other players' creativity and opinions for the sake of the discussion without being offended or becoming defensive or being concerned with who is right or wrong. Final judgment is not about being 'right,' but about being creative and open-minded.

Design case 3: Blob by Sam Janssen

Objectives: In this project, we wanted to focus on learning skills. To be more specific, we wanted to look at how the library can provide and enable children's curiosity for nature, inviting them to discover and explore their outdoor surroundings instead of experiencing the world only through digital interaction and using the computer. A second objective we had was to get children outdoors and to teach them skills of examining, questioning, unscrambling, and analyzing the world around them. The role of the library would be to 1) provide tools and devices to develop these skills; 2) be the caretaker and curator of the data collected and harvested; and 3) collect methods developed for and iterated by the users.

Description of design: *Night lamp Blob* becomes a child's friend and requests daily input about nature to be able to survive and shine its protective light and colors at night. Its functionalities are like those of 'Siri,' the intelligent personal assistant from Apple that helps you get things done (Aron 2011). In this case, communication and interaction are not only conducted through voice input, but also with the help of photos, audio, and ambient lighting (see Figure 12.9). The idea is that the child explores nature and takes pictures of an interesting object or specimen, after which the lamp 'asks' questions in order to comprehend the object and its larger context. The player learns to study objects more closely by reflecting on the questions asked by Blob:

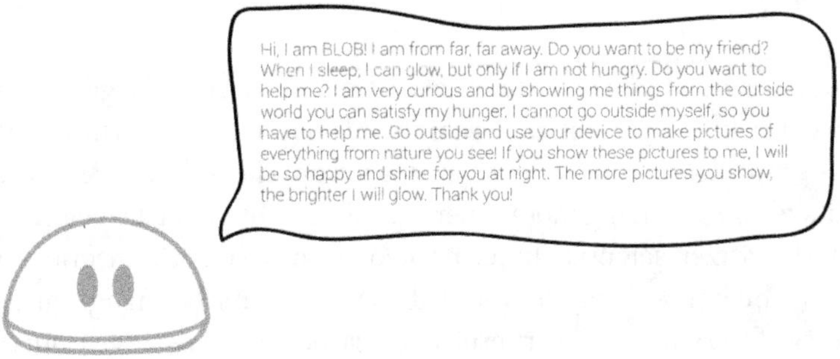

12.9: *Night lamp Blob* is a smart object that is able to serve as a knowledge base for children using Apple's Siri technology. The child presents photos and objects to Blob, after which the lamp gives back additional information pertaining to the objects shown.

how big, how heavy, what color, how soft? The child should be able to adopt an explorative attitude in order to acquire better learning skills.

Analysis: The child becomes motivated to connect with their very personal friend. After recognizing the benefits of knowledge, they learn to naturally explore on their own. Their efforts are rewarded by the increasing illumination of the night lamp. Meanwhile, the player becomes more aware, confident, and competent in nature since they learn about the outside world in a safe home environment with the Blob.

This collective, dynamic growth at the library will result in the collection of large amounts of big data including photos, questions, and answers. These data are literally 'food for thought' since the lamp will attempt to recognize patterns; what pictures are taken in which seasons and in what areas/locations (i.e. city or countryside) by what type of players. Little data gems can be found in the big data collected by the children who are primarily driven by curiosity to feed their night lamp. Players learn to become scientists without realizing it, since their motivation is to nourish the lamp, and only indirectly experience the growth of information. The product teaches you to question your environment and by asking you to contribute to the development of the science of nature. Moreover, the photos can also produce a lot of contextual information about natural phenomena such as seasonal characteristics and/or climate changes.

Conclusion

The goal of current citizen science practices is to encourage larger groups of users to contribute to scientific research. It is not hard to see the benefit for scientists as well as science. However, apart from the particular research topic and its results receiving more general public attention, little meaning is created for the citizen scientist, in terms of fostering a scientific worldview, as well as in the game design employed to make it more engaging. The functionality of the state of the art projects is gathering knowledge from the public to science and not the other way around. In order for citizen science to live up to its potential, a number of factors need to be addressed to better target citizens. The first we like to mention is the fun factor. Citizen science can be fun and motivate people to contribute to science. It seems that the main reason why people participate in citizen science projects is because they feel they can add value by contributing. Citizen science projects need to make citizen contributions more fun and more intrinsically motivating, as well as trying to create a longer lasting appeal by establishing communities and affinity spaces for the participants through meaningful gamification (making the interaction more playful and/or achievement based). A second important aspect is accessibility. Projects should be made more accessible by being web-based or smartphone-based. By doing this, citizens can contribute at any time and from any location.

Another aspect we would like to put forward is ownership. At the level of scientific values, we like to mention review, verification, and filtering. In some projects, field experts review, verify, and filter people's contributions; in other projects, those who contribute most are the ones that review, verify, and filter the contributions; and in still other projects, the contributions are filtered by a computer which compares the results to filter the 'odd ones out.' In order to improve the validity of collaborative citizen scientist reviews and verification processes in future participatory cultures, more care should be invested in fostering the scientific paradigm pertaining to the affinity space these citizen scientists are participating in. We contend that entrenching the communities of citizen science practices in intrinsically motivating and meaningful games can help in reaching such a sufficient scientific level.

Citizen science projects are usually designed to be accessible to ensure as many people as possible can contribute and participate. This is done by either making the subject or field more accessible, or by making the interaction (analysis/data entry) more simple and playful! And this brings us to the role of science institutes, in this case, the public library. In line with the arguments discussed above, it is the library that should encourage the opportunities to practice citizen science and as a result their role should shift from archiving information to processing information to allow citizens the opportunity to participate and create meaning. This new role focuses on 1) offering meaningful information at the right time and right place as part of everyday life; 2) contextualizing information using playful solutions; 3) bringing communities together to share and network information; and 4) enabling new scientific practice in other unexplored fields.

In this project, we focused and played around with the concept of a library practising science. Our starting point was the current behavior of citizens, their needs and desires, and how to encourage the curiosity of people and how to invite people to become engaged in pursuing knowledge and skills and building their own resources to become more autonomous and deal with life's problems around us. It is clear that curiosity engages citizens and elicits learning. Besides, by being connected to others with the same interest, users experience partnership and are willing to cooperate and co-create. This could eventually result in science (or public understanding, so to say) based on alternative theories and lines of thought different from current state of the art science practices.

We all need to play more in order to learn more and hone our skills and stimulate our interest. Citizen science has the ambition to invite and enable people to co-create, participate and explore.

Acknowledgments

This research is part of the project *Persuasive gaming. From theory-based design to validation and back*, funded by the Netherlands Organisation for Scientific Research (NWO; 2013-2018; project number 314-99-106). We are grateful to the City Council of Eindhoven for their financial support, as well as to the students who contributed to this chapter: Robert van Kampen, Milan Knust Graitchen, Doenja Oogjes, and Sam Janssen.

References

Aron, J., 2011. How innovative is Apple's new voice assistant, Siri? *New Scientist* 212 (2836): 24.

Bogost, I. 2007. *Persuasive games: The expressive power of videogames*. Cambridge, MA: The MIT Press.

Cornell Lab of Ornithology. 2008. *CamClickr.* [browser]. Cornell University. Game.

Deen, M., and B. A. M. Schouten. 2011. Games that motivate to learn: Designing serious games by identified regulations. In *Handbook of research on improving learning and motivation through educational games: Multidisciplinary approaches*, ed. P. Felicia, 330-351. Hershey: IGI Global.

—. 2014. The differences between problem-based and drill and practice games on motivations to learn. *International Journal of Gaming and Computer-Mediated Simulations* 7 (3): 44-59.

Gee, J. P. 2004. Learning by design: Games as learning machines. *Interactive Educational Multimedia* 8:15-23.

—. 2005. Semiotic social spaces and affinity spaces. In *Beyond communities of practice: Language, power and social context*, eds. D. Barton and K. Tusting, 214-232. New York: Cambridge University Press.

Hummels, C., and J. Frens. 2011. Designing disruptive innovative systems, products and services: RTD process. In *Industrial design: New frontiers*, ed. D. A. Coelho, 147-172. London: Intech Open Access Publisher.

Isbister, K. 2011. Emotion and motion: Games as inspiration for shaping the future of interface. *Interactions* 18 (5): 24-27.

Jenkins, H. 2009. *Confronting the challenges of participatory culture: Media education for the 21st century.* Cambridge, MA: The MIT Press.

Jonas, W. 2007. Design research and its meaning to the methodological development of the discipline. In *Design research now,* ed. R. Michel, 187-206. Basel: Birkhäuser.

Lévy, P. 1997. *Collective intelligence: Mankind's emerging world in cyberspace.* Trans. R. Bononno. Cambridge, MA: Perseus Books.

Lombardi, M. M. 2007. Authentic learning for the 21st century: An overview. *Educause Learning Initiative* 1:1-12.

Malone, T. 1981. Toward a theory of intrinsically motivating instruction. *Cognitive Science* 4:333-369.

Mojang. 2011. *Minecraft.* [multiplatform]. Mojang/Microsoft Studios. Game.

Oblinger, D., and J. Oblinger. 2005. Is it age or IT: First steps toward understanding the net generation. *Educating the Net Generation* 2 (1-2): 20.

Przybylski, A. K., C. S. Rigby, and R. M. Ryan. 2010. A motivational model of video game engagement. *Review of General Psychology* 14 (2): 154-166.

Robertson, M. 2010. Can't play, won't play. *Hide&Seek.* http://www.hideandseek.net/2010/10/06/cant-play-wont-play.

Ryan, R. M., and E. L. Deci. 2000. Self-determination theory and the facilitation of intrinsic motivation, social development, and well-being. *American Psychologist* 55 (1): 68-78.

Schouten B. A. M. 2015. Playful empowerment. Inaugural address at the Amsterdam University of Applied Sciences, 12 May 2015. Amsterdam: Amsterdam University Press.

Sein, M., O. Henfridsson, S. Purao, M. Rossi, and R. Lindgren. 2011. Action design research. *MIS Quarterly* 35 (1): 37-56.

Shaffer, D. 2006. Epistemic frames for epistemic games. *Computers & Education* 46 (3): 223-234.

Squire, K. 2003. Video games in education. *International Journal of Intelligent Games & Simulation* 2 (1): 49-62.

University of Washington Center for Game Science/Department of Biochemistry. 2008. *Foldit*. [browser]. University of Washington. Game.

Van der Spek, E. D. 2012. Towards designing for competence and engagement in serious games. In *Proceedings of the 3rd international conference on serious games development and applications, Bremen, September 26-29, 2012*, 98-109. Berlin, Heidelberg: Springer.

Voss, M. A., and C. B. Cooper. 2010. Using a free online citizen-science project to teach observation & quantification of animal behavior. *The American Biology Teacher* 72 (7): 437-443.

Wikipedia. 2015. Foldit. *Wikipedia*. http://en.wikipedia.org/wiki/Foldit.

Wired Differently. 2012. *Eyewire*. [browser]. MIT. Game.

Wouters, P., E. D. van der Spek, and H. van Oostendorp. 2009. Current practices in serious game research: A review from a learning outcomes perspective. In *Games-based learning advancements for multisensory human computer interfaces: Techniques and effective practices*, eds. T. Connolly, M. Stansfield, and L. Boyle, 232-255. Hershey: IGI Global.

Zimmerman, E. 2007. Gaming literacy: Game design as a model for literacy in the twenty-first century. *Harvard Interactive Media Review* 1 (1): 23-31.

About the authors

Ellis Bartholomeus started her career as an industrial designer at the Design Academy in Eindhoven. Via signage, graphic, web, and interaction design she became a game designer and created over 50 serious games in ten years with Laika.nl. In 2010, she became eager to become involved in greater depth with the use of gaming as a medium and a tool, in order to discover and research the magical features and mysteries in play that allow a player to become more autonomous, gain competencies, and become socially more connected to others. As a game researcher and game consultant, she spends all her time in Wonderland and learning about play and motivation.

Daniël Harmsen is a professional Game Designer at IJsfontein, based in Amsterdam, where he designs serious games for a broad audience and on a wide range of topics. One of his latest projects, The Canon of Dutch History for the Open Air Museum in Arnhem, the Netherlands, landed the Silver award at the European Design Awards 2018 and the International Award at the Museums + Heritage Awards for Excellence.

Ben Schouten is Full Professor of Playful Interactions in Intelligent Systems. In addition, he is scientific director of education at the Amsterdam University of Applied Sciences. He is an advisor for the European Commission on the Internet of Things as well as for the Dutch Cultural Media Fund, responsible for E-culture. Schouten is interested in games and play design for social innovations, citizen empowerment, and culture. Schouten was the general chair of the renowned CHI PLAY 2017 conference and co-founder of the Games for Health Conference series. He has co-edited several scientific volumes, such as the proceedings of the *5th International Joint Conference of Ambient Intelligence* and the thematic issue of the *Journal of Ambient Intelligent Systems* (2013) on playful interactions and serious games.

Erik van der Spek is Assistant Professor of Game and Play Design. He is the chair of the Industrial Design Department Council and secretary of the International Federation for Information Processing Technical Committee on Entertainment Computing (TC14). His research interests are the design of games and play for entertainment, learning, vitality, and empathy. From playful interaction to immersive VR experiences, Van der Spek tries to discover the elements that engage us to construct imaginary magic circles, to have cathartic mediated presence experiences in fantasy environments, and that stimulate us to see the world in a newfound light. In addition to his TC14 work, Van der Spek has been the student game competition chair for CHI PLAY and supervises more than 60 student games per year, some of which have won national or international prizes and recognition.

13. Laborious playgrounds: Citizen science games as new modes of work/play in the digital age

Sonia Fizek and Anne Dippel

Abstract

Via citizen science games, players are invited to contribute to the production of knowledge. In their chapter, Fizek and Dippel see the games as laborious playgrounds, with qualities associated previously with leisure or pastimes *and* with productive or useful time. The chapter investigates citizen science games as new modes of work/play, surpassing a strictly dualistic mode of thinking and showing how the capital-oriented logic of a productive human existence is encoded into play. Fizek and Dippel argue that such blurring lines lead us into an age of post-ludification, urging us to consider these playful technologies and phenomena as empowering, engaging, and participatory, or to observe them with caution, restraint, or even suspicion.

Keywords: Citizen science games, work/play interference, playbor, post-ludification, productive play, capitalism

If anything could be said to characterize new modes of work/play, it would be precisely this sort of interplay.
– O'Donnell 2014, 12

The computer screen gradually fills up with ever more complex geometrical patterns. Thousands of players go online to combine and rearrange colorful building blocks. With every level, the shapes become more refined, the patters harder to build, and the achievements more difficult to obtain. The leaderboards with the highest scores are published online and available

Glas, R., S. Lammes, M. de Lange, J. Raessens, and I. de Vries, eds. 2019. *The Playful Citizen. Civic Engagement in a Mediatized Culture.* Amsterdam: Amsterdam University Press.
DOI: 10.5117/9789462984523/CH13

to the entire playing community. The in-game mission outcomes are also shared via social media platforms.

The game outlined above would not differ substantially from other abstract online digital puzzles, such as *Bejeweled* (PopCap Games 2001) or *Candy Crush Saga* (King 2012), if it were not for one crucial detail—its collaborative drive for an external goal. *EteRNA* (Carnegie Mellon University and Stanford University 2010) constitutes a big data-driven digital laboratory ("Solve Puzzles. Invent Medicine"), where more than 38,000 citizen player-scientists assemble shapes representing ribonucleic acids (RNAs), tiny molecules that are the basis of every living cell. The best virtual RNA designs are selected and synthesized in the biochemistry laboratory at Stanford.

Like numerous other citizen science games (also known as serious games, human-based computation games, or games with a purpose, GWAP), *EteRNA* is an example of a much broader playful/laborious phenomenon. The term itself is opening up three significant fields for the understanding of citizen science games as playful collaborations for a common goal lying outside the game itself.

The 'citizen' emphasizes the importance of the collaborative social element, lying at the etymological heart of the Proto-Germanic word 'game' (*ga*—together, *mann*—man). In digital games such as *EteRNA*, large numbers of citizens are crucial, for their collaborative endeavors not only influence the gameworld, but more importantly reach outside of it, and contribute to the production of knowledge. The 'scientific' dimension provides an external goal for the citizen players. It is placed in the realm of seriousness, associated with work. The 'game' on the other hand, with its freedom of action within internal rules, achievement-based mechanics, and playful aesthetics, belongs to the realm of play performed for entertainment. Those three aspects become the points of departure in the analysis of this phenomenon as a work and play interference, where both qualities permeate each other.

Citizen science games can be discussed in terms of the gamification (Deterding et al. 2011) of science (introducing playful elements into an originally non-game context), but this explanation seems to be leading in one direction only—play entering the non-game domain and changing it into a playful entity. However, in this encounter, not only the gamified or ludified activity changes, but also play itself is undergoing transformation. Citizen science games may be perceived as laborious playgrounds, placed between the two poles of *ludus* and *labora,* oscillating between qualities associated previously with leisure or pastime and with productive or useful time.

In the following sections, drawing upon interdisciplinary academic approaches of game studies, media theory and socio-cultural anthropology, we are going to discuss this relationship, and analyze citizen science games as new modes of work/play, where both qualities overlap or even hybridize.

Collaborative gaming with a purpose

> We're calling on gamers to help connect the dots by playing a game to map the brain.
>
> – Wired Differently 2012

Large collaborative online environments, including some citizen science games, are the most recent incarnation of ideas that were put into practice already a few decades ago. The first attempts to use the collaborative power of humankind in combination with games were proposed at the beginning of the 1960s by Buckminister Fuller, who introduced the *World Game*, an educational simulation for solving problems of overpopulation and the uneven distribution of global resources. As the author himself claimed, he had played it without the assistance of computers since 1927. The *World Game* that Fuller envisioned was to be a place where individuals or teams of people compete, or cooperate, in order to "[m]ake the world work, for 100% of humanity, in the shortest possible time, through spontaneous cooperation, without ecological offense or the disadvantage of anyone" (Buckminister Fuller Institute n.d.). Fuller conceptualized a playful systemic tool that could engage large numbers of participants in a strategic game based on statistical data about the world, its minerals, manufactured goods and services, humans and their needs (Buckminister Fuller Institute n.d.). However, what he did not have at his disposal, were the essential components of today's collaborative digital games with purpose: big data, the calculating machine able to process the deluge of information, and a network that would connect thousands of minds. The turning point came in 1989 with the invention of the World Wide Web (at CERN by Tim Berners-Lee). Its emergence led to the development of a new gameplay phenomena—a massively multiplayer online game (MMOG).[1] It is only in the 1990s and the beginning of 2000s that a game world could be populated by millions of players simultaneously. One of the most

1 The first multiplayer real time virtual worlds, such as Multi User Dungeons (MUDs) emerged at the end of 1970s. They could be, however, played online exclusively as experiments in the ARPANET network or within internal university networks.

recognizable MMORPG titles, *World of Warcraft* (Blizzard Entertainment 2004), in its peak had twelve million active players (Statista, n.d.).

What if those millions of participants, instead of performing fictitious online battles, were united in order to solve existing and potentially problematic scenarios, following Fuller's vision? Collectively, we spend a few billion hours a week gaming. Why not turn this abundance of pastime into productive time, and collaborative gameplay into socially positive ends, —asks game designer Jane McGonigal (2010, 2011). In order to achieve this McGonigal used Alternate Reality Games (ARGs), combining the physical world with the online world, where she emphasizes role play turns into real-play. In 2007, ITVS Interactive launched *World Without Oil* online as "a massively collaborative imagining of the first 32 weeks of a global oil crisis." The players contributed with their own stories and possible scenarios via email, fora, uploading video material, or comics. The game attracted 1,800 players. *Evoke* (World Bank Institute 2010), the next collaborative ARG, brought together more than 20,000 people all over the world with a common goal to find solutions to the most urgent social problems, such as food shortages, water crises, or women's empowerment, among others.

The productive, anticipatory, and systemic real-play has been refined further in the most recent collaborative ludic phenomena—citizen science games. In contrast to previous ARGs, citizen science games unite all the players online within a consistent game platform with specific rules and tasks to perform. Within these big data collaborative play spaces, players solve puzzles, categorize, identify and tag data, participate in challenges, and by doing so contribute to the advancement of scientific research. The free digital labor (Scholz 2013) of thousands of amateur science-players helps researchers deal with various subjects, from biology, neuroscience, astronomy, high-energy physics, to linguistics and history of art, among others. With these citizen science games, the players can predict protein patterns (the earlier mentioned *EteRNA*), map neural retina pathways (*Eyewire*, Wired Differently 2012), classify the morphologies of galaxies (*Galaxy Zoo*, Galaxy Zoo Team 2007), program algorithms identifying the Higgs boson (*Higgs Boson Machine Learning Challenge*, CERN 2014), tag social language (*Metropolitalia*, Ludwig-Maximilian University of Munich 2012), and art works (*ARTigo*, Ludwig-Maximilian University of Munich 2010).

One of the first digital citizen science games was *Foldit* (University of Washington Center for Game Science/Department of Biochemistry 2008). It was developed as an online challenge of synthesizing molecules. The input from the online playful laboratory turned out to be so successful that its initial prototype, developed as a science project at Stanford and

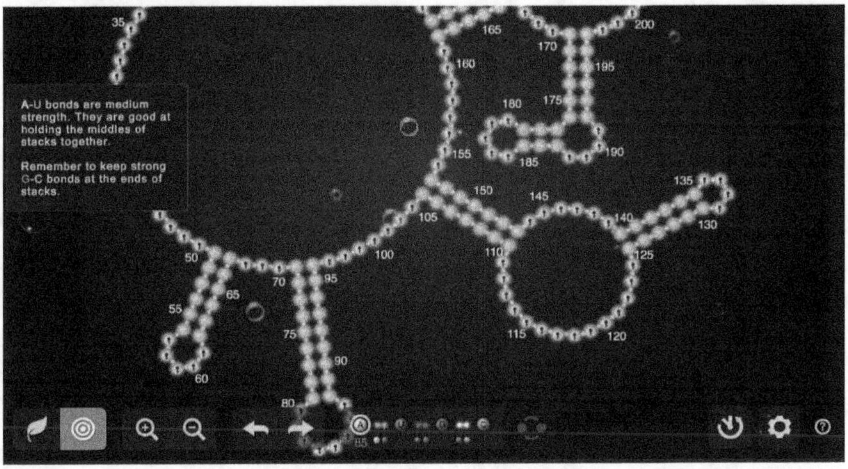

13.1: A screenshot showing gameplay in *EteRNA*.

Carnegie Mellon Universities, was transformed into a worldwide ludic experiment renamed *EteRNA* (see Figure 13.1). Its gameplay is based on the complex pattern recognition process. The player's task is to assemble shapes representing ribonucleic acids (RNAs). Since humans are currently much more efficient in deciphering and predicting the structures of proteins than existing computer algorithms, the initiators of the project decided to use the form of an online puzzle to attract potential participants. Their actions are collected in a big data assemblage with the aim to improve the development of algorithms for pattern recognition.

Big data collaborative games and challenges have become such an effective scientific tool in the past few years that they led to the development of entire online platforms for collaborative volunteer research projects such as *Kaggle* or *Zooniverse*, among others, where academic institutions and research centers create their own games and outsource the tasks to citizens around the world.

Those lofty and idealistic attempts to change the world by turning gaming into something productive embody what Alexander Galloway (2012) refers to as contemporary romantico-cybernetic understanding of play. On the one hand, play is perceived as a spontaneous, careless, and almost childlike activity. On the other hand, in many instances, it has become almost synonymous with complex iterative systems. Commercialization and systematization of play, gamification, or productive collective gaming operate in accordance with the systemic and structural quality of play. At the same time, they draw from the Huizingian spirit, associating play with something pure, almost poetic, and above all else meant to entice pleasure. And this romantico-cybernetic fusion invites people into the world of something they intuitively associate with pleasure and frivolity, all the while performing productive tasks for an external purpose.

Work and play interference

> Play turns to seriousness and seriousness to play.
> – Huizinga 1938/1992, 8

The process of blurring the lines of work-play and seriousness-playfulness was first described in the last chapter of *Homo ludens* (1938/1992), in which Johan Huizinga discusses the loss of purity of a frivolous playful experience and focuses on the confusion of where play ends and non-play begins. To support his claim, he uses the example of professional sports, which systematizes pure play and corrupts it through the principles of paid work. He then moves on to the world of commercial rivalry and emphasizes the *agon* element in business, noticing that "some of the great business concerns deliberately instill the play-spirit into their workers so as to step up production" (Huizinga 1938/1992, 200). By doing so, according to Huizinga, they turn business into play, and as a result play becomes business. The two allegedly mutually exclusive aspects of human practice, work and play, interfere and transform the everyday life. Their boundaries collapse and as a result playfulness leaks into labor, and the latter unfolds moments of drudgery within play.

The Huizingian distinction between play and work, and the portrayal of the latter as a productive and paid activity indirectly relates to the Marxist understanding of work ethics and productivity. For Karl Marx, work is defined as a useful and productive activity that may be translated into the value of commodities produced. It is also part of a natural human behavior, "a productive expenditure of human brain, muscle, nerve, hand, etc." (Marx 1887/2015). In the *Grundrisse,* he also points out the Abrahamic definition of work as toil that seems to have been placed on human shoulders at the moment of the ancestral sin: "In the sweat of thy face shalt thou eat bread, till thou return unto the ground; for out of it wast thou taken: for dust thou art, and unto dust shalt thou return" (Holy Bible 2011). While the foundational text of Abrahamic monotheism represents work in terms of a curse leveled upon humans by God, Marx departs from this perspective and defines work as a chance for the "individual's self-realization," an a priori act of utmost freedom, which encompasses happiness, even if throughout history mostly corrupted, self-alienated forms of work or "external forms of labour" have emerged (1858/1973, 611). In this, he rejects the understanding of Adam Smith, who argued that work "obtains its measure from the outside through the aim to be attained and the obstacles to be overcome in attaining it" (Elster 1999, 59).

The differentiation between work and play appears already in Aristotle's *Nicomachean ethics* (1971). Both qualities, according to Aristotle, are required in order to achieve happiness and freedom. Gregory Bateson (1972), on the other hand, differentiates between play and combat, drawing from the animal kingdom. Here, playing is opposed to serious activities required for the sustainment of life or defense from danger. With such dualisms, Brian-Sutton Smith (1997) notices the rhetoric of frivolity, which carries in itself an implicit work ethic, moving play into the domain of fun, non-seriousness, and nonsense. Salen and Zimermann notice that in modern times this sort of rhetoric inverts the classic work ethic view of play, "against which all the other rhetoric exist as rhetoric of rebuttal" (2004, 305).

Games and play seem to be determined by their self-sufficiency and closely defined "magic circle," which is creating a temporary world within the ordinary one (Huizinga 1938/1992, 10). They remain at the opposite end of drudgery as long as they are non-serious (Ibid.), unproductive (Caillois 1958/2001, 10), joyous (Scheuerl 1979, 69), and utterly absorbing (Huizinga 1938/1992, 10), making the players lose themselves in the constellation of playful time and space. The magic element within the play experience points toward the very suspension of time, as if past and future did not exist. The time within play is defined and perceived as pastime, for the players need to be entirely captured by the game in order to play it. Pastime seems to synchronize permanence and simultaneity and encloses them within what the German pedagogue Hans Scheuerl (1979, 69) defines as presence and inner endlessness. The experience of being suspended in time and lost within the game, yet not necessarily in the magic circle, has also been theorized from the perspectives of flow (Csikszentmihalyi 1990/2008) and incorporation (Salen and Zimmerman 2004; Calleja 2011).

Following the above logic, we may come to the conclusion that play itself makes no sense, but simply exists within its internal logic. Play creates sense and meaning and presents this to its players. In contrast to work, it does not need any external references to be defined as such. Play carries its goal in itself. It is *autotelic*.

Unlike play, work is perceived a productive activity, which leads to meaningful, often profit-oriented goals. The Middle Ages had associated work with till and hardship. In the thirteenth century, labor (from Latin *laborem*) designated a task to be performed. By the late fourteenth century, it was mostly associated with exertion of the body, possibly originating from the notion of 'tottering under a burden' (from Latin *labere*). Not without a reason, in the Anglo-Saxon linguistic tradition, the term also designates the suffering women experience while 'in labor.' Etymologically, labor seems to be connected with productivity, effort, and suffering, qualities which fundamentally differ from play. The laborious effort is undertaken for the value of work lies outside of it and is encapsulated in its produced commodities. Work is therefore *exotelic*.

In the digital age, the differentiation between work and play gradually disappears and dissolves into playbor (Lund 2015), and while doing so, it encodes the Protestant and capital-oriented logic of a productive human existence into play. As much as play enters the allegedly play-free domains of life, such as the workspace, seemingly non-ludic practices pervade playgrounds. And it is precisely at the intersection between those ostensibly distinct practices of play and work, or playfulness and seriousness, where new spaces and forms come into being; where the lines between the imaginary, the symbolic and the real are blurred.

The digital machine itself unites those two seemingly mutually exclusive qualities. On the one hand, a computer is a digital calculator based on mathematical game theory (Von Neumann 1928), performing work-related tasks; on the other hand, it is an entertainment center used in free time. From its early years the computer has found itself entangled at the intersection between work and leisure-related playful activities. It served as a computing and simulating aid at governmental departments, universities, research and cultural institutions. At the same time, that very same assemblage of hardware and software was used to program the first games. In 1961, a group of researchers at the Massachusetts Institute of Technology developed *Spacewar!* (Russel 1961), a space combat simulation, in order to demonstrate the capacities of the computing machines to the public in a compelling way. Today, in the developed parts of the world, the most popular digital machines (personal computers, smartphones, or tablets) are an indispensable part of work and leisure, permeating both spaces.

As Joost Raessens (2010, 6) notices when discussing the ludification of culture, play is not only characteristic of leisure, but also now turns up in domains that were hitherto considered the opposite of play, such as education (e.g. educational games), politics (playful forms of campaigning, using gaming principles to involve party members in decision making processes) and even warfare (interfaces resembling computer games, the use of drones—unmanned remote-controlled devices—introducing war à la PlayStation). This flooding of life with game elements leads naturally to the presence of play (the activity of play) and playfulness (the attitude of play) in the domains previously reserved for or associated with serious endeavors, such as work. However, in order to understand these play-centered dynamics we need to realize that the process of ludification of culture is not a one-way street. Our everyday life and work practices might resemble play. But equally, our playgrounds seem to be turning into workspaces. As Alexander Galloway emphasizes, "labor itself is now play, just as play becomes more and more laborious" (2012, 29).

This reciprocal effect has also been discussed in Walz and Deterding's work entitled *The gameful world* (2015), which is devoted to the ludification of various domains of life. They hold that not only games and play are moving toward the center of our cultural, social, and economic existence, but also other realms of life impress their forms onto play (Walz and Deterding 2015, 7). Games migrate into new, also non-leisure, territories and, while doing so, undergo changes. The latter phenomenon, in contrast to the ludification of culture is referred to as the cultivation of ludus. Following the same logic, we have introduced the concept of *laborization* (Dippel and Fizek 2015) as a contrasting term to that of gamification (Deterding et al. 2011)[2] or ludification (Raessens 2006, 2010, 2014; Mäyra 2015). It denotes the process of the permeation of play with work elements. However, the work-play relationship is neither fully embraced by the concepts of gamification and ludification, nor that of laborization.

In order to cover the overlay of the work-play relationship, we are proposing the concept of *interference*, borrowing a term that originally was used in the field of physics to denote the superposition of waves. This concept allows us to describe the interactions between phenomena, and their transformative character. The elements, dynamics, and logics of play are moved into the workspace, and by doing so they modify it (ludification). At the same time the opposite process of influencing play with the elements of work is taking place (laborization). The proposed *work/play interference model* (see Figure 13.2) delineates the relation between supposedly non-productive playful activities and productive work-related behaviors. It illustrates the dissolving distinction between the two qualities, and surpasses a strictly dualistic mode of thinking. By doing so it has the chance to characterize the complexities and impurities of social praxis more accurately.

2 In its purely mechanistic understanding, gamification is described as the implementation of game design elements into originally non-game contexts with the aim of influencing human behavior.

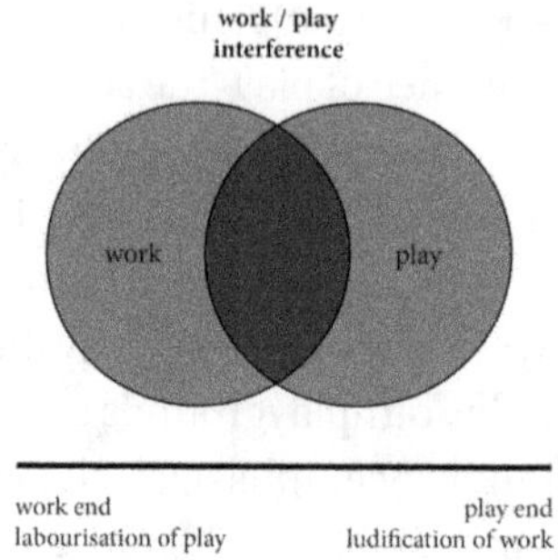

13.2: A diagrammatic visualization of the work and play continuum as a work/play interference model created by the authors.

Within the model of interference, work and play appear as polar modalities of human interaction. On the one hand, they may be described separately from each other. On the other hand, they influence each other reciprocally, and within the moment of hermeneutical analysis and empirical research may be observed in their overlaying condition (Dippel and Fizek 2015). When the seriousness of work turns into jolly playfulness, and when the playful frivolousness transforms back into serious work, one may observe the processes of work-play interference.

Online citizen science ludic laboratories are considered a priori pleasurable and leisure-oriented game spaces, they are especially successful in enabling "productive activities of connected human minds" (Terranova 2013, 42). The players make a voluntary decision to contribute to the digital economy. They are not motivated by monetary compensation for hours of their immaterial work. Like other participants in the digital economy (fan fiction writers, 'modders,' amateur web designers), they are acting out of the desire for cultural production. They are willingly contributing to the development of knowledge, being motivated and rewarded at numerous levels from the internal elements of the game's system itself, including points, levels, and badges, to their status among the gaming community. *EteRNA* operates according to reinforcement strategies based on leveling up. The player folds the ever more complex patterns and is awaiting the results, while watching the animated test-tube simulating a chemical process. Such animations introduce a dramatic climax that may be resolved in the epiphany of a successful protein assemblage, and allow the players to experience little eureka moments within the game. Those scientific discoveries reinforced by the numerical system give the player a luring promise of completion. The motivation to perform playful citizen science is also enticed by external factors, such as the will to contribute to something greater than the game itself. The scientists recognize the citizen community's efforts, and test the protein fold-up results of the best players in their laboratories or acknowledge the players in academic papers. This immediate leverage of a playful and pleasant activity with socially productive outcome, the element of competition in a large collaborative environment, and the feeling of belonging to a research community with a common goal, form the basis of citizen science games as examples of the work/play interference.

What remains fascinating in this work/play constellation is the relationship between the human, the machine, and the data. The human agents contributing to research in the big data collaborative online games for science are of two kinds—the scientist and the citizen science player. Their roles played out in the human-machine assemblage are distinct and contrasting although both of them rely upon ludic simulation. A team of scientists in the laboratory analyze the already sieved data in search of significant pieces. The deluge of data is beforehand classified, labeled, and identified by players, each sitting in front of their own computer, which together with thousands of other calculating machines form a networked production line. In this sense, citizen science games resemble virtual assembly lines where big data is mined in an iterative factory-like system. The machine, on the other hand, stores the big data, runs the game, calculates the results delivered by thousands of players, communicates between the players and the scientific team, and networks the whole community. Most importantly, it learns from human behavior.

Into the age of interferences and postludification

> [W]hat becomes of games when the sharp line dividing their ideal rules from the diffuse and insidious laws of daily life is blurred?
>
> – Caillois 1958/2001, 43

Playing is a fundamental human activity (Tomasello 1999, 91). There is no culture known to ethnologists, historians, archaeologists, or missionaries that has been devoid of games (Bally 1966, 61; Mäyra 2008, 37). Some researchers argue that play itself is a mode of fun and as such a universal quality, not only an attribute of humans (Graeber 2014). The proclaimed century of play we are currently experiencing is not necessarily a novelty. Already in 1751 Daniel Bernoulli, a Swiss mathematician and physicist, wrote, "The century that we live in could be subsumed in the history books as: Free Spirits' Journal and the Century of Play" (Bernoulli 1751/1769, 387;

quoted in Bauer 2006, 377 and Fuchs 2014, 131).[3] Moreover, a few decades before Zimmerman wrote the 'Manifesto for a ludic century' (2014) and the ludification of culture entered academic discourse (Raessens 2006, 2010, 2014), Huizinga and Brian Sutton-Smith were analyzing play as a universal cultural element or state-of-mind, permeating other domains of our lives—from language, myths, rituals (Huizinga 1938/1992, 13) to thought games, television, theater, sexual intimacy, humor, celebrations and festivals, or gossip (Sutton-Smith 1997, 5).

The above examples point to a great diversity of play and the extension of play through other domains of life. They all, however, belong to the sphere of free time and entertainment. What has changed in our digital times is not so much the extent to which games permeate our everyday, but more importantly the interfering spaces of this permeation. As we have shown with the example of citizen science games, play has entered domains that previously had little to do with joyousness. In the case of games with purpose, play is as much a frivolous as a productive activity.

Also, such free-time activities as fan fiction writing, modifying existing software and video games (developing 'mods'), managing communities, or sharing content via social networks, are being monetized and respectively 'laborized.' Those leisure-related, playful and free activities are assigned monetary value and become products of the digital economy. After all, free labor is not only based upon the idealism of creative abundance and community building, but also on the capitalistic understanding of knowledge as added value. More importantly, free digital labor is performed voluntarily and is perceived as a pleasant activity—"[i]t does not feel, look, or smell like labor at all" (Scholz 2013, 2). And this aspect is particularly interesting as it further blurs the distinction between playfulness and work.

The complexities of work and play and their mutual interdependencies and superpositions are also the subject of a recent anthropological study, describing and analyzing the collaborative work practices among video game developers and the significance of play in their workspace respectively (O'Donnell 2014). Building upon the work of T. L. Taylor (2006, 72-73), O'Donnell refers to this playful labor or laborious play dimension as *work/play interplay*, and observes the overlaps on numerous levels, from the collaborative team work and the playful work conduct to the very arrangement of space in companies, where employees can climb,

3 In its original form: "Das gegenwärtige Jahrhundert konnte man in den Geschichtsbüchern nicht besser, als unter dem Titel: Das Freygeister-Journal und Spielsaeculum nennen" (Bernoulli 1751/1769, 387).

play volleyball, or lift weights. As idyllic as this vision of labor may seem, O'Donnel emphasizes that the new modes of work practice, based on the blurred distinction between what is work and what is play, may as well dissolve into "destructive work practices" (2015, 31). For as much as such playful work scheme encourages people to think creatively, it also pushes them to invest more time into work, giving the video game producers and publishers the possibility of extending the developer's work week even up to 80 hours.

Caillois considered this blurring of fictitious boundaries and the permeability of the magic circle as a contamination and corruption of play. In his reasoning, the four elements of play (*agon, alea, mimicry, ilinx*) when devoid of playful convention transform into destructive activities, such as violence (the corruption of competition), superstition (the corruption of chance), alienation (the corruption of simulation), or alcoholism and drug addiction (the corruption of vertigo) (Caillois 1958/2001, 53-54).

The capital-oriented forms of laborized play or ludified work and the destructive human drives described by Caillois introduce yet another form of skepticism with regards to citizen science games. Here, it is the interference between human and non-human players that may cause concerns. Currently, humans are excelling at solving puzzles and predicting patterns—skills, which form the basis of citizen science gameplay. However, the unparalleled power of the human brain in pattern recognition may soon be challenged by such algorithms as EteRNAbot, which is already on its way to synthesizing excellence. The learning digital machine is enticing fears born in the age of industrialization. The uncertainties of the past are mirrored in the digital age as journalists paint bleak visions of future games, in which humans are not competing against one another, not even against the machine, but in which we all serve as "intelligence-gathering slaves" in a playful factory simulated by a digital brain, playing with human pawns (Koerner 2012). We should realize, however, that such fearsome visions are still deeply rooted in the model of human-machine co-existence, where the main role of people is to supervise the machines, and the main role of the machines is to obediently perform upon the human command. In the digital times, when the machines and algorithms are ever more present and refined, we need to constantly re-negotiate and re-think our place in the playful and laborious places of everyday.

It is precisely such interferences, interplays, transgressions, crossed boundaries, or blurred lines, which paint a large part of the present ludic landscape, and lead to the rise of the new modes of play. And these are possibly taking us into the age of *postludification*. The age in which we are not only saturating the everyday with playful forms of expression, but also immersing frivolous play in productivity and labor. Or as Sicart also puts it, moving play into the realms of efficiency, seriousness, and technical determinism (Sicart 2014, 5). At the outbreak of the *postludic* era proposed here, we need to decide whether we are embracing the transgressing playful technologies and phenomena as empowering, engaging, and participatory, or observing them with caution, restraint, or even suspicion in Caillois' spirit.

References

Aristotle. 1971. *Nikomachische Ethik*. Leipzig: Reclam Verlag.

Bally, G. 1966. *Vom Spielraum der Freiheit. Die Bedeutung des Spiels bei Tier und Mensch*. Basel/Stuttgart: Schwabe.

Bateson, G. 1972. *Steps to an ecology of mind*. Chicago, IL: University of Chicago Press.

Bauer, G. 2006. Mozart, Kavalier und Spieler. In *Mozart: Experiment Aufklarung*, ed. H. Lachmayer, 377-388. Ostfildern: Hatje Cantz.

Bernoulli, D. 1751/1769. In *Anonym, Die Kunst die Welt erlaubt mitzunehmen in den verschiedenen Arten der Spiele, so in Gesellschaften höhern Standes, besonders in der Kayserlich-Königlichen Residenz-Stadt Wien üblich sind*, Bd. II, Nürnberg.

Blizzard Entertainment. 2004. *World of Warcraft*. [Windows/OS X]. Blizzard Entertainment. Game.

Buckminster Fuller Institute. n.d. *World Game*. [browser]. Buckminster Fuller Institute. Game.

Caillois, R. 1958/2001. *Man, play, and games*. Trans. M. Barash. Chicago, IL: University of Illinois Press.

Calleja, G. 2011. *In-game: From immersion to incorporation*. Cambridge, MA: The MIT Press.

Carnegie Mellon University and Stanford University. 2010. *EteRNA* [browser]. Carnegie Mellon University/Stanford University. Game.

CERN (Conseil Européen pour la Recherche Nucléaire). 2014. *Higgs Boson Machine Learning Challenge*. [browser]. Game.

Csikszentmihalyi, M. 1990/2008. *Flow: The psychology of optimal experience*. New York: Harper Perennial Modern Classics.

Deterding, S., R. Khaled, L. E. Nacke, and D. Dixon. 2011. Gamification: Toward a definition. http://gamification-research.org/wp-content/uploads/2011/04/02-Deterding-Khaled-Nacke-Dixon.pdf.

Dippel, A., and S. Fizek. 2015. Playful laboratories. The significance of games for knowledge production in the digital age. Paper presented at *DiGRA: Diversity of Play, Lüneburg, Germany, May 14-17, 2015*.

Elster, J. 1999. *Karl Marx: A reader*. New York: Cambridge University Press.

Fuchs, M. 2014. Predigital precursors of gamification. In *Rethinking gamification*, eds. M. Fuchs, S. Fizek, P. Ruffino, and N. Schrape. Lüneburg: meson press.

Galaxy Zoo Team. 2007. *Galaxy Zoo*. [browser]. The Citizen Science Alliance. Game.

Galloway, A. 2012. *The interface effect*. Malden, MA: Polity Press.

Graeber, D. 2014. What's the point if we can't have fun? *The Baffler*. January. http://thebaffler.com/salvos/whats-the-point-if-we-cant-have-fun.

Holy Bible. 2011. Genesis 3:19. In *Holy Bible: King James version*. New York: HarperCollins Publishers.

Huizinga, J. 1938/1992. *Homo ludens: A study of the play-element in culture*. Boston, MA: Beacon Press.

ITVS Interactive. 2007. *World Without Oil*. http://worldwithoutoil.org. Multimedia.

King. 2012. *Candy Crush Saga*. [multiplatform]. King. Game.

Koerner I. B. 2012. New videogame lets amateur researchers mess with RNA. *Wired*. http://www.wired.com/2012/07/ff_rnagame.

Ludwig-Maximilian University of Munich. 2010. *ARTigo*. [browser]. http://www.artigo.org.

—. 2012. *Metropolitalia*. [browser]. http://www.metropolitalia.org.

Lund, A. 2015. A contribution to a critique of the concept playbour. In *Reconsidering value and labour in the digital age*, eds. C. Fuchs and E. Fisher, 63-79. Houndmills: Palgrave Macmillan.

Marx, K. 1858/1973. *Grundrisse: Introduction to the critique of political economy*. Trans. M. Nicolaus. New York: Random House.

—. 1887/2015. The fetishism of commodities and the secret thereof. In *Capital: A critique of political economy*. http://www.marxists.org/archive/marx/works/1867-c1/ch01.htm#S2.

Mäyra, F. 2008. *An introduction to game studies: Games in culture*. London: Sage Publications.

—. 2015. Playful culture: Are we undergoing a ludic turn? Keynote lecture at Clash of Realities, Cologne, Germany, Nov. 4, 2015.

McGonigal, J. 2010. Gaming can make a better world. http://www.ted.com/talks/jane_mcgonigal_gaming_can_make_a_better_world.

—. 2011. *Reality is broken: Why games make us better and how they can change the world*. New York: Penguin Press.

O'Donnell, C. 2014. *The developer's dilemma: The secret world of video game creators*. Cambridge, MA: The MIT Press.

PopCap Games. 2001. *Bejeweled*. [multiplatform]. PopCap Games. Game.

Raessens, J. 2006. Playful identities, or the ludification of culture. *Games and Culture* 1 (1): 52-57.

—. 2010. *Homo ludens 2.0: The ludic turn in media theory*, Inaugural Address. Faculty of Humanities, Utrecht University.

—. 2014. The ludification of culture. In *Rethinking gamification*, eds. M. Fuchs, S. Fizek, P. Ruffino, and N. Schrape, 91-114. Lüneburg: meson press.

Russel, Steve. 1961. *Spacewar!*. [PDP-1]. Steve Russel. Game.

Salen, K., and E. Zimmerman. 2004. *Rules of play: Game design fundamentals*. Cambridge, MA: The MIT Press.

Scheuerl, H. 1979. *Das Spiel: Untersuchungen über sein Wesen, seine pädagogischen Möglichkeiten und Grenzen*. Weinheim/Basel: Beltz.

Scholz, T. 2013. Introduction: Why does digital labor matter now? In *Digital labor: The internet as playground and factory*, ed. T. Scholz, 1-9. New York: Routledge.

Sicart, M. 2014. *Play matters*. Cambridge, MA: The MIT Press.

Statista. n.d. Number of World of Warcraft subscribers from 1st quarter 2005 to 3rd quarter 2015 (in millions). *Statista*. http://www.statista.com/statistics/276601/number-of-world-of-warcraft-subscribers-by-quarter.

Sutton-Smith, B. 1997. *The ambiguity of play*. Cambridge, MA: Harvard University Press.

Taylor, T. L. 2006. *Play between worlds: Exploring online gaming culture*. Cambridge, MA: The MIT Press.

Terranova, T. 2013. Free labor. In *Digital labor: The internet as playground and factory*, ed. T. Scholz, 33-57. New York: Routledge.

Tomasello, M. 1999. *A natural history of human cognition*. Cambridge, MA: Harvard University Press.

University of Washington Center for Game Science/Department of Biochemistry. 2008. *Foldit*. [browser]. University of Washington. Game.

Von Neumann, J. 1928. Zur Theorie der Gesellschaftsspiele. *Mathematische Annalen* 100 (1): 295-320.

Walz, S. P., and S. Deterding, eds. 2015. *The gameful world: Approaches, issues, applications*. Cambridge, MA: The MIT Press.

Wired Differently. 2012. *Eyewire*. [browser]. MIT. Game.

World Bank Institute. 2011. *Evoke*. http://www.urgentevoke.com. Multimedia.

About the authors

Sonia Fizek is a digital games and media scholar. Since 2016, she has been holding a lectureship position at the Division of Games and Arts at Abertay University. Her current research focuses on the relationship between digital games and automation. She looks at self-playing games, automated gameplay, and algorithmic players to understand the essence of self-acting playful systems and the fascination with these systems. She is also an active member of the game studies research community as an associate editor of the *Journal of Gaming and Virtual Worlds*, and a board member for multiple initiatives and journals, such as the Digital Games Research Association (British DiGRA), the *Digital Culture and Society Journal, The Polish Journal of Game Studies*, and the *Journal of the Philosophy of Games*.

Anne Dippel is an anthropologist, historian, and poet. In 2015, she published *Dichten und Denken in Österreich: Eine literarische Ethnographie*, a literary ethnography based on two years of field work in Austria. Dippel is a lecturer at the department of European Ethnology and Socio-Cultural Anthropology at the Friedrich-Schiller University Jena and a researcher in the Cluster of Excellence at the Humboldt University of Berlin. She is also a visiting scholar at the Institute for the Advanced Study in Media Cultures of Computer Simulations at Leuphana University Lüneburg. Her most recent research (see www.annedippel.com) focuses on epistemic practices and anthropological conditions of knowledge production at CERN. Playfulness in science is one of multiple aspects she is exploring there.

Part III

Ludo-politics

Introduction to Part III

René Glas, Sybille Lammes, Michiel de Lange, Joost Raessens, and Imar de Vries

In Part III of this volume, the discussions in all the chapters converge on forms of political action enabled by playful media technologies. In the chapter *On participatory politics as a game changer and the politics of participation*, philosopher of technology Mercedes Bunz notes that we cannot simply take the alleged participatory nature of digital media technologies as self-evident. She addresses a similar point to Ingrid Hoofd in Part I, namely how discourses about participatory media are all too easily co-opted. How radical is this gesture really, Bunz asks. She critically unpacks claims about the revolutionary impact of digital technology on society and shows how digital media both facilitate increased participation and the splintering of the public. The idea of playfully 'hacking politics' may help to turn political problems into challenges that can be solved through public participation, but advocating participation can then easily morph into the outsourcing or offloading of state responsibilities onto citizens. Bunz notes how as a corollary many participatory projects have become non-monetary-centered organizations.

With her contribution, Bunz opens up the debate on the potential scope of 'true' political change that playful media can instigate. The chapters that follow take the play perspective to provide new insights into the relationships between digital technology and political action. Critical geographer Sam Hind's contribution, *Playing with politics: Memory, orientation, and tactility*, investigates political agency by highlighting the jovial and carnivalesque qualities of anti-austerity demonstrations in London in 2011. During the March for the Alternative, which attracted over 250,000 protesters, people carried a giant Trojan Horse with them that variously served as a dynamic landmark used in identifying and directing the group of protesters, as a satirical comment, and as a seemingly frivolous 'incident.' In Hind's analysis, such ludic political interventions constitute a playful, material, and performative relationship between digital technology and embodied political action. Hind analyzes three ways in which social media are instrumental in making this work: they enable the production and preservation of memories of protests, they enable the orientation and the navigation of protesters, and they provide a tactile combination of body and action during events. Even though the Trojan Horse was burned afterwards, its political memory lives on thanks to the various social media that captured and commented on its existence.

In *Meaningful inefficiencies: Resisting the logic of technological efficiency in the design of civic systems*, civic media scholars Eric Gordon and Stephen Walter pick up Bunz's notion of digital participation technology as preformatting citizen engagement by highlighting the rhetoric of efficiency that is present in many civic media platforms. Participatory media profess to make interacting with the government more 'user-friendly' or 'customer-friendly,' but in opposition to this narrative Gordon and Walter argue that the true productive power of public engagement lies in creating participatory technologies that do not aim at smooth and seamless usability as their main objective. Building upon the distinction made by Hannah Arendt between labor, work, and action, Gordon and Walter propose that the notion of 'meaningful inefficiency' offers an escape from the co-optation of civic participation as productive labor and work. Meaningful inefficiency as found in play, they argue, allows for truly participatory civic action as it opens up a way of "expanding technological civic systems to accommodate more than just the 'good user' of systems, but also the marginalized, the emergent, and the playful."

Continuing this focus on the range of possibilities and limitations that participatory technology can offer to playfully operating citizens, media theorist Douglas Rushkoff begins his chapter *Permanent revolution: Occupying democracy* by historically contextualizing and critically discussing the 2008 Obama presidential campaign as a landmark event that is often referred to as having redefined citizens' political engagement for the better, thanks to the widespread use of social media. Given that the Obama administration seemed to still largely act as a 'read-only government' and today's net culture seems to reward participation with hits, likes, and binary answers instead of knowledge or insight, Rushkoff disputes the idea that digital media inevitably promote participatory communication. Still, he identifies certain characteristics of digital media —feedback, deconstruction of narrative, prototyping, and programmer/player—that do help to rethink expectations of agency, participation, and change in the digital environment that we live in, perhaps as catalyzers for creating meaningful inefficiencies. Studying the Occupy Movement as a prime example embodying these characteristics, Rushkoff claims that it reflects "values and insights of twenty-first-century science and technology" and that it stands for a form of political engagement that is much more inclusive and iterative—and therefore playful—than was possible in previous media environments.

In his chapter about playful urban planning, *The playful city: Citizens making the smart city*, media scholar Michiel de Lange argues that play and games can help foster smart citizenship. In recent years, many cities have embarked on what is termed smart city policies, deploying ICTs to optimize a variety of urban processes. Many authors have noted that these smart city policies often leave little room for civic action and agency. De Lange proposes the notion of the 'playful city' as an alternative vision for leveraging the smartness of people in creating more livable and lively cities. Play, he argues, should not be positioned as offering potential solutions to urban problems. Instead, as an alternative narrative about city-making, play allows the future of smart cities to be made political again instead of technocratic and tech-driven.

While Rushkoff and De Lange see ways to approach existing systems of governance as 'hackable' and therefore as enabling playful counter-narratives or co-creative narratives to gain ground using digital technologies, the contribution *Dissent at a distance* by The Janissary Collective (composed of digital media and journalism scholars Mark Deuze and Lindsay Ems) argues that while protest movements and civic groups may indeed benefit from 'mediatization,' their playful character is less the result of a conscious strategy than it is the outcome of the performativity of means-over-ends focused engagement, which manifests itself in the 'slacktivism' inherent in participating online only, and the gaming of the telecommunication system. In this, The Janissary Collective is also skeptical about generalizing the transformative role of new media tools, and proposes to regard today's political and social movements as thriving on the unruly and affective ecologies of media that mostly emphasize the 'feeling' of belonging to a community instead of actually being part of one. Participation in these movements, according to the Collective, is an expression of a playful way of being and therefore a mode of being human.

This playful mode of being human in a mediatized world, finally, is explored further by media scholar Alex Gekker, who aims to extend the vocabulary of the field of digital game studies—and casual game studies in particular—to the realm of political studies. In *Playing with power: Casual politicking as a new frame for political analysis*, Gekker's argument picks up on the Janissary Collective's notion of mediatization and notes that this is a meta-process in which the molding forces of games congregate and operate within political spheres, which in turn makes politics today less about fully fledged participation than about playful and casual types of engagement. Echoing Bunz's take on the outsourcing of governmental decision-making to citizens via digital technologies, Gekker's notion of casual politicking sees citizens being enticed to participate in politics *because* it is regarded as a game, one that does not ask too much of the player and is easily discarded when a certain goal is reached. By analyzing the 'gameful designs' of the

Obama 2008 and Trump 2016 presidential campaigns, Gekker attempts to lay bare the possibilities of casual politicking to overcome a range of common dichotomies: between passive and active citizenship, between sender and receiver, and between citizenship as a duty and citizenship as a vocation.

14. On participatory politics as a game changer and the politics of participation

Mercedes Bunz

Abstract
In this chapter, the revolutionary impact of digital technology on society is unpacked and critically assessed. Bunz asks how digital media can facilitate the increased participation of citizens, but can at the same time be used as a means for diffusion that is far less radical in its political outcomes. The idea of playfully 'hacking politics' may help to turn political problems into challenges that can be resolved through public participation, but advocating participation can just as easily change into the contracting out of state responsibilities onto citizens. As is argued in this chapter, citizens' participation does not necessarily allow for radical transformation and often does not offer enough tension and discussion to kickstart societal changes.

Keywords: Citizens' participation, hacking, politics, digital media, political gestures

"Forms of organization are inseparable from technical gestures": this proposition by Bruno Latour (1999, 210) was written right at the time when the internet was about to become a mass medium. As digitalization spread, a new technical gesture was on the rise (Bunz 2014, 55-59). The aim of my contribution is to follow Latour's proposition and explore it with regards to a specific type of organization: the field of politics. For this, I plan to take a general look at the effects of the technical gesture of digitalization commonly identified as "decentralization" or "fragmentation" (Castells 1996; Galloway 2004, 46; Hayles 2009, 68; Lovink 2012; Bruns et al. 2015).

Glas, R., S. Lammes, M. de Lange, J. Raessens, and I. de Vries, eds. 2019. *The Playful Citizen. Civic Engagement in a Mediatized Culture.* Amsterdam: Amsterdam University Press.
DOI: 10.5117/9789462984523/CH14

Being at times discussed as promising models of anti-capitalism (Srnicek and Williams 2015; Scholz and Schneider 2017), I will specifically describe new forms of participatory politics to analyze how they have influenced a shift in the concept of the political. After some introductory remarks about the relation of organization and technology, my contribution will look at three examples that put new forms of participatory organization into play and will explain why this can be conceived as the gamification of politics (e.g. Deterding et al. 2011, Fuchs et al 2014) or casual-politicking (Gekker, see Chapter 20 in this volume). It will also describe the consequences on citizens that come with the shift from representational politics to participatory politics. Finally, it will turn to a discussion of the political 'game' itself, in order to ask, how radical is this gesture, how political is this new form of organization? Is it a game changer, or is it just the same old story, now in just a new, fancy light of participation?

Organization and technology

Organization has an odd and indirect relation to technology. As the American philosopher of technology Langdon Winner noted, there is a "technical constitution of society" (1986, 47). This is an interesting remark, as Winner did not write "technical dependence." Obviously, the means of our social organization cannot be directly deduced from technology or vice versa. However, Winner holds that they are fundamentally linked. In the era of industrialization, the link of technology and the political was widely debated via the means of production. In the era of digitalization on the other hand, we are about to shift our focus away from production and instead stress the matter of organization (Srnicek and Williams 2015; Virno 2006, 36; Baecker 2011). The Dutch philosopher of technology Peter-Paul Verbeek (2011) for example has explicitly shown how design always imposes a certain organization and with it a morality of things.

On an abstract level, the link between organization and technology reads as follows: everything that is organized has a pattern and a structure. To form a structure and hold on to a certain pattern, it requires communication, and communication is based on a technical element. A crowd or an individual is never simply there. Connections and distances are constantly communicated, negotiated, acknowledged, or denied: this is the work of a society, a work done with the help of a symbol, a paper form, or a poster, a meeting room, a telephone, a membership card, a digital platform, or a specific thing (Marres 2012). With the help of those communication tools, we form as multitudes (Virno 2004, 84), create assemblages (DeLanda 2006), or coordinate ourselves on platforms (Srnicek 2017).

If we apply this perspective to citizens, we can see the state as an "apparatus" (Althusser 1970) that produces a loose group, connected by the symbol of a passport. In Western societies, passports grant citizens certain responsibilities and rights, including, among others, the right that they may register to vote. This form of participatory power—the vote—has been the most important political act of the citizen; it represents his or her ability to control politics since in representative democracies we vote someone in and out of an office. However, if we compare the length of time it takes a citizen to cast a vote with the length of time a government is in power, the unbalance of this political division of labor becomes apparent: after the brief active moment of voting, we find that voters (i.e. 'us') are generally passive, while the politicians ('them') make the decisions. To overcome this division, participatory politics—getting the citizen to take a more active part via public campaigning or in local initiatives—has been a recurring theme. Especially in the 1960s this turned into a strong participatory impulse, which was also expressed in art and culture (Debord 1967; Bishop 2006). Thus, we can say that in our most recent past, participation has been discussed as an emancipatory act. Not any more. Now that new forms of participation have evolved with digitalization, the positive rhetoric seems to have changed: Srnicek has denounced certain forms of participation as 'platform capitalism' (2017). Before him Schäfer (2009) already pointed out the misuse of participation as a replacement for market research. Since new digital forms of participatory politics continue to emerge in great scale, it is important to try to understand this more precisely: how does the increase in participatory politics and its transformation from an exception to a new norm affect the set-up of the political? Let us look at some examples from the recent history of digitalization.

Forms of participation

In 2009, the platform RaceOnline2012.org was created by Martha Lane Fox, co-founder of Lastminute.com. Its aim was to tackle the digital divide and bring millions of people, who had never been online, in touch with the internet. Bearing the gamification of politics in its name, the website made use of an interface that acquired details from people willing to help regarding on which weekday and time they or their seminar room or their computer would generally be available each week; or if they felt more comfortable with teaching a group or an individual person, making available a work place, a work tool, or working time. As we can see here, the interface was programmed to connect humans and “nonhumans” (Latour 1999, 174) as directly and detailed as possible.

Data.gov.uk is another example of early participatory politics. The UK government project, which started in 2010 and relaunched in 2018, enables developers to freely access non-personal data the state acquired for official purposes, from traffic sector data to crime statistics to the governments central accounting system. Initiated by the founder of the World Wide Web Sir Tim Berners-Lee and the computer professor Nigel Shadbolt, the website was launched in January 2010. A few years later, in 2013, some 9,000 data sets were available, and more than 2,500 developers had signed up to the project. The result of their experimental data use was the creation of many applications and websites, among them for example the ‘Care Home Map,’ which helps to evaluate the services of Care Homes for elderly relatives or friends, or ‘Road Works,’ which informs about planned government traffic works and helps to optimize logistics. With these projects, data.gov.uk became committed to the idea of government transparency and proclaimed it would open up government. It did this in parts, since most of us cannot handle this kind of raw data.

Here, digital participation introduces an interesting dilemma (see also Tkacz 2012). It can be summed up as follows: while data sets are of tremendous use to developers, they are of no use to the general public. Being able to use data depends on having digital skills, so making it available simultaneously triggers a digital divide. Paradoxically, digitalization introduces more participation, but it splinters the public—obviously the fragmentation of digitalization also affect publicness itself. To correct this, tools exist that lower the tech barriers and make app building and programming easier. These are ways to tackle this new digital exclusion, as the relapse to an equal but passive position is not an attractive alternative.

Finally, there is the interesting example of the Social Innovation Camp, a project that was founded in 2008 by, among others, the then global manager of Amnesty International Dan McQuillan, a scholar for creative and social computing at Goldsmiths University. The Social Innovation Camp brings digital solutions to social challenges by following the approach of what is known among coders as a ‘hackday’: by applying existing code to a new problem, programmers rapidly find creative solutions and are able to swiftly build a prototype. As digitalization allows new connections and a far more detailed administration of our world, this can be applied to real life, or as McQuillan puts it, we can “combine rapid prototyping with asset-based community development, using the ability of the Internet to aggregate and mash-up solutions to social issues" (2012). One outcome of this new approach is GoodGym.org, a project that mashes up participation with digital technology; instead of becoming a member at a gym, the service pairs runners with isolated and less mobile people in their area. Runners then jog to their house, deliver something nice, have a brief chat, and are on their way again.

Participation and the citizen

Let us now take a step back from the examples and focus on the political ethos these projects bring into play when addressing their issues. Firstly, we can notice that these issues do not have a political motive at all, whether in the traditional sense of politics as the activity of government, nor in the more recent radicalized conception of politics as 'post-politics.' This movement, represented by philosophers as different as Rancière, Badiou, Mouffe, and Žižek, aims for a new radical approach toward politics from the standpoint of equality, when finding politics proper reduced to social administration. Instead of compromise and consensus, they stress friction, debate, disagreement, and allowing the unheard voice to be accounted for (see Rancière 1999, 27ff). Both approaches, however, when compared to the 'gamification of politics,' do not seem to apply. Here, the social and political issues tackled have not moved back under the administrative wings of the government, but they also do not seem to be an issue in the post-political sense. All of them address urgent social problems but there is no friction or debate, there is no voice that makes itself heard, or a strong notion of inequality.

The problems present themselves as challenges that citizens can face and take part in, in case they are interested. Like in the setting of a game, political issues appear as simple fragments of a much bigger picture; there is also the opportunity with these game-like politics to take part, but there is no obligation. Instead of a political idea or ideology, there is a simple challenge; instead of tackling common problems in the world as a whole, we stick with solving a demarcated field or question or problem; instead of asking the citizen to believe in a political program, the issues at stake ask us to take part in finding a solution to a particular problem: join the club and play with us! Now Wittgenstein (1953) rightly observed that we may not be able to clearly define what a game is, but there are enough family resemblances between this new approach of tackling a social problem and the setting of a game: it is structured, a challenge, circumscribed in time and place, and although it is not fictitious it connects you with a different reality from your own. Do not let the elderly feel isolated. Help people who have no digital literacy. Open government and make it accessible for others. Fight for the survival of your planet. Save Lara Croft. The seamless gliding between both spheres makes it apparent that we can indeed claim the 'gamification of politics' when we define gamification as "the use of game design elements in non-game contexts" (Deterding et al. 2011, 10). If we explore the effect of this kind of gamification further, however, new questions arise: what are its consequences for politics? Does the gamification of politics not only change politics, but also change the approach of the state toward its citizens, and if so in what way?

As I have emphasized above, the social is not an obligation for everyone anymore, but a challenge that is optional, in which one can take part as if it were a game. Here, the gamification of politics changes the notion of the political in a very specific way, and the new notion of the political is triggered when the technical constitution of society (Winner 1986, 47) becomes visible. Clearly, the technical gesture (Latour 1999, 210) of digitalization is at work: fragmentation has dismantled the notion of 'everyone.' This leads to an urgent political question: What will happen to a state that is subjected to the logic of gamification when in the past it was a democratic apparatus set to ensure the values of justice, freedom, and equality *for everyone*? Let us ponder this question for a moment.

Replacing the war of 'all against all' while respecting the plurality of its people, the democratic state ideally provides its citizens with equal opportunities to live in freedom, so that *everyone* gets a fair chance to take part in society—Jacques Rancière has, among others, discussed equality as an essential and complex democratic value "on which any social order rests" (Rancière 1999, 16). The actual way that the social order is based on equality, however, changes in a digitalized society. Instead of facilitating just one equal opportunity for all (i.e. through voting), the state can now also offer a range of different possibilities to directly participate in its politics. Consequently, instead of 'a people' we have a plurality of different participants. This means while 'a people' can now be more active, they also find themselves divided into different groups, each one with different skills to 'play politics' at different levels—an interesting dilemma that needs to be discussed.

It becomes apparent that the rise of digital technology confronts the state with an interesting problem: to enable digital participation will necessarily mean the state is *not the same for all*. In a society fragmented into citizens with different skills, the idea of equality is without question still important but needs to be newly adjusted. While every one of its citizens should be able to browse the knowledge of the internet, not everyone necessarily needs to know how to code; everyone should, however, get an opportunity to learn this important and powerful task. Here, the state needs to struggle with the division of its people, for it should not deny its citizens the technical chance of taking a more active part in politics. Yet, the attractive option of opening government up has another flipside: when is a state enabling its citizens to participate politically and when is it simply outsourcing its responsibilities? This is a serious problem which this chapter will now turn to in order to discuss the potential of participatory politics as a game changer.

Participatory politics as game changer?

If we return for a moment to the beginning of this chapter, where we were introduced to Latour's proposition that "[f]orms of organization are inseparable from technical gestures" (1999, 210), we can now finally focus on the question of *how inseparable* these two phenomena are. Can a technical gesture initiate new forms of organization? Does it change the organization of our societies with regard to being socially truly revolutionary? Regarding technology, a revolutionary connotation has often been addressed. For a long time, philosophers have been especially fascinated by the deep impact technical change has had on society. Besides Marx, it was Walter Benjamin who most explicitly linked technology to a social revolution. When in Moscow in 1927, he wrote for example that "the revolutionary work of this hour is not conflict, not civil war, but canal construction, electrification, and factory building. The revolutionary nature of true technology is emphasized ever more clearly" (Benjamin 1927, 45). Langdon Winner also addresses technologies as a basic cause of social change (1986, 31), much like Corlann Gee Bush, who points out that technological change stimulates social change (1983). Let us now finally explore the ability of digital technology to change societies, as well as the participatory politics, and start with the obvious question: Does digital technology really change the way we organize our societies, or does it simply automatize it?

Analyzing digital technology, one can notice the potential of far more detailed organization than ever before, in which logistics is turned into an integral element of production (Thrift 2004, 182). Online interfaces automatically manage details and notify issues that, before the existence of algorithms, a human person had to ask, such as: When is this room free?

When do you have some spare time? What skills do you have? When is a computer available? Or, when can this object be used? Again, it becomes obvious that digitalization connects and manages the world in far greater detail, and this will increasingly become the case with the further growth of the Internet of Things (Bunz and Meikle 2018). For instance, by using RFID chips not only humans, but also objects are able to answer inquiries (Hayles 2009) and this enables millions of new connections. This technical innovation takes the Internet of PCs to a next level since it makes objects digitally addressable.

The political potential of these new connections, as I have shown elsewhere in great detail (Bunz 2014, 109-115; Bunz and Meikle 2018), has fascinated media scientists, some even predict the emergence of a new media ontology (Kittler 2009). The human geographer Nigel Thrift, for example, writes about our new ability of tracking and tracing: "If things are showing up differently, we can do different things too, energetically opening up the new order of being" (2004, 188). McQuillan discusses this potential further as "hacking social reality": as the digital allows to transform pre-existing elements to evoke meanings not originally intended in the raw material, he argues that "we can prototype parts of a new society in the shell of the old" (2012). As Latour has indicated, the new digital technical gesture does not simply apply to automatize tasks, but truly opens up new forms of social organization since the change even goes further than what has existed. In effect, it interrupts existing mechanisms in their tracks: regarding organization digitalization is—again—skipping the intermediaries, or rather one intermediary, namely money.

If one analyzes the above-mentioned examples from the Social Innovation Camp to RaceOnline2012 more closely, it becomes apparent that they set the logic of money aside. Compared to websites of The Red Cross, Amnesty International, or Greenpeace, their homepages do (or did) not have a clearly visible donate button. Instead they stressed the notion of 'get involved.' This is symptomatic. Since they focus on connecting things and skills, humans and nonhumans directly, money is not at the center of their organization but just one means among others to reach their goal. And this is also the case with thepublicschool.org, Rynda.org, and many other examples leading to the conclusion that a new type of organization indeed has emerged in the digital era. Referring to 'non-governmental organizations' (NGOs) this new type can be categorized as 'non-money centered organizations' (NMCOs). These new possibilities, which have been described and supported by Trebor Scholz and Nathan Schneider (2017), introduce a potential for massive change. For example, before digitalization and its technical gesture of fragmentation had reached organization, the size of a budget clearly defined the size of an organization. Now this has changed. With the rise of NMCOs, the potential of playing a different game, one that might escape the logic of money, becomes apparent. While the new technical gesture gave rise to this new form of organization, it does not however dictate its political interpretation. Here the link of technical organization and social revolution, one that escapes the ruling logic of money, profit, and efficiency, comes to an end. Technology and organization are inseparable, but their political interpretation is not. Or, to put it differently, the fact that technology enables new forms of organization does not mean the direction of change is automatically set for a revolution. Participatory politics are pushed further by the technical gesture of digitalization so they can be a game changer, but they can also be used as a means to outsource social responsibilities from the state to its citizens. For example, 'Do It—Volunteering made easy' is a website from the charity YouthNet supported by the UK Cabinet Office which enables citizens to find voluntary work in their area. After the public sector job cuts in the UK heavily affected social services—the Office for Budget Responsibilities report showed that by the second quarter of 2011 General Government Employment fell by 80,000—there were obviously many opportunities to volunteer. This work was often being done by professional social workers who had at one time been employed by the state. In April 2018, a search limited to a five-mile area in East London displayed 1475 volunteer opportunities, including helping sixteen- to nineteen-year-olds in their local school or college, being the weekend receptionist in a hospital, or joining clean-ups in the local area. Here, participatory technology does not innovate, but simply helps to replace a retracting state. Participatory technology is simply being used to keep on reproducing the same social situations instead of creating new ones that may unlock a new becoming.

Conclusion

While exploring Latour's proposition in the era of digitalization and looking into new forms of organization like participatory politics, it became apparent that his statement is still relevant: "forms of organization are inseparable from technical gestures." The fact that technology is inseparable from organization *influences* but does not *determine* politics. In other words, digital technology opens up new forms of organization, but the question of the political remains. When do we play a new game? And when do we just change the rules in order to replay the old game on a new board?

References

Althusser, L. 1970. Idéologie et appareils idéologiques d'État (Notes pour une recherche). *La Pensée* 151.

Baecker, D. 2011. Technik und Entscheidung. In *Die technologische Bedingung. Beiträge zur Beschreibung der technischen Welt*, ed. E. Hörl, 179-192. Berlin: Suhrkamp.

Benjamin, W. 1927. Moscow. In *Selected writings volume 1, 1927-1934*. Trans. R. Livingstone and others, 22-46. Cambridge, MA: Harvard University Press.

Bishop, C. 2006. *Participation*. Cambridge, MA: The MIT Press.

Bruns, A., G. Enli, E. Skogerbo, A. O. Larsson, and C. Christensen, eds. 2015. *The Routledge companion to social media and politics*. New York: Routledge.

Bunz, M. 2014. *The silent revolution: How digitalization transforms knowledge, work, journalism, and politics without making too much noise*. Houndmills: Palgrave Macmillan.

Bunz, M., and G. Meikle. 2018. *The internet of things*. Malden, MA: Polity Press.

Bush, C. G. 1983. Women and the assessment of technology: To think, to be; to unthink, to free. In *Machina ex dea: Feminist perspectives on technology*, ed. J. Rothschild, 151-170. New York: Pergamon Press.

Castells, M. 1996. *The rise of the network society. The information age: Economy, society and culture vol. I.* Oxford: Blackwell.

Debord, G. 1967. *Society of the spectacle*. New York: Zone Books.

DeLanda, M. 2006. *A new philosophy of society: Assemblage theory and social complexity*. London, New York: Continuum.

Deterding, S., D. Dixon, R. Khaled, and L. Nacke. 2011. From game design elements to gamefulness: Defining "gamification". In *Proceedings of the 15th international academic MindTrek conference: Envisioning future media environments, Tampere, September 28-30, 2011*, 9-15. New York: ACM.

Fuchs, M., S. Fizek, P. Ruffino, and N. Schrape. 2014. *Rethinking gamification*. Lüneburg: meson press.

Galloway, A. 2004. *Protocol: How control exists after decentralization*. Cambridge, MA: The MIT Press.

Hayles, K. 2009. RFID: Human agency and meaning in information-intensive environments. *Theory, Culture & Society* 26 (2-3): 47-72.

Kittler, F. 2009. Towards an ontology of media. *Theory, Culture & Society* 26 (2-3): 23-31.

Latour, B. 1999. *Pandora's hope: Essays on the reality of science studies*. Cambridge, MA: Harvard University Press.

Lovink, G. 2012. *Networks without a cause*. Malden, MA: Polity Press.

Marres, N. 2012. *Material participation: Technology, the environment and everyday publics*. London: Springer.

McQuillan, D. 2012. Could prototyping be the new policy? *The Guardian*. http://www.guardian.co.uk/culture-professionals-network/culture-professionals-blog/2012/may/28/prototyping-replaces-policy-arts-culture.

Rancière, J. 1999. *Disagreement: Politics and philosophy*. Trans. J. Rose. Minneapolis, MN: University of Minnesota Press.

Schäfer, M. T. 2009. Participation inside? User activities between design and appropriation. In *Digital material: Tracing new media in everyday life and technology*, eds. M. van den Boomen, S. Lammes, A. Lehmann, J. Raessens, and M. T. Schäfer, 147-158. Amsterdam: Amsterdam University Press.

Scholz, T., and N. Schneider, eds. 2017. *Ours to hack and to own: The rise of platform cooperativism, a new vision for the future of work and a fairer internet*. New York: OR Books.

Srnicek, N. 2017. *Platform capitalism*. Malden, MA: Polity Press.

Srnicek, N., and A. Williams. 2015. *Inventing the future: Postcapitalism and a world without work*. London: Verso Books.

Thrift, N. 2004. Remembering the technological unconscious by foregrounding knowledges of position. *Environment and Planning D: Society and Space* 22 (1): 175-190.

Tkacz, N. 2012. From open source to open government: A critique of open politics. *Ephemera, Theory and Politics in Organization* 12 (4): 386-405.

Verbeek, P. 2011. *Moralizing technology: Understanding and designing the morality of things*. Chicago, IL: University of Chicago Press.

Virno, P. 2004. *A grammar of the multitude*. Boston, MA: The MIT Press.

—. 2006. Reading Gilbert Simondon: Transindividuality, technical activity and reification. *Radical Philosophy* 136:34-43.

Winner, L. 1986. *The whale and the reactor: A search for limits in an age of high technology*. Chicago, IL: University of Chicago Press.

Wittgenstein, L. 1953. *Philosophical investigations*. Hoboken, NJ: Blackwell Publishing.

About the author

Mercedes Bunz is Senior Lecturer at the Communications and Media Research Institute, University of Westminster. Her research focuses on digital technology and how it affects society, especially regarding knowledge and work. Her publications include *The internet of things* (2018), written together with Professor Graham Meikle, in which she explored new skills that things have, such as 'seeing' and 'speaking' gathered through artificial intelligence. She also wrote *The silent revolution: How digitalization transforms knowledge, work, journalism, and politics without making too much noise* (Palgrave 2014), and co-edited *Terra critica: Symptoms of our planetary condition* (Meson Press 2017).

15. Playing with politics: Memory, orientation, and tactility

Sam Hind

Abstract

The focus of this chapter is how playfulness can be a constitutive part of political activism. Analyzing the anti-austerity demonstrations in London in 2011, Hind looks at the carnivalesque and ludic qualities during the March for the Alternative, which attracted over 250,000 protesters. One of the highlights of this march was a giant Trojan horse that people carried with them. In Hind's analysis, ludic political interventions such as the Trojan horse constitute a playful, material, and performative relationship between digital technologies and embodied political actions. Hind draws attention to the fact that political events are not solely human-driven, but that technologies form an intrinsic part of how they unfold. Through a reading of Stiegler, he examines the material and affective dynamics of contemporary protest events.

Keywords: Political activism, ludic interventions, the carnivalesque, mobility

In this chapter, I want to propose that protest events are not solely human-driven. Although this might seem a rather modest task to undertake, it is a rather bold proposition. Think of the affective nature of all manner of demonstrations, rallies, marches, occupations, and even riots. Think also of the objectives. Protest events are designed to change human thinking and acting. Some are anti-war campaigns to rally fellow citizens. Others are full-scale revolutions designed to shift power from autocratic leaders to the people. In essence, they might be witnessed as wholly human accomplishments.

Glas, R., S. Lammes, M. de Lange, J. Raessens, and I. de Vries, eds. 2019. *The Playful Citizen. Civic Engagement in a Mediatized Culture.* Amsterdam: Amsterdam University Press.
DOI: 10.5117/9789462984523/CH15

But what is often missing from accounts of these moments is a nuanced consideration of the role of technology. Although it is now commonplace to suggest that social media has become a conduit for organization of, and solidarity with, demonstrations the world over, it is less common to chart these technologies in action. Platform-specific messages do not necessarily invoke a change in thinking. Nor do they magically cause citizens to assemble. While a tweet, a Facebook notification, or a Firechat message may stimulate action this cannot be presumed in advance of its happening. What is of interest in this chapter is how platform-specific messages affect the playful, material, and performative dimensions of protest events. In order to situate this, I will first provide a brief introduction to social media and protest. Then, I will turn to Bernard Stiegler (1998, 2009) and his work on the mnemotechnical and navigational developments in contemporary society. In other words, I will examine his work to address the importance of memory and orientation. To these I will also add a discussion on the tactile nature of protest events to draw out the more recent shifts at the interface between technology and protest.

In order to show the specificity of these dynamics I will make reference to one particular incident; the parading of a Trojan Horse that took place during an anti-austerity demonstration in London, on 26 March 2011. Organized by the umbrella organization, the Trades Union Congress (TUC), it was known as the March for the Alternative, and attracted over 250,000 protesters (BBC News 2011)—including myself. Photographic evidence and contributions from social media collected both during and after the event will serve as the empirical basis for this contribution. The playful, material, and performative relation between the Trojan Horse and digital technology will become clearer as this chapter proceeds.

Social media and protest: The delusional citizen?

> Although some may wager that the exercise of rights now takes place quite at the expense of bodies on the street, that Twitter and other virtual technologies have led to a disembodiment of the public sphere, I disagree.
>
> – Butler (2011, n.p.)

As Juris (2012) points out, network-based forms of social movement organization are nothing new. The New Social Movements of the 1970s were characterized by less hierarchical arrangements of command that were not predicated upon a centralized organizational form (Buechler 1995). Protestors have also been using forms of digital communication to coordinate action since the late 1990s. The global justice movement utilized listserve networks during this period to communicate with followers across the world. They allowed computer users from disparate locations to connect with the cause of global justice. But, as Juris (2012, 260) further contends, this was far from a revolutionary overhaul in organization, but more simply an incorporation of new forms of media into "ongoing practices of core groups of activists," with the aim to "diffuse new dynamics of activism."

Fast-forward, and the mobilization of activists via Twitter during the various Occupy protests (see Constanza-Chock 2012; Pickerill and Krinsky 2012; Gleason 2013) is but a more recent example of the entanglement of such events with new technological capabilities. Again, it is important to note that although such advances in access to (and speed, performance, and mobility of) such technologies are undoubtedly contributing to a radical shift in protest operation, there are still a number of caveats. While it may seem that access is open and universal to social media platforms such as Twitter, divides do remain. Geography, class, age, race, and gender continue to be barriers to online participation (see Zook and Graham 2007; Crutcher and Zook 2009; Thatcher 2013), suggesting that the infrastructural, social, and political bases for contribution are highly uneven—this despite widespread discussion on the 'democratization' of data in the 'Web 2.0' era (Morozov 2011; Haklay 2013).

Moreover, the efforts of groups such as Anonymous and Lulzsec (Gallagher and Arthur 2011), while synonymous with more natively digital protests such as hacks and distributed denial-of-service (DDoS) attacks, have also spawned collective, urban action (Gekker, see Chapter 20 in this volume). The widespread use of Guy Fawkes masks made popular in the *V for Vendetta* film (McTeigue 2005) during the Occupy protests was a striking example of the visible solidarity between contemporary protesters (see Elden 2011). This is what the journalist Jonathan Jones has called a kind of 'festive citizenship' (Jones 2011); drawing on the public image of an amorphous hacktivist group to re-constitute the carnivalesque in a new technological age (see Sicart 2014, 10-11).

Gerbaudo (2012, 2) explicitly asked: "Is this all just an activist delusion?" In other words, can we really draw causal links between social platform content and on the ground action? Are the dynamics outlined above really constitutive of a new arena of civic engagement? Or do they constitute a kind of technological fetishism in which a causal link between message and action is presumed a priori? The next three sections will draw out the parameters of the debate by drawing on the work of Bernard Stiegler (1998,

2009). Social media, it is argued here, are used in three ways to stimulate action on the ground: to form a recallable and recoverable depository of moments *within* events; to construct a navigational orientation *toward* moments during events; and to forge a co-constitution of body and action *in* events.

Memory and event

One of the ongoing discussions surrounding new technological devices is the effect on the human capacity to remember. Nicholas Carr (2008) theorized in his infamous article 'Is Google making us stupid?' on how Google was helping to shape "the process of thought" by becoming a conduit for information-gathering. This, Carr suggests, is leading to a reduction in people's mental capacity to concentrate, to contemplate, and their ability to engage in deep learning.

Digital devices like personal computers, mobile phones or tablets, or online platforms like Google, Twitter, or Facebook constitute a materialization of thought, or what Bernard Stiegler (1998) terms 'tertiary forms of memory.' These "technical objects," as Stiegler refers to them, sift, collect, store, structure, catalogue, and re-present information exterior to the human body so that thoughts become "inscribed in the non-living body" of technical objects (Stiegler 2009, 4). It is through these objects that we, as humans, are comprised especially in spatial terms as Kinsley (2014) and Ash (2010, 2012) have explored. It is this inscription that becomes a valuable technique for those participating in protest events, as the content of such objects far outlives their producers.

This has implications for what is known as primary and secondary forms of memory. The former constitutes the "original impression" (Stiegler 2009, 246) of an event or a moment; that initial period of perception in which people capture and process everyday occurrences. For instance, at the moment an activist encounters other fellow protesters during a demonstration. The latter forms what we know as human memory; the fragmentation of past experiences constituted in the mind afterwards. Say, in the days, weeks, months, and years after a particularly memorable protest event. These are naturally partial, reconstituted, and re-imagined fragments that together with primary perceptual impressions form 'protensions,' the projection of past thoughts and perceptions into everyday life.

But while primary and secondary memories cease to exist when a life form dies, memories supplanted and registered in digital devices and online platforms continue on. Stiegler's (1998) general claim therefore, is that technology acts as a third type of human memory, one that, despite laden with a degree of human knowledge, is nonetheless exterior to, and independent of, human memory. It is for this reason that it becomes a powerful tool during protest events, providing the ability for others to collect, search, and recall particular moments otherwise 'lost.' Moreover, critically, that tertiary forms of memory come to constitute both primary and secondary forms of memory in the first instance. In other words, digital devices and online platforms *precede* and therefore *wholly shape* the types of experiences and capacities for thought that Carr (2008) suggested earlier. It is only through tertiary forms of memory—technologies that enable us to store and recover moments—that our primary and secondary forms can function.

Stiegler (2009, 8) calls this relationship between tertiary memory, individual, and environment 'mnemotechnics.' Put otherwise, all forms of media—from printed books to social media platforms—allow for a kind of memory to be developed and inscribed. The primary function of this is to reduce the cognitive load on the human. If something becomes inscribed there is little need to remember it in full—it is safe and secure written, drawn, photographed, or copied down in some other way. Such is the power of this material independence that it is capable of outliving all other forms of memory, and evolving in an altogether unique way. However, these dynamics of technical evolution, Simondon (1958/1980) maintains, have been criminally misinterpreted, representing a prosthetic, developmental necessity of human life. By extension we can understand how digital technology within protest events has constituted a prosthesis of action. However, this is not the form of technological fetishism questioned previously. For although Stiegler holds that technology is a prosthetic, developmental necessity of human life, he does not believe that because of this we are married to any *specific* technology per se. We can still propose the former without slipping into the latter, thus avoiding the technological determinism highlighted by Gerbaudo (2012).

In the conceptualization of a tertiary memory, Stiegler (2009, 12) grapples firstly with what he calls "the orthographic age." In constituting the practice of writing as the foremost prosthesis of technical memory, Stiegler is able to comprehend the role technical objects have in shaping and remembering human politics. As he says:

> It is philology's business to establish the authenticity of source materials; once they have been established, I no longer doubt having access, as if I were there, to Plato's or Heidegger's orthographic thoughts, constituted in the very possibility of a certain after-the-fact re-constitution. (Ibid., 8)

We do not question, in everyday matters, the medium of the written word, only the veracity of the message written within. For Stiegler, the words of Plato and Heidegger do two things. In the first instance, they suffice for either two, working *as* Plato and Heidegger, so that we correlate the words of either as they themselves speaking the very same words. This is despite the existence of any intonation, rhythm, or accent. Not least to mention either authors' physical or mental state that would have had a bearing on how the words were transmitted. Then, in the second instance, they work *beyond* either author, lasting far longer than either could have imagined or indeed realized. The writings of both Plato and Heidegger thus serve as lingering artefacts of human thought and endure as objects of a technical memory.

One particular moment during the March for the Alternative demonstration exemplifies Stiegler's argument. Consider the photographic evidence of a cumbersome, wood and cloth Trojan Horse crafted and paraded by protesters along the official march route (see Figure 15.1). Its progression was marked by Twitter users as messages were sent and photos uploaded of its whereabouts along the march route. What was particularly interesting was the way in which the Trojan Horse was variously constituted through different, mediated accounts. The protest application Sukey (2011)[1] was the first to note its presence, tweeting an image from a feeder point in Kennington Park, south of the route (Sukeyio 2011a) along with the message "Fake Stallions Unite." As it made its way into central London, the Metropolitan Police's communication team (CO11) urged protesters to "continue on the march past the Trojan Horse effigy in [sic] Downing Street" (MetPoliceEvents 2011) in order to avoid the demonstration slowing down. But as protesters began to congregate around the unwieldy object, Sukey responded to the Metropolitan Police by satirically suggesting that David Cameron, the UK Prime Minister at that time, could not come out to bring it inside with such a large number of protesters gathered around (Sukeyio 2011b). Meanwhile, in a factual tone, the organizers of the event, the TUC, simply alluded to an "incident at Downing St."[2]

The nature of each communication, as a result, went some way in shaping both the general perception of, and re-action to, the event. If users were to solely take the CO11's account of the Trojan Horse seriously, they might be urged to continue past a jovial expression of public outrage against public

1 Sukey is a "multi-platform, news, communications and logistical support system" (Sukey 2011) for protesters.

2 The tweet in full: "March is held up due to incident at Downing St. #26march." Retrieved from personal records collected during the event. The account has since been deleted.

15.1: The Trojan horse at the March for the Alternative, London, UK (Twitter user @smithsam).

sector cuts. If users were entertained by Sukey's take on the incident, they might well have made their own satirical remarks on David Cameron's predicament and joined in the chorus of disapproval. Further still, if fellow Twitter users had taken to the TUC's social media account for updates about the protest, they might well have mistaken the disruption for an unspecified, insignificant, and momentary event. But as Rieder (2012) suggests, some tweets receive more coverage due to their conversational spin on events. The TUC's account is a coded reading intended to avoid conflict. The CO11 message, however, has an expressive tactical meaning. It is an instruction to move. A command to continue along the pre-designated route at a pre-defined speed. The Sukey account is different again; appealing to the jovial, carnivalesque nature of the protest event. Even though each message has a "refractive capacity" (Rieder 2012, n.p.) to spin, twist, or frame the story, only the Sukey account succeeds in mobilizing it fully. While it is possible to trace back the logistical narrative of the event through the TUC and CO11 accounts, it is a bare, functional story—one devoid of the transgressive nature of protest events and their ability to challenge or at least 'temporarily relieve' (Lane Bruner 2005) oppressive political power. Neither the CO11, nor TUC accounts were set up to facilitate such action and, as such, refrained from providing any kind of spin, other than a rote account of the incident.

If we understand Stiegler correctly, and we are to follow his thesis on mnemotechnics, then we are to say that the Trojan Horse that was paraded around London was a kind of tertiary memory inscribed with the thoughts and actions of the people who devised and constructed it. Even within the same media platform—in this case, Twitter—this constructive process has the potential to be markedly different depending on the account of such events. In this way, the Trojan Horse was materially coded, stored, and re-constituted courtesy of the digital medium, this despite its ceremonial burning at the busy road junction hours later. Although the object ceased to exist, it lived on through the platform—remembered and recoverable far beyond the spatio-temporal constraints of the event itself. It is only through these mnemotechnical inscriptions that the event itself is now actually composed; through and prior to all other forms.

Orientation and event

In the first instance, this refractive capacity concerns a temporal quality: the ability to witness, remember, and spin events. Now I want to move on to the Trojan Horse's *navigational* character. In other words, I want to consider how those who constructed the Trojan Horse—and I include here the Twitter users and photographers just as much as the joiners and painters of the horse—became key protagonists in constituting the Trojan Horse as a geospatial event itself.

The employment of spatial metaphors throughout the history of the web has helped in conceptualizing its networked infrastructure to unfamiliar users. Discussions on 'cyberspace' were the first to use such terminology during the late 1990s, when it was believed that the cyber-era would overthrow the tyranny of materiality, open up new freedoms and allow for the "unfettered circulation of abstract free-floating information" (Stevenson 2013, 45). As Nunes (2006, 8) suggested, "[t]he 'space' of cyberspace [...] remained firmly within scare quotes"—in cybernetic terms it was meant to be boundless and without physical constraint. But at a time when computers were heavy, immobile, and accessible only in specific places (i.e. internet cafes, libraries, etc.), spatial metaphors had to be mobilized to describe the nature of connections and 'virtual' actions. Desktop computers, chained to the desks of users, would paradoxically act as portals to a boundary-less world. As Graham (2013, 179) suggests, "common prepositions associated with internet use (e.g to go *to* a website, or to get *on* the Internet) imply a certain spatiality" despite claims in the cyber-era to the contrary. This cyberspace, however ethereal, abstract, and boundless, nevertheless strongly held to spatial metaphors in order to aid users in conceptualizing the types of actions required to engage with such technology.

However, the *interactive* nature of the social media era shattered this fixed, singular notion of abstract digital space. Material and digital worlds have forever been inextricably linked (Graham, Zook, and Boulton 2012). Place and space are thoroughly constituted through a relation with the digital. Interactions commonly cross, loop back into, and affect the material world. They augment and, in some cases, completely constitute the make-up of everyday experience. Kitchin and Dodge (2011) have been the most persistent in making this academic argument of the intermingling of code and space, employing Gilbert Simondon's notion of 'transduction' in order to argue for the (spatially) transformative nature of modern technologies (see also MacKenzie 2002; Dodge and Kitchin 2005). Stiegler, also a reader of Simondon, again provides an adequate framework for this understanding.

In *Technics and time, 2* Stiegler (2009, 65) talks of a "genesis of disorientation." In the first instance, technologies involve a delegation of authority from the *who* to the *what*; a delegation that has progressively distanced humans from their own knowledge. As Leroi-Gourhan (1975, 65 quoted in Stiegler 2009, 78) remarks, this delegation is split into five stages; "of oral transmission, of written transmission with tablets or indices, with simple filing systems, with mechano-graphics, and with electronic seriation." With each advance, Leroi-Gourhan contends, an even greater collective memory is constructed, contributing to the "progressive exteriorization of individual memory" (1975, 65). In this ensuing process, the only logical way for humans to then begin to orientate themselves—bearing in mind Stiegler's (1998) earlier claim that humans are always-already constituted through technical objects—is to attempt to articulate the demands of technical evolution. This involves an orientation at two levels.

First, it is an orientation between ethnic knowledges—those constructed by particular cultures at specific times—and technical objects. This is orientation *qua* memory, covered in the previous section. Second, though, it is a spatiotemporal orientation of *rhythmicity*. This is an orientation that calls forth the relationship between program (technical object) and speed. Consider, for example, the way in which social media platforms and 24-hour news channels have re-constituted news-making by drawing out and speeding up the news cycle. Central to this argument is the relationship between technical object and space. We can call this orientation a *navigational* dynamic in order to make this claim more explicit.

As Stiegler has detailed, the evolution of technology (oral, written, filing, mechano-graphics, and electronic seriation) has led to a colonization of the speed of change. Rhythms of the natural world (stars, seasons, days, bodily functions, heartbeats) are supplemented with rhythms of a human world bound to a technical world in speech, writing, and now coding. Spatial rhythms of a technically-arranged human world might include airport security checks (Kitchin and Dodge 2009), or quotidian driving experiences (Thrift 2004; Sheller 2007; Hind and Gekker 2014). Humans, thus, are orientated toward an industrial space and time that introduces the notion of 'real-time' that forces the human to match the speed of technical evolution, moving as part of a generalized socio-technical system. To put it another way, they are coerced into keeping up with technological evolution.

For the purposes of this chapter, then, the spatial dynamics of contemporary events are co-constituted by the real-time nature of social media platforms. As Leroi-Gourhan suggests:

> [t]he individual functions like a cell, an element of the collective program, in a network of signals that not only control his gestures and the process of his effective thought, but which also control his right to absence, that is, to his rest or leisure time [...] Space then exists only as a function of the requirement of time. Socialized time implies a humanized space, integrally symbolic, such that day and night take place in cities at fixed hours [...] and in which the relations between individuals and their place of activity are instantaneous. (1975, 131 as quoted in Stiegler 2009, 89-90)

To return to our story, the construction of the Trojan Horse consisted of multiple tools. Not only the tools for its mechanical construction; the wood and cloth material, the hammers and nails that secure it together, or the paint and brushes that help carry its message, but also the tools of an 'evental' construction (Shaw 2012), or what Stiegler (2009, 115) calls "event-ization." These included the messages sent by Sukey, the TUC, and CO11. Each message either directly or obliquely referred to the same Trojan Horse (an 'effigy' or 'incident'). A horse thus made by combining wood, cloth, hammers, nails, paint, brushes, and people, but also a horse made by the organizational accounts of Sukey, the TUC, and CO11. This was a horse constructed by a medium and co-opted by a vast array of actors, ostensibly human and technological. A medium restricted in its possible message by an inherent structure ('no more than 140 characters please!'), online protocol (Galloway 2004), and real-time architecture. In other words, it is through this selective process of deciding "what happens" (Stiegler 2009, 115) and thus what matters, that the event itself is actually constructed. As Stiegler writes, "[t]he preservation of memory, of the memorable [...] is always already also its elaboration: it is never a question of a simple story of 'what happened'" (Ibid.).

Despite these restrictions, the messages helped to literally orientate protesters to the existence of the Trojan Horse, and did so through the programmatic tendencies of the tool. Furthermore, the Trojan Horse was constituted in space and time by the digital platform, allowing not only debate and discussion, but also physical action to take place. Real-time updates facilitated the navigation of protesters to the Trojan Horse's position. Transforming the space in which to rally around, whether positioned outside the home of David Cameron, or in Oxford Circus. Either as a political object for directing anger at anti-austerity measures or as a (literally) burning, symbolic reminder of the inequalities of capitalism. In other words, the program helped to structure the Trojan Horse, the urban space, and the event for which it was constructed.

Tactility and event

> [U]nder conditions when those with cameras or Internet capacities are imprisoned or tortured or deported, then the use of the technology effectively implicates the body. Not only must someone's hand tap and send, but someone's body is on the line if that tapping and sending gets traced.
>
> – Butler (2011, n.p.)

To understand how the spatio-temporal mechanics of a digitally mediated protest event are utilized, we must consider the *tactility* of such action. This is where we must make a break from Stiegler and instead turn to the work of those most interested in the haptic nature of technology, as well as those furthering a more phenomenological approach to bodily movement. If, as Frith contends, it is through the interface of the mobile phone that "the individual is able to exert control over signifiers and construct a semi-narrative out of the fractured city streets" (2012, 140), then what does this mean for a type of protest predicated on solidarity, togetherness, and symbolic holism? Moreover, from a bodily perceptive, how are our senses being retuned to adapt to these kind of hybrid, interfacial instances?

In a world dominated by 'occularcentrism,' as Jay (1994) famously noted, conceptions of touch have been largely neglected. There are numerous types of touch, however, and we are only concerned with one here, at least for the purposes of this chapter. If we are to make a rather academic distinction between 'close' and 'deep' touch then we might say that one 'touches' us, quite literally as in body to body, but we might also say that one 'touches us' emotionally and metaphorically. 'Tactility' is the former; a cutaneous sensing of body to body. A form of sensing that relates primarily to the skin "as a sense organ" (Paterson 2007, ix). One particular appendage is most closely connected to the notion of touch, namely the hands. Like the eyes that work as the primary visual organ, so the hands work as contact points for the human body engaging with the world through touching and feeling.[3]

How can tactility help people to orientate themselves? A hypothetical problem posed by philosopher William Molyneux to John Locke in 1690 asked whether an individual born blind and taught to distinguish between two differently shaped objects by touch could do the same by sight alone should they be able to see. The empirical psychologist Marius von Senden (1960) believed that the visual senses had a monopoly on spatial representation, arguing therefore that the blind had no spatial faculties at all since this was solely a preserve of the visual sense. This was to do with Von Senden's insistence that perception was not, what is now called, 'inter-modal.' In other words, the different senses (touch, vision, etc.) would interact with each other through a transcendental perceptual system. Fellow psychologists Gibson (1950), Piaget (1955), and Jones (1975), however, systematically refuted the claim that without sight people lack any spatial cognition whatsoever. They understood perception to be an inter-modal process constituting a "mutually supportive system of the senses" (Paterson 2007, 40). Touch can help mould spatial form, knowledge and experience as much as the visual, and this data can inform, and can be informed by, any of the other senses.

In a traditional sense, orientation concerns our ability to reference waypoints or landmarks like a hill walker might do. In Stieglerian (2009) terms, orientation refers to the openings and affordances we grant to our interaction with technology and the world-at-large. The former is a kind of orientation focused on a distanced vision, a view of far-away reference points that can help to ground the individual, situate their body and place their actions. The latter is employed by Stiegler (2009) to make a more general point about the transformative nature of referencing one particular technological assemblage instead of another. For instance, say, in purposing dominant social media platforms (Twitter, etc.) for a particular need, rather than using outdated machines that fail to carry out the required task as quickly or efficiently as possible (semaphore lines, Morse code, telephones, etc.).

3 Of course, the feet are also another appendage associated with notions of touch, especially in regard to walking. As I primarily wanted to explore the connections between prehensility and technology, and related fieldwork involved the operation of a mobile phone device, I felt I should narrow my focus to include only the hands. Although I do not detail the many ways in which walking is an embodied and haptic experience in this chapter, Ingold (2004), Solnit (2006), and Ingold and Vergunst (2008) provide useful introductions.

Touch, however, is a 'near-view' orientation, an 'egocentric' (Kitchin, Blades, and Golledge 1997, 233) spatiality that places the subject at the center of the map. This 'performative cartography' (Verhoeff 2012, 13) is opposed to the distancing nature of the visual. In a sense, new digital technological apparatuses allow us to manipulate content like never before. The ability to pore over, stretch, zoom, and pan across objects is in stark contrast to the way in which modern inventions of the panorama, the arcade, the world exhibition, and the plate-glass shop window facilitated the "visual spectacle alone" (Pickles 2000, 9). Tactile interaction is thus, arguably, the primary orientation of contemporary digital society; marking a rather radical shift from phantasmagorical fetishes of the modern era. It is this 'double-tap' philosophy (Hind and Lammes 2015) that drives our interaction with the world and its phenomena.

What does this say about the spatiality of protest as wired through a multi-touch mobile device? The mobile smartphone market is now dominated by devices with large, slate-sized screens. Handsets made by Apple, Huawei, and Samsung give preference to 'multi-touch gestures' over the ubiquitous keypad. We are witnessing a technological transition that is re-constituting the human body in an entirely new way. In a passage that now can be applied to the mobile phone, although originally in reference to high-value desktops and industrial machines, Paterson notes:

> Whereas the keyboard is a passive mechanical channel between the computer and user, haptics enables a more active exploration and allows the user not just to *see* three-dimensional shapes represented on the screen, but also to *feel* them and interact with them. (2007, 128, emphasis in original)

This corresponds to Paterson's later analysis of the 'proximal tactile interaction' (Ibid., 129) of new haptic technologies. Multi-touch phones allow the user to bridge the distance between visual data and the self, and instead interact with it via cutaneous sensing. This is, arguably, how protesters have sought to comprehend the rather overwhelming size, symbolism, and aims of collective action in the digital age.

A stream of near-live updates from a Twitter account straight to a mobile device gives the protester an ability to calibrate their place in the greater narrative and the wider spatio-temporal extent of the event. Take Sukey, the protest application mentioned previously, which when deployed during demonstrations displayed a digital map replete with the location of essential services for protesters (first aid tents, legal advisors, toilet facilities, Wi-Fi) as well as the shifting points of conflict during a march (police lines,

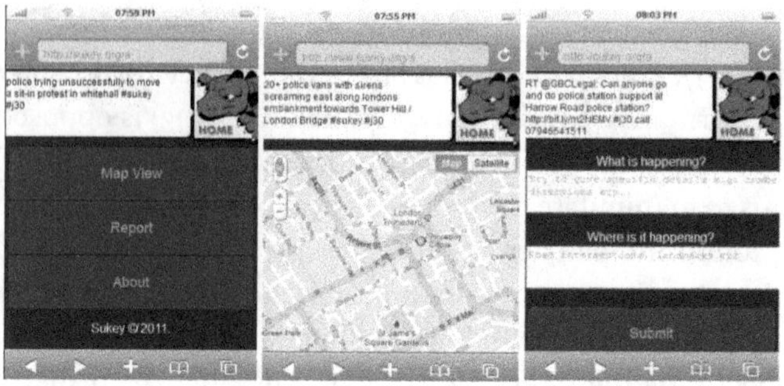

15.2: The Sukey application homepage (left), map view (center) and incident submission form (right) as it was in 2011. Twitter updates are displayed in the box above each screen (author screenshots).

mounted officers, riot vans, a containment), thus allowing users to make navigational decisions (see Figure 15.2). The multi-touch gestures involved in navigating such devices thus enable the protester to be present and 'of the moment.' The egocentric orientation of touch is intertwined with the growing individualization, processual and 'event-centered' framing of mapping, all central to the use of mobile devices during protest events (see Brown and Laurier 2005; Kitchin and Dodge 2007; Perkins 2009). With this combination users are central pivots for navigational duties. Tactile interaction allows events to be brought back to the body itself.

Conclusion: What tools for which citizens?

Let us return to the pertinent question concerning technological determinism posed by Gerbaudo (2012) earlier: "Is this all just an activist delusion?" The answer, following the analysis in this chapter, should be a qualified no. But, as above, we must continue to steer clear of a technological fetishism that proposes that all and everyone is under the universal spell of technological evolution. The question that remains from this analysis—and one that should replace Gerbaudo's above—is: what tools are appropriate for which citizens? In other words, having hopefully exemplified how digital technology plays a critical role in augmenting protest events, the question of whether their involvement is but a 'delusion' should be answered. Instead, we need to evaluate the extent to which particular technologies can and do generate political power for activists around the world.

In this chapter, I have proposed, through a reading of Stiegler (1998, 2009) and those working at the interface of phenomenological thought and technology, that there are three notable dynamics that come to constitute contemporary shifts in protest action. Changes are occurring in our ability to remember, which although not new, is now happening in near real-time. Material devices are providing an instantly referable archive of events that outstrip human capacities. Changes are also being witnessed in our ability to orientate toward real-world incidents. These affordances allow us to be attentive to happenings outside our immediate sensory field. But it is only through a shift to a 'double-tap' philosophy (Hind and Lammes 2015) that allows this to become a reality. The haptic capabilities of the digital device allow us to interact with, manipulate, and re-constitute our worlds. The modernist distancing of the visual is no longer applicable. As the quotes from Judith Butler have iterated throughout this chapter, we must consider how such advancements have created a new co-constructive, hybrid space where citizens are being forced to re-learn their position in the world in order to make their own voices heard.

Acknowledgments

Thanks to Sam Smith for permission to use his image of the Trojan Horse. The research leading to these results has received funding from the European Research Council under the European Community's Seventh Framework Programme (FP7/2007-2013) / ERC Grant agreement n° 283464.

References

Ash, J. 2010. Teleplastic technologies: Charting practices of orientation and navigation in videogaming. *Transactions of the Institute of British Geographers* 35:414-430.

—. 2012. Technology, technicity, and emerging practices of temporal sensitivity in videogames. *Environment and Planning A* 44:187-203.

BBC News. 2011. Anti-cuts march: Tens of thousands at London protest. *BBC*. http://www.bbc.co.uk/news/uk-12864353.

Brown, B., and E. Laurier. 2005. Maps and journeys: An ethno-methodological investigation. *Cartographica* 40 (3): 17-33.

Buechler, S. M. 1995. New social movement theories. *The Sociological Quarterly* 36 (3): 441-464.

Butler, J. 2011. Bodies in alliance and the politics of the street. *Transversal: A Multilingual Web Journal*. http://eipcp.net/transversal/1011/butler/en.

Carr, N. 2008. Is Google making us stupid? *The Atlantic*. http://www.theatlantic.com/magazine/archive/2008/07/is-google-making-us-stupid/306868.

Costanza-Chock, S. 2012. Mic check! Media cultures and the Occupy Movement. *Social Movement Studies* 11 (3-4): 375-385.

Crutcher, M., and M. Zook. 2009. Placemarks and waterlines: Racialized cyberscapes in post-Katrina Google Earth. *Geoforum* 40 (4): 523-534.

Dodge, M., and R. Kitchin, 2005. Code and the transduction of space. *Annals of the Association of American Geographers* 95 (1): 162-180.

Elden, S. (2011). V for visibility. *Interstitial Journal* 1-4.

Frith, J. 2012. Splintered space: Hybrid spaces and differential mobility. *Mobilities* 7 (1) (February): 131-149.

Gallagher, R., and C. Arthur. 2011. Inside lulzsec: Chatroom logs shine a light on the secretive hackers. *The Guardian*. http://www.guardian.co.uk/technology/2011/jun/24/inside-lulzsec-chatroom-logs-hackers.

Galloway, A. 2004. *Protocol: How control exists after decentralization*. Cambridge, MA: The MIT Press.

Gerbaudo, P. 2012. *Tweets and the streets: Social media and contemporary activism*. London: Pluto Press.

Gibson, J. J. 1950. *The senses considered as perceptual systems*. London: George Allen & Unwin.

Gleason, B. 2013. #Occupy Wall Street: Exploring informal learning about a social movement on Twitter. *American Behavioral Scientist* 57 (7): 966-982.

Graham, M., M. Zook, and A. Boulton. 2012. Augmented reality in urban places: Contested content and the duplicity of code. *Transactions of the Institute of British Geographers* 38 (3): 464-479.

Graham, M. 2013. Geography/internet: Ethereal alternate dimensions of cyberspace or grounded augmented realities? *The Geographical Journal* 179 (2): 177-182.

Haklay, M. 2013. Neogeography and the delusion of democratisation. *Environment and Planning A* 45 (1): 55-69.

Hind, S., and A. Gekker. 2014. 'Outsmarting traffic, together': Driving as social navigation. *Exchanges: The Warwick Research Journal* 1 (2): 1-17.

Hind, S., and S. Lammes. 2015. Digital mapping as double-tap: Cartographic modes, calculations and failures. *Global Discourse* 1-19.

Ingold, T. 2004. Culture on the ground: The world perceived through the feet. *Journal of Material Culture* 9 (3): 315-340.

Ingold, T., and J. Vergunst, eds. 2008. *Ways of walking: Ethnography and practice on foot*. Aldershot: Ashgate.

Jay, M. 1994. *Downcast eyes: The denigration of vision in twentieth-century French thought*. Berkeley, CA: University of California Press.

Jones, B. 1975. Spatial perception in the blind. *British Journal of Psychology* 66 (4): 461-472.

Jones, J. 2011. Occupy's V for Vendetta protest mask is a symbol of festive citizenship. *The Guardian.* http://www.guardian.co.uk/commentisfree/2011/nov/04/occupy-movement-guy-fawkes-mask.

Juris, J. S. 2012. Reflections on #Occupy everywhere: Social media, public space, and emerging logics of aggregation. *American Ethnologist* 39 (2) (May): 259-279.

Kinsley, S. 2014. The matter of 'virtual' geographies. *Progress in Human Geography* 38 (3): 364-384.

Kitchin, R., M. Blades, and R. G. Golledge. 1997. Understanding spatial concepts at the geographic scale without the use of vision. *Progress in Human Geography* 21 (2): 225-242.

Kitchin, R., and M. Dodge. 2007. Rethinking maps. *Progress in Human Geography* 31 (3): 331-344.

—. 2009. Airport code/spaces. In *Aeromobilities: Theory and method,* eds. S. Cwerner, S. Kesselring, and J. Urry, 96-114. London: Routledge.

—. 2011. *Code/space: Software and everyday life.* Cambridge, MA: The MIT Press.

Lane Bruner, M. 2005. Carnivalesque protest and the humorless state. *Text and Performance Quarterly* 25 (2): 136-155.

Leroi-Gourhan, A. 1975 [1964-65]. *Le geste et la parole.* Vol. 2 *Le mémoire et les rhythmes.* Paris: Broché.

MacKenzie, A. 2002. *Transductions: Bodies and machines at speed.* London: Continuum Press.

McTeigue, J. (dir). 2005. *V for Vendetta.* Warner Bros. Film.

MetPoliceEvents. 2011. Please can you continue on the march past the Trojan Horse effigy in Downing Street #march26 #TUCnews #march-26march #Demo2011 #sukey. *Twitter.* http://twitter.com/MetPoliceEvents/status/51634253125009409.

Morozov, E. 2011. *The net delusion: How not to liberate the world.* London: Allen Lane.

Nunes, M. 2006. *Cyberspaces of everyday life.* Minneapolis, MN: University of Minnesota Press.

Paterson, M. 2007. *The senses of touch: Haptics, affects, and technologies.* New York: Berg.

Perkins, C. 2009. Performative and embodied mapping. In *International Encyclopedia of Human Geography,* eds. R. Kitchin and N. Thrift, 126-132. Oxford: Elsevier.

Piaget, J. 1955. *The child's construction of reality*. London: Routledge & Kegan Paul.

Pickles, J. 2000. Cartography, digital transitions, and questions of history. *Cartographic Perspectives* 37:4-18.

Pickerill, J., and J. Krinski. 2012. Why does Occupy matter? *Social Movement Studies* 11 (3-4): 279-287.

Rieder, B. 2012. The refraction chamber: Twitter as sphere and network. *First Monday* 17 (11). http://www.firstmonday.dk/ojs/index.php/fm/article/view/4199/3359.

Shaw, I. G. R. 2012. Towards an evental geography. *Progress in Human Geography* 36 (5): 613-627.

Sheller, M. 2007. Bodies, cybercars and the mundane incorporation of automated mobilities. *Social & Cultural Geography* 8 (2): 175-197.

Sicart, M. 2014. *Play matters*. Cambridge, MA: The MIT Press.

Simondon, G. 1958/1980. On the mode of existence of technical objects. Trans. N. Mellamphy. London, ON: University of Western Ontario.

Solnit, R. 2006. *Wanderlust: A history of walking*. London: Verso Books.

Stevenson, M. 2013. *The Web as exception: The rise of new media publishing cultures*. PhD thesis University of Amsterdam.

Stiegler, B. 1998. *Technics and time, 1: The fault of Epimetheus*. Stanford, CA: Stanford University Press.

—. 2009. *Technics and time, 2: Disorientation*. Stanford, CA: Stanford University Press.

Sukey. 2011. Introducing Sukey. *Sukey*. http://sukey.org.

Sukeyio. 2011a. Fake Stallions Unite http://twitpic.com/4dg61j #sukey #march26. *Twitter*. http://twitter.com/sukeyio/status/51599597990187008.

—. 2011b. Met are asking people to move on past the Trojan horse at Downing St. Else David can't go out to bring it in. #FSU #sukey #march26#26march. *Twitter*. http://twitter.com/sukeyio/status/51634902193541120.

Thatcher, J. 2013. Avoiding the Ghetto through hope and fear: An analysis of immanent technology using ideal types. *GeoJournal* 78 (6): 967-980.

Thrift, N. 2004. Driving in the city. *Theory, Culture & Society* 21 (4-5): 41-59.

Verhoeff, N. 2012. *Mobile screens: The visual regime of navigation*. Amsterdam: Amsterdam University Press.

Von Senden, M. 1960. *Space and sight: The perception of space and shape in the congenitally blind before and after operation*. London: Methuen.

Zook, M., and M. Graham. 2007. The creative reconstruction of the internet: Google and the privatization of cyberspace and DigiPlace. *Geoforum* 38 (6): 1322-1343.

About the author

Sam Hind is a Research Associate in Locating Media at the University of Siegen. His research interests include digital navigation and playful methodologies. As a constituent of this work he is keen to develop a conceptual understanding of what he calls 'disruptive cartography.' In more general terms, his research interests stretch across technology, space, and politics to include an interrogation of risk, calculation, and failure as they manifest themselves in and between such worlds. He is currently investigating the limits and limitations of autonomous vehicle technology. He is the co-author of *Playful mapping in the digital age* (Institute of Network Cultures 2016) with the Playful Mapping Collective, and co-editor of *Time for mapping* (Manchester University Press 2018).

16. Meaningful inefficiencies: Resisting the logic of technological efficiency in the design of civic systems

Eric Gordon and Stephen Walter

Abstract

The promise of smart cities is that Big Data and the Internet of Things will transform them into efficient, productive machines. But the smart city is a rather rational proposition where technological efficiency is the primary indicator of success. This chapter advocates a counterpoint to this emphasis on efficiency. Borrowing from game design, where players are provided with goals, and confronted with unnecessary obstacles that make their striving for that goal meaningful, the chapter suggest that 'meaningful inefficiencies' are necessary for making cities smart. When there is room for play in the systems with which we interact, there is opportunity for people to form relationships, build trust, care for one another, and make shared meaning, all of which comprise the foundation for resilient communities.

Keywords: Smart city, meaningful inefficiency, civic media, datafication, civic work

> We are making government more user-friendly.
> – San Francisco's Mayor Ed Lee (Innovate SF 2013)

In the early 2000s, the City of Baltimore became the first large American city to organize all its major services under a single digital system and to utilize the collection and reporting of big data to increase efficiency in all aspects of government (O'Connell 2001). This program, called CitiStat, winner of the

Glas, R., S. Lammes, M. de Lange, J. Raessens, and I. de Vries, eds. 2019. *The Playful Citizen. Civic Engagement in a Mediatized Culture*. Amsterdam: Amsterdam University Press.
DOI: 10.5117/9789462984523/CH16

2004 Innovations in American Government Award, originally made use of existing, yet closed, data streams collected by sixteen agencies across the city. However, CitiStat would make two paradigm-shifting enhancements to the system. The first was the opening of a new, citizen-sourced data stream, a 311 citizen-reporting hotline—similar to 911 but for non-emergency calls—that linked directly to city service management; the second was in opening up the data to the public and using it as a 'civic communication tool.' This helped usher in a new age of e-reporting that soon spread to related data programs in New York, Chicago, and elsewhere. Now, as both data producers and data consumers, citizens ostensibly became partners to the government in making the basic functioning of the city more efficient (Ackerman 2004). This model of co-governance was met with much praise by tech-industry leaders. The IBM Center for the Business of Government sponsored a report praising the City of Baltimore for becoming "increasingly customer-friendly" as a result of its data-driven programs and for "the higher level of agency performance in delivering critical goods and services to citizens in the metropolitan area" (Henderson 2003, 6).

In the decade that followed, social networks such as Facebook and Twitter, publishing platforms from Patch to Tumblr, and mobile web-connected smart devices all worked to set new standards for how people communicate with each other. In April 2015, partly facilitated by these connective technologies, multiple videos captured by onlookers went viral showing an unarmed black man named Freddie Gray as he was dragged screaming into a police van by Baltimore police officers. Freddie Gray would later die due to injuries he sustained during his arrest.

Inspired by the videos captured by smartphones and amplified on social media, these same technologies were then utilized to coordinate widespread protests against police brutality across Baltimore, which would ostensibly 'shut the city down.' Certain city services were canceled, and a curfew was imposed. These events, and the often disquieting and extraordinary images, stories, and commentaries produced and shared from them, pushed the national conversation and media coverage about police brutality, mass incarceration, and urban inequality, to the center of attention. In a marked shift from other episodes of police brutality in the United States (e.g. in Ferguson, MO, and New York City), the state's attorney for the City of Baltimore, Marilyn Mosby, conducted a news conference where she both publicly ruled the death a homicide, charging the six officers involved, and, in unity with the protestors, openly acknowledged the "structural and systemic" racial issues present in policing, and the need for them to be broadly changed (Democracy Now! 2015). Although the decision was a result of many disparate current and historical factors, connective technologies played a part in the telling and reflection of the story. Without the capturing of video, without the amplification on social media, and without the tech-coordinated protests, this may have become another buried case of police brutality. Instead, it became a highly visual moment of reflection on the inequality inherent in Baltimore's systems of governance.

CitiStat in the early 2000s and the protests in 2015 represent two starkly different cases of the use of technologies to 'efficiently' enhance or intervene in civic systems. With CitiStat, the notion of efficiency is born out of the technical and industrial sectors, defined by cost-effectiveness, speed, and market distribution. These efficiencies were intentionally designed into the system by a central design team. With the protests, efficiency is tied to what John Dewey (2011) has called 'civic efficiency,' or the ability to get things done with others, even if disruptive, messy, and unpredictable. In this case, existing technology was appropriated for an unexpected context, and civic efficiency emerged through its unique use by disparate actors. These two cases bring up important questions as to what efficiency means, for whom systems are efficient, and how efficiencies are designed into a civic technology. When the application of technology to civic life is celebrated purely for its expediency, transactionality, and instrumentality, then other uses and users are potentially sidelined. Civic technology is running on two parallel tracks—technological efficiency and civic efficiency—where an emerging technology sector is forming around streamlining government operations, and worldwide social movements are forming around unexpected uses of existing technology. While the latter track often produces dramatic images and stories that draw media attention and public conversation, the former track is becoming increasingly profitable and, we argue, dangerously overtaking the narrative of civic technology *design* and shifting the intentional mobilization of efficiency by designers, implementers, and funders to focus more on helping users of a technological system rather than citizens of a democracy.

The philosopher Hannah Arendt, writing in the 1950s in response to postwar industrialism in Europe and the United States, provides important insight into the logic of human systems, specifically the way tools and functions conceive of and mobilize their human users. Arendt (1998) argues that all human activity falls within three categories: *labor, work,* and *action*. Labor is a fundamental activity that maintains human life, an activity that caters to biological needs of production and consumption (the actual human effort that is mobilized toward work); work is an activity that contributes to the world that humans occupy (everything from building tools to thinking ideas); finally, action is the birth of a new political current in the world, a social means for change with no neatly predictable or prescribed ends.

The problem with many contemporary systems built purely with a focus on labor or work is that they too often view humans as interchangeable units, and imposed civic *behavior* replaces civic action. Arendt criticizes the rationalizing systems under which modern humans live for their tendency to elicit "from each of its members a certain kind of behavior, imposing innumerable and various rules, all of which tend to 'normalize' its members, to make them behave, to exclude spontaneous action or outstanding achievement" (1998, 41). Technology critic Evgeny Morozov echoes this in 2013 in the context of digital technology: "recasting all complex social situations either as neatly defined problems with definite, computable solutions or as transparent and self-evident processes that can be easily optimized—if only the right algorithm is in place!" is likely not even to achieve its predicted purpose, for the 'solutions' are often more tied to techno-utopian values than the realities of a messy, real world democracy (Morozov 2013, 5).

It is perhaps an irony then that modern web technologies might be the most effective medium ever to exist to facilitate action as Arendt defines it. Open, interconnected, mobile, complex, chaotic: the web not only provides potential for action through its ability to connect disparate people and to propagate ideas at a level never before realized, but it is also perfectly fitted to integrate into the contours of a democratic system—one complex pluralistic system intertwined with another. The job of civic systems can be to promote and curate this action while at the same time establishing stable "islands of predictability" through institutions, laws, and promises (1998, 244). When we invoke 'civic systems,' we mean any designed series of social interactions aimed at facilitating collective governance or action, be it a constituted system of national government aimed at sustaining integral institutions, a grassroots collective aimed at radically altering how voices are counted in a deliberative process, or an online forum dedicated to establishing and maintaining the rules and etiquette of a website. It is imperative that the designers of civic systems leverage web-based technology not for imposing behaviors, but for facilitating action.

In this chapter, we analyze the narrative of technological efficiency in the civic space. Contributing to what Elizabeth Losh calls the "Virtualpolitik," the narrative of technological efficiency has become part of everyday governance, impacting decisions made by the "managers of the nation state" (2009, 12). We seek to recognize where the narrative is challenged through alternative actions and designs. We introduce what we call *meaningful inefficiencies* as an emerging design paradigm for civic technology, which accommodates the possibility of messiness, disruption, and playing with rules and boundaries. Borrowing from the fields of game design and game studies, meaningful inefficiencies is a way of thinking about civic systems that are open to the affordances of play—what Roger Caillois refers to as an "occasion of pure waste" (1958/2001, 5)—where users have the option to *play* within and with rules, not simply to *play out* prescribed tasks (Sutton-Smith 1997; Sicart 2014). While we argue for the value of play in the design and implementation of civic systems, we do not want to suggest that there is something inevitable in the playful (or ludic) paradigm (Raessens 2006, 2014; Walz 2010; Zimmerman 2015). Instead, we seek to understand play not as a paradigmatic shift, but as a characteristic of systems that has been overlooked in the current discourse surrounding technology and governance. Ultimately, in this chapter we present a call to action to understand civic technologies not simply in terms of what they do, but what people do with them. Designing for meaningful inefficiencies is a way of expanding technological civic systems to accommodate more than just the 'good user' of systems, but also the marginalized, the emergent, and the playful.

User-friendliness

While civic technology, or civic tech, in its current form is a new phenomenon, the insertion of technological efficiency into civic life is hardly new. Consider the design of cities. Twentieth-century urbanism has ushered in an understanding of cities as complex and rational systems (Mumford 2010) wherein the networks of building and roads could be conceptualized as a structure or language with which humans could interact (Alexander et al. 1977). But the end logic of the modernist city, the master-planned Brasilia or Robert Moses's rationalized sanitation of New York City, is what by today's standards would be called a dumb city, as they were systems designed and fixed in place with the premise of full automation without responsiveness to their human occupants. These mid-century modernist utopias were human systems designed for the abstracted and generic human user (Gordon 2010). More recently, discourses of the smart city, or the smarter city, have dominated contemporary city planning efforts around a simple premise—data generated through users of systems can inform the design and iteration of such systems (IBM 2012; Townsend 2013). In a big data environment, where mobile devices and sensors can capture movements, purchases and, social interactions, and where data from property, crime, and taxes are available and usable in aggregate, the promise of data-driven design is motivating change in urban systems and their governance (Caragliu, Del Bo, and Nijkamp 2009; Ratti and Townsend 2011). The individual is no longer the primary subject of governance; instead, governments have sought to become responsive to the aggregate data traces they leave behind (de Souza e Silva and Gordon 2013; Whitson 2015). Data sourced in aggregate, and the users that enable efficient data access, are the subjects directly addressed by government and organizations all within the celebrated framework of the 'user-friendly city.' This rhetoric was apparent in Baltimore's early CitiStat program, but questions about which customer was being served, and to whom the government was being friendly, arose with dramatic poignancy during the 2015 protests. The only people that get counted in aggregate, it would seem, are those who are good users of the systems provided.

Inequality and access have been insufficiently addressed in the context of 'smart' governance and city building, largely because it has been so heavily influenced by private sector-sponsored infrastructure projects, including IBM's Smarter Cities initiative, or contemporary master-planned city environments such as New Songdo City in South Korea. While the modernist representations of urbanism are apparent in these projects—skyscrapers, plazas, and highways—a central part of the infrastructure is the data scraped from citizens as they occupy these representations. Residents are conceived as users of systems, and most importantly, creators and users of data. Governing this smarter city, therefore, requires access, production, and analysis of data, and the conceptualization of the citizen as a producer of data within the confines of systems.

The city as system, much like any designed technical system, is designed for the user who uses the system well, or one who enters into the system in good faith to accomplish prescribed tasks. Users of technological systems often accommodate those systems *in order* to use them well (Lanier 2010) and the underlying code of systems becomes a kind of hidden legal framework that shapes social actions (Lessig 2006). For example, users learn how to navigate automated telephone lines in order to speak to a human being or learn how to use Facebook to reach their friends. Technological systems are always guiding and 'reskilling' their users as much as they are facilitating pre-mediated social actions (Latour 1988). Thus, technology that focuses only on designing more efficiency into civic life runs the risk of altering, without deliberation or oversight, the very constitution of what a citizen is and what they can or cannot do.

So when city government is framed as a user-friendly technological system, the characteristics of the 'good user' become the legible stand-in for the citizen. The concept of the 'good user' is based on normative structures of citizenship that situate the user solely within abstracted procedures, such as attending a meeting or voting or registering a complaint about a pothole. The users, conceived within the systems they use well, are necessarily articulated outside of any other modes of social integration such as place or cultural lineage that might otherwise compose political and civic identities (Habermas 2001), and determine patterns of inclusion or exclusion (Fraser 1990). Mechanisms of crafting citizenship such as formal or informal education (Callan 1997; Guttman 1999) and civic voice and activism (Manin 1997; Habermas 2001; Bennett 2008) are potentially sidelined in the minds of system architects to accommodate those already producing the appropriate data or those data-producing practices that can best accommodate new technological systems. The 'good user' is the rational, self-interested customer who demands efficient services toward prescribed ends. Similar to the concept of 'political consumerism,' or the buying or boycotting of products for political purposes (Stolle, Hooghe, and Micheletti 2005), the production or use of aggregate data is a form of consumerism that has direct impact on one's sense of engagement (or lack of same) in civic life (de Zúñiga, Copeland, and Bimber 2013).

Hackability

One of the first major instances with a city actively publicizing its ability to leverage private sector innovations occurred with CompStat in New York City. Originally developed for the NYPD in 1994, CompStat aimed to modernize the department through a "continuous improvement of performance" by employing "a variety of corporate strategies" to make its organizational structure more efficient (O'Connell 2001). At the core of CompStat is the requirement of routine data-based meetings where field commanders were mandated both to report and react to data generated from their precincts. This data resulted from a requirement that all precincts record a number of crime statistics on a neighborhood basis. The reaction to the data would trigger a street-by-street response, with the goal of rewarding commanders not by the number of arrests their staff made, but according to a drop in specific crime statistics.

Winner of the 1996 Innovations in American Government Award from the Harvard Kennedy School of Government, CompStat represents one of the first major city systems to fully embrace an emerging focus on the private sector: the collection and leveraging of big data. Soon, this data-driven approach to service management was adopted by other New York

City departments—*ParkStat* for the Department of Parks and Recreation, *TrafficStat* for the traffic division, *JobStat* for the Human Resources Administration, and *HealthStat* for health insurance enrollment—and by other cities throughout the United States. It was Baltimore that fused all these various departments together in CitiStat.

E-government, Government 2.0, and open government are all terms used to describe the 'digital revolution' in government function and operation which have been influenced in no small way by CitiStat (Misuraca 2009; Ressler 2009; Poje 2011). Chun et al. (2010) identify several stages of e-government, ranging from the basic digitization of government records, to simple web-based transactions with available data, to more complex transactions such as paying taxes and fines. These early stages of e-government were focused solely on the efficiency of transactions at the municipal level, as we saw with the first 311 services. The current stage, they argue, is focused on interaction. It is about the quality of citizen interaction with government and the opportunities for collaborative decision-making through social media and open data. These three stages make clear the logical slippage between the digitization of records and citizen engagement. For e-government practitioners, these very different activities are placed under the umbrella of government efficiency and speak directly to the rhetorical promise of networked, web-based technologies for everyday governance.

This declarative position is in part fueled by the Obama administration's 2009 open government initiative, which established three principles for governing in the digital age: transparency, participation, and collaboration. According to the document, governments should make more data available to the public; they should make it easy to access basic services and information; and they should foster possibilities for interdepartmental and interagency collaboration. The initiative was directed to the federal government, but it has served as a justification for municipal government to devote resources to 'opening up.' As these principles of open government translate to the local level, they have maintained their focus on internal efficiency and appropriation of private sector rhetoric, but have also been refined to focus on direct service provision and citizen participation.

'Opening up' and empowering citizens has dominated the discourse of civic technology. But just as the civic tech community has celebrated these possibilities, they have also situated that openness within a language of control, specifically, in the discourse of technology, through the metaphor of *hacking*. According to Shannon Spanhake, San Francisco's Deputy Innovation Officer, "[c]ities are like living machines, and policy making in government is like writing the code that governs how a city operates. This city is the most complex machine I have ever had the opportunity to hack and it is what inspired my shift from the private sector to the public sector. #helloworld" (Innovate SF 2013). Big data production and consumption has enabled the opening up of channels of communication, but at the same time, it has enabled designers of civic systems to control and hack the system. As a result of this conceptual framing, the citizen as a user of a hackable system, is disciplined through procedures of what philosopher Michel Foucault (1991) describes as governmentality, whereby under the promise of collaboration governments redouble their hold on power by dispersing it to the governed. In the actual operation of governments, this does not represent "a diminishment or a reduction of state sovereignty and planning capacities but a displacement from formal to informal techniques of government and the appearance of new actors on the scene of government (e.g. NGOs), that indicate fundamental transformations in statehood and a new relation between state and civil society actors" (Lemke 2002, 11). In this sense, government power can be maintained far more efficiently and pervasively not through external force, but by tacitly managing the possible forms of self-government and fields of action available to citizens (Söderström, Paasche, and Klauser, 2014). Hackability, according to the discourse of the smarter city, is often employed as a means of exerting control, as opposed to challenging it. It invokes an internal to government strategy that becomes a way of managing social difference, including race, class, and gender, by streamlining the good user into normative, technical activities.

Civic labor and civic work

The designers and proponents of civic technology too often articulate participation and openness within the framework of efficiency and control. This approach to governance is premised on defining a very specific user, one that is compelled to operate as an individual, presumably for personal benefit, but in the service of a system. Hannah Arendt's conceptions of labor and work provide useful frameworks for understanding this design paradigm.

When civic technologies are designed for labor, users are conceived as components of an efficient system, as laborers in achieving prescribed ends (i.e. 311 non-emergency systems). Systems designed to cultivate civic labor tend to be transactional, focusing on the curation of good habits and slipping into the background of everyday routine. Citizen mobile reporting apps and APIs such as Boston 311, NYC 311, or Chicago Works outsource the identification of problems directly to laborers. According to Arendt, to labor is "meant to be enslaved by necessity, and this enslavement was inherent in the conditions of human life" (1998, 83-84). Labor is the basic contribution to the maintenance of survival. No longer needing to attend extensively to biological survival, modern labor in post-industrial nations can be equated to the continual repetitive processes with which the status quo of any system is maintained. Not only does outsourcing labor to citizens increase efficiency and decrease costs for government if done correctly, but it also defines citizenship in transactional terms and as something done purely 'in service' to the basic continuation of the status quo and its existing power structures.

Systems designed with civic work in mind tend to consider the outcomes of labor and the use of those outcomes in the world. For example, public planning processes are typically framed as a collective effort toward designing a particular policy document through input and analysis. Contrary to simply using citizens as laborers for increasing the efficiency of civic life, civic designers deploy interventions that help to *fabricate solutions* and *make* citizens better users of existing civic systems. Whether traditional public information campaigns, education programs, mandatory requirements for participation, or web-enabled education and discussion apps, civic work aims to construct an artifice of efficient citizenship required by all in order to optimize the way civic systems are used. As opposed to using citizens to generate big data, here data is used to optimize citizens through systems of education or activity. For example, the attempt at crowd-sourcing a new constitution in Iceland after the protests in 2008-2009 is a good illustration of civic tech directed toward a specific work product. While the effort was ultimately rejected by Iceland's parliament in 2012, the process of using networked technology to steer collective labor toward specific ends is clearly represented in this example. However, the value of such efforts needs to be questioned given that the ratification of the new constitution, which was supported by 67 percent of voters, ended up being rejected because of only a few disenchanted MPs. Despite the 'opening up' through consolidating work efforts, the system remained *hackable* by its architects, essentially under the control of those already in power. Iceland, perhaps because of its highly connected (95 percent broadband use) and highly homogenous population, has continued to explore and support similar civic tech efforts such as *Better Reykjavik*, which is a mobile input system that has sourced since its start in 2010 over 1700 policy recommendations (with over 400 of them formally considered by the government). The example of Iceland demonstrates both the extraordinary affordances of streamlining civic work and the risk of it simply reifying existing power structures through governmentality.

Increasingly, practitioners in and out of government are looking to behavioral science for insights and for approaches to encouraging civic labor and work. In the UK, for example, the Behavioral Insights Team (sometimes called the 'Nudge Unit') was established in 2010 through the Prime Minister's Office to apply behavioral science to policy enforcement and service delivery. In the United States, the Obama administration established a similar office in 2014 called the Social and Behavioral Science Team (SBST). The notion of 'nudging' people as an approach to social policy was popularized by economist Richard Thaler and former Administrator of the White House Office of Information and Regulatory Affairs, Cass Sunstein. Nudging seeks to alter "people's behavior in a predictable way without forbidding any options or significantly changing their economic incentives" so that "consistent and unwavering people, in the private or public sector, can move groups and practices in their preferred direction" (Thaler and Sunstein 2009, 58). With the subtle coercion of citizens to govern their behaviors more efficiently through the internalization of mechanisms of control (as in governmentality), the citizen again takes on the qualities of a good user: predictably acting within a pre-defined system and pushed to act primarily in their own self-interest.

Many of these efforts have produced clear outcomes. For example, the benchmark program for the new SBST, in partnership with the United States Department of Education, sought to increase rates of federal loan repayment among those who had fallen behind. The team experimented with email communication to understand what form of address and frequency of email had the most impact on loan repayment. The results of the pilot demonstrated that sending emails to borrowers in delinquency for 90-180 days resulted in a statistically significant increase in repayment applications, with 6000 additional completed applications in the first month. These sorts of results hold significant promise for making government more efficient insofar as they seek to understand and iterate on the measurable behaviors of citizens. But they also reinscribe the notion of a citizen as a user of a system, as a consumer of services, while engaging in labor and work. In so doing, they bracket out the nuance, the unmeasurable, and the actions through which citizens construct meaning and form identities. By making civic systems more user-friendly, they ultimately make users friendlier to civic systems.

Civic action and meaningful inefficiencies

Democracy does not always appear to be efficient. As the events in Baltimore demonstrate, anger and feelings of exclusion can lead to disruption of otherwise streamlined systems. But those same feelings, bolstered by social media and connective technologies, create what John Dewey (2011) calls 'civic efficiency,' or working with others to achieve public ends. "If democracy has a moral and ideal meaning," Dewey notes, "it is that a social return be demanded from all and that the opportunity for development of distinctive capacities be afforded all [...] the adoption of the narrower meaning of efficiency deprives it of its essential justification" (Ibid., 117). Dewey here is distinguishing 'technological efficiency' from the kind of 'civic efficiency' that makes social experiences valuable and educative. Both technological efficiency and civic efficiency are present in any democratic context, even as civic technologies push to produce and reproduce the former. The activities associated with Dewey's version of civic efficiency are born of Arendt's third category: *action*.

Democracy needs to allow for unpredictable, chaotic, novel *civic action* to occur, in which even "the smallest act in the most limited circumstance" and even "one deed, and sometimes one word, suffices to change every constellation" (Arendt 1998, 190). Action, as Arendt defines it, is the birth of a new political current, as small as a word or as large as a declaration, that reverberates through a human collective and interacts with everything and everyone, often imperceptibly. Allowing the freedom and providing a medium through which these waves can flow, enables the chaotic emergence of new ideas, new experiences, and new actions that a single individual, a group, or a data model could never achieve. The consequences are "boundless, because action, though it may proceed from nowhere, so to speak, acts into a medium where every reaction becomes a chain reaction and where every process is the cause of new processes" and that "no matter what its specific content, always establishes relationships and therefore has an inherent tendency to force open all limitations and cut across all boundaries" (Ibid.). An action can be set into motion by a single person, but it reverberates and grows in the social world where it takes on a character that transcends its initial design or intention through pluralistic, collective force. A system that permits action in Arendt's sense allows for collective contributions to a process or a cause to become more than the sum of its parts. From people in the Roxbury neighborhood of Boston commandeering the 311 system to focus the city's attention on blighted properties, to a simple hashtag, #blacklivesmatter, created by a few activists after the acquittal of George

Zimmerman in the wrongful death trial of African American teenager Trayvon Martin in Sanford, Florida—each action is a meaningful inefficiency with clear outcomes. One forced a city government to act on long ignored blighted properties and the other mobilized a global campaign to highlight racial injustices. While vastly different in scale, each is disrupting norms and challenging efficiencies in systems of governance.

In order to counteract technological efficiency as the dominant design value of civic systems, we suggest a concerted effort to design meaningful inefficiencies into human systems. Meaningful inefficiencies represent the design of systems for civic action, not behaviors. They can be civic tools, systems, or events, etc., that temporarily halt normal civic processes and create a delineated time or place in which play, disorder, messiness, and the ability to experiment and fail are safely utilized in productive—though not necessarily practical—ways. The results of these types of play can be increased civic learning, reflection, empathy, and increased awareness of civic systems and their effects—which citizens can then leverage in creating new forms of action in the normal processes of civic life.

A meaningful inefficiency, like Dewey's civic efficiency, ultimately aims to increase "neither more nor less than capacity to share in a give and take of experience. It covers all that makes one's own experience more worthwhile to others, and all that enables one to participate more richly in the worthwhile experiences of others" (Dewey 2011, 116). In the near dominance of technological efficiency in the design of civic systems today, meaningful inefficiency is necessarily an oppositional term, bringing to light the collapsing of the "range and accuracy [of a citizen's] perception of meanings" into machine-readable, hackable, and simplistic *features* (Ibid., 119).

We are not suggesting the design or cultivation of inefficiencies out of context. The fundamental requisite for a civic inefficiency to be 'meaningful' is that it is productively *in tension* with a new or existing efficiency. It would not necessarily be meaningful to create more inefficiencies where inefficiencies run rampant, such as in a situation where basic civic and social services do not exist. An inefficiency only becomes meaningful once it either provides a respite from efficiency, where citizens can share in a give and take of experience and increase their range and perception of meanings with each other, or when it provides a new view of the efficiency, where citizens are able to more fully understand how they are being shaped by the system—or how they might in turn be able to shape it. By doing so, this prompt allows for systems to make the uncertainties of variables fertile; the unexpectedness of outcomes revelatory; the opportunities for waste and the failure of resources and efforts constructive; the stakeholder complexities of interests and goals nourishing; and the deliberate misuses of the system constructive. Common to all meaningful inefficiencies, as we shall see below, is an element of play, or playfulness.

Play

Play is, in a sense, the mechanism of action in meaningful inefficiencies. Play can be defined as an activity in which the means are more valuable than the ends—that is, it is *autotelic*, it is done first and foremost for its own sake. Cultural historian Johan Huizinga writes: "in play there is something 'at play' which transcends the immediate needs of life and imparts meaning to the action. All play means something" (1950, 1). Thus, regardless of outcome—which certainly can be important—play itself is its own point. Players voluntarily enter into a system ostensibly in pursuit of some goal, but participation is not wholly dependent on the outcome of achieving that goal. For example, in a good game, players elect to play and the reward for playing is play itself. If one were to start a game of chess and beat their opponent in less than two minutes, the game would likely be unsatisfying for both the loser and the winner, because while the goal of winning provides direction, the goal of simply playing is not achieved. The uneven game of chess disallows the experience of play. The good user of chess is the one who beats her opponent in less than two minutes. The good player, however, is one that generates meaning from actions taken within the inefficiencies in the system—the circuitous paths one often takes to achieve victory in the face of unnecessary obstacles (Suits 2005).

While play is "an action accomplishing itself outside and above the necessities and seriousness of everyday life," at the same time it can, and often is, employed as a "helping-out of the action" of everyday life, beyond traditional play contexts (Huizinga 1950, 26, 15). Miguel Sicart suggests the term *playfulness* to apply to play in a "context that is not created or intended for play" (2014, 27). Fundamental to this act is the "appropriation of what should not be play." It is this act of appropriation, of bringing to bear on a serious situation in life, play—a mode of experience so fundamental to how we make meaning in the world as we grow, but so stamped out of adult life—that "we bring freedom to a context." Play is "personal, and playfulness is used to imbue the functional world with personal experience," while at the same time "revealing the seams of behaviors, technologies, or situations that we take for granted" (Ibid., 29).

When playfulness is recognized and accommodated within civic systems, the result is a meaningful inefficiency, where the good user is propelled toward action, not just work and labor. In this sense, the notion of a user of a meaningfully inefficient civic system is not sufficient; when a system enables playfulness, either by design or accident, the user acts as a player with freedom to explore meaning well beyond the confines of the system in which they are operating. As such, the recognition of meaningful inefficiencies suggests the recognition of a playful citizen, not simply a good user.

The playful citizen, as a subject of civic systems, is more able to fully participate in the give and take of experience that Dewey declares so fundamental to democratic and personal growth. Acknowledging the playful citizen means recognizing that people actively play with and within systems, which necessitates being adaptable and responsive to unpredictable appropriations. This means that one should not, as internet scholar Yochai Benkler puts it, utilize "a straightforward, uncomplicated theory of human nature that reduces our actions as simple, predictable responses to punishments and incentives and helps us explain away confusing and even disturbing behaviorism," but that designers of civic technologies and citizens alike can learn from each other in a constant play of inventive meanings (Benkler 2011, 18).

"Vibrancy and efficiency may not be diametrically opposed," says Ethan Zuckerman, "but the forces are clearly in tension" (2013, 220). This tension can be productive; and, while challenging for designers, it is only through designing for the play of these and the other forces that facilitate and are moved by citizen action that it is possible to think about and build systems that "let our humanity find a fuller expression; systems that tap into a far greater promise and potential of human endeavor than we have generally allowed in the past" (Benkler 2011, 26). Instead of using new technological innovations to structure behavior so as to impose transactionality, efficiency, and predictability operating on that technology's own terms, it is possible to commission the chaos and emergent play of appropriations when new technology enters civic life, and to use citizen action to steer systems in new, unconventional directions.

Meaningful inefficiencies: An (im)practical example

The concept of disruptive design is nothing new. In the art world, examples abound in the twentieth century, from the Dadaists to the Situationists. Or more specifically in the realm of design, Carl DiSalvo's (2012) concept of adversarial design or Dunne and Raby's (2013) concept of speculative design each point to an interventionist practice in relation to dominant systems. What is unique about the concept of meaningful inefficiencies is its distinct focus on play and civic action taking, not only as an interventionist and deliberate act of design, but also as a characteristic that is inherent within existent systems. Our own experience in designing civic technologies is illustrative of the relevance of meaningful inefficiencies.

Motivated by a lack of community feedback systems in urban planning, in 2010 we were funded by the Knight Foundation to build a public dialog game. The project, in the end called *Community PlanIt* (Engagement Lab 2012), was an online social network meant to bring the public planning meeting online, increase the diversity of those who participated, and to scaffold the process with learning in order to enhance deliberation (Gordon and Baldwin-Philippi 2014). We were interested in making people more informed about the planning issues at hand, more capable of understanding the nuances and rules of a public planning process, and more congenial and empathetic toward other deliberators and decision makers. Following this, our goal, ultimately, was to create a new public planning process and to concurrently cultivate a good user of it. In other words, if we were to successfully introduce a new platform for public engagement, we would need to engage the public in using the platform well.

But, as happens in the early days of a design project, our focus lingered on all the bad users we seemed to be getting, and how we might be able to make them go away. Because of this, many of our early design iterations were about stamping out opportunities where bad users could unexpectedly appropriate our system and do something that we had not planned on. After some pilot tests in the Boston area, we set out to design a system that was more efficient, had more features, and eliminated uncertainty—not so much with the content people could put in to the system, but rather the *way* in which people could use the system. The value of the system, we suspected, was the layering of the social values of the internet (efficiency, archivability, searchability) onto the practical outcomes of most planning processes (conflict avoidance, ephemerality, and confusion).

However, as we deployed the game in two initial implementations (in Boston as part of a school policy planning process and in Detroit as part of an urban planning process), it was clear that the efficiencies so painstakingly built into the system were perhaps the least interesting (and least impactful) qualities of the game experience. While the efficiencies of online participation were an appealing selling point to funders and partners (each game attracted over a thousand players), in fact, the inefficiencies of gameplay created the greatest amount of interest. Ranging from humorously spamming the system with good-natured community event posts (which then created another tangent where participants deliberated about the unsaid rules of civil internet etiquette), to stepping away from the planning issues and talking about the game system itself, the role of youth in civic planning, what it meant to digitally engage with stakeholders or to imbue serious issues with a sense of fun, etc.—these actions were intentional means of appropriating the system to bring some other meaning to it. The best conversations and the most interesting insights did not occur from prompts by the designers, but rather the prompts or provocations created when users disrupted the normal use of the system and did something slightly different with it.

This sort of thing had occurred with virtually all the games or game-like systems we had created for civic engagement up to this point (Gordon and Manosevitch 2010; Gordon and Schirra 2012). But never was it clearer than in this experiment that perhaps our use of games was actually inadvertently doing something else that we were not taking into account; perhaps it was not the games themselves that offered the biggest value to these civic engagement processes, but rather something that emerged because of the very use of a game in this particular sociotechnical context. When tasked with organizing and finding a pattern to the most impactful moments for participants during the process, we realized it was not when the system was working fully, or during the moments when it was working but doing nothing more than facilitating simple transactional interactions such as liking comments or answering yes or no to a prompt; it also was not when a part of the system was simply broken, or was functionally pointless or redundant. The most impact, defined as opportunities to increase trust and efficacy, occurred in moments that were meaningfully inefficient—where either an existing inefficiency itself prompted the user to appropriate it to create some new meaning or action within the system, or when users were able to bring in some inefficiency of their own, and use that to temporarily disrupt the system and cause others to reflect upon what it is that is happening under their noses—how they have been *designed* and how they might be able to build off, or resist, such a design. If this observation was correct, and in fact community engagement matters most when the systems through which people engage are intentionally inefficient (in the technological sense), then our challenge became how to design for these meaningful inefficiencies. Indeed, in the years since *Community PlanIt* was first deployed, there has been a marked increase in the desire to see technologically efficient systems in processes of public engagement and civic life more generally. The use of games or game mechanics to achieve these ends was gaining popularity among marketing consultants and policy makers alike (McGonigal 2011; Zichermann and Cunningham 2011), even as it developed its very vocal critics in academia (Bogost 2015). But what made our project unique, and perhaps not as scalable as other solutions, was the inherent inefficiency in the system that compelled the user to explore alternative meanings. It was the experience of play, buried within our own gamified design and replete with messiness and ambiguity, that positioned us, inadvertently, in a discursive battle emerging within the conflation of technological efficiency and civic life.

Thus, when we set out to design a game to make planning more efficient, we found ourselves pushing up against the very affordances of games. Games are built to be inefficient as the player seeks to overcome unnecessary obstacles to reach the goal and to engage in the process of play for itself (Suits 2005). Civic tech, on the other hand, is steeped in the discourse of efficiency, with a laser focus on the instrumentality of activity. We became very aware of the tensions inherent in the system we designed—wanting to cultivate civic action through play, and at the same time appeal to funders and partners (foundations, municipal governments, and development organizations) to appease their sense of value through efficiency.

Applied games are often characterized as gamified systems (Deterding et al. 2011). In 2011, the term gamification saw a significant surge in popularity, most commonly applied to the use of game mechanics for specific behavior modifications, ranging from business to healthcare. The early location-based social network, Foursquare, used points and badges to motivate digital check-ins, and major corporations began using similar social incentives to increase productivity in the workforce. Gamified systems are widely considered to do three things: 1) they give users motivation to do something; 2) they give users the ability to complete the action; and 3) they give users a trigger or cue to complete the action (Laja 2012). Gamified systems, by this definition, are no different than the ideal systems conceived through the lens of civic tech. This is what makes our early design work with *Community PlanIt* so contradictory: it was a gamified system that promised some level of increased efficiency, yet was framed around the possibilities of play.

We began teasing out these distinctions very slowly. Our initial studies of *Community PlanIt* were focused on its capacity to increase efficiency in what we understood to be a dangerously inefficient system of urban planning (Gupta, Bouvier, and Gordon 2012). We sought to measure participation rates, reciprocity on the part of government stakeholders, and trust among users. It was not until later implementations and years of being steeped in discourses of gamification, that all the fissures and intentional ellipses that *Community PlanIt* brought to planning narratives demonstrated their value. The messy data of deliberation, the playful competition, and the creative storytelling were not simply artifacts of a system, but were central to its design.

The tensions that emerged in the implementation of *Community PlanIt* have been central to our evolved understanding of what it takes to recognize and design for civic action. Characteristics of play and playfulness were emergent within this system. While clearly also designed for labor and work, valued for the data produced by users, the system's incorporated elements of play, of encouraging exploration and discovery, were meaningful inefficiencies that came to define it. Or at least came to define our sense of what made it valuable. With the promise of the good user so persistent in civic tech discourse—a user self-disciplined through data production and consumption—the playful citizen became a necessary design prompt for us as a means of cultivating better, more humane systems that are scalable, meaningful, and allow for novel action to emerge.

Conclusion

The example of *Community PlanIt* represents our 'aha moment' in designing technologies that are meaningfully inefficient. We do not present it as a case study with particular observable outcomes, but as a study in process, wherein our expectations were subverted by the logics we had inadvertently designed into the system. Civic life is composed of actions, even if they are masked by the efficient presentation of labor and work. And civic technologies, properly conceived, should acknowledge and nurture the actions that are expressive and potentially transformative. We began this chapter by talking about the contrast present in the civic technology landscape of twenty-first-century Baltimore. On one hand, CitiStat represents a triumph of technological efficiency, where good users are effectively defined and governed through promises of 'user-friendliness' and 'hackability.' And on the other hand, the 2015 protests prompted by the unlawful death of Freddie Gray represent a triumph of civic efficiency led by those historically excluded from the category of 'good user.' The latter definition of efficiency is often realized in opposition to existent systems of governance, and for that reason, it is, in practice, a meaningful inefficiency. Civic technologies have the capacity to cultivate meaningful inefficiencies within a system that enables playful citizens to electively explore, experiment, resist, and reimagine the systems that govern their collective actions.

We advocate for policymakers and civic technologists alike to incorporate meaningful inefficiencies into the design of civic systems in order to allow for emergent qualities and experiences beyond those prescribed to the good user. Civic systems should accommodate play through embracing: 1) uncertainties (of variables); 2) unexpectedness (of outcomes); 3) opportunities for waste and failure (of resources and efforts); 4) stakeholder complexity (of interests and goals); and 5) deliberate non-use or misuse (of the system). These qualities of play function as a kind of safety valve for the dominance of technological efficiency in civic design and encourage an evolution of democratic practices not absolutely contained by the rational means of their distribution.

We do not mean to suggest that technological efficiency lacks importance or that programs like CitiStat cannot contribute productively to civic life. The efficient delivery of basic services such as access to housing, policing, and healthcare, is essential. This sort of efficiency is a fundamental and important part of civic life and human activity, and certainly something not to be snuffed out. The danger is when technological efficiency goes unchecked, and the rigid systems are designed only for 'good users'—where the slightest unexpected use of the system by a user operating outside of the accepted norms is not accommodated or acknowledged. Ultimately, we suggest that designers, implementers, and funders of civic technologies take into account the existent qualities of labor, work, and action to more accurately pinpoint the function(s) of human activity they are meant to address. The future of civic technology needs to be critical of its ascending values of technological efficiency and not allow a technomentality to obscure relevant intervention points, contexts, and communities in need that may not play well with the rules of good use that have been articulated by the technology of the time. The basic question in civic tech today—how can we make civic life more efficient with technology—must be changed to, how can we use technology to make civic life more meaningful.

Acknowledgments

This chapter is based on a manuscript written in 2013, which since then has also been published in Gordon and Mihailidis (2016).

References

Ackerman, J. 2004. Co-Governance for accountability: Beyond 'exit' and 'voice'. *World Development* 32 (3): 447-463.

Alexander, C., S. Ishikawa, M. Silverstein, M. Jacobson, I. Fiksdahl-King, and S. Angel. 1977. *A pattern language: Towns, buildings, construction.* Oxford: Oxford University Press.

Arendt, H. 1998. *The human condition.* Chicago, IL: University of Chicago Press.

Benkler, Y. 2011. *The Penguin and the Leviathan: How cooperation triumphs over self-interest.* New York: Crown Business.

Bennett, W. L. 2008. Changing citizenship in the digital age. In *Civic life online: Learning how digital media can engage youth*, ed. W. L. Bennett, 1-24. Cambridge, MA: The MIT Press.

Bogost, I. 2015. Why gamification is bullshit. In *The gameful world: Approaches, issues, applications*, eds. S. P. Walz and S. Deterding, 65-79. Cambridge, MA: The MIT Press.

Caillois, R. 1958/2001. *Man, play, and games.* Trans. M. Barash. Chicago, IL: University of Illinois Press.

Callan, E. 1997. *Creating citizens.* Oxford: Oxford University Press.

Caragliu, A., C. Del Bo, and P. Nijkamp. 2009. Smart cities in Europe. *Serie research memoranda 0048*, VU University Amsterdam, Faculty of Economics, Business Administration and Econometrics. http://ideas.repec.org/p/vua/wpaper/2009-48.html.

Chun, S. A., S. Shulman, R. Sandoval, and E. Hovy. 2010. Government 2.0: Making connections between citizens, data and government. *Information Polity* 15 (1, 2): 1-9.

de Zúñiga, H. G., L. Copeland, and B. Bimber. 2013. Political consumerism: Civic engagement and the social media connection. *New Media & Society* 16 (3): 488-506.

Democracy Now! 2015. WATCH: Baltimore prosecutor charges six police officers, calls Freddie Gray's death a "homicide". http://www.democracynow.org/blog/2015/5/1/watch_baltimore_prosecutor_charges_six_police.

Deterding, S., D. Dixon, R. Khaled, and L. Nacke. 2011. From game design elements to gamefulness: Defining "gamification". In *Proceedings of the 15th international academic MindTrek conference: Envisioning future media environments, Tampere, September 28-30, 2011*, 9-15. New York: ACM.

Dewey, J. 2011. *Democracy and education.* New York: Simon and Brown.

DiSalvo, C. 2012. *Adversarial design.* Cambridge, MA: The MIT Press.

Dunne, A., and F. Raby. 2013. *Speculative everything.* Cambridge, MA: The MIT Press.

Engagement Lab. 2012. *Community PlanIt.* [browser]. Emerson College. Game.

Foucault, M. 1991. Governmentality. In *The Foucault effect: Studies in governmentality*, eds. G. Burchell, C. Gordon, and P. Miller, 87-104. Chicago, IL: University of Chicago Press.

Fraser, N. 1990. Rethinking the public sphere: A contribution to the critique of actually existing democracy. *Social Text* 25/26:56-80.

Gordon, E. 2010. *The urban spectator: American concept-cities from Kodak to Google.* Hanover, NH: Dartmouth University Press.

Gordon, E., and J. Baldwin-Philippi. 2014. Playful civic learning: Enabling lateral trust and reflection in game-based public participation. *International Journal of Communication* 8:759-786.

Gordon, E., and E. Manosevitch. 2010. Augmented deliberation: Merging physical and virtual interaction to engage communities in urban planning. *New Media and Society* 13 (1): 75-95.

Gordon, E., and P. Mihailidis, eds. 2016. *Civic media: Technology | Design | Practice.* Cambridge, MA: The MIT Press.

Gordon, E., and S. Schirra. 2012. Playing with empathy: Digital role playing games in public meetings. In *Proceedings of the 5th international conference on communities and technologies, Brisbane, June 29-July 2, 2011*, 179-185. ACM: New York.

Gupta, J., J. Bouvier, and E. Gordon. 2012. Exploring new modalities of public participation: An evaluation of digital gaming platforms on civic capacity and collective action in the Boston public school district. http://placeofsocialmedia.com/projects-2.

Guttman, A. 1999. *Democratic education.* Princeton, NJ: Princeton University Press.

Habermas, J. 2001. *The postnational constellation: Political essays.* Trans. M. Pensky. Cambridge, MA: The MIT Press.

Henderson, L. 2003. The Baltimore CitiStat program: Performance and accountability. *IBM Center for The Business of Government.* http://www.businessofgovernment.org/report/baltimore-citistat-program-performance-and-accountability.

Huizinga, J. 1950. *Homo ludens: A study of the play-element in culture.* Boston, MA: Beacon Press.

IBM. 2012. *Smarter, more competitive cities: Forward thinking cities are investing in insight.* New York: IBM Corporation.

Innovate SF. 2013. *The San Francisco Mayor's Office of Civic Innovation: A start-up called government—Our first year in retrospect.* http://ofti.org/wp-content/uploads/2013/05/2012Retrospective.pdf.

Laja, P. 2012. How to Use Gamification for Better Business Results. *Kissmetrics*. http://blog.kissmetrics.com/gamification-for-better-results.

Lanier, J. 2010. *You are not a gadget: A manifesto*. New York: Thorndike Press.

Latour, B. 1988. Mixing humans and non-humans together: The sociology of a door closer. *Social Problems* 35 (3): 298-310.

Lemke, T. 2002. Foucault, governmentality, and critique. *Rethinking Marxism* 14 (3): 49-64.

Lessig, L. 2006. *Code: Version 2.0*. New York: Basic Books.

Losh, E. 2009. *Virtualpolitik: An electronic history of government media-making in a time of war, scandal, disaster, miscommunication, and mistakes*. Cambridge, MA: The MIT Press.

Manin, B. 1997. *Principles of representative government*. New York: Cambridge University Press.

McGonigal, J. 2011. *Reality is broken: Why games make us better and how they can change the world*. New York: Penguin Press.

Misuraca, G. C. 2009. E-Government 2015: Exploring m-government scenarios, between ICT-driven experiments and citizen-centric implications. *Technology Analysis & Strategic Management* 21 (3): 407-424.

Morozov, E. 2013. *To save everything, click here: The folly of technological solutionism*. New York: PublicAffairs.

Mumford, L. 2010. *Technics and civilization*. Chicago, IL: University of Chicago Press.

O'Connell, P. E. 2001. Using performance data for accountability: The New York City Police Department's CompStat model of police management. http://businessofgovernment.org/sites/default/files/CompStat.pdf.

Poje, J. 2011. Gov 2.0: Interaction, innovation and collaboration. *Public Lawyer* 19 (1): 2-11.

Raessens, J. 2006. Playful identities, or the ludification of culture. *Games and Culture* 1 (1): 52-57.

—. 2014. The ludification of culture. In *Rethinking gamification*, eds. M. Fuchs, S. Fizek, P. Ruffino, and N. Schrape, 91-114. Lüneburg: meson press.

Ratti, C., and A. Townsend. 2011. Harnessing residents' electronic devices will yield truly smart cities. http://www.scientificamerican.com/article.cfm?id=the-social-nexus.

Ressler, S. 2009. The rise of Gov 2.0: From GovLoop to the White House. *Public Manager* 38 (3): 10-14.

Sicart, M. 2014. *Play matters*. Cambridge, MA: The MIT Press.

Söderström, O., T. Paasche, and F. Klauser. 2014. Smart cities as corporate storytelling. *City* 18 (3): 307-320.

de Souza e Silva, A., and E. Gordon. 2013. The waning distinction between private and public: Net locality and the restructuring of space. In *The international encyclopedia of media studies*, ed. A. N. Valdivia, 195-214. Malden, MA: Wiley-Blackwell.

Stolle, D., M. Hooghe, and M. Micheletti. 2005. Politics in the supermarket: Political consumerism as a form of political participation. *International Political Science Review* 26 (3): 245-269.

Suits, B. 2005. *The grasshopper: Games, life and utopia*. Peterborough, Ont.: Broadview Press.

Sutton-Smith, B. 1997. *The ambiguity of play*. Cambridge, MA: Harvard University Press.

Thaler, R., and C. Sunstein. 2009. *Nudge: Improving decisions about health, wealth, and happiness*. New York: Penguin Books.

Townsend, A. 2013. *Smart cities: Big data, civic hackers, and the quest for a new utopia*. New York: W. W. Norton & Company.

Walz, S. P. 2010. *Toward a ludic architecture: The space of play and games*. Pittsburgh, PA: ETC Press.

Whitson, J. 2015. Foucault's Fitbit: Governance and gamification. In *The gameful world: Approaches, issues, applications*, eds. S. P. Walz and S. Deterding, 339-358. Cambridge, MA: The MIT Press.

Zichermann, G., and C. Cunningham. 2011. *Gamification by design: Implementing game mechanics in web and mobile apps*. Seabastopol, CA: O'Reilly.

Zimmerman, E. 2015. Manifesto for a ludic century. In *The gameful world: Approaches, issues, applications*, eds. S. P. Walz and S. Deterding, 19-22. Cambridge, MA: The MIT Press.

Zuckerman, E. 2013. *Rewire: Digital cosmopolitanism in the age of connection*. New York, NY: Norton W. W. & Co. Inc.

About the authors

Eric Gordon is the founding director of the Engagement Lab and a Full Professor in the Department of Visual and Media Arts. He is particularly interested in the transformation of civic institutions, including government and journalism, in the wake of technological disruption, and the emerging tensions between technological efficiency in 'smart city' solutions and democratic governance. In addition to this research, Gordon works with cities and organizations around the world to design creative media approaches to public participation, using games, augmented reality, and virtual reality. He is the author of two books: *Net locality: Why location matters in* *a networked world* (Blackwell 2011, with Adriana de Souza e Silva) and *The urban spectator: American concept cities from Kodak to Google* (Dartmouth 2010), and the editor (with Paul Mihailidis) of *Civic media: Technology | Design | Practice* (The MIT Press 2016). His new book, tentatively titled *Meaningful inefficiencies: Democracy and public value in the smart city*, will be published by Oxford University Press.

Stephen Walter researches and designs civic media, technology, and spaces. At the Mayor's Office of New Urban Mechanics, he helps lead efforts around experiments in civic engagement, storytelling, technology, and research. Previously, Walter was the founding managing director of the Engagement Lab, an applied research lab for reimagining civic engagement in a digital era. He has conducted action research projects in places like Detroit, Boston, Philadelphia, Moldova, Zambia, Egypt, and Bhutan, and has worked at the International Red Cross/Red Crescent Climate Centre, the United Nations Development Program, the US Department of State, and the PBS television shows *Frontline* and *Nova*. His research also appears in the book *Civic media: Technology | Design | Practice* (The MIT Press 2016), and he is a research affiliate at the Berkman Klein Center for Internet and Society at Harvard.

17. Permanent revolution: Occupying democracy

Douglas Rushkoff

Abstract

The Occupy movement constitutes an upgrade of political activism from campaign to prototype. This shift from the traditional narrative, goal-oriented movement to activism as 'infinite game' is consistent with the changing media environment informing this activity. As we move from a culture defined by the book and broadcast media to one expressed more through the net and peer-to-peer media, our approaches to politics and our expectations for its results change. We are transitioning from a spectator democracy, in which citizens project their hopes and dreams onto charismatic leaders, to a participatory democracy, in which citizens enact change through their real-time interactions. This shift reflects more than a change in communications technologies; it marks a change in the mode and dimensional level of activism.

Keywords: Occupy movement, political activism, peer-to-peer media, participatory democracy, global justice movement, prototyping

Back in the late 1990s, I became interested in the potential of interactive and networking technologies to enhance the potential for democratic and civic participation. I wrote a short book entitled *Open source democracy* (Rushkoff 1998), in which I outlined what I saw as the opportunity for deeper levels of public intervention in not just electoral politics, but ongoing civic affairs. At the time, most visions of electronically enabled democracy were still stuck in what we might call the Ross Perot phase: use the net to let people vote or participate in what the third-party presidential candidate called "electronic town halls" (Simon 1992). Perot envisioned citizens watching

Glas, R., S. Lammes, M. de Lange, J. Raessens, and I. de Vries, eds. 2019. *The Playful Citizen. Civic Engagement in a Mediatized Culture.* Amsterdam: Amsterdam University Press.
DOI: 10.5117/9789462984523/CH17

television programs that informed them about the issues, and then voting yes or no to proposals through their remote controls.

Meanwhile, Clinton pollster Dick Morris (Martinson 2000) saw in the internet a new path to polling accuracy. Instead of calling people and asking them questions, internet pollsters could send emails and monitor existing discussion groups and comments sections. While feedback from users would not directly influence policy, at least lawmakers would be able to gauge (and presumably change messaging in order to influence) public opinion.

My own hope was for a deeper level of participation. Just as the internet allowed former television viewers to create something very much like programming, the internet could allow former voters to create something very much like policy platforms. The law might come to resemble less a set of bound volumes than a participatory wiki.

The 2004 Howard Dean campaign was among the first to respond to this call for a more net-enabled democracy. Dean's campaign manager, Joe Trippi, used the language of open source democracy to energize the first sustained and successful internet political fundraising campaign. Instead of taking large sums from a small group of donors, Dean drew support from thousands upon thousands of individuals whose donations averaged just $80. Nevertheless, the $50 million Dean raised made him the first presidential candidate to forgo federal matching funds (Trippi 2004).

Eventually, the Obama campaign followed suit, using Facebook, Twitter, Meetup, forums, and a state-of-the-art website to solicit campaign donations, organize on-the-ground get-out-the-vote activities, and generate peer-to-peer support for his candidacy. He, too, raised enough money to reject federal campaign funds, and managed to leverage the internet's metaphorical value as a participatory medium to cast his candidacy as a bottom-up people's revolution.

However, after Obama won, the stirring idea that 'we are the change we have been waiting for' quickly devolved into politics as usual. While Obama the net-enabled campaigner offered many ways for people to get involved by donating money or getting others to donate money, Obama the net-enabled office-holder used the net much less aggressively. The administration offered greater transparency than its predecessors, making it easier for citizens to find pending legislation on the web. But for the most part, it was still a read-only government. The net was used to gather the troops for the campaign, but not to solicit or enable their participation as citizens in an ongoing way. For those who may have risen to the call to "be the change" (Sullivan 2008) this was a disappointment.

But the media attention garnered through YouTube-sponsored debates and national net-organized Meetups spurred dozens of pop culture and commercial copycats. Internet-style democracy founds its expression in everything from American Idol (where viewers use text messaging to vote for their favorite singers) to a campaign for Mountain Dew called 'Dewmocracy' where consumers campaign for name and color of the next Mountain Dew beverage offering (Rushkoff 2009). This gamification is not an entry point for democratic participation, but rather vulgarizes democracy as some form of consumer decision. Instead of using the net to increase opportunity, engagement, and levels of knowledge, the net seems to be used in the opposite fashion: Internet-style democracy encourages impulsiveness, impatience, siloing, and closed-minded hostility (Pariser 2011). CNN and other news networks now use scientific-looking 'people meters' to gauge instantaneous audience responses to candidates' speeches and debates. A line at the bottom of the screen indicates male and female enthusiasm for whatever a candidate is saying in that moment—as if the immediate reaction and the considered response were one and the same (Goodman, Rushkoff, and Dretzin 2003).

Meanwhile, the amateurization encouraged by the net leads users to believe that access means ability (Keane 2007). Just because someone has access to a blog does not mean he or she has the ability to write researched, considered or even logical posts. Since a Wordpress template can now make anyone's posts appear—at least superficially—as authoritative as anyone else's, it is up to readers to distinguish between the veracity and sense of different voices, including their own.

But in a media environment where sensationalism still trumps sense, the reward for participation is not to gain or share knowledge or insight, but to be credited with hits. Bloggers get attention for saying outrageous things, or linking to those who have. With the tools to publish becoming equated with the skill to write, the amateur is rendered incapable of distinguishing his own off-the-cuff output from the considered, researched, or reported product of trained professionals. This in turn leads to a misplaced disgust for professional journalism—a sense that those who earn column space in *The New York Times* or airtime on the BBC do not offer anything of greater intrinsic value than people posting in the comments sections or unvetted Tumblr blogs. I have more than once been questioned by college students wanting to know why I should be paid for doing "exactly the same thing" that they are doing for free.

Of course, the notion that no one should be paid for journalism misses the fact that corporations and governments will continue to pay billions to public relations firms and advertising agencies to obfuscate the truth. If society invests nothing in professional journalism, there will be no one left with the time, resources, and ability to deconstruct the fictions, pursue leads, evaluate sources, and confirm facts (Rushkoff 2010). Instead, we get an internet-inspired ontological relativism where everyone's opinions matter as much as everyone else's facts. Again, without some discipline and direction—some conscious sense of the structural biases of digital media—the promise of some kind of constructive, open source democracy moves ever further away.

In my own experience, I was scheduled to deliver a talk at an American college and received an email from a young woman who wanted to know whether or not I was a "leftist." It seems she had been retained by an organization headed by right-wing activist David Horowitz to protest the hiring of leftist speakers and professors at American colleges (Horowitz 2006). The young woman had spent a bit of time on my website reading articles, but had been as of yet unable to ascertain if I was, indeed, a leftist. "Could you just tell me if you are a leftist, so I know whether to protest your appearance?"

I responded that it would be difficult for me to answer. I had read much of Marx and understood the extraction of value from the worker, but I was not convinced that large-scale labor unions were the best vehicle for correcting the wrongs of corporate capitalism. She replied, asking if I could give her a simple "yes or no answer." I told her "yes and no." She declined my invitation to appear with me to discuss all this on stage during my appearance. This young woman was ready to protest based on my binary response, but unprepared to have an extended conversation—even through email—where she could become educated or even just hone and advance her own argument. She wanted something as easy as the like button on Facebook.

By amplifying the more gamified, amateur, and impulse-driven qualities of the net, e-democracy has not only missed the mark as an opportunity for a more participatory electorate and civic body, but also exacerbated some of the least productive elements of spectator democracy so many believed would be obsolesced by the internet (McLuhan 1992). However, while the net may have failed democracy as a tool or platform, it may have succeeded on a more subtle yet ultimately deeper level as a media environment. That is, while the keyboards and websites and blogs and streaming video and social networks actually comprising the internet may not be directly impacting the ways in which citizens engage in civics, digital technology as a cultural landscape is beginning to have a profound effect on the way people conceive of themselves in relationship to one another and institutions.

Most significantly, as I'll attempt to show in the case of the Occupy Wall Street movement, the net suggests new metaphors and demonstrates new principles that inform a novel amalgam of activist practices.

In short, the 'playful citizen' now being discussed in many forums and collections like the one in which this chapter appears, is most interesting—and ultimately promising—as a style of inquiry into the ways that the emergence of the net and accompanying changes in the social-scientific paradigm have altered our expectations of agency, participation, and change.

Digital environment

The digital environment, like any other media environment, is embedded with certain values that inform the culture within it. The textual environment encouraged new ways of thinking about accountability (written contracts), human interaction (written law) and even religion (the written Covenant with God—the Torah) (Logan 1987; Ong 2002). The printing press likewise changed the way people related to business (central banking), government (the Enlightenment), and the authority of the Church (personal Bibles and the Protestant reformation) (McLuhan 1962).

To parse the impact of the digital environment is a bit more difficult since we are currently living within its effects. I identify four of the most pronounced conceptual shifts accompanying digitality in order to demonstrate the ways the Occupy movement has utilized them as central operating principles for its new approach to activism and democratic participation.

Feedback. The first is the notion of feedback. Traditionally, what we think of as feedback is simply the latent results of particular causes. Farmers plant in one season, and get feedback months later in the yield of crop. Plant seed too close together, and the crop compete for resources. This data is then incorporated into the next year's planting. Likewise, businesses send a product to market and then wait for sales reports to determine if the design and marketing were appropriate or could be improved upon. Each new iteration of planting or product design was based on the feedback from the one before.

In the dawn of the digital era, Cyberneticist Norbert Weiner (1965) saw in feedback a way of developing robots that could instantaneously 'feel' and respond to changing conditions in the real world. Just as a thermostat senses the temperature in order to turn a heater on or off, and an elevator 'feels' for indicators at each floor instead of attempting to measure the distance between one floor and another, robots could be taught to rely to no greater extent on their programming than to the things around them. Each piece of feedback could be iterated into the next action.

With the help of systems theorists aided by computers (Miller and Page 2007), much more complex systems could be analyzed in terms of feedback and iteration. The screech one hears when placing a microphone too close to an amplified speaker—what we call feedback—is really just the cyclical loop of uncontrolled feedback, iterating back to the microphone and again to the speaker. It is analogous to any of the many chaotic systems from the weather to the stock market that evade the analysis of our normal faculties.

Computers give us a way to see such systems in terms of their feedback and iteration. Fractals—the paisley graphics churned out by computers—are really just visualizations of the feedback and iteration of non-linear equations. Their power is in their ability to render previously incomprehensible systems in graphics that make sense to the human viewer. As a result, we become increasingly ready to understand feedback as an ongoing phenomenon rather than some occasional event.

In politics, for example, feedback used to occur primarily in four-year cycles. The populace would vote for a president, that president would go about his job, and then four years later he would get feedback in the form of being granted another term or kicked out of office. Pollsters arose to obtain feedback at tighter intervals, so that a politician could adjust policy (or even just his communication about policy) during his term. Digital technology—from live Twitter feeds to real time people meter results—now allows for instantaneous feedback. In a digital environment, feedback and iteration fold into one another.

Deconstruction of narrative. Likewise, in a digital environment, narratives no longer work quite like they used to. Thanks to the remote control, the DVR, the joystick, and the mouse, traditional stories are deconstructed, channel surfed, and fast-forwarded (Rushkoff 1995). The effects of the Aristolean arc and the hero's journey alike depended on a captive audience. With escape as close as the push of a button, audiences of all kinds become intolerant of the anxiety associated with the rising tension of a story.

In the deconstructed, cut-and-paste mash-up of digital media, the messianic, ends-justify-the-means values of traditional journeys no longer find an environment consonant with their value systems. This is the realm of ongoing fantasy role-playing, not tragically terminal heroes. The digital environment is not a place for extended struggles, charismatic leaders followed by masses, or winner-takes-all campaigns. The structure of digital entertainment and problem-solving is less like agonistic play with victors and vanquished than it is like James Carse's "infinite game" (Carse 1997)—one played for the sake of play. The object of the game is to keep the game going as long as possible.

Prototyping. This sensibility extends to the third characteristic of the digital media environment, its emphasis on prototyping over product. The shareware culture of the internet led to what are known as 'public betas'—the release of unfinished software to the public for testing and improvement. As Media Lab director Joichi Ito has explained (Ito 2011), there is no point testing a product in-house when there is a willing population of users out there ready to bang on one's programs. Besides, there is no time (see feedback and iteration above) to finish a product before seeing how people are going to react to it. Better to incorporate feedback into one's software in an ongoing fashion.

Programmer or player. Fourth and finally, the digital environment blurs the boundary between users and programmers. In a computing environment (unless a program is intentionally and artificially encrypted and protected) one's level of participation is only limited by one's willingness to learn more and dig deeper. One can play music through iTunes, or become a DJ whose selections are listened to by others. He can go deeper and use Garage Band to make new music, or another program to create new instruments for Garage Band. Or he can learn to program a new kind of music sequencer altogether.

Or, as I (Rushkoff 2012) and Julian Kücklick (2004) have explored separately, one's level of participation in any system can now be understood through the lens of a programmer or player. One can play a computer game out of the box; one can learn the 'cheat' codes to play the game on a new level; one can learn to 'mod' his own level of the game; or one can become a programmer and develop his own game. In a digital society, people participate on all these levels, and their limitations are either voluntary or visibly imposed.

Occupy movement

The Occupy movement bears all four of these characteristics of the digital media environment—and its success may have less to do with any immediate goals being met or elections being won than the extent to which these values are internalized by politics at large. As an Editor-at-Large for *Adbusters* magazine in the 1990s and later author of the book *Life inc* (Rushkoff 2009), which deconstructed the corporation and sought new bottom-up solutions to capitalism, I was at least tangentially involved in laying some of the groundwork for this movement's ethos and methodology.

When the Occupation was first announced, I decided to remain a distant supporter—so as not to either take credit for what was going on, or to unduly influence a movement of young people who I believed deserved to do this for themselves. In short, I fully believed the Occupiers would be capable of planning and interacting in ways beyond my own ability or foresight.

The first time I visited Zuccotti Park, during the first week of the Occupation, I had originally intended to speak and offer support. But on my arrival, I saw not just one but several cultural heroes of the 1960s through the 1990s, all preaching to the assembled activists, or singing songs with guitars, or giving interviews to the press. From my perspective, these folk figures meant well—but were ultimately usurping the moment from their ideological successors. So instead, I spent that day and several more simply observing the proceedings, asking questions, participating in teach-ins, and keeping my identity to myself.

My participation was entirely 'real world.' I did not check any of the social networks or Facebook pages for news, as I seemed to be learning enough on the ground. In fact, it did not even occur to me to use Facebook to learn what I could in real life. While this may imply a certain elitism, in that only those with the means to get to Zuccotti Park could experience what it was, the notion that this entire demonstration was enabled by social media implies that participants came entirely from one side of the digital divide. Yet, the fact that both real world and virtual means of participation remained available throughout at least this phase of Occupy suggests that neither is true. Social media competency was not a prerequisite for participation. This is not to say Occupy was divorced from social media at all. The activities I saw on site, however, mirrored the kinds of insights and behaviors garnered from what I believe were the participants' experiences—both direct and indirect—of the digital media environment.

For instance, Occupiers have an altogether new relationship to feedback than traditional political movements. Although they occasionally march and shout, the majority of activity is not directed *at* or *to* anyone. Rather, it is lateral. Occupiers are more focused on one another than the stockbrokers who may curse their encampment from the periphery. The Occupation is a form of self-education. Rather than looking for signs that their message has been 'heard' by a politician or incorporated into some party's platform, they seek instead to develop coherence together.

The result is less like the feedback and iteration of an election cycle, where the constituency feeds back to the elected official, and more like the feedback and iteration of a fractal or dynamic system. As such, it remains unrecognizable as a form of politics to those still entirely within the printing press or broadcast modality, yet absolutely activist to participants within a digital environment.

Likewise, the Occupy movement is non-narrative, perhaps even to a fault given the practicalities of our still largely broadcast-centric media culture. The main critique by mainstream media of the Occupy movement is its seeming inability to articulate clear goals or demands. This is at least part of why mainstream television news reporters appeared so determined to cast Occupy Wall Street as the random, silly blather of an ungrateful and lazy generation of weirdos. As if defending against the coming obsolescence of their own truncated news formats, television journalists reported that the movement's inability to articulate its agenda in ten seconds or less meant there was no agenda at all. CNN business anchor Erin Burnett covered the goings on at Zuccotti Park in a segment called Seriously?! (Burnett 2011) "What are they protesting?" she asked, "nobody seems to know." Like *Tonight Show* comedian host Jay Leno's testing random mall patrons on American History, her main objective was to prove that the protesters did not know that the United States government had been reimbursed for the bank bailouts. More predictably, a Fox News reporter appeared flummoxed when the occupier he interviewed refused to explain how he wants the protests to "end." Attempting to transcend the standard political narrative, the protester explains: "As far as seeing it end, I wouldn't like to see it end. I would like to see the conversation continue" (Christopher 2011).

In this sense, whether or not its economic agenda is grounded in reality, Occupy Wall Street does constitute the first truly post-narrative political movement. Unlike the civil rights protests, labor marches, or even the Obama campaign, it does not take its cue from a charismatic leader, it does not express itself with bumper-sticker-length goals, nor does it understand itself as having a particular endpoint. The lack of specific goals makes it hard to maintain focus. The movement may be attempting to embrace too wide an array of complaints, demands, and goals: the collapsing environment, labor standards, housing policy, government corruption, World Bank lending practices, unemployment, increasing wealth disparity, and so on. Different people have been affected by different aspects of the same system—and they believe they are symptoms of the same core problem. What upsets banking's defenders and traditional Democrats alike is the refusal of this movement to state its terms or set its goals in the traditional language of campaigns.

But the Occupiers are simply native to a different media environment than its detractors. Unlike a political campaign designed to get some person in office and then close up shop (as in the election of Obama and subsequent youth disillusionment), this is not a movement with a traditional narrative arc. It is not about winning some debate point and then going home. Rather, as the product of the decentralized networked-era culture, it is less about victory than sustainability. It is not about one-pointedness but inclusion. It is not about scoring a victory, but groping toward consensus. It is not like a book or television, it is like the internet.

The Occupy movement is also imbued with digital culture's emphasis on prototyping. The encampments are no more a form of symbolic protest than they are a workshop for prototyping new methods and reviving old methods of political engagement. They are beta tests. Occupy's 'General Assembly' methodology, for example, is a highly flexible approach to group discussion and consensus building borrowed from the Ancient Greeks. Unlike parliamentary rules that promote debate, difference and decision, the General Assembly forges consensus by 'stacking' ideas and objections as they arise, and then making sure they are all eventually heard. The whole thing is orchestrated through simple hand gestures. Elements in the stack are prioritized, and everyone gets a chance to speak. Even after votes, exceptions and objections are incorporated as amendments.

Strangers to the process are justifiably alienated by the General Assembly, and a certain facility with its processes is required. Those who do not know the hand signals cannot readily participate. But from what I observed, newcomers quickly came to understand the General Assembly's rules, either through observation and osmosis, or the ready instruction by peers. In fact, the last place I had seen 'newbies' so quickly and deliberately oriented by more experienced participants was on the early internet.

And like many online processes, such as the 'collaborative filtering' done to bring popular results to the top of a web page, the General Assembly seems like an evolutionary leap forward in consensus-building. Dispensing with preconceived narratives about generating policy demands or settling the score between Right vs. Left, this process eschews debate (or what Enlightenment philosophers called 'dialectic') for consensus. It is a blatant rejection of the binary, winner-takes-all, political operating system of the thirteenth century.

The approach of the Occupiers is more like a university than a political movement. Both online and offline spaces consist largely of 'teach ins' about the issues they are concerned about. Young people teach one another or invite guests to lecture them about subjects such as how the economy works, the disconnection of investment banking from the economy of goods and services, possible responses to mass foreclosure, the history of centralized interest-bearing currency, and even best practices for civil disobedience.

It is unwieldy and unpredictable, but oddly consistent with the values of a post-narrative landscape. The Occupy ethos replaces the zero-sum, closed-ended game of financial competition with a more sustainable, open-ended game of abundance and mutual aid. In the traditional political narrative, this sounds like communism—but to the Occupiers, it is a realization of the peer-to-peer sensibility of the social net. It is not a game that someone wins, but rather a form of play that—like a massive multiplayer online game—is successful the more people get to play, and the longer the game is kept going.

Finally, the Occupiers embody the player or hacker's approach to the political process. Each member of the movement is as capable and likely as any other to write or edit the operating system through which all of this activity takes place. Whether joining a general assembly, leading a working group, taking a role in developing or sustaining the infrastructure, or organizing an entirely new encampment, each member is free to author his or her own contribution to the total effort.

Conclusion

In the internet age, occupation could become less a form of conditional, temporary, discrete political activism than a new normative behavior. The culture of the net dissolves the boundaries between consumer and producer, programmer and user and instead promotes more of a peer-to-peer relationship between all members of the network. In a similar fashion, Occupy eschews hierarchies and defined roles in favor of modeling a new normative behavior for its participants. The occupation of Zuccotti or any other encampment is just the most pronounced version of the occupation of reality itself.

As Occupiers become conscious of the consonance of their approach with the greater emerging digital landscape, the loss of Zuccotti and other encampments becomes less significant. As McLuhan might argue, the protest encampment is merely the 'figure'—the particular content at one moment in time. The occupation concerns the 'ground'—the greater environment in which this activity is taking place. The individual players and their temporary roles mean less than the changes to the playing field itself, our understanding of the extra-political means through which the socio-economic landscape can be revised, and the trivial value of recognition from either the political parties or the mainstream corporate media.

The Occupy movement is indeed revolutionary, but not in the sense of victory, overthrow, and replacement of authority. That cycle seeks simply to entrench a new regime (figure) within the same environment (ground). The Occupiers appear to be groping instead for something more sustainably iterative than the steady state of a single solution. The only sort of permanence in the occupation is the ongoing process of revolution, itself.

This is a politics consonant with the values and insights of twenty-first-century science and technology. Unlike the innovations of the industrial age, which fostered production, accumulation, central authority, and empire, those of the digital era are biased toward replication and self-modification. Robotics, genomics, nano-machines and digital programming do not render completed technologies but self-replicating, iterative systems. We program them now, but they continue themselves, learning from experience, iterating new versions, and carrying on the intentions of their original creators in novel ways.

So while the majority of public encampments and protests appear to have died down, new forms and mutations of the Occupiers' presence emerge every day. It is as if the movement is on an entirely different calendar, operating in a parallel dimension. Given the tremendous differences between the digital media environment and what went before it, this may not be an inaccurate perception. The original occupation may be 'over' as far as it is officially recognized by extant media and political authority. But as an emergent narrative, digital prototype, cultural norm, and style of play, it has only just been born.

References

Burnett, E. 2011. Out front. *CNN Out Front*, 3 October (E. Burnett, interviewer).

Carse, J. 1997. *Finite and infinite games.* New York: RandomHouse.

Christopher, T. 2011. Van Susteren explains why anti-Fox clip with Occupy Wall St. protester got cut. *Mediaite.* http://www.mediaite.com/tv/van-susteren-explains-why-anti-fox-interview-with-occupy-wall-st-protester-got-cut.

Goodman, B. (dir. and writer), D. Rushkoff, and R. Dretzin (writers) 2003. *The Persuaders.* PBS Frontline. Film.

Horowitz, D. 2006. *The professors: The 101 most dangerous academics in America.* New York: Regenery Publishing.

Ito, J. 2011. In an open source society, innovating by the seat of our pants. *The New York Times*, 5 December.

Keane, A. 2007. *Cult of the amateur: How today's Internet is killing our culture.* New York: Currency.

Kücklick, J. 2004. Play and playability as key concepts in new media studies. *STeM Centre, Dublin City University.* http://pdfs.semanticscholar.org/9ee4/25c40d353f61f7a0bc8832dbc696d26497d5.pdf.

Logan, R. K. 1987. *The alphabet effect: The impact of the phonetic alphabet on the development of Western civilization.* New York: St. Martins Press.

Martinson, J. 2000. Online politics proves a turn-off. *The Guardian,* 27 August.

McLuhan, M. 1992. *Laws of media: The new science.* Toronto: University of Toronto.

—. 1962. *The Gutenberg galaxy: The making of typographic man.* Toronto: University of Toronto Press.

Miller, J. H., and S. E. Page. 2007. *Complex adaptive systems: An introduction to computational models of social life.* Princeton, NJ: Princeton University Press.

Ong, W. 2002. *Orality and literacy.* New York: Routledge.

Pariser, E. 2011. *The filter bubble: What the internet is hiding from you.* New York: Penguin.

Rushkoff, D. 1995. *Playing the future: How kids' culture can teach us to thrive in an age of chaos.* New York: HarperEdge.

—. 1998. *Open source democracy: How online communication is changing offline politics.* London: Demos.

—. 2009. *Life inc: How corporatism conquered the world and how we can take it back.* New York: RandomHouse.

—. 2010. There's more to being a journalist than hitting the "publish" button. *Nieman Reports* 64 (2): 39-40.

—. 2012. *Monopoly moneys: The media environment of corporatism and the player's way out.* Utrecht: Utrecht University Dissertation. http://dspace.library.uu.nl/handle/1874/250622.

Simon, R. 1992. A Perot presidency and a La-Z-Boy lawmaking. *Baltimore Sun,* 13 May.

Sullivan, A. 2008. We are the ones we've been waiting for. *The Atlantic,* 28 February.

Trippi, J. 2004. *The revolution will not be televised.* New York: William Morrow.

Weiner, N. 1965. *Cybernetics, second edition, or the control and communication in the animal and the machine.* Cambridge, MA: The MIT Press.

About the author

Douglas Rushkoff is a writer, documentarian, and lecturer whose work focuses on human autonomy in a digital age. He is the author of fifteen bestselling books on media, technology, and society, including *Program or be programmed* (OR Books 2012), *Present shock* (Current 2013), and *Throwing rocks at the Google bus* (Portfolio 2016). Rushkoff is the recipient of the Marshall McLuhan Award for his book *Coercion*, The Jacques Ellul Award for his documentary *The Merchants of Cool*, and the Neil Postman Award for Career Achievement in Public Intellectual Activity. Named one of the world's ten most influential intellectuals by MIT, he is responsible for originating such concepts as 'viral media,' 'social currency,' and 'digital natives.' Today, Dr. Rushkoff serves as Full Professor of Media Theory and Digital Economics at CUNY/Queens, where he recently founded the Laboratory for Digital Humanism and hosts its TeamHuman podcast. He is also a research fellow at the Institute for the Future, and an advisor to Meetup, Shareable, and Codecademy.

18. The playful city: Citizens making the smart city

Michiel de Lange

Abstract

This chapter about playful urban planning argues that play and games can help foster smart citizenship. In recent years, many cities have embarked on what is termed smart-city policies, deploying ICT to optimize a variety of urban processes. Various authors have noted that these smart-city policies often leave little room for civic action and agency. This contribution proposes the notion of the 'playful city' as an alternative vision for leveraging the smartness of people in creating more livable and lively cities. Play, it is argued, should not be positioned as offering solutions to urban problems. Instead, play offers alternative narratives about the potential futures of city-making, and reinserts the 'political' into smart city-making.

Keywords: Smart city, playful city, city-making, smartness, civic engagement

How can play and games entice urban stakeholders to become involved in making their city? In the nineteenth century, urban design became a professionalized discipline in reaction to the new machine era, the explosive growth of cities, and an impoverished class of new citizens lacking adequate housing (Hall 1988). With the current wave of 'smart technologies' pervading the urban realm, we observe how, once again, the shifting technological conditions of urban life affect the ways cities are made and the role of citizens in such processes. Today, municipalities all over the world seize the omnipresence of digital technologies as an opportunity to make their city 'smart.' In the wake of creative city policies popularized in the late 1990s (Landry and Bianchini 1995; Florida 2004, 2012; Landry 2008), smart city agendas aim to improve services and livability through ICTs and

Glas, R., S. Lammes, M. de Lange, J. Raessens, and I. de Vries, eds. 2019. *The Playful Citizen. Civic Engagement in a Mediatized Culture.* Amsterdam: Amsterdam University Press.
DOI: 10.5117/9789462984523/CH18

supporting infrastructures. Large technology companies, including IBM, CISCO, Siemens, Microsoft, Philips, General Electric, among others, are forming coalitions with municipalities and knowledge institutions in 'triple helix' smart city consortia. Among the problems that smart city policies seek to address are mobility, clean energy, water and food production and distribution, health, living standards, and public participation (Hollands 2008).

Smart city visions and discourses have received much criticism (e.g. Hemment and Townsend 2013; De Lange and De Waal 2013; Söderström, Paasche, and Klauser 2014; Vanolo 2014; Calzada and Cobo 2015; Hollands 2015). These criticisms can be broken down in three major strands. The first strand of criticism focuses on the ill-defined notion of 'smartness.' What does 'smart' actually mean? Who is supposed to be smart? How can digital technologies be used for a pedagogy of smart urban life? The second strand targets the technocratic solutionism of these visions and the lack of agency ascribed to 'smart citizens.' All too often, technology-centric smart city visions assume that there are easy technological fixes for complex urban problems. They fail to leverage citizen creativity and smartness in more participatory ways of city-making. The third strand critically questions underlying simplistic views of what cities are or should be. What makes a city? Do we want city life and the urban experience to be about control, efficiency and predictability, or do we also value serendipity, friction, and playfulness?

To address these shortcomings, a variety of alternative notions have been coined. Many of them stress inclusivity and citizen agency. Quite a few of these build on the notion of playfulness to seek people-centric alternatives to the tech-driven smart city. Terms coined include the 'playable city' (Nijholt 2016), the 'ludic city' (Feirreis 2007; Stevens 2007), the 'gameful city' (Alfrink 2015), and the 'playful city' (De Lange 2014, 2015; Sicart 2016). At stake in these notions is the question of how games and play can help foster a smarter civic engagement. In this chapter, I further develop the idea of the 'playful city' as an alternative imaginary for utilitarian smart city agendas. This chapter investigates how playful media technologies can help to engage citizens in playing with and testing future city scenarios, and how as a result this can make cities and citizens smarter. I claim that the playful city is a productive concept to help conceptualize truly smart cities. This claim rests on three interconnected arguments, each addressing one of the above-mentioned criticisms. As I have argued elsewhere (De Lange 2013, 2014, 2015), play and games can be used first to leverage citizen creativity (*smartness*). Second, games and play can help to organize engagement, create collectives and strengthen people's agency (*citizen participation*). Third, games and play can be used to experiment with possible urban futures that are much more solidly rooted in a fertile substratum of theorizing urban culture instead of technology-driven efficiency (*cityness*). The notion of the playful city addresses civic agency in relation to professional disciplines. It aims to develop a perspective on playful citizens *and* playful urban planners.

The structure of the chapter is as follows. In the next section, I juxtapose two approaches to citizen engagement in urban planning. This section serves to articulate the central concerns of my argument that deal with new technologies, civic participation, smartness, and cityness. Furthermore, it traces how playfulness slowly entered its way into city-making with the advent of creative city policies. Next, I take a look at some historical strands of conceptualizing city life in terms of play, in order to construct a more solid conceptualization of the 'playful city.' The section exposes five different playful city themes, each harboring a different kind of playful civic smartness. The section also zooms in on the notion of play. The chapter then turns to a concrete case study of *Rezone the Game*, a game about vacant urban spaces in which I have been involved as a researcher, in order to find out how play can engage citizens in co-creating their urban environment. In the conclusion, I suggest that the concept of play serves to account for shifts in city-making and urban design practices. It is proposed that the tripartite ontology of play as material object, rule-based algorithm, and situated action offers a fruitful perspective on the changing roles of various stakeholders in shaping the future of the media city.

What is at stake in this contribution is how people can become engaged in their urban environment and with urban issues through 'playful media technologies' (see Frissen et al. 2015). The early days of digital media technologies bred in many commentators a gigantic optimism about their creative and democratizing potential to involve non-professionals in areas of professional expertise. For example, speaking about the field of design Mieke Gerritzen and Geert Lovink programmatically declared that "everyone is a designer in the age of social media" (Gerritzen and Lovink 2010). Similarly, Chris Anderson in his book *Makers: The new industrial revolution* claimed that "we are all designers now" (Anderson 2012, 53). We can and should doubt whether this is truly the case. As is argued in several chapters in this volume, there are many problems with the assumption that new media fuel more egalitarian and participatory societies, the end of expert knowledge, and a blossoming of high quality user generated content. There is little doubt, however, that digital media technologies profoundly shape new practices of city-making. 'Civic media' or 'civic technology' are terms that have recently gained considerable traction to designate the potential of media technologies to foster civic engagement (Gordon and Mihailidis 2016).[1] The challenges of dealing with digital media technologies and citizen-driven city-making in the field of urban planning have become more urgent in the light of accelerating urbanization, a worldwide financial crisis that hit the sector particularly hard, and the rise of a DIY (do-it-yourself) maker culture. Like many other disciplines, urban design is faced with a tilting balance between professionals and amateurs, a decline in legitimacy of expert knowledge, and the rise of networked collective or 'connective' action (Varnelis 2008; Bennett and Segerberg 2012). This contribution argues that playful technologies and the ludification of (urban) culture (Raessens 2006, 2014) provide momentum and opportunity to productively address such questions of citizen engagement in city-making.

Planning cities

Citizen participation is by no means a new phenomenon in urban planning. In the 1970s, architects and planners already experimented with engaging communities in 'placemaking' and collective ownership through participatory design techniques (e.g. Landry 2008, 208). Only one century before, the inverse had happened in western societies, when a major professionalization took place in how cities were made (Hall 1988). In reaction to the industrialization of the city and the squalid living circumstances of a pauperized class of new urbanites, urban planning became a professional and academic discipline. Ever since, urban planning has been concerned with realizing visions of a better future. Dreams of a better tomorrow were frequently driven by fears and anxieties about city life today (Andraos et al. 2009). Urban design produced spaces that prescribed how people should behave. It was assumed, for instance, that the creation of healthier, greener, cleaner, and more aesthetically pleasing urban environments would lead to more societal stability (Huxley 2006, 774). Thus, planning became an instrument for superimposing order and control. The design of these 'governable spaces' would discipline and rationalize the minds and bodies of people, instill higher moral standards in them, and mold them into good citizens (Huxley 2006; Watson 2009). Central to the late Peter Hall's magnum opus *Cities of tomorrow: An intellectual history of urban planning*

1 Also see, for instance, reports by the Knight Foundation (2013) or various programs by UK-based Future Cities Catapult (2018).

and design in the twentieth century (Hall 1988) is this continual struggle between planners who want to impose a top-down totalitarian planning logic onto the populace in the belief that a better society is never designed by committee, and those who take an on the ground perspective of people's everyday needs and desires, and wish to empower them. Best exemplifying these extremes in city-making is the often-recounted antagonism between New York City's modernist municipal planner Robert Moses and urban activist Jane Jacobs. Moses built bridges that were deliberately too low for public transportation, thus preventing racial minorities and low-income groups without private cars to get to Long Island Jones Beach (Winner 1980). Jacobs, on the other hand, made passionate pleas for messiness and diversity (Jacobs 1961/1992). As an activist, she took it to the streets and defended Greenwich Village against Moses' demolition plans to make space for a highway. In the humanities, a similar opposition is expressed in Michel de Certeau's well-known juxtaposition of a birds-eye city view from high above, and a city walker perspective at street-level (de Certeau 1984). We briefly look at how the Situationist art movement addressed this tension later on.

An apparent break from old ideals of urban planning as instruments for superimposing social order took place in the second half of the 1990s with the rise of the 'creative city' paradigm. Building explicitly upon the legacy of Jane Jacobs, creative city proponents valued city life for being pleasantly chaotic, unpredictable, emergent, and self-organizing. Chaos is not to be curbed but cherished. In fact, in moderate doses it is a necessary precondition for creativity to blossom, via serendipitous encounters and exchanges. In the new paradigm, socio-economic prosperity of cities goes hand-in-hand with fostering their playful qualities. Cities with many playful 'third spaces' provide nurture beds for creativity and, ultimately, monetary revenue. Neither private domestic spaces nor utilitarian work spaces for rationalized productivity, these playful civic spaces were hotbeds for new ideas to blossom and come to fruition (Oldenburg 1989; Rifkin 2000; Thrift 2008). Creative city discourses fit very well with the rise of the information economy and the rhetoric of disruptive innovation.

Several points in the discussion above are relevant for this chapter. The first point is about 'smartness' in civic participation. The recurrent tension between city-making *for* the people and city-making *by* the people reflects opposing views of citizenship and participation. One involves a liberal view that highlights 'passive' individual rights ("the right to have rights"), while the other entails a republican communitarian view that emphasizes 'active' collective participation and civic duty (Somers 2008, 5, 14). Today's technology-driven smart cities seem to recombine these two types into a new type of participatory liberal citizenship, while at the same time stripping away their respective empowering potential and political agency. In many smart city visions, the good citizen is no longer a collectively organized and vocal political agent, or somebody protected by individual rights, but primarily a mute collector of data. Civic participation equals producing economic value. Although this is often touted to exemplify a new branch of participatory and entrepreneurial urban citizenship predicated upon a collectivized 'sharing economy' (Davidson and Infranca 2016), in terms of political agency it is very limited. No longer communal duty or individual rights, citizenship becomes individualized duty. You shall be a productive citizen. How then, can the notion of the playful city contribute to an active kind of 'smart' civic participation in which people can help shape the future of their cities?

The second point is about media technology and civic participation. When we think about smart cities, and indeed more generally about media and citizenship, we need to pay attention to the 'politics' of technologies and artifacts (Winner 1980). Technologies and their material and institutional arrangements may serve both as enabling devices and as instruments of control. Smart city technologies do not bring equal civic participation for everyone. They can empower some while posing insurmountable thresholds for others, in terms of accessibility or literacy. Like Moses' NYC bridges half a century ago, the institutional arrangements that come with smart cities might lead to social sorting and a splintering of urban public life (see Graham and Marvin 2001). So, one may ask how can we think of a more inclusive kind of civic participation through the notion of the playful city?

The third point is about what is called 'cityness,' or what constitutes city life (for example, Brenner and Schmid 2015). The brief discussion above sensitizes us to the fact that every well-meant vision about better urban futures is infused with ideological assumptions about city life and the role of citizens. This rhetoric of change conceals a deep core of what should remain stable. In the case of the industrial city, urban planning professed to bring positive change to the housing conditions of the masses and endow people with individual citizen rights to adequate living circumstances and—in many European cities—institutionalized welfare. The implication, however, was that the working class through a variety of new institutions were fixated and made controllable for the sake of the societal status quo. City life in the machine age was to be neat and orderly, and everything and everyone had to behave like a cog in it. Likewise, the smart city's emphasis on controlling and optimizing flows and environments through data means it perpetuates existing systems. It is, in a sense, a return to the modernist conception of the city as a controllable machine, or to be more precise, a smart cybernetic system controlled through feedback loops and self-learning capacities. The case of the smart city control center in Rio de Janeiro illustrates this drive toward centralized real-time control. The Rio Operations Centre was built by IBM and allows the municipality to gather data from 30 different agencies, display them on screens in a room-size 'urban dashboard,' and remotely manage processes like natural disasters or big public events (Townsend 2013, 65; Mattern 2015). The critical question then is what remains fixated through the rhetoric of smart urban change? To what extent do attempts at optimizing existing systems allow us to step outside of the box and conceive of radically new alternative visions for the future of cities? As I will argue in more detail below, I propose that the playful city imaginary is not only a productive notion to conceive of a more participatory smart citizenship, but also acts as a meta-reflective notion that opens up the space to critically question its own foundations.

Playful cities in a historical context[2]

In order to better understand how playful technologies can help engage people in participatory city-making, let us trace several historical themes in understanding the city as playful. Indeed, play and games have been part and parcel of city life (Stevens 2007). I identify five major playful city themes: the city as a center of entertainment; the city as everyday theater; the city as civic learning space; the city as a subversive playground; and urban simulation. First, from Roman bread and games (*panem et circenses*) to the present 'experience economy' (Pine and Gilmore 1999), cities have long been conceived as centers of entertainment and fun experiences. According to this view, the city is a locus for genuine playful behavior and activities, and for enjoying games or other forms of entertainment in designated settings. Second, with the rise of the modern metropolis, people's interactions in newly conceived public spaces came to be understood in theatrical metaphors. Theorists like Georg Simmel, Erving Goffman, and Lyn Lofland argued that urbanites in public situations engage in role-playing and information games using various props as a way to deal with life among strangers in highly segmented roles and situations (Goffman 1959; Lofland 1973; Simmel 1997). In this view, city life itself is conducive to everyday role-playing. Third, a historical strand of 'ludic architecture' connects play and games to the

2 This section is based in part on de Lange (2009, 2015).

physical design of cities. In the Netherlands after the second World War, Dutch architect Aldo van Eyck dotted the ruined cityscapes with outdoor play spaces as a way to counter top-down functionalist planning policies and to open up room for people's own creativity (Oudenampsen 2013). Play served the pedagogical goal of teaching new generations to deal with conflict and tensions without resorting to destructive violence. Besides, what better way to make traumatized people smile again than watching children playing? According to this view, play spawns learning and *Bildung* ideals of civilization. Accompanying the restoration of the physical *urbs*, play mends the social bonds of *civitas*. A related fourth historical strand takes play as downright subversive. The artistic movement of The Situationists International criticized mass consumer society and sought to reclaim the right to the city through subversive counter-play and everyday spatial tactics, like *dérive* and *detournement* (drift and diversion) (Debord 1955, 1958, 2005; de Certeau 1984). A friend of Van Eijck, Constant Nieuwenhuys's New Babylon was an attempt to imagine a non-conformist city of play in which ever-changing environments would foster citizen creativity and engagement (Nieuwenhuys 1974; De Mul 2009). More recently, several studies in the same tradition focus on subcultural or countercultural urban practices like skateboarding or *parkours* (Borden 2001; Mould 2009). In this view, play is an everyday tactic to counter dominant structures by reclaiming agency and 'the right to the city' (Lefebvre 1996; Mitchell 2003). Fifth, while not strictly playful, terms from the world of informatics like networks, simulation, feedback, algorithms, and virtuality have come to profoundly influence architectural theory and practice as new ways to imagine, represent and design cities with digital tools (see Wigley 2001; Picon 2008). Cybernetics and systems theory have been very influential in understanding the city as emergent rule-based systems, which can be simulated and 'played' through creative recombinations and generative, algorithmic, responsive, or parametric design (see Berry 1964; Beesley and Khan 2009; Tan 2014).

What we can take from this, first, is a more nuanced and plural understanding of the notion of 'smart.' In the views above there is fairly clear conception of 'smartness' at play, each different from the other. Smartness in everyday role-playing means being clever, persuasive and having self-confidence. In the case of Van Eyck's urban playgrounds smartness is didactic and self-empowering. The smart playful tactics of the Situationists evoke shrewdness and unorthodox associative thinking. And the smartness in urban simulations is of an almost demiurgic ambition as it attempts to confer sentience or intelligence to systems to aid in problem-solving and learning. As for the 'entertainment city,' it may be a bit more difficult to discern smartness among those seeking a temporary carnivalesque inverse of normalcy (indeed it is easy to dismiss this as childish, stupefying, or opium for the masses). Yet, many of these urban play activities simultaneously aid in developing problem solving skills and fostering communal and situated experiences (not to mention that it takes creativity and originality to produce or curate such engaging experiences). There is a whole genre of mobile urban games with labels like pervasive/ubiquitous/location-based mobile/hybrid reality/alternate reality/urban games that frame the city as a playing board and escape the confines of the screen to be played in hybrid space (Chang and Goodman 2006; Montola, Stenros, and Waern 2009; de Souza e Silva and Hjorth 2009; de Souza e Silva and Sutko 2008, 2009). Hence, the 'playful city' complements the majority of smart city visions that equate 'smart' with automation and efficiency. It also vastly broadens our perspective of what 'smart citizenship' in relation to urban life could be.

A second point, made by many already, is that the modern separation of play and everyday life is not the default but the exception (see Ehrmann, Lewis, and Lewis 1968). Clearly, Van Eijck, Constant, Débord, and others, felt the need to go against the dominant mode of thinking with their integrated views. Recently, play and everyday life are (again) being understood as inextricably intertwined (Raessens 2006, 2014). This is largely driven by the pervasive presence of digital technologies in the urban realm, by the creative city agenda, and by the current search for smart city alternatives. It is imperative therefore that we consider playfulness not as some exotic idealistic notion far removed from the nitty-gritty of city-making, but as an inherent part of it. In fact, urban designers are turning to play to develop more diversified and resilient modes of urban planning (see Venhuizen 2011; Holleman, de Kort, and Lindemann 2012; Tan 2014).

A third point is that we must pay closer attention to the myriad of understandings of play and games. Conceptual clarity is needed to push the playful city as a productive idea to explore participatory smart city-making. Although there is infinitely more to say about play and games, for sake of brevity, I shall stick to the well-known conceptualization of French sociologist and philosopher Roger Caillois. Caillois identified four types of play: competition (*agôn*), chance (*alea*), make belief (*mimicry*), and sensory delusion (*ilinx*) (Caillois 1958/2001). He further differentiated between two opposing poles in play attitudes: spontaneous and intrinsically motivated free play (*paidia*) versus rule-based and goal-oriented gaming (*ludus*). While other play theorists have better situated play in everyday reality (for instance Ehrmann, Lewis, and Lewis 1968; Sutton-Smith 1997), Caillois offers a powerful scheme to analyze how since the rise of the modern city, play in various guises has been a central element in imagining urban culture.[3] More importantly for our purposes here, however, is that this scheme allows us to analyze and theorize playful city-making with more rigor.

Caillois' distinction between *paidia* and *ludus*, I argue, coincides with two stances toward the citizen engagement in the smart city. This helps us to better articulate the differences between the smart city and the playful city when it comes to citizen engagement. Citizen engagement in the majority of technology-driven smart city agendas tends toward the *ludus* pole: it is contractual and rule-governed, goal-oriented, and favors rationalized efficiency.[4] The playful city serves to emphasize the *paidia* pole: free spontaneous play, not so much instrumental and goal-oriented but *autotelic*, that is, the joy of the activity in itself constitutes the major reason for engaging. Furthermore, smart city initiatives tend to use technologies (including games) in a very *ludus*-like way. Tech is understood as goal-oriented: it aims at solving problems and thus ending the engagement. I want to make a plea here for playful smart city interventions that instead lean toward the *paidia* pole: aimed at continuing engagement and self-motivated action. As we will see below, such playful interventions do not necessarily use games with the aim of solving a problem, but to ask questions about the underlying mechanisms and to create the conditions for people to come up with smart ideas.[5] Additionally, Caillois' fourfold game typology allows us to establish that smart city interventions are mostly of the competitive *agôn* type. Complex urban problems like sustainability, crime, or congestion are agonistically framed as 'challenges' that can be solved via data and apps. As a city-branding strategy, smart cities are continually competing with each other in a host of global rankings. According to this view, smartness

3 *Agôn* underlies the 'ecological' views of the Chicago School that took urban life as a competition for scarce resources, and the post-industrial city engaged in competition with other cities vying for the attention of the creative industries. *Alea* connects to common views of urban life as serendipitous and is present in terms used to describe high or late modernity as a 'risk society' (Beck 1992) or in terms of radical uncertainty. *Mimicry* informs the view of urban life as constant theatrical role-playing. And *ilinx* can be recognized for example in the flaneur who loses himself in the crowd, Walter Benjamin's shock experiences brought about by visual media, Simmel's metropolitan blasé attitude caused by 'intensification of nervous stimulation,' and the Situationist legacy of psycho-geography.

4 One only needs to take a look at some of the corporate videos made by IBM Industries (2013) to understand that the rhetoric about citizen engagement is skin deep and only serves the functional needs of the municipality and corporate stakeholders.

5 See for instance Games for Cities (2018), a database that contains a mix of goal-oriented games and more playful interventions, several of them developed in the context of smart city policies.

is of a competitive nature: it means 'outsmarting' the system, other people, or other cities. Competitive problem-solving is in my view a very narrow understanding of 'smart.' By contrast, I argue for playful city interventions that involve a broad range of game types, including *alea*, *mimicry*, and *ilinx*, to nurture and leverage different kinds of civic smartness. That could mean embracing and anticipating aleatory radical uncertainty, engaging in creative and cooperative make-belief, or seeking pleasurable experiences and deeply valuable "occasions of pure waste" (Caillois 1958/2001, 5) or "meaningful inefficiencies," as Gordon and Walter write in Chapter 16 of this volume.

Rezone the Game: Playing against vacancy

Armed with these directions and insights, I want to move from these theoretical and historical explorations of the playful city to a more concrete case, in order to see how participatory smart citizenship may work in practice. *Rezone the Game* is a project to help address the complex urban issue of vacancy.[6] Two cultural organizations from Den Bosch in the Netherlands, the Bosch Architecture Initiative and art organization Wave of Tomorrow, collaborated with a game design school to create *Rezone the Game* (www.rezone.eu), challenging players to 'fight blight.' In the game, players work together to keep the city safe from deterioration by salvaging real estate from decline. There are four player roles: the proprietor (owner of the real estate), mayor (representing the municipality), engineer (urban designer), and citizen (neighbors). *Rezone the Game* is composed of a physical board game with a number of 3D printed iconic buildings that represent the neighborhood, an augmented reality layer of real-time information about these buildings projected on a screen, and a computer algorithm programmed to let buildings descend into vacancy like a wildfire. A camera above registers the players' moves by scanning QR codes on pawns. The game engine continually adapts to changes. To beat the system players must strategically collaborate instead of pursuing self-interests. The game was tested during a series of events including *The Playful Arts Festival* (2013) and *Rezone Playful Interventions* (2014), with the mayor of Den Bosch participating in playing. The large Dutch construction company Heijmans became interested. Their involvement initiated a new collaboration and lead to a follow-up game concept. Part of the motivation for the development of *Rezone the Game* was that it is hard to address complex questions like vacancy through conventional means.

6 I have been involved in this project as a paid advisor and researcher.

Traditional parties involved in urban development are not inclined to invest in initiatives with uncertain outcomes and often wait for others to take the first step. It was believed that in a game stakeholders would feel freer to experiment without immediate (financial) consequences.

Again, this informs the three elements of smartness, civic participation, and cityness mentioned at the start of this chapter. First, in this case playful smartness is fostered on multiple levels. Players have to manage their different stakeholder roles, they must forge coalitions with other players and quickly negotiate, they must unpack the underlying mechanisms of vacancy, and think of ways to address this issue. *Rezone the Game* involves all of Caillois' play types: competition, role-playing, chance, and even dizzyingly speedy interactions with the computer system. The competitive element exists not between players but between players and the system. Playing together forges trust and connections between players. Real world stakeholders can meet each other in a playful atmosphere instead of at the negotiation table. The game is fun and acts as a catalyst for ensuing discussions and reflections among players (a crucial part of the play sessions), and even potential follow-ups. It is a deliberately simplified and artificial safe setting where real emotions and desires emerge. It invites people to temporarily stand in their adversaries' shoes. This could lead to better understanding of each other's standpoints through embodied experience and affects, instead of mere argumentation and deliberation. No longer passive as users of the city, players temporarily become smart planners.

Second, *Rezone the Game* helps to foster citizen engagement around the issue of vacancy. The game was used to invite real world stakeholders to the table. This happened during special play sessions and events such as *The Playful Arts Festival* (2013) and the *Rezone Playful Interventions* event (2014). Stakeholders met in a joyous atmosphere instead of tense town hall meetings or around the negotiation table. Playing together allowed relationships to form based on trust. Importantly, *Rezone the Game* is not a 'solutionist' attempt to solve a complex urban problem via technology. Playing the game helps people to become incentivized and take ownership for an otherwise abstract issue like vacancy. Playing makes the issue tangible via personal lived experiences and provides possible horizons for further action. The game mechanics and dynamics are deliberately aimed at stimulating social interactions and experimentation through collective action. Hence, we can conclude that this playful intervention strengthens a new hybrid liberal/ communal type of citizenship: people's individual rights to the city are extended to include a collective right to the smart city.

Third, *Rezone the Game* represents a particular take on the notion of cityness. A superficial reading might suggest that it is a game that helps to solve the issue of vacancy. The underlying notion of cityness in such a view, would be one of a playable system with citizens as productive problem-solvers. According to this view, a complex urban problem can have an optimal solution, which leads the city into a state of equilibrium. By contrast, I understand the game to actually have a deeper narrative, which tells that urban issues like vacancy are far too complex to model, let alone solve, by simple technological means.[7] Previously, I suggested that the special quality of playful city interventions like *Rezone the Game* is that they act on a meta-level. Gregory Bateson famously theorized that play always consists of a level of meta-communication. When monkeys in the zoo engage in play-fighting, they exchange signals that communicate that what they are doing is not fighting. In his words, we face "two peculiarities of play: (*a*) that the messages or signals exchanged in play are in a certain sense untrue or not meant; and (*b*) that that which is denoted by these signals is nonexistent" (Bateson 1972/1987, 141). In my view, this is precisely the strength of playful city interventions like *Rezone the Game*: it questions its own solutionist promise by overtly signaling to not actually do what it purports to do (solving vacancy). Instead, the game impels players to stake claims about what kind of city they actually want, to negotiate the underlying issue, and to agree on how to address it collectively. This involves a view of the city as a commons, a space of perpetual tension and conflict and at the same time a space that allows for negotiation and collaboration (Foster and Iaione 2016, 288).

As I have argued above, understanding city life in terms of play and games has a long tradition. Arguably, this connection has become even more important today. For an increasing number of people playing games is part of their cultural repertoire. They have grown up playing video games and are 'ludo-literate' (see Part I of this volume). Moreover, as outlined in the Introduction and in earlier work, we live in a playful media culture (Frissen et al. 2015). We are continuously surrounded by a plethora of technologies that offer spaces for playful experimentation, and shape our understanding of the world as playful. Playing means acquiring knowledge about the world and the capacity to act in it, in what can be called 'ludo-epistemology' (see Part II of this volume). Therefore, it no longer seems strange to have various organizations turn to games to address serious issues.

7 See also the notion of 'procedural rhetoric,' which designates how arguments can be created and unpacked using computer models, thus making claims about how things work (Bogost 2007, 1-64; 2011, 13-14).

Reflection and discussion

This chapter dealt with the question of how play and games can help foster a smarter civic engagement. The current challenge of making our cities smart impels us to ask not just what is technically feasible or economically viable, but what is also socially desirable. Do we want smart tech programmed by companies to make decisions for us? Or do we want to include the 'smartness' of actual people? Do we want efficient cities, or also generate other values like sustainability, democratic legitimacy, playfulness, and a sense of ownership? Do we consider technologies as just utilitarian solutions, or far more broadly as part of our everyday culture and experiences? The notion of the playful city, I argue, helps to do this by conceptualizing 'smart cities' in terms of smartness, civic participation, and cityness. The playful city opens up a people-centric and plural perspective on 'smartness,' instead of just a technologically driven one. If we want citizens to be smart alongside cities, we need to better understand how people already possess the capacity to act smart in a multitude of ways and how we can leverage this to make better and more interesting cities. The playful city also helps to think about citizen participation. Play and games themselves are not solutions for urban problems. They do however change the ways we address complex urban issues through more inclusive, participatory (and also more 'messy') approaches. Play also provides a far richer outlook on cityness. Play highlights the importance of creativity, curiosity, and culture in city life.

Play redefines roles and relations between professionals and citizens in processes of making cities. It has become clear that the making of cities no longer is the exclusive domain of architects and planners. Rather, it is one of the domains shaping, and being shaped by, playful citizenship. Gamemakers, media artists, app developers, and a variety of other urban dwellers are becoming the designers of today's cities (De Lange 2015). Cities are facing ever more complex issues. This requires smart strategies to tap into the pool of citizen smartness and leverage civic participation. Games and play seem great ways to do so. However, this requires policy makers and planners to relinquish control, accept uncertain and ambiguous outcomes, and to allow the possibility of failure. Games are ontologically multifaceted: they are composed of a set of constitutive rules, a material setting, and actualized through the embodied activities of the players. This is comparable to what urban designers recognize as program, design and use, but with a twist. Game designers create rules and can influence the setting yet the game is only actualized in play. People playing are not merely end users. They are active participants. They frequently play with the (rules of) the game (see

Chapter 11 by Glas and Lammes in this volume), discuss the issues raised in the game through the use of strong concepts (Schouten et al. 2016), or even question the very foundations of the game as we have seen above. According to Dutch cultural historian Johan Huizinga, author of the seminal *Homo ludens*, play is not just part of culture, but it is central to its origin (Huizinga 1955). Play generates culture because it provides room for innovation. Play offers a safe space for experiment and collaborations in which failing does not immediately have grave consequences. Huizinga's observation that culture (which he used in the narrow sense of 'civilization') emerges from play, suggests that playful interventions like the one discussed in this chapter may contribute to a new urban planning culture and participatory urban culture (Van Westrenen 2011; De Lange, Van Boxmeer, and Peters 2014). In addition to governments, corporations and (design) professionals, playful citizens are key in creating smart urban futures. If we are serious about making our cities smarter, we need to understand them as playful.

As already mentioned, the playful city also allows us to consider more critical issues. A first consideration involves the fine balance between persuasion and manipulation. *Rezone the Game* persuades people to address the issue of urban vacancy through collaboration, but it could easily become manipulative if outcomes are used by one party for their own profit. A closely related second consideration involves the exploitation of people's free efforts in what is known as 'playbor,' a portmanteau of play and labor (Kücklich 2005; Rheingold 2012, 134-135; Walz and Deterding 2015). Several authors argue that play in late capitalism has been absorbed by work itself through the conflation of labor and leisure time, and the concomitant self-disciplining ethics of the creative class (e.g. Rifkin 2000; Scholz 2013; Fortunati 2015). Play risks becoming absorbed in goal-oriented utilitarian practices, and neoliberal and self-disciplining discourses of labor as play. While this has not received much attention here, this should be born in mind when studying and designing the playful city. Quasi-participation is a third consideration. Who can play, who may actually decide? What will happen to the outcomes of games like *Rezone the Game*? What suggestions are being made? To what extent should we consider games like these a kind of 'tokenism' if nothing really profound happens with them (Arnstein 1969)? A fourth critical question about 'civic media' is how a technology-driven participatory citizenship might reshuffle or even bypass legitimate democratic institutions (see Foster and Iaione 2016, 339). How desirable is it if civic tech only serves the interests of groups of people capable enough of making productive use of these technologies (for a discussion of public values in the 'platform society,' see Van Dijck, Poell, and De Waal 2018)?

For future research, I suggest that the playful cities agenda should be pushed along the following lines: 1) Research: What urban issues lend themselves to being addressed by play and games, and what are the key considerations? 2) Design: What type(s) of games, and which mechanics-dynamics-aesthetics, can be employed for particular complex urban issues? 3) Validation: How can we assess and validate the role of play and games in urban culture? 4) Governance: How can we up the scale and appropriately institutionalize the use of games for complex urban issues (i.e. stakeholder coalitions, toolkit, best practices)?

References

Alfrink, K. 2015. The gameful city. In *The gameful world: Approaches, issues, applications*, eds. S. P. Walz and S. Deterding, 527-560. Cambridge, MA: The MIT Press.

Anderson, C. 2012. *Makers: The new industrial revolution*. New York: Crown Business.

Andraos, A., D. Wood, Y. Vobis, M. Alexander, H. Zaic, J. Esparza, A. Menke, S. Dufaux, J. L. Andersen, A. Maymind, and W. Boning. 2009. 49 cities. *Storefront for Art and Architecture*. http://www.storefrontnews.org.

Arnstein, S. R. 1969. A ladder of citizen participation. *JAIP* 35 (4): 216-224.

Bateson, G. 1972/1987. *Steps to an ecology of mind: Collected essays in anthropology, psychiatry, evolution, and epistemology*. San Francisco, CA: Chandler Publishing Co.

Beck, U. 1992. *Risk society: Towards a new modernity*. London: Sage Publications.

Beesley, P., and O. Khan. 2009. Responsive architecture/performing instruments. In *Situated Technologies Pamphlet series*, eds. O. Khan, T. Scholz, and M. Shepard. New York: The Architectural League of New York. http://www.situatedtechnologies.net/files/ST4-ResponsiveArchitecture.pdf.

Bennett, W. L., and A. Segerberg. 2012. The logic of connective action: Digital media and the personalization of contentious politics. *Information, Communication & Society* 15 (5): 739-768.

Berry, B. J. L. 1964. Cities as systems within systems of cities. *Papers in Regional Science* 13 (1): 147-163.

Bogost, I. 2007. *Persuasive games: The expressive power of videogames*. Cambridge, MA: The MIT Press.

—. 2011. *How to do things with videogames*. Minneapolis, MN: University of Minnesota Press.

Borden, I. 2001. *Skateboarding, space and the city: Architecture and the body*. New York: Berg.

Brenner, N., and C. Schmid. 2015. Towards a new epistemology of the urban? *City* 19 (2-3): 151-182.

Caillois, R. 1958/2001. *Man, play, and games*. Trans. M. Barash. Chicago, IL: University of Illinois Press.

Calzada, I., and C. Cobo. 2015. Unplugging: Deconstructing the smart city. *Journal of Urban Technology* 22 (1): 23-43.

Chang, M., and E. Goodman. 2006. Asphalt games: Enacting place through locative media. *Leonardo Electronic Almanac* 14 (3).

Davidson, N. M., and J. J. Infranca. 2016. The sharing economy as an urban phenomenon. *Yale Law & Policy Review* 34 (2): 216-279.

de Certeau, M. 1984. *The practice of everyday life*. Berkeley, CA: University of California Press.

De Lange, M. 2009. The mobile city project and urban gaming. *Second Nature: International journal of creative media* 1 (2): 160-169.

—. 2013. *Rezone the Game*: Playing for urban transformation. *BIJT.org*. http://www.bijt.org/wordpress/2013/04/24/rezone-the-game-playing-for-urban-transformation.

—. 2014. Playful planning: Citizens making the smart and social city. *ECLECTIS report: A contribution from cultural and creative actors to citizens' empowerment*. http://www.dedale.info/_objets/medias/autres/publication-eclectis-corrigee101214-965.pdf.

—. 2015. The playful city: Using play and games to foster citizen participation. In *Social technologies and collective intelligence*, ed. A. Skaržauskienė, 426-434. Vilnius: Mykolas Romeris University.

De Lange, M., R. van Boxmeer, and T. Peters, eds. 2014. *Rezone playful interventions: Spelen voor de toekomst*. Den Bosch: BAI & bART/DW.

De Lange, M., and M. de Waal. 2013. Owning the city: New media and citizen engagement in urban design. *First Monday* 18 (11). http://firstmonday.org/article/view/4954/3786.

De Mul, J. 2009. Database architecture: Anthropological reflections on the art of the possible. *The Journal of Asian Arts & Aesthetics* 3:1-14.

de Souza e Silva, A., and L. Hjorth. 2009. Playful urban spaces a historical approach to mobile games. *Simulation & Gaming* 40 (5): 602-625.

de Souza e Silva, A., and D. M. Sutko. 2008. Playing life and living play: How hybrid reality games reframe space, play, and the ordinary. *Critical Studies in Media Communication* 25 (5): 447-465.

—. 2009. *Digital cityscapes: Merging digital and urban playspaces.* New York: Peter Lang.

Debord, G. 1955. Introduction to a critique of urban geography. *Les Lèvres Nues* 6.

—. 1958. Theory of the dérive. *Internationale Situationiste* 2.

—. 2005. *Society of the spectacle.* London: Rebel Press.

Ehrmann, J., C. Lewis, and P. Lewis. 1968. Homo ludens revisited. *Yale French Studies* 41:31-57.

Feirreis, L. 2007. New Babylon reloaded: Learning from the ludic city. In *Space time play: Computer games, architecture and urbanism: The next level*, eds. F. Von Borries, S. P. Walz, and M. Boettger, 332-334. Boston, MA: Birkhauser Verlag AG.

Florida, R. L. 2004. *The rise of the creative class: And how it's transforming work, leisure, community and everyday life.* New York: Basic Books.

—. 2012. *The rise of the creative class: Revisited.* New York: Basic Books.

Fortunati, L. 2015. New media, play, and social identities. In *Playful identities: The ludification of digital media cultures*, eds. V. Frissen, S. Lammes, M. de Lange, J. de Mul, and J. Raessens, 293-305. Amsterdam: Amsterdam University Press.

Foster, S. R., and C. Iaione. 2016. The city as a commons. *Yale Law & Policy Review* 34 (2): 280-349.

Frissen, V., S. Lammes, M. de Lange, J. de Mul, and J. Raessens, eds. 2015. *Playful identities: The ludification of digital media cultures.* Amsterdam: Amsterdam University Press.

Future Cities Catapult. 2018. Home: Future cities catapult. *Future Cities Catapult.* http://futurecities.catapult.org.uk.

Games for Cities. 2018. City-game database. *Games for cities.* http://gamesforcities.com/database.

Gerritzen, M., and G. Lovink, eds. 2010. *Everyone is a designer in the age of social media.* Amsterdam: BIS Publishers.

Goffman, E. 1959. *The presentation of self in everyday life.* Garden City, NY: Doubleday.

Gordon, E., and P. Mihailidis, eds. 2016. *Civic media: Technology | Design | Practice* Cambridge, MA: The MIT Press.

Graham, S., and S. Marvin. 2001. *Splintering urbanism: Networked infrastructures, technological mobilities and the urban condition.* New York: Routledge.

Hall, P. 1988. *Cities of tomorrow: An intellectual history of urban planning and design in the twentieth century.* Oxford: Basil Blackwell.

Hemment, D., and A. Townsend, eds. 2013. *Smart citizens.* Manchester, UK: FutureEverything Publications.

Hollands, R. G. 2008. Will the real smart city please stand up? Intelligent, progressive or entrepreneurial? *City* 12 (3): 303-320.

—. 2015. Critical interventions into the corporate smart city. *Cambridge Journal of Regions, Economy and Society* 8 (1): 61-77.

Holleman, E., R.-J. de Kort, and S. Lindemann, eds. 2012. *Balkan in de polder: Naar organische gebiedsontwikkeling in Nederland?* Amsterdam: Mondriaanfonds.

Huizinga, J. 1955. *Homo ludens: A study of the play-element in culture*. Boston, MA: Beacon Press.

Huxley, M. 2006. Spatial rationalities: Order, environment, evolution and government. *Social & Cultural Geography* 7 (5): 771-787.

IBM Industries. 2013. IBM Smarter Cities Intelligent Operations Center 1.6 Demo. *Youtube*. http://www.youtube.com/watch?v=3yVe1DL2qjs.

Jacobs, J. 1961/1992. *The death and life of great American cities*. New York: Vintage Books.

Knight Foundation. Knight foundation: Trends in civic tech. *Knight Foundation*. http://knightfoundation.org/features/civictech.

Kücklich, J. 2005. Precarious playbour: Modders and the digital games industry. *The Fibreculture Journal* 5. http://five.fibreculturejournal.org/fcj-025-precarious-playbour-modders-and-the-digital-games-industry.

Landry, C. 2008. *The creative city: A toolkit for urban innovators*. London: Comedia.

Landry, C., and F. Bianchini. 1995. *The creative city*. London: Demos.

Lefebvre, H. 1996. *Writings on cities*. Trans. E. Kofman and E. Lebas. Cambridge, MA: Blackwell Publishers.

Lofland, L. H. 1973. *A world of strangers: Order and action in urban public space*. New York: Basic Books.

Mattern, S. 2015. Mission control: A history of the urban dashboard. *Places Journal*. http://placesjournal.org/article/mission-control-a-history-of-the-urban-dashboard.

Mitchell, D. 2003. *The right to the city: Social justice and the fight for public space*. New York: Guilford Press.

Montola, M., J. Stenros, and A. Waern. 2009. *Pervasive games: Theory and design*. Boston, MA: Morgan Kaufmann.

Mould, O. 2009. Parkour, the city, the event. *Environment and Planning D: Society and Space* 27 (4): 738-750.

Nieuwenhuys, C. 1974. *New Babylon: A nomadic town*. The Hague: Haags Gemeentemuseum. http://www.notbored.org/new-babylon.html.

Nijholt, A., ed. 2016. *Playable cities: The city as a digital playground*. London: Springer.

Oldenburg, R. 1989. *The great good place: Cafes, coffee shops, community centers, beauty parlors, general stores, bars, hangouts, and how they get you through the day.* New York: Paragon House.

Oudenampsen, M. 2013. Aldo van Eyck and the city as playground. *MO.* http://merijnoudenampsen.org/2013/03/27/aldo-van-eyck-and-the-city-as-playground.

Picon, A. 2008. Toward a city of events: Digital media and urbanity. *New Geographies* 0:32-43.

Pine, B. J., and J. H. Gilmore. 1999. *The experience economy: Work is theatre & every business a stage.* Boston, MA: Harvard Business School Press.

Raessens, J. 2006. Playful identities, or the ludification of culture. *Games and Culture* 1 (1): 52-57.

—. 2014. The ludification of culture. In *Rethinking gamification,* eds. M. Fuchs, S. Fizek, P. Ruffino, and N. Schrape, 91-114. Lüneburg: meson press.

Rheingold, H. 2012. *Net smart: How to thrive online.* Cambridge, MA: The MIT Press.

Rifkin, J. 2000. *The age of access: The new culture of hypercapitalism, where all of life is a paid-for experience.* New York: J. P. Tarcher/Putnam.

Scholz, T. 2013. *Digital labor: The internet as playground and factory.* New York: Routledge.

Schouten, B., G. Ferri, M. de Lange, and K. Millenaar. 2016. Games as strong concepts for city-making. In *Playable cities: The city as a digital playground,* ed. A. Nijholt, 23-45. London: Springer.

Sicart, M. 2016. Play and the city. *Navigationen* 16 (1): 25-40.

Simmel, G. 1997. The metropolis and mental life. In *Simmel on culture: Selected writings,* eds. D. Frisby and M. Featherstone, 174-185. London: Sage Publications.

Söderström, O., T. Paasche, and F. Klauser. 2014. Smart cities as corporate storytelling. *City* 18 (3): 307-320.

Somers, M. 2008. *Genealogies of citizenship: Markets, statelessness, and the right to have rights.* New York: Cambridge University Press.

Stevens, Q. 2007. *The ludic city: Exploring the potential of public spaces.* New York: Routledge.

Sutton-Smith, B. 1997. *The ambiguity of play.* Cambridge, MA: Harvard University Press.

Tan, E. 2014. Negotiation and design for the self-organizing city: Gaming as a method for urban design. Delft: Delft University of Technology, Faculty of Architecture and the Built Environment, Department of Urbanism.

Thrift, N. J. 2008. *Non-representational theory: Space, politics, affect.* New York: Routledge.

Townsend, A. 2013. *Smart cities: Big data, civic hackers, and the quest for a new utopia.* New York: W. W. Norton & Company.

Van Dijck, J., T. Poell, and M. de Waal. 2018. *The platform society: Public values in a connective world.* Oxford: Oxford University Press.

Vanolo, A. 2014. Smartmentality: The smart city as disciplinary strategy. *Urban Studies* 51 (5): 883-898.

Varnelis, K., ed. 2008. *Networked publics.* Cambridge, MA: The MIT Press.

Venhuizen, H., ed. 2011. *Game urbanism: Manual for cultural spatial planning.* Amsterdam: Valiz Book and Cultural Projects.

Walz, S. P., and S. Deterding. 2015. *The gameful world: Approaches, issues, applications.* Cambridge, MA: The MIT Press.

Watson, V. 2009. 'The planned city sweeps the poor away…': Urban planning and 21st century urbanisation. *Progress in Planning* 72 (3): 151-193.

Westrenen, F. van. 2011. Urbanism game. In *Game urbanism: Manual for cultural spatial planning*, ed. H. Venhuizen. Amsterdam: Valiz Book and Cultural Projects.

Wigley, M. 2001. Network fever. *Grey Room* 4:82-122.

Winner, L. 1980. Do artifacts have politics? *Daedalus* 109 (1): 121-136.

About the author

Michiel de Lange is Assistant Professor in New Media Studies, Department of Media and Culture Studies, Utrecht University. He is co-founder of The Mobile City, a platform for the study of new media and urbanism, an advisor on E-culture at Mediafonds, and works as a researcher in the field of (mobile) media, urban culture, identity, and play. He is a researcher in the NWO Creative Industries funded project *The Hackable City*, about the ways digital media shape the future of city-making.

19. Dissent at a distance

The Janissary Collective (*Mark Deuze and Lindsay Ems*)

Abstract

The contribution by The Janissary Collective argues that while protest movements and civic groups may indeed benefit from 'mediatization,' their playful character is less the result of a conscious strategy than the outcome of the performativity of means-over-ends focused engagement. This manifests itself in the 'slacktivism' inherent in participating online only. The Janissary Collective takes a skeptical stance towards generalizing the transformative role of new media tools, and proposes to regard today's political and social movements as thriving on the unruly and affective ecologies of media that mostly emphasize the *feeling* of belonging to a community instead of actually being part of one. Participation in these movements is an expression of a playful way of being and therefore a mode of being human.

Keywords: Political protests, social movements, public dissent, mediatization, affect

Asked for advice on what it takes to become president when speaking with a group of fourteen- and fifteen-year-old students on 8 September 2009, United States President Barack Obama answered:

> I want everybody here to be careful about what you post on Facebook, because in the YouTube age, whatever you do, it will be pulled up again later somewhere in your life. And when you're young, you make mistakes and you do some stupid stuff. (Stewart 2009)

Such advice seems to make sense—as employers reportedly check social network sites to research job candidates. Countries including Germany and Spain have attempted to curtail such practices, seeking to make it illegal for

---

Glas, R., S. Lammes, M. de Lange, J. Raessens, and I. de Vries, eds. 2019. *The Playful Citizen. Civic Engagement in a Mediatized Culture.* Amsterdam: Amsterdam University Press.
DOI: 10.5117/9789462984523/CH19

prospective employers to check up on applicants' private postings—clearly assuming that since we live through networks of mass self-communication sometimes we may need to be protected from ourselves (O'Hear 2010). Although such efforts may be noble, there is perhaps something to be said for not opting out, for enthusiastically embracing the recording, storing, and sharing potential of present-day media. Ironically, this insight was also shared by former President Obama; when one considers his statement (on 28 January 2011) in response to the mass demonstrations across Egypt, referring directly to the Egyptian government's attempts to shut down the country's internet and mobile communication services at the time, in which he said:

> I also call upon the Egyptian government to reverse the actions that they've taken to interfere with access to the internet, to cell phone service and to social networks that do so much to connect people in the 21st century. (BBC News 2011)

This call cannot be seen as separate from the global surveillance conducted by United States government agencies and other nations through the services and networks that support but can also potentially subvert social order. Considering the amplifying and accelerating role that mobile phones (outfitted with digital cameras) and online social networks have played, and continue to play in ongoing processes of social change. Such movements include, but are not limited to, events in Ukraine in 2004, Moldova and Iran in 2009, Tunisia in 2010, Egypt in 2011, in Syria since 2012, around the world under the banner 'Planet Occupy' (Schneider 2012), since 2013 in the US under the Black Lives Matter movement, and the #TimesUp and #MeToo movements which were jump-started in 2017. As a result of the widespread visibility of these high-tech social movements, it seems as if the future belongs to those clearly not shying away from telling everyone about their life and passions (Hermida 2014).

There seems to be a direct link between specific kinds of contemporary global protests, our current media ecology, and the role of individualized (yet connected) citizens in everyday life. To some extent, this link is benchmarked by a claim to citizen's power through both physical and virtual action. Escaping neat categorization, much of today's activism exists in a networked, 'foamy' format that lives in and mirrors the infrastructure of the internet. Yet, this mimicry is not just with a series of servers, wires, nodes, and access points—it is also articulated with values and practices that shape technologies, just as much as these values and practices are shaped by such technologies. Referring to the Occupy movement, Steve Anderson, director of the non-profit organization OpenMedia, wrote in a column for the Canadian weblog *Rabble* (on 1 November 2011): "[the Occupy movement] feels like an ongoing space infused with web values and practices. Their structure of participation mirrors that of the online encyclopedia Wikipedia [...]. Will it last? I have no idea, but I think these social practices are addictive and contagious" (Anderson 2011). One could argue that the viral and networked nature of social protest as well as the commodification of social networks (through digital marketing) reduces people to a faceless multitude (or data clusters representing specific consumer markets)—an aimless horde waiting to be divided and conquered by targeted advertising. In effect, we become zombies. Sarah Juliet Lauro (excerpting her work for the *io9* weblog on 13 January 2012) linked the Occupy movement to a zombie-like quality of contemporary society. She suggests that the collective disruption of public spaces takes its cues from zombies—more specifically, zombie walks occurring more or less regularly around the world: "These events seem to me to incarnate the youth culture's lament for its lack of real social power, and perhaps signal a willingness to change this" (Lauro 2012).

In a talk given at a symposium on zombies at Winchester University (on 28 October 2011), British Romanticist Gary Farnell endorsed the zombie as "the official monster of the moment," suggesting that the zombie signifies "an image of the truth of the current conjunctural crisis of global capitalism" (Farnell 2011). Relating zombies to a link between worldwide protests and the role of (social) media, scholars like Lauro and Farnell feel that zombies put a face on a widespread sense of crisis. Yet, it is not the face of the individual human being concerned about privacy or personhood, but rather the face of people being neither human nor machine. Once we are reduced to a *multitude* in Paolo Virno's sense, we are capable of engaging in a different way with being in the world that is essentially pluriform. Instead of being reduced to a singular mass of *people*, the era of Big Data, omnoptic surveillance and post-humanism reproduces us as a multitude, "a plurality which persists as such in the public scene" (Virno 2004, 21). Approaching the increasing interdependency between technology and life-world from a more positive point of view, Don Ihde reaches a similar conclusion in suggesting that the mediating technologies of the information age make possible an "essential pluricultural pattern" (1990, 156) in people's understanding of themselves and each other. According to Ihde, our global pluriculture gets established through the various ways in which media expose us to ideas, beliefs, cultures, rituals, up to and including culinary and architectural traditions different from our own. In media we cannot help but see and experience the lives of others (and they can see us, either through surveillance or our ongoing oversharing of it). Perhaps it is counterintuitive to suggest that the pluriculture of the multitude constitutes a zombie society, assuming that zombies are all the same (and therefore one). The point, however, is not that zombies are identical: it is just that their differences do not make a difference.

The protesters around the world do share certain characteristics that could remind one of zombies: first, they tend to be based on social movements without leaders, lacking clear hierarchical structures, and generally having no clear goals. Social movements such as the Arab Spring, the Indignados in Spain, the globally dispersed Occupy movement, and the Black Lives Matter and #MeToo movements have playful properties in that they have all share certain performative elements (concerts, costumes, cosplay, clever signage celebrations), that get creatively promoted, expressed, and shared in media (especially via social media such as YouTube, Twitter, Instagram, and Facebook). In this context, we understand a social movement to be playful when participation is self-directed and when the activities involved tend to be meaningful unto themselves rather than evaluated toward some specific end and can therefore considered to be *autotelic* (Csikszentmihalyi 1990). They are also considered playful when such activities at least to some extent are somewhat non-serious and somewhat performative (particularly regarding the omnipresent personal media documenting and sharing the activities). Second, these and other contemporary spontaneous movements involve people from all walks of life: from East to West, North to South, black and white, men and women, old and young—again negating distinct classifications—at least temporarily as these protest tend to erupt as rapidly as they dissipate. Finally, not only does the social arrangement of these protests rely heavily on the use of media (which in turn enable the active involvement of people not necessarily present)—they seem similarly infectious and as viral as media can be. We argue that what makes our being in the world in media more resonant with zombie life is its embodiment of the man-machine hybrid, rather than, as suggested by Parikka (2010), analogous with insect or bacterial life which similarly contains no structures, clear leaders and goals (swarms), expresses equality in diversity (the beehive), and is contagious (like a virus). The zombie forces us to question the false dichotomy—the endless remix—of the living and the dead.

Like our current media ecology, the nature of zombified social movements today has a distinctly remixed and remixable character, both in terms of media praxis—mashing up video and audio, culture jamming, online sharing and forwarding, up to and including hacking—and insofar as the people involved, forming a blend of often disparate backgrounds, life phases, and ideals. Following Miguel Sicart (2014), one could argue that participation in these movements—whether online or offline, either on the ground or through telepresence—is an expression of a playful way of being and therefore a mode of being human.

It is our goal in this contribution to suggest that the organization, technologies, and outcomes particular to contemporary forms of social movements and global protests differ in significant ways from those in the past, while stipulating there always has been a co-creative link between public protest, media use, and socio-political context. In other words: while our time is different, it is not necessarily new.

New social movements

It seems that hardly a day goes by without news coverage of some type of activist social movement being staged throughout the world. While the notion that we live in a 'movement society' (Meyer and Tarrow 1998) is not new, the pace and frequency of these group actions seems to have intensified. Not surprisingly, there has been a surge of research and popular debate on the connections between newer networked media, citizen engagement, and movement dynamics. Popular and academic interest in what makes these movements tick is fueled by their often dramatic and playful character—including zombie walks, cosplay, and gaming telecommunication systems by organizing protests via social media—challenging the status quo. These and other forms of public (and publicized) dissent can serve society as an equivalent form of our news media when they refuse to perform the tasks we expect of them: we seem to become aware most only once there is a breakdown. Social movements that propel forms of dissent in the public's eye, in effect, bring forth society, make it visible and open it up to intervention. As Snow and Soule put it, "understanding our own society, as well as the larger social world in which it is embedded, requires some knowledge and understanding of social movements and the activities with which they are associated" (Snow and Soule 2009, 5-6).

The newer networked media presence—the tweets from the streets, the dramatic YouTube videos, the Facebook groups—in many of these movements is unmistakable. Generally, mediated communication is important for its role in several key features of movements, such as social networking, collective identity formation and maintenance, sharing of ideas, and playful protest. The communicative power of newer media would seem to add particular affordances for movement participants. Protests and dissent in many forms can be coordinated and communicated globally, quickly, and more easily with newer networked media (Cottle and Lester 2011). Yet, we must caution against generalizing the transformative role of new media tools in social movements (Bennett 2003). Traditional media continue to play a critical role in defining, framing, and narrating dissent. There exists a reciprocal relationship between legacy media, mobile and networked media, and social movements, where each has a shaping role on the cognitions, attitudes and behaviors of the others. This ecological view of mediated dissent posits that 'old' and 'new' media work in concert as movements emerge, climax, and fade in particular cultural contexts:

> Social networking and other forms of Internet-based communication may provide new means to participate, new styles of protest and new ways to mobilize support, but they cannot fully relocate the mediated politics of dissent away from mass media news platforms. All political actors are now present in both the 'old' media and what Manuel Castells calls 'networks of mass self-communication,' and all undoubtedly will continue seeking to find bridges between the two. (Cottle and Lester 2011, 291)

The world of social movements and dissent seems to be changing with those bridges. That is because recent social movements "both draw upon and also challenge the socio-technical properties of the new media" (Loader 2008, 1921).

The formative features of social movements can be conceptualized in terms of five key elements. Movements tend to be collective efforts to challenge or defend some existing cultural, political, or economic authority. They are somewhat organized, in the sense that they usually include informal networks with shared beliefs and some solidarity. Movements tend to be sustained over time, although activities and participation may ebb and flow. Most social movement research emphasizes non-institutional means of mobilization and protest. It is further important to emphasize the fluidity of contemporary social movements in terms of membership, tactics, structure, and aims (Della Porta and Diani 1999; Snow and Soule 2009).

Mediatization (Hjarvard 2013) supports the features of social movements, in terms of both mobilization and media coverage. In the context of our lives as lived in media (Deuze 2012), it can be said of social movements that if they do not make it into media, then they do not really exist. When movement participants engage with newer media as part of their strategies and tactics, could this media use instantiate different social movement dynamics?

Recently, various social movements have emerged with characteristics that are out of sync with dominant social movement theory. These characteristics include: no clear hierarchy with often multiple (and varying) crowd-sourced leaders; no clearly defined demands or goals; no clear nation-based ideological framing; no coherent collective identities based on national politics; diversity and heterogeneity within an already fluid group; and, last but not least, a heightened role for emotions and identity dynamics. Moreover, all of these characteristics find expression in the kind of media such movements tend to use: generally mobile, networked, remixed personal media (next to, and at times instead of, mass media).

Walgrave's (1998, 2001) trenchant analysis of the Belgian White Movement may have set the stage for discussions about movements that start off as emotional movements only to become more instrumental and conventional later on, a pattern that seems prevalent today. Emotions have long been important for understanding social movements, but emotions have not been the target of much research on social movements, perhaps because of the difficulties with obtaining measurements and conducting analyses. Emotions are not only tough to operationalize, they are challenging for movement participants to talk about as well. Fortunati (2009) wonders whether this oversight in the social sciences has made the way in which people, media, and society are analyzed seem to be without a heart. She advocates for an increase in the investigation of (electronic) emotion.

At the beginning of the twenty-first century, there is a surge in research into affect theory since emotions are increasingly being considered as an important purpose of social movements, even as a key reason for their existence or maintenance (Polletta and Amenta 2001). People often participate in movements in order to meet affective and emotional needs that cannot easily be fulfilled elsewhere. Social networks, important catalysts or even requirements for collective action, are themselves built on affective bonds (Goodwin, Jasper, and Polletta, 2001). In other words, people join a network because it makes them feel good. These affective ties hold the network together, paving the way for group action (Ibid.). Feelings for a group can make participation itself pleasurable and meaningful, even if separate from the movement's aims. It is through emotions, then, that people can potentially discover their capacity for collective action.

Emotions may be the main reason people participate in movements in the first place, which in turn makes the kinds of dissent recently witnessed around the world—whether it is the Arab Spring, UK riots, street protests in Brazil, or the Tea Party Movement—harder to classify along earlier lines.

The link between contemporary media, new social movements, *glocalized* forms of dissent, and emotional immersion as a catalyst is further explored by Jodi Dean. In her article 'Affective networks' she maintains that people's use of social media, like Twitter and Facebook, constitutes an affective network, eliciting feelings of community. Dean writes:

> Affect [...] is what accrues from reflexive communication, from communication for its own sake, from the endless circular movement of commenting, adding notes and links, bringing in new friends and followers, layering and interconnecting myriad communications platforms and devices [...] Every little tweet or comment, every forwarded image or petition, accrues a tiny affective nugget, a little surplus enjoyment, a smidgen of attention that attaches to it, making it stand out from the larger flow before it blends back in. (2010, 21)

According to Dean, these affective attachments to media are not enough to produce actual communities, but the feeling of community matters since they enable mediated relationships that can take a variety of evolving, interconnected forms.

Could these new mediated emotions catalyze collective actions? Papacharissi and Oliveira (2011) argue for the importance of understanding affect in media use during contemporary social movements. Using centering resonance analysis and discourse analysis, the authors analyzed storytelling forms on Twitter for a period of time during the Arab Spring. Based on their findings, they characterize Twitter feeds during the Arab Spring as affective news streams, since they "blend opinion, fact, and emotion into expressions uttered in anticipation of events that have not yet been reported in mainstream media" (Papacharissi and Oliveira 2011, 24). Such affective news streams sustain and nurture affective involvement, connection, cohesion, and awareness. This is especially relevant, the authors suggest, in authoritarian regimes where speech is heavily controlled. In such oppressive contexts, these affective statements in social media can become political statements and a challenge to authorities (Papacharissi and Oliveira 2011).

The idea that aggrieved groups, brought together by shared, mediated emotions yet lacking substantive plans for social change might occupy the streets, infuriates some observers. In an opinion for the *New York Times*, columnist David Brooks (2012) responded to the viral YouTube video, 'Why I Hate Religion But Love Jesus.' Brooks used the performance art video as a window to explore the state of youth activism, protest forms, and social change. He argues that ill-informed, media-saturated youth lack the historical knowledge, contextual understanding, and well-laid, directed plans to carry out social change. He opines: "If you go out there armed only with your own observations and sentiments, you will surely find yourself on very weak ground." Yet, armed with just those mediated sentiments, people around the world seem to be discovering a momentum for collective action. They are strangers who meet to become a fluid 'we' in media. Powered by these affective ties, social movement dynamics, including knowledge building and sharing, can and do emerge. Perhaps some are just not comfortable with this order or, rather, disorder. The unruly nature of these affective ecologies bypasses the scripts, standards, and protocols of news industries, political parties, and social institutions. Their post-gender qualities (dynamically combining feminine elements of inclusivity and exchange with more masculine characteristics of confrontation and aggression) also escape carefully established ways of sense-making processes. Perhaps the newer forms of dissent, in conjunction with charged emotions and social media, are indeed as irreducible as zombies are.

It may be too reductive to label the recent collective actions throughout the Middle East, Northern Africa, Latin America and the United States as media-fueled emotional movements. There is no mistaking the triggering, expressing, and sharing of emotion that newer media, and social media in particular, have allowed in these contexts. This circulation of affect (Dean 2010) in media, intense and alluring as it is for people, is ripe for cultural analysis. And perhaps we need some unreason to really make sense of the cases before us.

Contemporary media and dissent

Scholars in a number of disciplines investigating the relationships between new social movements, dissent, and newer networked media tend to pitch their intellectual tents in one of two camps. Some argue that media have had a significant impact on social movements' successes or failures (Castells 2007; Shirky 2008; Allagui and Keubler 2011; Elseewi 2011; Howard, Agarwal, and Hussain 2011; Segerberg and Bennett 2011; Wall and El Zaheed 2011). Other observers emphasize the social forces responsible for the uprisings and downplay the importance of communication tools (Agre 2002, 2003; Christiansen 2011; Etling, Faris, and Palfrey 2010; Hofheinz 2011; Newsom, Lengel, and Cassara 2011). Still others argue that both of these two perspectives are essential to understanding recent phenomena, somehow suggesting one should move back and forth between the tents in both of the camps (Hara and Huang 2010; Aouragh and Alexander 2011; Shklovski and Kotamraju

2011). Interestingly, all authors (even those who call for a more holistic approach) view these two entities as separate in their discussions of social media and social change. This has implications for what kinds of questions investigators ask and what types of findings they achieve. By sidestepping this distinction and, by instead seeing media as both technological and emotional infrastructures that reveal the motivations and actions of the people and institutions using them, researchers can begin to observe and analyze the circulating intensities that instantiate current social movements.

By observing and analyzing the use of social media tools in recent social movements in this way, it becomes clear that social media are extremely versatile tools put to use in multiple ways by different groups of protesters and governments; there is not only one single use or result of Twitter-use in protest events. Social forces and technical forces are intertwined. Technical forces are social forces that have been fixed through a decision-making process for a certain time period into a non-biological infrastructure. They are decisions with lasting impact. Social forces are constantly changing with fluctuations in the local ecosystem. This is a new advantage for observers and analysts of human behavior. When a tool can be used in multiple ways to achieve a wide variety of different outcomes, one can look at the way the tool is used and the resulting outcome to identify the user's intentions and ambitions. Social media tools today help make protester's actions, motivations and expressions more visible on a global scale which can be benefitial in a way that was not possible before.

For example, news media in the United States became transfixed by the protests that broke out after the 2009 Iranian elections. They broadcasted updates continuously despite the limited access Western journalists had to events on the street. Because of this limited access, news outlets became very dependent on the information generated by Iranians. The BBC's Persian-language television channel reported receiving about five videos a minute from amateurs, even though the channel was blocked within Iran and 4,000 emails and hundreds of phone calls a day (Landler and Stelter 2009). Along with this information, news outlets turned to Twitter for information including images and video along with eyewitness accounts of events on the streets. On 16 June CNN's Wolf Blitzer and Abbi Tatton used conversations on Twitter to help them construct a view of what was unfolding on the ground in Iran (Tatton 2009). In a similar case, a BBC web article also embedded user generated video footage of a man wounded after the Revolutionary Guard fired shots on the streets of Tehran (BBC News 2011). Perhaps the most frequently circulated story from the Iranian protests plays out in a video of an Iranian woman named Neda Agha-Soltan, dying after being shot while walking with her singing instructor on the street. A bystander caught her death on video and posted it to the internet. This video became the source of much inspiration for Moussavi supporters in Iran and around the world (Fathi 2009). The video link was distributed frequently through Twitter.

Moreover, the United States government asked the CEO of Twitter to leave its service up in Iran during the 2009 protests when it was scheduled to be taken down for regular service maintenance (Landler and Stelter 2009). This was an explicit diplomatic move on the part of the United States government who was acting out politically against its enemy, the incumbent Ahmadinejad regime, by securing the communication tools of the anti-government protesters on the streets in Iran.

On the other hand, the United States government went so far as to arrest Elliot Madison, a protester who was tweeting the location of police blockades in Pittsburgh, Pennsylvania during the 2009 G-20 Summit protests just a few months later (Goodman 2009). In the G-20 Summit protests, the use of Twitter by protesters was altogether different. In Iran, Twitter was used primarily to get information out to Western journalistic outlets, as evidenced by the small number of Twitter users in Iran at the time and the large number of tweets in English instead of Farsi. At the 2009 G-20, Twitter was used by protesters to avoid the police in the streets. Elliot Madison was one of these protesters. When he was arrested, he was in a hotel room that was raided by a brigade of armed police officers. His charges were for hindering apprehension or prosecution, criminal use of a communication facility, and possession of instruments of a crime. Eventually all of these charges were dropped (DMLP 2010). It was intended he be used as an example of what protesters should not do.

These apparently contradictory moves show that the Obama administration's actual goals were not to secure the freedom of speech of Iranian citizens, as it was claimed (Landler and Stelter 2009), nor to stop violence in the streets of Pittsburgh (Singel 2009). Instead, the United States government was trying to gain some leverage over its international adversaries and suppress dissent at home. The governments' actions can also be considered to be attempts to extend this control over communication channels and information flows across media.

An additional affordance made possible by the new socio-technical arrangements of today, is that people who are not geographically located where the protests are taking place can still participate in the protest events. In effect, these online protest participants are providing resources in the currency of emotional support, interest and sympathy. These are invaluable resources that help motivate the physical participants to keep fighting even when it seems that they might not achieve their goals. In this way, new communication tools and the socio-technical arrangements in which they are embedded provide ways for people to participate in protest events from a distance—their non-presence becomes a significant (and sustaining) element of the social movement. Online participants help those on the ground circumvent firewalls. They re-tweet, forward and share information from protesters on the ground with their social networks. They learn about police brutality and express sympathy on personal forums such as Facebook and Twitter newsfeeds. All of these actions contribute to the multi-faceted form of today's social movements. Two essential components, however, can be identified. One is geographic and offline, the other is online and virtual. One cannot exist without the other. Mediated participation fuels motivation and determines the functional potential of the geographically located protests. That the online component is essential to today's movements is understood by the autocratic regimes outlined above. In efforts to suppress and dissolve the movements, there was an attempt to curtail communications via the internet and/or SMS by taking down infrastructure and/or content.

These ever-changing circulating intensities are now visible and recorded for observers of human behavior in new ways. The channels of information flow—the infrastructure and how messages travel—shed light on how human power struggles play out. Today, we can see the utilization of social structures more visibly, which can have implications for future outcomes of protest events and social power struggles between governments and dissenters in the connected world.

Conclusion and discussion

Although turning to media in moments of social upheaval and unrest is not a new phenomenon, the traits of today's media technologies and the social arrangements that have emerged in conjunction with our media provide new channels through which to witness, participate in and take responsibility for today's social movements. Social movements both shape and reflect qualities of the media that are used to motivate and sustain them. Just as our media can be seen as neither dead nor alive—as neither the internet, nor our cell phones or what we do with them determines our lives, yet at the same time our lives have become quite unimaginable without them—contemporary forms of mass protest for social change feel like zombie movements. There are—or seem to be—no leaders, no hierarchies, few or no particular individuals running the show, even though there definitely seems to be a show taking place. This mediatized aspect of public (and, to some extent, private) life is paramount, tending to make forms of social protest more about the disruption of social order in and of itself rather than the achievement of some clear goal beyond it. Sherry Turkle (2011) is among those warning that our emotional life is becoming increasingly performative and controlled by the influence of technology. Media may act as amplifiers and accelerators of affect in the context of new social movements, and in the process also act to amplify the playful aspects of participation, such as the at times non-seriousness of joining in, the 'slacktivism' inherent in participating online only, and the gaming of the telecommunication system.

The protesters, as a relatively amorphous and generally temporary collective, seem pretty good at tearing things down—yet tend to be less than effective at building anything anew. Instead of capitalism's central tenet of creative destruction, we observe a purposeless passion at work—signaled as a crucial quality of the multitude by Virno (2004), engaged as we are in production time without producing anything (analogous with Marx's concept of activity-without-end-product). Similarly, the performativity of means-over-ends focused engagement can be seen as a playful act of citizenship. Raw emotions drive these new movements, locally spurred on by viral forms of engagement from anywhere on the planet. The good, bad and the ugly become visible in power negotiations like never before—we can see each other (trying to) live. Next to mass media reporting hastily (and somewhat grudgingly) on outbreaks all over the world, a new system of communicative practices emerges, based on peer-to-peer connectivity and a phatic digital culture (Miller 2008) consisting of small communicative gestures that are distinctly social and produce communal forms, but are generally not intended to transmit substantial information. Most importantly for scholars, new socio-technical configurations represent new lenses with which to observe human activity, forcing us to question age-old assumptions about (possibly false) dichotomies between engagement and apathy, participation and witnessing, production and consumption—and indeed between affect and effect in processes of (mediated) social change. The zombie, both as an analogy and a metaphor, is a helpful conceptual tool to question such categories. In media, there is a new visibility of everyone's actions (Thompson 2005), both among the powerful and the powerless. This emerging struggle to publish and publicize our lives makes socio-technical configurations the new artifacts that reflect our current social state at this point in time, providing a new object for media studies.

It is impossible to generalize about the transformative role of new media in dissent around the world. What we can analyze and discuss, though, are fissures in power and why particular groups of people in particular contexts seem to discover and widen those cracks. As we have discussed, this is ultimately not just a story about social life but about media life (Deuze 2012), about mediated outbursts of anger, fear, hope, play, courage, sacrifice, and creativity.

References

Agre, P. E. 2002. Real-time politics: The internet and the political process. *The Information Society* 18 (5): 311-331.

—. 2003. P2P and the promise of internet equality. *Communications of the ACM* 46 (2): 39-42.

Allagui, I., and J. Keubler. 2011. The Arab Spring and the role of ICTs. *International Journal of Communication* 5:1435-1442.

Anderson, S. 2011. The Occupy movement is making the world more like the web. *Rabble*. http://rabble.ca/columnists/2011/11/occupy-movement-making-world-more-web.

Aouragh, M., and A. Alexander. 2011. The Egyptian experience: Sense and nonsense of the internet revolution. *International Journal of Communication* 5:1344-1358.

BBC News. 2011. In quotes: Reaction to Egypt protests. *BBC*. http://www.bbc.com/news/world-middle-east-12316019.

Bennett, L. 2003. New media power: The internet and global activism. In *Contesting media power*, eds. N. Couldry and J. Currans, 17-37. Lanham, MD: Rowman & Littlefield.

Brooks, D. 2012. How to fight the man. *The New York Times*, 3 February.

Castells, M. 2007. Communication, power and counter-power in the network society. *International Journal of Communication* 1 (1): 238-266.

Christiansen, C. 2011. Discourses of technology and liberation: State aid to net activists in an era of "Twitter revolutions". *The Communication Review* 14:233-253.

Cottle S., and L. Lester, eds. 2011. *Transnational protests and the media*. New York: Peter Lang.

Csikszentmihalyi, M. 1990. *Flow: The psychology of optimal experience*. New York: Harper & Row.

Dean, J. 2010. Affective networks. *Media Tropes eJournal* 2 (2): 19-44.

Della Porta, D., and M. Diani, 1999. *Social movements: An introduction*. Cambridge, MA: Blackwell Publishers.

Deuze, M. 2012. *Media life*. Malden, MA: Polity Press.

DMLP, 2010. United States v. Madison. *Digital Media Law Project*. http://www.dmlp.org/threats/united-states-v-madison.

Elseewi, T. A. 2011. A revolution of the imagination. *International Journal of Communication* 5:1197-1206.

Etling, B., R. Faris, and J. Palfrey. 2010. Political change in the digital age: The fragility and promise of online organizing. *SAIS Review, Summer-Fall.* http://dash.harvard.edu/bitstream/handle/1/4609956/SAIS%20online%20organizing%20paper%20final.pdf?sequence=1.

Farnell, G. 2011. For a symposium on zombies. *Nettime mailing list archives*. http://www.nettime.org/Lists-Archives/nettime-l-1110/msg00106.html.

Fathi, N. 2009. In a death seen around the world, a symbol of Iranian protests. *The New York Times Online*. http://www.nytimes.com/2009/06/23/world/middleeast/23neda.html?ref=middleeast.

Fortunati, L. 2009. Theories without heart. In *Cross-modal analysis*, eds. A. Esposito and R. Vích, 5-17. Berlin: Springer.

Goodman, A. 2009. Watch what you tweet. *TruthDig.com*. http://www.truthdig.com/report/item/20091006_watch_what_you_tweet/?ln.

Goodwin, J., J. Jasper, and F. Polletta. 2001. *Passionate politics: Emotions and social movements*. Chicago, IL: University of Chicago Press.

Hara, N., and B. Huang. 2010. Online social movements. *Annual Review of Information Science & Technology* 45:489-522.

Hermida, A. 2014. *Tell everyone: Why we share and why it matters*. Toronto: Doubleday.

Hjarvard, S. 2013. *The mediatization of culture and society*. London: Routledge.

Hofheinz, A. 2011. Nextopia? Beyond revolution 2.0. *International Journal of Communication* 5:1417-1434.

Howard, P. N., S. D. Agarwal, and M. M. Hussain. 2011. When do states disconnect their digital networks? Regime responses to the political uses of social media. *The Communication Review* 14:216-232.

Ihde, D. 1990. *Technology and the lifeworld: From garden to earth*. Bloomington, IN: Indiana University Press.

Landler, M., and B. Stelter. 2009. Washington taps into a potent new force in diplomacy. *The New York Times Online*. http://www.nytimes.com/2009/06/17/world/middleeast/17media.html.

Lauro, S. J. 2012. Did zombie flash mobs help pave the way for Occupy Wall Street? *Gizmodo*. http://io9.gizmodo.com/5875897/did-zombie-flash-mobs-help-pave-the-way-for-occupy-wall-street.

Loader, B. 2008. Social movements and new media. *Sociology Compass* 2 (6): 1920-1933.

Meyer D., and S. Tarrow, eds. 1998. *The social movement society: Contentious politics for a new century*. Lanham, MD: Rowman & Littlefield.

Miller, V. 2008. New media, networking and phatic culture. *Convergence* 14 (4): 387-400.

Newsom, V. A., L. Lengel, and C. Cassara. 2011. The Arab spring, local knowledge and the revolutions: A framework for social media information flow. *International Journal of Communication* 5:1303-1312.

O'Hear, S. 2010. Germany to outlaw employers checking out job candidates on Facebook, but Googling is OK. *TechCrunch*. http://eu.techcrunch.com/2010/08/23/germany-to-outlaw-employers-checking-out-job-candidates-on-facebook-but-googling-is-ok.

Papacharissi, Z., and M. Oliveira. 2011. The rhythms of news storytelling on Twitter: Coverage of the January 25 Egyptian uprising on Twitter. Paper presented at *WAPOR 64th annual conference: Public opinion and the internet, Amsterdam, September 21-23, 2011*.

Parikka, J. 2010. *Insect media*. Minneapolis, MN: University of Minnesota Press.

Polletta, F., and E. Amenta. 2001. Second that emotion? Lessons from once-novel concepts in social movement research. In *Passionate politics*, eds. J. Goodwin, J. Jasper, and F. Polletta, 303-316. Chicago, IL: University of Chicago Press.

Schneider, N. 2012. Planet Occupy. *Harper's Magazine*. http://harpers.org/blog/2012/01/planet-occupy.

Segerberg, A., and W. L. Bennett. 2011. Social media and the organization of collective action: Using Twitter to explore the ecologies of two climate change protests. *The Communication Review* 14:197-215.

Shirky, C. 2008. *Here comes everybody: How change happens when people come together*. New York: Penguin Books.

Shklovski, I., and N. P. Kotamraju. 2011. Online contribution practices in countries that engage in internet blocking and censorship. *CHI, Session: Inter-cultural Interaction*, 1109-1118.

Sicart, M. 2014. *Play matters*. Cambridge, MA: The MIT Press.

Singel, R. 2009. Fed's search of twittering anarchist upheld. *Wired*. http://www.wired.com/threatlevel/2009/11/twitter-anarchist-search-uphel.

Snow D., and S. Soule. 2009. *A primer on social movements*. New York: W. W. Norton.

Stewart, P. 2009. RPT-Obama warns U.S. teens of perils of Facebook. *Reuters*. http://www.reuters.com/article/obama-facebook-idUSN08285822200909 08.

Tatton, A. 2009. The situation room. *CNN.com*. http://www.cnn.com/video/#/video/politics/2009/06/16/srm.protest.online.cnn.

Thompson, J. 2005. The new visibility. *Theory, Culture & Society* 22 (6): 31-51.

Turkle, S. 2011. *Alone together.* New York: Basic Books.
Virno, P. 2004. *A grammar of the multitude.* Boston, MA: The MIT Press.
Walgrave, S. 1998. De 'nieuwe emotionele bewegingen' en de arbeidersbeweging. *De Gids op Maatschappelijk Gebied* 89 (10): 753-762.
—. 2001. The Belgian white movement: Between identity and instrumentality. Paper presented at *The 1st general conference of the European consortium for political research, Canterbury, September 6-8, 2001.*
Wall, M., and S. E. Zaheed. 2011. "I'll be waiting for you guys": A YouTube call to action in the Egyptian revolution. *International Journal of Communication* 5:1333-1343.

About the authors

Mark Deuze is Full Professor of Media Studies, specializing in Journalism at the University of Amsterdam's (UvA) Faculty of Humanities. From 2004 to 2013, he worked at Indiana University's Department of Telecommunications in Bloomington, United States. Publications of his work include over ninety papers in academic journals and books, including the monographs *Media work* (Polity Press 2007) and *Media life* (Polity Press 2012). He co-authored and co-edited the books *Beyond journalism* (Polity Press 2018; with Tamara Witschge) and *Making media* (Amsterdam University Press 2018; with Mirjam Prenger). He is also the bass player of post-grunge band Skinflower.

Lindsay Ems is an Assistant Professor in the College of Communication at Butler University, where she teaches courses in the Department of Human Communication and Organizational Leadership. Her research and teaching explore social changes and the role new, digital communication technologies play in accelerating or inhibiting them. In her dissertation, *Divine design: Configuring Amish communication in a high-tech world,* she studied the calculated (non-)use of new information communication technologies in Amish communities. This project identifies strategies for preserving cultural autonomy among marginalized groups in the information age. In 2015, she completed her PhD in the Media School at Indiana University. She has also published research on ethnographic techniques for studying technology non-users, Twitter use by protesters and social and mobile media use for public health communication among high-risk groups. Among other outlets, her research has been published in *First Monday, New Media & Society* and *Media Culture & Society.*

20. Playing with power: Casual politicking as a new frame for political analysis

Alex Gekker

Abstract

The chapter examines the entanglement of play and politics through digital media. By analyzing the Obama 2008 and Trump 2016 presidential campaigns, it proposes a new term for examining political engagement, namely 'casual politicking.' Building on mediatization theories, the chapter takes the affordances of causal video games as a template to analyze the actions performed by citizens, politicians, and organizations attempting to alter behaviors. The resulting characteristics of the political process are presented through four key aspects: the role of ICT platforms with intuitive interfaces, the prevalence of issue-centered rather than ideological action, a perpetual political engagement undeterred by failure, and socially focused networks orientated towards fun. When applied to the two campaigns, surprising similarities can be seen, despite the different messages and personalities of the candidates.

Keywords: Casual politicking, casual games, mediatization, elections, Obama, Trump

This chapter deals with the tricky duality of politics and play for the contemporary citizen. Arguably, politics is and always has been playful. In his famous treatise on playfulness, Johan Huizinga sees the playful (agonistic) origins of law in the courts of the Greek and Roman lawyer-politicians. In a later chapter, he analyzes the playfulness of war and peace in medieval society and mourns the loss of such playfulness in contemporary times (Huizinga 1970). Brian Sutton-Smith (2005) calls this type of interaction 'play as power,' hailing from ancient sporting events and contests. Similarly, mediatization scholar Stephen Coleman (2006, 2011) tracks the changes

Glas, R., S. Lammes, M. de Lange, J. Raessens, and I. de Vries, eds. 2019. *The Playful Citizen. Civic Engagement in a Mediatized Culture.* Amsterdam: Amsterdam University Press.
DOI: 10.5117/9789462984523/CH20

in the voting and participation habits of young people with the advent of televised voting for *Big Brother*-style reality shows. However—as I will argue below—political play has changed considerably since it merged with the digital affordances of new media platforms, resulting in autotelic political play that is centered on issues and platforms rather than concrete ideologies. To illustrate this, I highlight two turning points in world politics: the campaign that led to the election of Barack Obama as President of the United States in 2008, and the campaign that elected his successor, Donald Trump. Provocatively, I claim that these campaigns were *identical* in their underlying principles, despite the differences in the ideology and personality of their respective candidates.

In doing so, I aim to offer a view of playful political processes through the contemporary lens of digital media by bridging the gap between two disciplines that have rarely met, namely game and play studies on the one hand and political communication on the other. In an introductory chapter to the influential anthology *Political communication in postmodern democracy: Challenging the primacy of politics*, the editors warn that "as readers, listeners and viewers learn to recognize the manufactured nature of news, cynicism and disillusionment with politics grows and with it a dramatic erosion of trust and political engagement" (Brants and Voltmer 2011a, 6). The word 'users' is absent from this warning, yet users are perhaps the most common conceptualization of the masses to date and, in fact, as pointed out by visualization guru Edward Tufte, "[t]here are only two industries that call their customers 'users': illegal drugs and software" (Whitlatch 2015, n.p.). Unlike in narcotics industries, however, political-socio-technical processes are in a constant state of flux and renegotiation between various parties, users and producers alike. 'Usage' does not imply unidirectionality, as research has shown that in complex technological processes designers and users 'co-configure' each other continuously (Woolgar 1990; Bruns 2007). Therefore, I argue that to understand the remaking of what it means to be engaged in contemporary mediated politics, we must look at *users* and even more so at *players*.

This chapter is divided into two sections. The first section introduces my main theoretical framework. Utilizing the hybrid human/nonhuman perspective of the Actor-Network Theory (ANT), I conceive mediatized political engagement as shaped through playful performative practices and enabled by casual devices. Unlike the sporting metaphors or grand battles associated with political play, I suggest that *casual games* should be used as our primary analogy. The second section outlines my concept of *casual politicking*, and its properties of reliance on ICT platforms, issue networks, perpetual engagement, and social media sites. Throughout this chapter, I will discuss the 2008 Obama app and Trump's 'Great Meme War' in 2016 as two poignant historical case studies exemplifying casual politicking mechanisms. Ultimately, I offer a view of the ludification of politics in which action is contingent on the perceived enjoyment of—and affordance to—users.

Games as mediatization of politics

This section will show that a type of video game referred to as 'casual games' can be used as a productive prism for understanding certain types of political engagement. In the first subsection, I briefly problematize classic theories of political communication in relation to current modes of media consumption, and suggest mediatization theory as a solution. Mediatization presupposes the existence of certain 'molding forces' whereby media technologies and institutions mold previously non-mediated spheres of life. In the second subsection, I argue that casual games are a type of medium that can and should be examined in relation to political mediatization.

Mediatization

Video games are an example of networked media, becoming widespread through the convergence of platforms and technologies (Jenkins 2006a; Jenkins 2006b; Moore 2011; Sicart 2014; Walz and Deterding 2015). The field of game studies that has emerged around them is multifaceted and conflicted, hailing from computer science, cultural studies, play studies, and Human-Computer-Interface (HCI) studies. In this chapter, video games are postulated as an established communication medium, rendering it possible to examine the potential of games and game studies as a prism for political research. This follows the notion of political agents as tactical producers and consumers of media, as has been conceptualized in recent scholarship (Fuchs et al. 2014; Tufekci 2017).

Agenda setting and framing are two fundamental theories for political communication in general, and for my notion of casual politicking in particular. Ever since McCombs and Shaw (1972) published their ground-breaking research on what they dubbed *the agenda-setting effect*, researchers have studied the media's ability to set agendas for the public and political establishment by putting certain topics in the spotlight while downplaying others. Or, as McCombs and Shaw quote Cohen in the opening pages of their work:

"[T]he press may not be successful much of the time in telling people what to think, but it is stunningly successful in telling its readers what to think *about*" (Cohen 1963, 13, emphasis in original). While the findings regarding the agenda-setting effect vary in terms of the strength, directedness, and homogeneity of effects, it is generally agreed that media are responsible for highlighting a set of topics that influence public opinion (Scheufele and Tewksbury 2007). Increased public concern subsequently influences the attention given to those issues by public officials, who consequently try to attract the media's attention with topics fitting their own interests, and so on, ad infinitum.

The second theory, framing, was developed through the application of psychologist Erving Goffman's (1974) frame analysis theory. Goffman suggests that our daily experience is organized through a series of 'frames,' or referential models with which we approach each situation. We use different 'keys' to refer to different frames, depending on our heuristics and predispositions. Such frames might include, for example, 'play' or 'rehearsal' as opposed to 'serious situation.' In other words, a person is able to make a distinction between their understanding of an argument in the frame of a theater play and an argument in the frame of observing an incident in the street. Framing as media theory (Entman 1991, 1993; Iyengar 1994) builds upon this and suggests that the media repackages certain aspects of stories for their audiences in a way that influences the broader context within which the stories are understood. These aspects may include words, photographs, or interviews emphasizing certain things, but also elements such as the color chosen for the graphics or the visual arrangement of material on the page or the screen. Word choices, the placement of photographs, or even the colors used on a page or during the newscast invoke certain referential frames for an audience. One famous example of frame analysis was conducted by communication researcher Robert Entman (1991), who examined two similar aerial tragedies, the shooting down of a Korean civilian airplane by the Soviets and the shooting down of an Iranian civilian airplane by United States troops. He shows how the American press framed one case as a tragic mistake (using words such as "tragedy" and "plane passengers") and the other as a deliberate crime ("attack," "victims," and portraying the plane in crosshairs).

Agenda-setting and framing theories are considered the cornerstones of modern political communications, yet they represent a research paradigm no longer sufficient for understanding modern mediated communication. As economic and technological networks converge to offer a personalized (political) experience (Jenkins 2006b; Couldry and Hepp 2016; Chadwick

2017), the networked society supplements mass communication with mass self-communication (Castells 2007). Such structures are dominated by a flat network of internet peer-to-peer communication, rooted in social media sites, email, online games, and micro-blogging rather than by the hierarchies of traditional media—though still reliant on them for broader appeal. While traditional media institutions still set the agenda and frame it, everyday users today have much greater ability to do the same, by 'poaching' and 'repackaging' meanings provided by mainstream sources (Jenkins 2006a, 2012; Schäfer 2011). This greatly undermines the power of such traditional media institutions to set and frame agendas, as can be seen through the massive bottom-up activist campaigns of #BLM and #MeToo that originated on Twitter. Facebook, for example, has emerged as a dominating force on the web, inducing a significant change in how information is exchanged and evaluated (Gerlitz and Helmond 2013; Helmond 2015). And while scholars and activists have long warned about the ramifications of an algorithmically curated public sphere, it took several years and Facebook's own admission of unwilling compliance with Russian interference in United States elections to cement awareness of this change in the public's mind.

There seems to be an increased enveloping of different social spheres within mediated communications. This, in turn, affects how those spheres behave and what sort of discourse arises, a process that is referred to as mediatization. While 'convergence,' a concept used to describe the media changes mentioned above, brings to mind a technical term and a process of one-sided integration, 'mediatization' on the contrary implies elasticity and reciprocity: the web affects political discourse as much as corporate mergers affect televised content distribution methods. In it, we find traces of globalization anthropologist Arjun Appadurai's (1996, 2001, 2013) views of the world's composition as constantly shifting and changing *scapes* (ethnoscapes, technoscapes, financescapes, mediascapes, and ideascapes), multiple geographies that are *leaking through each other*—thus creating a global blur of cultures and images. Building on the notion of imagined communities (Anderson 1983), Appadurai raises the importance of *imaginary spaces* as global social practices that tend to weaken the nation states and lead to the creation of deterritorialized communities of immigrants and 'wannabe nations.' Such modern practices, I argue in response, have an inherent resistance to the classic agenda-setting and framing effects of the media because they are dispersed, multi-modal, and constantly reconfiguring.

Prominent communication researchers Bennett and Iyengar (2008) suggest that the changes in audience fragmentation, media authority, and news consumption are leading to a change in the way audiences form opinions and interact with political processes. According to them, communication research continues to be "adrift theoretically, seldom looking back to see where foundational modern theory needs to be adapted and, in some cases, overthrown, in order to keep pace with the orientations of late modern audiences, and new modes of content production and information delivery" (Bennett and Iyengar 2008, 713). They argue for a return of a 'minimal effects' era in research, concentrated on the diminishing power of institutions to dictate agendas, alongside the growing significance of choice in media consumption and the ability to surround yourself with reinforcing political attitudes in an 'echo-chamber' or distance yourself from political discourse and conduct altogether. They lament the fixation on "findings-driven controversies in political communication" (Ibid., 709) and instead propose focusing on developing a theoretical framework "that may reconcile the paradox between the growing centrality of media in governance processes and its shrinking credibility and attention focus in the lives of citizens, particularly given the waning of mass media influence in the lives of most citizens" (Ibid., 714). This highlights the problem of traditional communication research, with its imposition of unidirectional effects-driven findings, when applied to modern modes of political mediation.

Such entanglements of political and media institutions have come to be known as part of the research direction referred to as *mediatization research.* According to sociologist and mathematician Friedrich Krotz (2007), mediatization is a *metaprocess* that occurs in parallel to and with other metaprocesses (globalization, migration) and informs knowledge construction, identities, social relations, and organizational structures. It takes into account longitudinal shifts in communicative processes *mediated* by various forms of technological mass media and new media. While diverse and not free from internal debates, the mediatization perspective recognizes that there is an ongoing entanglement of media infrastructures and institutions with other, previously separate social spheres. The resulting change is that certain fields that could previously be separated into their own analytical domains, for example politics, religion, or family life, are becoming increasingly modified by the way they are mediated (Hjarvard 2008, 2013; Lundby 2009; Brants and Voltmer 2011b; Hepp 2012, 2013; Couldry and Hepp 2016). Some have argued that this perspective faces the peril of descending into the pitfall of media-centric technological determinism, particularly focused on new technologies (Deacon and Stanyer 2014). The proponents of the approach retort that, while disagreeing on the extent of mediatization in terms of historic continuity and the role of certain platforms, the goal is to focus scholarly attention on distinguishing

> [b]etween being 'media-centric' and 'media-centered.' Being 'media-centric' is a one-sided approach to understanding the interplay between media, communications, culture, and society, whereas being 'media-centered' involves a holistic understanding of the various intersecting social forces at work at the same time as we allow ourselves to have a particular perspective and emphasis on the role of the media in these processes. (Hepp, Hjarvard, and Lundby 2015, 316)

Andreas Hepp clarifies in an earlier work that mediatization is not "a question of a 'causal effect' of a certain media (technology). Media as such only become concrete in communicative action; however, they offer a certain 'potentiality of action' in such a figuration, which can be called the 'molding forces' of the media, and have to be analyzed in a contextualized way" (2012, 17). He utilizes concepts from Actor-Network Theory (ANT) (Latour 1987; Latour 2005b; Law 1992) to strengthen this theoretical framework, since its scope aims for the exploration of social processes involving the conjunction of humans and technology. ANT argues that in order to understand modern society, a researcher must follow the 'work-nets' of human and non-human actors—or rather, actants (Latour 2005b)—in producing cultural-material artefacts, referred to as chains of associations. We can thus facilitate meanings by tracing and relating the different actors to one another, wherein agency is distributed among them. Such a theory of mediatization presents technological endeavors as "coagulated actions" (Hepp 2012, 16) of human and non-human actants. Hepp argues that mediatization should be viewed as a metaprocess where media are not transparent instances of communications but institutionalized sociocultural processes, consisting of the coagulated actions of press institutions, governmental actors, the technologies that allow them, and relevant idiosyncratic uses of them in each case by the users (viewers, participants). This conceptualization of mediatization is built not on a specific media logic, or even logics, but on "the moulding force of the media" (Ibid., 17). This mediatization framework infused with ANT is what allows me to contextually analyze the respective campaigns of Obama and Trump in the section below on casual politicking. It presupposes that socio-technical changes in modes of communication are fueled by a combination of (1) developing technological practices and (2) the institutional changes of political and media organizations in response to these practices. Moreover, it draws attention to the necessary shift in what it means to 'do politics' when examined through the prism of such shifts.

Games

Here, we return to the appropriation of games and the field of game studies for cultural enquiry. By tracing specific manifestations of the mediatization metaprocess, I show how the molding forces of digital play congregate and operate within political spheres. One can no longer talk of unidirectional effects on the public, as in the case of agenda setting and framing, but on how the media penetrates, infuses, and resonates along with various other social practices. Thus, as mediatization implies, the continued growing entanglement of additional spheres of life with specific media logics leads to the hybridization of communicative and cultural practices. I follow Joost Raessens's (2006, 2014) suggestion that games and other digital technologies facilitate playful goals and identities, leading to the "ludification of culture." This idea was summarized by the prominent game developer and theoretician Eric Zimmerman in an interview for Jesper Juul's book on casual games (2010). In the interview, Zimmerman notes:

> [a]s digital technologies and networks of information, the Internet, computers, mobile technologies, more and more pervade our lives, [and] the ways in which we socialize and flirt and communicate and learn and work and do our taxes and engage with our government and manage our finances, and many, many other important aspects of our lives, the more I think our culture becomes primed for play and particularly, games as the dominant form of leisure. Because games are the form of culture that is most intrinsically related to those things, to systems, technology, information, and mediated communication, [...] play becomes a more dominant paradigm for culture rather than the moving image. (Juul 2010, 215)

Here Zimmerman evokes the idea of playfulness as a major component of various human activities, underlying modes of being beyond leisure, later reinforced in his *Manifesto for a ludic century* (Zimmerman 2015). Moreover, he draws a conceptual link between the abstract idea of play and the notion of play as embedded in computerized systems, making computation itself playful, in what Sebastian Deterding defines as the 'rhetoric of systems' (Deterding 2015), which is explored further below. It is built on the argument of play as a prerequisite for culture, drawing from *Homo ludens* (published originally in 1938) in which the Dutch historian and anthropologist Johan Huizinga (1970) suggested the then-revolutionary notion that play is present in most areas of human activity. It is the basis for law, politics, religion, commerce, war, and most other human endeavors. To support this argument, he pointed to the 'play-element' of ancient Greek and Indian mythology, riddle-games in ancient civilizations, medieval tournaments, and carnivals, as well as the beatification process of Christian saints. The French sociologist, critic, and philosopher Roger Caillois (1958/2001) later criticized and refined Huizinga's overtly broad definition of play. Caillois made a distinction between ludic activities centered on competition, such as sports or gambling, and activities of free play, such as theater, music, or carnivals. He introduced the idea of play as a *voluntary activity* and tied the act of playing to make-believe—which was lacking in Huizinga's original definition.

Following on from these two pioneers, the debate on the role of play in various human activities has been extended to include biologists, sociologists, psychologists, historians, mathematicians, and designers. In particular, play has been examined by game designers, a profession emerging with the growth of leisure time in post-industrial societies and the culture built around tabletop games and later on computer games. Designers took a specific, practical interest in the notion of play, trying to understand how play is present in games and what sorts of rules and guidelines games should follow in order for them to be an enjoyable, playful activity. As digital (and to some extent, tabletop) games have become distinct cultural artefacts, academics have started to pay interest as well. In 2003, the Digital Games Research Association (DiGRA) was established and its first conference was held, further demarcating games from play. The field of game studies (Aarseth 2001; Raessens 2016) builds on play research by combining classic notions of play with modern insights taken from the fields of HCI and interactive design as well as cultural analysis rooted in film and television studies.

Katie Salen and Eric Zimmerman (2004) note that as digital technologies, computers, and video games develop, a familiar definition is sneaking into the field: that of *games as systems* coined by writer and game designer Chris Crawford (1982). Building on Crawford, Salen and Zimmerman suggest that a game is "a system in which players engage in an artificial conflict, defined by rules, that results in a quantifiable outcome" (2004, 80). Another elaboration of Crawford's definition was proposed by Juul (2003, 35): "A game is a rule-based formal system with a variable and quantifiable outcome, where different outcomes are assigned different values, the player exerts effort in order to influence the outcome, the player feels attached to the outcome, and the consequences of the activity are optional and negotiable."

What I find interesting about these supplemental definitions is that they could just as easily apply to modern political processes, especially when these processes take place in a mediatized environment. The fact that so much of our contemporary political jargon rests on metaphors of a contest, a race or a game is not a trivial thing, since metaphors—as Lakoff and Johnson (1980, 1999) remind us—are more than just words; they represent our experience in the world, which is shaped and framed by the signs we use. Elections are a simple example. The players and the rules are there, while the results are certainly quantifiable: e.g. election win percentages and the number of seats in parliament. Regarding the artificiality of the conflict, this is mostly a question of worldview. However, even as we turn away from this very obvious example (after all, election campaigns have long become synonymous with 'games' or 'races'), the elusive association remains. The 'system' in the definition contributes a great deal to this. 'System' (together with 'network' or 'algorithm') is the organizational metaphor of the network society (Castells 2001, 2007; Galloway 2004; Van Dijk 2005). This idea lies in the specific understanding of play as systematic (Deterding 2015) and it reminds us of computers, communication infrastructures, logical patterns, and mathematical topographies—all those things that were not necessarily associated with politics but now are. Perpetual campaigns, media monitoring, polling, and calculated political advertising are all part of news management strategies undertaken by contemporary establishments (Brown 2011), as fully revealed in the Cambridge Analytica scandal and its reliance on psychometric data collected from Facebook users for political campaigning (Graham-Harrison and Cadwalladr 2018). Journalistic practices are becoming similarly systematic, quantifiable, and algorithmized via web metrics, ratings, subscription figures, and opinion polls (Christin 2018). As noted above, digital games do seem to be the cultural form most closely associated with our digitalized-networked age by modern play theorists. To understand the role of the digital game within mediatized society, let us trace its characteristics.

Unlike other media, the technological affordance of games allows multiple participants to engage with content repeatedly under similar conditions, individually or through collaborative effort. In this context, a single playthrough has diminished significance compared with the broader game capital and meta-game practices such as socializing or asking other players for help (Steinkuehler 2004; Consalvo 2007; Shaw 2010; Corliss 2011). As Simon, Boudreau, and Silverman (2009) have shown with their exploration of players of the game *Everquest* (Sony Online Entertainment 1999), performance is never calculated simply as a momentary score of kill points, but is instead a confluence of game mechanics, personal track record in relation to others, online social experience, and offline understanding of the play context, over a period of time. This accumulation of social capital via engagement with playful systems is what draws me to examine video games through the prism of mediatization theory. I claim that as the political becomes increasingly mediatized, games become an expanding, different type of media, reaffirming within themselves characteristics associated with the network society as a whole. The continuous ludification of culture (Raessens 2006, 2014; Jahn-Sudmann and Stockmann 2008; Pargman and Jakobsson 2008; Roig et al. 2009; McGonigal 2011; Fuchs et al. 2014; Walz and Deterding 2015) is exhibited in the trickling spread of digital games beyond the boundaries of the home and arcade parlor and into broader cultural forms. From a separated, dedicated activity associated with a certain gender and class (Cassell and Jenkins 2000; Flanagan 2009), games have grown into a mainstream media consumption practice, to the point that "games have become so successful in 'colonizing' the sphere of everyday activities that playing them becomes transformed into a mundane act, comparable to watching television (to kill time) or cooking (to fill one's belly)" (Pargman and Jakobsson 2008, 234).[1]

In parallel, games and game elements are frequently being incorporated as design methodologies in computerized fields as distinct as advertising, education, and corporate training, resulting in the paradigm of 'gamification'—the inclusion of game elements in non-game systems (Deterding, Dixon et al. 2011; Deterding, Sicart et al. 2011; Fuchs 2012; Fuchs et al. 2014). This aspect of games as a widespread cultural phenomenon is thoroughly explored by Jesper Juul's (2010) foray into the phenomenon of 'casual games,' the immediate precursor to the adoption of gamification. He combines ethnographic studies of players, interviews with developers, and comparative analyses of the game industry, and stresses that the abundance of such games has made the format accessible and accepted over multiple platforms and devices. Today, Juul notes, "[t]o play video games has become the norm; to not play video games has become the exception" (Juul 2010, 8). Digital games, from the workplace time-killers *Solitaire* and *Minesweeper* to smartphone staples like *Angry Birds* (Rovio 2009) and *Candy Crush Saga* (King 2012) to the top-selling ('Triple-A') blockbuster *Grand Theft Auto* and *Call of Duty* series, can thus be seen across various audiences, across age groups, gender, and income brackets. They are at the forefront of the new digital economy's

1 Arguably, Pargman and Jakobsson refer to ethnographic studies of hardcore gamers here, but as discussed next, those definitions are becoming blurred: 'casual' players occasionally spend growing amounts of time on games, while 'hardcore' players switch to 'casual' games due to lack of time.

business model, extracting value from the experience of media in new (and often troubling) ways, from micro-transactions to behavioral tracking (Philips 2016).

The casual game is an important paradigm shift in video gaming culture, which highlights producers' attempts to address wider audiences on the one hand and audiences' growing familiarity with digital game interfaces on the other. Juul notes that from a market perspective, the modern 'hardcore' game industry (which is aimed at dedicated players who can devote time and effort to complex game learning curves) has reached saturation. Still, the inclusion of simple digital games in a variety of products (from watches to movie players) has made basic games into a common pastime of millions. Since many hardcore games are difficult to get into for casual players while casual games seem to be accessible to all, several game developers have attempted to 'casual-ize' some of the features of games, leading to simplified controls for hardcore games or the inclusion of mini-games as part of the main game. Intuitive controls on consoles like the Nintendo Wii/3DS and AR/VR applications with three-dimensional body tracking, music games from the *Guitar Hero* or *Rock Band* series, the rise of intuitive touch screen controls and the overall dominance of smartphones as personal media devices, as well as the waxing and waning popularity of Facebook and the social games played through it, are all developments that have made digital gaming more accessible and acceptable for most people.

To conclude this section, I view the proliferation of digital games as an indication of the ludic attributes of our culture, previously identified in play studies. As (casual) games become the *lingua franca* of the digitally engaged, certain modes of behavior associated with playing games are becoming dominant. Mediatization theory suggests that politics is affected by the molding forces of the media, and while the theory initially pinpointed television as the medium 'to blame,' later replacing it with the web and associated ICTs, I suggest that games, and especially casual games, are the direction in which mediatization theorists should be looking now. Game studies and political communication have rarely been combined until now, and I hope to provide additional food for thought by creating a new conceptual framework for studying topics of engagement, participation, and information transmission that traces the different forms of *ludic political communication*. I suggest this form is present in both top-bottom and bottom-up relations between the public, media, and governing officials, and I call it 'casual politicking'.

Casual politicking

According to Juul (2010), the term 'casual game' developed over the last two decades to denote a type of entertainment software aimed at popular audiences rather than video game hobbyists. The genealogy of the casual game can be drawn from parlor card games such as *Solitaire* and family board games like *Monopoly*, alongside such early staples of video gaming as *Myst* (Cyan 1993), which was more concerned with the aesthetic experience than with complex game mechanics. The term is often contrasted to that of 'hardcore' games and their players, who are interested in developing complex gaming skills and willing to commit to a major time investment. However, Juul points out that the introduction of new distribution platforms has created a new economy of play time, one where simple games can be played repeatedly in short bursts, but taking up many hours over the day. Instead of focusing on time investment, Juul provides a breakdown of the design elements most strongly associated with casual games.

This section is dedicated to a two-stage argument about the applicability of Juul's design elements to the study of contemporary politics. In the previous section, I argued that digital games are an expression of the ludification of culture in digital media. Moreover, I showed that mediatization theory suggests how certain 'molding forces' in the media shape entangled social spheres, and I presented casual games as a possible venue for such an analysis. Here, I wish to operationalize this analytical framework by first synthesizing the characteristics of casual games according to Juul, and then providing certain parallels with processes of political communication. I compare the Obama 2008 election app to Trump's 'Great Meme War' strategy as a comparative case study to be analyzed within this framework. Here it must be stressed again that I do not claim any unidirectional or bidirectional effects between casual games and the political shifts I describe. Rather, the two reflect a similar trend in the information consumption and distribution practices of ICT-reliant audiences in the developed world. To begin with, I briefly introduce the two case studies and their significance before extrapolating the principles of casual politicking by synthesizing Juul's characteristics into four distinct categories.

The official Barack Obama 2008 mobile application for the iOS and Android mobile operating systems is an example of casual politicking true to its time (Ritchey 2008). Mobile communications, text messages, and applications were instrumental in the success of Barack Obama's 2008 campaign (Kiyohara 2009; Pick 2010) and the app was a major part of this

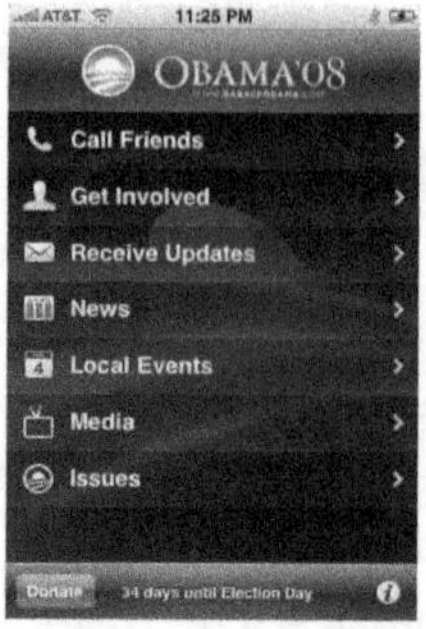

20.1: Obama '08 app home screen.

effort. The app was released after a collaborative effort by ten volunteer coders, who had decided to donate their time and skills in order to support their presidential candidate (Sagolla 2008; Pick 2010). The developers acknowledged the innovativeness of their own emergent method of contributing to the campaign and stated that the same emergent principles helped build the features they implemented in the app, saying that "[t]he app was designed as a means to donate your time in discreet segments—we call it 'micro-volunteering'" (Sagolla 2008). The application includes seven main functions (see Figure 20.1) and a "Donate" button, which played an important part in Obama's unique campaign funding method of obtaining a multitude of small donations.

Ironically, the very same principles that went into the design of the Obama app and its surrounding campaign can be identified in the making of Donald Trump's 'Great Meme War' (Nagle 2017; Lovink and Tuters 2018)—the word 'meme' here refers to the practice of creating and spreading (visual) content online (Shifman 2014), while the word 'war' evokes the character and tone of Trump's presidential campaign. This semi-facetious term, which references bloody conflicts of old yet is filled with purposefully self-deprecating humor, was favored by online supporters of Trump, claiming to have "actually elected a meme as a president" (Ohlheiser 2016, n.p.) While Trump's campaign also featured the option to donate money in a similar fashion to the Obama app, the main conceptual innovation of Trump's campaign was utilizing micro-volunteering for cultural meaning-making (see Figure 20.2), and cross-pollinating various political right-wing groups (loosely identified as the 'Alt-Right') by Trump's chief strategist Steve Bannon. The latter presided over the popularization of the Alt-Right identity in his previous position as the editor of Breitbart News, and maintained ties to this community throughout the campaign until his later departure from Trump's White House team (Neiwert 2017).

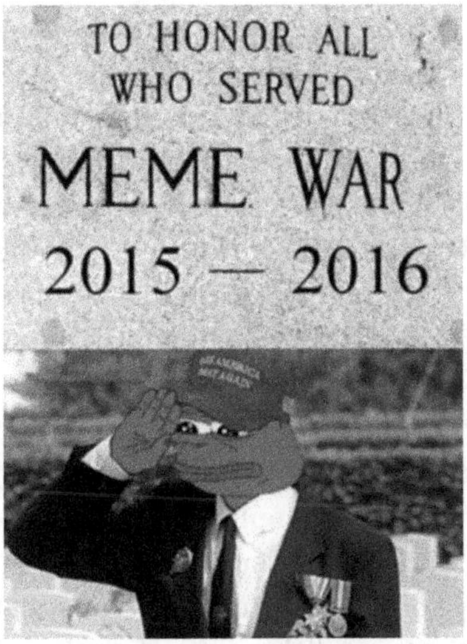

20.2: One of the images from the titular page on the 'Great Meme War' *Encyclopediadramatica* website, depicting Pepe the Frog (an unofficial mascot of online Trump supporters) saluting the 'fallen'.

Understanding these two pivotal moments in political participation requires us to take a brief detour to the world of casual games, and their unique properties for capturing and holding the user's attention (see Table 1, left column). First and foremost is the concept of 'juiciness,' relating to these games' design patterns. Juiciness is embodied in the visceral interfaces that prioritize immediate visual and aural gratification, intuitive control, simplification of tasks, and a clear definition of goals. Usability is a major component in juicy design.[2] Games in general have outstanding interaction design methodologies, communicating their objectives via tutorials and gameplay rather than through external training. Unlike other kinds of software, casual games are developed for quick and easy play, aimed at a non-technical audience, in a context where complex instructions are impractical. A juicy interface values simple controls with immediate feedback, often in non-diegetic form as in text that appears on the screen congratulating players on successful actions. A second characteristic is interruptibility, which means designing the game in such a manner that a play session requires little effort. Casual games are designed to be played in short bursts. Be it a social network game that runs server-side through the

2 Although Juul separates juiciness from usability, the former is reliant on the latter, as a usable and intuitive interface will determine whether the juicy elements become apparent. For my discussion, it is sufficient to include both terms under one category.

website interface and requires no save/load functions, or a console game that breaks play into small segments (levels, missions, mini-games), such games allow users to adjust the playing time to suit their schedule rather than vice versa.[3] Thirdly, casual games exhibit a forgiving attitude toward mistakes. This is not to say the games are not hard, but they are designed in such a way as to avoid making players have to repeat large portions of game play if they make a mistake. Finally, all casual games exhibit a tendency to involve social connections as part of the game design, either by making the game multi-player or by promoting features such as leader boards and providing bonuses for inviting friends and family (Juul 2010).

Similar principles can be applied to tracing casual politicking. To date, many critics of online modes of political engagement depict them as shallow and non-consequential. Terms like 'slacktivism' or 'clicktivism' (Morozov 2014) highlight the low threshold of computer-mediated political engagement, both on the side of the political establishment and on that of ordinary citizens. To engage with the political *only* online, in other words, is not serious politics. Instead, I offer the term 'casual politicking' as a more nuanced alternative to the pessimistic view of contemporary political participation online. With this term, I wish to evoke—in conjunction with the aforementioned characteristics of casual games—an unplanned, emergent, and self-organizing mode of conduct, rather than a binary, rigid structure of serious versus non-serious politics. It relies on four key aspects, which we can equate with the four casual gaming operating principles discussed earlier (see Table 1, right column).

First, such modes are facilitated by ICT platforms that exhibit interface and affordance equivalents to the juiciness elements of casual game design. Second, casual politicking relies on issue-centered rather than ideology-centered conduct, which, when coupled with ICT platforms, generates an interruptible political mode for various actors. Users follow and connect with those issues that are relevant to them, contributing in each case according to their time and resources. Third, users exhibit perpetual political engagement, resonating with the low price of failure characteristic of casual games. In other words, there is a fluid and continuous engagement with issues on the side of politicians and citizens alike that allows for a quick recuperation in case of failure, while avoiding major disappointments and a sense of

3 'Casual players' can still spend long hours on games. Juul's survey indicates that fourteen per cent of casual players dedicate more than 40 hours a week to playing games. Similarly, almost one third of baby-boomer gamers in the United States spend 20 hours playing a week (Pearce 2008). The game simply allows for shorter individual play sessions.

setbacks. Lastly, just like in casual gaming, sociability is the driving force of casual politicking. This is reflected by involving networks of like-minded people in the political process, heavily relying on the social capital aspect of actions rather than on the perceived outcome.

Table 1: Comparison between involvement principles underlying casual gaming and those underlying casual politicking

Casual gaming	Casual politicking
Juiciness: Rich visceral interfaces for immediate gratification	Intuitive interfaces: Accessible, reliable, and highly visualized interface for immediate information and engagement, with a high level of affordance
Interruptibility: Intended to be played in short bursts, minimal save/load compatibility	Issue-centered: Engagement for the shorter political/media attention span through clictivism and meme wars
Forgiving attitude toward mistakes: A game may be hard, but failure does not result in a massive setback	Low price of failure: Perpetual processes minimize each engagement's cost and reduce the entry barriers
Socially driven: Existing ties are important parts of the play experience	Socially driven: Existing ties and networks are important parts of the participatory experience, which underscores fun rather than ideology

Accessible interfaces in ICT

ICT networks with high-affordance accessible interfaces facilitate direct and visceral experiences that require little in the way of technical or political education. More and more political content migrates to platforms where ideologies are simplified in infographics and participation is achieved by signing an e-petition or sharing a link on your social media site profile, such as the embedding of Facebook's 'Like' buttons on an external website that lets users 'like' a certain topic or personality and then receive communication about it in their feed (Helmond 2015).

Moreover, this ubiquitous access to information is provided by constantly simplifying and homogenizing access to digital data. This is done through a better understanding of computer-mediated usability (Nielsen and Pernice 2008) as well as through the growing distribution of mobile wireless devices, which become embedded in the urban experience, manifesting a renewed connection between the city, its inhabitants, and the information they produce/consume (Mitchell 2003; Nunes 2006; de Souza e Silva 2006; de Souza e Silva and Hjorth 2009). For the first time in history, mobile communication means that both the information carrier and the information itself are mobile—creating the possibility for the individual to be on the move while transmitting and receiving large quantities of data (Poster 2004). Casual politicking requires fast and simple access to data, and the ability to communicate while being on the move, often involving swarming (dispersed, self-organizing) modes of operation. Such traits are achieved through the imagined technological affordances (Gibson 1977; Norman 1988, 2002; Nagy and Neff 2015) of the interface, where agency results from the conjunction of a sentient (human) actor pursuing a goal and the perceived qualities of objects in the immediate vicinity that allow the actor to perform an action. Digital interfaces are often built with affordance design principles in mind, to hint, guide, and drive users. Contemporary interfaces thus create affordances for fast two-way communication, location-based action, viral news consumption, and the like.

The Obama app exemplifies this well. The first option on the app's main screen—Call Friends—links the app to the user's phone book, sorting their contact list according to U.S. states (with an emphasis on contested ones), and prompts the user to call contacts and discuss the upcoming vote. This most innovative feature allows users to track their call efforts, post notes in relation to each friend, and eventually compare their statistics to nationwide lead callers. In effect, this function alters a friendly discussion about politics, turning it into a quantifiable measure and, more importantly, comparable set of statistics. While its developers may not have thought of it at the time, this function was probably one of the first attempts at gamification in national politics. The second menu choice—Get Involved—gives contact details for the nearest campaign headquarters using geolocation. They both rely on the unique technological affordances of the smartphone as a mediator of sociality and space. The smoothness and immediacy of the afforded function contributes to the speed of action.

This all occurs in an atmosphere of 'post-broadcast democracy' (Prior 2007), where citizens have an increasingly selective interface with news media. Those who are interested in political information tend to be more partisan, and devote their time to searching and consuming politically oriented news material. Others have the opportunity to avoid the consumption of political news altogether, occupying themselves with entertainment content (which increasingly also includes video games). This leads to a widening gap between involved and uninvolved citizens, as knowledge is a prerequisite for public participation (Bennett and Iyengar 2008), with fatigue from the constant need to participate creating the need to find alternative means of self-expression (Schölzel 2017). To state the obvious, neither of the campaigns discussed in this chapter would have been possible without the ICT infrastructure available today. But such foundations include not only the oft-praised speed and horizontality, but also the embedded socio-technical affordances of such websites as 4Chan, Reddit and YouTube that were instrumental in the formation and subsequent distribution of various forms of memetic content. And while an attempt to understand Trump's 'Great Meme War' as *only* technological reeks of 'solutionism' (Morozov 2014), ignoring this component is also foolhardy.

To sum up, ICT platforms let casual politicking practitioners create interfaces for quick information provision and mobilization, which often require no—or minimal—previous knowledge or training. This opens up the opportunity for multiple actors to engage in interruptible, issue-centered political conduct.

Interruptible issue-networks

Just as game designers tend to create gradual experiences that allow players to choose their level of involvement, casual politicking is about selective levels of participation according to the individual's abilities, desires, and availability. The prime promise of this type of engagement is that of choice—for the individual, the politician, and the media. Actors in mediatized environments are constantly exposed to a multitude of topics, interpretations, focuses, analyses, framings, and counter-framings.

The marketplace of ideas has become more than just a metaphor. In a multitude of global distractions, the active citizen has an abundance of choice and can select from a wide spectrum of economic, human rights, and environmental issues, from Black Lives Matter to #MeToo. But this also means that public interest quickly diminishes and moves onto the next hot 'issue of the day.' Consequently, many organizations focus on certain issues, rather than on an ideological bundle, 'selling' certain ideas or beliefs, while constantly framing and reframing those issues in order to take advantage of momentary alliances, public opinion shifts, a beneficial media landscape, and the like. This notion follows from the work of Richard Rogers and Noortje Marres, who developed and implemented a digital humanities tool named *Issue crawler* that follows web URLs based on certain keywords, tracking the amalgamation of issues between different websites (Marres and Rogers 2000; Rogers 2002, 2013; Marres 2006, 2017). What emerges from their research is a reflection of how politics works in the networked age: unsurprisingly, via networks. Rogers and Marres name them 'issue networks' after the term coined by political scientist Hugh Helco in the late 1970s. While Helco and others used this term to refer to the cynical practice by civil society organizations of combining forces on certain issues for purely populist goals, Marres argues that issue networks are in fact an affirmative framework, which we can use to examine activism and decision-making mechanisms.

Such networks, with their recognizable hashtags and domain names, also help concretize the debate (Burgess and Matamoros-Fernández 2016). Latour (2005a) famously criticized political scientists for being too preoccupied for too long with how to conceptualize the representational procedures in debating issues, rather than the issues (things) themselves. He argues that political contestations around topics like global warming or the war in Iraq have rendered the classic agreements on the rules and boundaries of debate null and void and that there is a need to "bring into the centre of the debate the proof of what it is to be debated" (Ibid., 8). Issue networks do just that, by allowing publics to form around a token, while still debating the exact boundaries of the issue in question (Bruns et al. 2016). Obama's app presented a quick 'cheat-sheet' of election issues, broken down by categories such as Foreign Affairs or Energy-Environment. Inside each category, a list of stances and quotes was presented, to give an idea of the candidates' approaches but also to make use of during discussions with others. By the time Trump's supporters rallied for their candidate, the issues were generated bottom-up, rather than dictated from above. An infamous example of an issue can be seen in 'Pizzagate,' where the 4Chan community cultivated a conspiracy theory claiming that Hillary Clinton, Trump's rival for presidency, supported a hidden child-abuse ring (Bach, Jokubauskaite, and Tuters 2018). While the full details of this endeavor are beyond the scope of this chapter, suffice it to say that it ended up with an assault-rifle-wielding Trump supporter entering a pizza parlor in Washington D.C., aiming to put a stop to the abuse, an incident that was picked up and discussed in mainstream media sources. Clinton's team had to respond to those events, becoming implicated in them and shifting the discourse onto 'Pizzagate' itself, rather than the broader political issues of the campaign.

Overall, the disjointed nature of issue networks, coupled with the affordances provided by modern ICT, allow the various casual politicking practitioners to engage with selected issues and provide their followers (but subsequently, also opponents) with rapid means of interfering with the agendas of both decision-makers and the media.

Perpetual processes

In the aftermath following Foucault's dissection of the premodern and modern societies of punishment and discipline respectively, Gilles Deleuze noted that the postmodern is the society of control (Deleuze 1992). The defining moment of the move from enforced discipline to embedded control is the perpetualness:

> [I]n the disciplinary societies one was always starting again (from school to the barracks, from the barracks to the factory), while in the societies of control one is never finished with anything—the corporation, the educational system, the armed services being metastable states coexisting in one and the same modulation, like a universal system of deformation. (Ibid., 5)

Game researcher David Nieborg identifies mainstream Triple-A games as an "unfinished commodity" (2011, 36), arguing that by utilizing "branched serialization" (Ibid., 38), publishers turn the single game into a perpetual release cycle, generating constant additions to the original game content in the form of smaller and cheaper *paid-for download packs* or more content-filled and expensive *expansions*.

Casual games show even stronger 'unfinished' characteristics, as the casual game revenue model resembles a service rather than a product. First, they are developed on the basis of existing and well-known genres and mechanisms (Juul 2010) to appeal to the broadest base possible. In addition, the game is often 'freemium,' meaning that it is free to play, but allows for additional (usually small) payments to unlock layers of the game previously inaccessible or to speed up the game progress (Evans 2015). The design of such games often presupposes the introduction of additional goods, and thus the game is intentionally left incomplete, with more features added as the life cycle of the game continues (Hamari 2011). Much of the freemium content consists of 'vanity items' that have no real gameplay value, and many vanity items are seasonal, such as Christmas decorations or clothing for the player's avatars or virtual domains (Fields and Cotton 2011), tied to the player's real-world time. Casual game companies often compete with one another by copying successful game elements, and because distribution is mostly online and development cycles much shorter, audiences occasionally move *en masse* to a more successful clone of an older game, forcing the latter's designer to embark on a new, fast-paced development and marketing campaign. Games as an industry are a very fitting illustration of the Deleuzian never-finishing condition that is prevalent in societies of control.

The same perpetualness exists similarly in the realm of politics, and using the epistemic prism of casual games helps us to conceptualize it. With the growth of mass self-communication and the loss of legitimacy, politicians have adopted further methods of perpetual and horizontal campaigning (Manin 1997; De Beus 2011). Instead of issuing focused messaging to the public during election time, mediatized politics constantly strives to present a vivid spectacle[4] to the ever-hungry press and the judgment of their constituents. My claim here is that understanding the ways casual games capitalize on their players' desire for short-cycle repetitive patterns of use can help us shed light on such political developments. In an increasingly information-saturated world, games and politicians may face similar challenges: to stand out among the crowd and draw attention (Terranova 2012). Both Obama's app and Trump's campaign have done so, to varying degrees of success. To do this, both of these actants seek to rally users through 'social' methods of engagement.

Sociable and collaborative

The last defining characteristic of casual politicking is the tendency to orchestrate political action as social and collaborative. What I mean by this is that modern politics is reliant on 'social' elements as they are understood today in the popular digital discourse, as a design principle or technology powering many of our mediatized environments—from news to entertainment to education. Social elements, which are often tied to the 'Web 2.0' concept (O'Reilly 2005), include reliance on sharing and crowd-sourced elements, distributed and decentralized models, platforms rather than services, and the like.[5] Social capital is a major driving force behind casual games, especially those with the free-to-play model. They use a player's computerized social connections to facilitate cooperation or completion, prompting an exchange of virtual crops or tracking a friend's progress on a leader board. Similarly, the social component of causal politicking is reliant on playful and subversive massive engagement with political content

4 Manin uses the metaphor of the theater to describe postmodern politics: politicians perform, citizens watch, journalists review.

5 For a broader discussion of the term and the associated practices, see Kylie Jarret's (2008) critical paper on Web 2.0 terminology.

and stands in direct relation to the collapse of traditional representative parliamentary democracy and the rise of issue networks.

Communication outlets are increasingly consciously aligning themselves with certain political and/or economical actors' ideologies (Brown 2011). In this environment, framing information becomes a game of sorts. Individuals and groups are approaching the glocal (Meyrowitz 2005) and translocal (Hepp 2013) media spaces as puzzles: what is the given information, what is hidden, what is the bias of each source, how can we deconstruct, recombine, and supplement the news provided in order to make sense of the world? This approach is inherently social and ludic, and many online news communities in fact act as if they are current affairs 'fans': inquisitive, critical, fanatical, and collaborative (Gray, Sandvoss, and Harrington 2017). The gamification of various political spheres is built on such a perception of fan (and fun) engagement with the political process, for example in the practice of 'fake' social media accounts that are now widely used to parody public figures (Wilson 2011).

In the case of the Obama app, it allowed those who used it to organize themselves (independently or through Obama's local headquarters) to participate in the broadening of the network. The people using the app do this of their own volition, contributing themselves as additional nodes to Obama's network and obtaining in return the perceived benefits of connectedness. Some features, such as the leader-board caller functions, appeal directly to the users' sense of competition, whether among themselves or in the greater context of the presidential race: talk to your friends, as the winning conditions of this race can be quantifiable, and each call matters.[6]

Eight years later, the same principles fueled the 'Great Meme War.' The practice of 'shitposting'—creating random and deliberately annoying memes—was about playful socialization. Many of the participants in the 'war' did it, primarily, to have fun as part of a bigger community, jokingly seeing themselves as rebels and outcasts in the light of classic science fiction and fantasy tropes (Banis 2018). Just like the touch-screen game or app, innocuously taking up more and more of people's time without them realizing (Gekker 2016), the meme war grew and became serious business.

6 It is interesting to note the progress of this leaderboard approach toward the 2012 presidential elections when supporters were given the option of creating their own customizable fundraising page, which further increased the campaign personalization and potentially fostered an internal competition in terms of design, operation, and success metrics of each page. It remains to be seen whether such a distributed approach will be effective in the long run.

Some Trump online supporters admit they regretted their actions after the election results were announced. It is conceivable to imagine them perceiving their participation through the prism of the screen, concentrated more on the immediate results—make a successful meme to antagonize the 'normies' (non-supporters)—than on the final outcome.

Conclusion: Toward the ludification of politics

At the annual Game Developers Conference in 2010, game designer Jesse Schell gave a talk in which he outlined his vision of the continued process of the ludification (and especially gamification) of society (G4TV 2010). It is not so farfetched, he argued, that the future will feature gameful elements everywhere: in our taxes, health insurance, cars, social interaction, and so on (e.g. Zimmerman 2015). He calls it the 'gamepocalypse,' a term that registers the concern he has for this state of affairs, although both he and some of his supporters noted the positive opportunities of this situation. This future is, however, uncertain, with others pointing out the backlash of people against the gameful systems, and the hyped nature of the gamification field, which may subdue the enthusiasm for implementing such design mechanisms in additional societal systems.

While gamepocalypse may be a contested vision, I wish to complicate the discussion yet further with the proposition of *gamocracy* as a form of political organization. It will not necessarily happen in the way Schell envisioned it, with leader boards for the best performing politicians, graphic interfaces through which parliament members could battle opposing factions, or 'political experience points' with which you could 'level up' for voting or participating in referenda (although those are some interesting experiments). It will, however, prioritize the aforementioned modes of engagement so characteristic of games and their audiences: playfulness, immediacy, and casual burst-like activity. This will result in the need for a new research framework from cultural studies and the humanities to supplement traditional tools of communication. Such a framework will focus on the citizen not only as a sender or receiver of information, but as a subject embedded in a ludic culture whose motives in the political realm may rely on the notions of fun and play no less than on ideological rational choice.

References

Aarseth, E. J. 2001. Computer game studies, year one. *Game Studies* 1 (1): 1-15.

Anderson, B. 1983. *Imagined communities: Reflections on the origin and spread of nationalism*. London: Verso Books.

Appadurai, A. 1996. *Modernity at large: Cultural dimensions of globalization*. Minneapolis, MN: University of Minnesota Press.

—. ed. 2001. *Globalization*. Durham, NC: Duke University Press Books.

—. 2013. *The future as cultural fact: Essays on the global condition*. London: Verso Books.

Bach, D., E. Jokubauskaite, and M. Tuters. 2018. The deep vernacular web. *Digital Methods Initiative*. http://wiki.digitalmethods.net/Dmi/WinterSchool2018DeepVernacularWebAltRight.

Banis, D. 2018. Fictiocracy: Media and politics in the age of storytelling. *Institute of Network Cultures*. http://networkcultures.org/longform/2018/02/22/fictiocracy-media-and-politics-in-the-age-of-storytelling.

Bennett, W. L, and S. Iyengar. 2008. A new era of minimal effects? The changing foundations of political communication. *Journal of Communication* 58 (4): 707-731.

Brants, K., and K. Voltmer. 2011a. Introduction: Mediatization and decentralization of political communication. In *Political communication in postmodern democracy: Challenging the primacy of politics*, eds. K. Brants and K. Voltmer, 1-16. Houndmills: Palgrave Macmillan.

—. 2011b. *Political communication in postmodern democracy: Challenging the primacy of politics*. Houndmills: Palgrave Macmillan.

Brown, R. 2011. Mediatization and news management in comparative institutional perspective. In *Political communication in postmodern democracy: Challenging the primacy of politics*, eds. K. Brants and K. Voltmer, 59-74. Houndmills: Palgrave Macmillan.

Bruns, A. 2007. Produsage. In *Proceedings of the 6th ACM SIGCHI conference on creativity and cognition, Washington, DC, June 13-15, 2007*, 99-106. New York: ACM.

Bruns, A., B. Moon, A. Paul, and F. Münch. 2016. Towards a typology of hashtag publics: A large-scale comparative study of user engagement across trending topics. *Communication Research and Practice* 2 (1): 20-46.

Burgess, J., and A. Matamoros-Fernández. 2016. Mapping sociocultural controversies across digital media platforms: One week of #gamergate on Twitter, YouTube, and Tumblr. *Communication Research and Practice* 2 (1): 79-96.

Caillois, R. 1958/2001. *Man, play, and games*. Trans. M. Barash. Chicago, IL: University of Illinois Press.

Cassell, J., and H. Jenkins, eds. 2000. *From Barbie to Mortal Kombat: Gender and computer games*. Cambridge, MA: The MIT Press.

Castells, M. 2001. *The internet galaxy: Reflections on the internet, business and society*. New York: Oxford University Press.

—. 2007. Communication, power and counter-power in the network society. *International Journal of Communication* 1 (1): 238-266.

Chadwick, A. 2017. *The hybrid media system: Politics and power*. New York: Oxford University Press.

Christin, A. 2018. Counting clicks: Quantification and variation in Web journalism in the United States and France. *American Journal of Sociology* 123 (5): 1382-1415.

Cohen, B. C. 1963. *The press and foreign policy*. Princeton, NJ: Princeton University Press.

Coleman, S. 2006. How the other half votes: *Big Brother* viewers and the 2005 General Election. *International Journal of Cultural Studies* 9 (4): 457-479.

—. 2011. Representation and mediated politics: Representing representation in an age of irony. In *Political communication in postmodern democracy: Challenging the primacy of politics*, eds. K. Brants and K. Voltmer, 39-56. Houndmills: Palgrave Macmillan.

Consalvo, M. 2007. *Cheating: Gaining advantage in videogames*. Cambridge, MA: The MIT Press.

Corliss, J. 2011. Introduction: The social science study of video games. *Games and Culture* 6 (1): 3-16.

Couldry, N., and A. Hepp. 2016. *The mediated construction of reality*. Malden, MA: Polity Press.

Crawford, C. 1982. *The art of computer game design*. http://www.vancouver.wsu.edu/fac/peabody/ game-book/Coverpage.htm.

Cyan. 1993. *Myst*. [multiplatform]. Brøderbund. Game.

De Beus, J. 2011. Audience democracy: An emerging pattern in postmodern political communication. In *Political communication in postmodern democracy: Challenging the primacy of politics*, eds. K. Brants and K. Voltmer, 19-38. Houndmills: Palgrave Macmillan.

de Souza e Silva, A. 2006. From cyber to hybrid: Mobile technologies as interfaces of hybrid spaces. *Space and Culture* 9:261-278.

de Souza e Silva, A., and L. Hjorth. 2009. Playful urban spaces a historical approach to mobile games. *Simulation & Gaming* 40 (5): 602-625.

Deacon, D., and J. Stanyer. 2014. Mediatization: Key concept or conceptual bandwagon? *Media, Culture & Society* 36 (7): 1032-1044.

Deleuze, G. 1992. Postscript on the societies of control. *October* 59 (January): 3-7.

Deterding, S. 2015. The ambiguity of games: Histories and discourses of a gameful world. In *The gameful world: Approaches, issues, applications*, eds. S. P. Walz and S. Deterding, 23-64. Cambridge, MA: The MIT Press.

Deterding, S., D. Dixon, R. Khaled, and L. Nacke. 2011. From game design elements to gamefulness: Defining "gamification". In *Proceedings of the 15th international academic MindTrek conference: Envisioning future media environments, Tampere, September 28-30, 2011*, 9-15. New York: ACM.

Deterding, S, M. Sicart, L. Nacke, K. O'Hara, and D. Dixon. 2011. Gamification. Using game-design elements in non-gaming contexts. In *Proceedings of the 2011 annual conference extended abstracts on human factors in computing systems, Vancouver, BC, May 7-12, 2011*, 2425-2428. New York: ACM.

Entman, R. M. 1991. Framing U.S. coverage of international news: Contrasts in narratives of the KAL and Iran air incidents. *Journal of Communication* 41 (4): 6-27.

—. 1993. Framing: Toward clarification of a fractured paradigm. *Journal of Communication* 43 (4): 51-58.

Evans, E. 2015. The economics of free freemium games, branding and the impatience economy. *Convergence: The International Journal of Research into New Media Technologies* 22 (6): 563-580.

Fields, T., and B. Cotton. 2011. *Social game design: Monetization methods and mechanics*. Waltham, MA: Morgan Kaufmann.

Flanagan, M. 2009. *Critical play: Radical game design*. Cambridge, MA: The MIT Press.

Fuchs, C. 2014. Hacktivism and contemporary politics. In *Social media, politics and the state: Protests, revolutions, riots, crime and policing in the age of Facebook, Twitter and YouTube*, eds. D. Trottier and C. Fuchs, 88-106. New York: Routledge.

Fuchs, M. 2012. Ludic interfaces. Driver and product of gamification. *G|A|M|E Games as Art, Media, Entertainment* 1 (1). http://www.gamejournal.it/ludic-interfaces-driver-and-product-of-gamification.

Fuchs, M., S. Fizek, P. Ruffino, and N. Schrape. 2014. *Rethinking gamification*. Lüneburg: meson press.

G4TV. 2010. DICE 2010: "Design out of the box" presentation. *G4tv.com*. http://www.g4tv.com/videos/44277/dice-2010-design-outside-the-box-presentation.

Galloway, A. 2004. *Protocol: How control exists after decentralization*. Cambridge, MA: The MIT Press.

Gekker, A. 2016. Casual power: Understanding user interfaces through quantification. *Digital Culture & Society* 2 (1): 107-122.

Gerlitz, C., and A. Helmond. 2013. The like economy: Social buttons and the data-intensive Web. *New Media & Society* 15 (8): 1348-1365.

Gibson, J. J. 1977. The concept of affordances. In *Perceiving, acting, and knowing: Toward an ecological psychology*, eds. R. Shaw and J. Bransford, 62-82. Hillsdale, NJ: Lawrence Erlbaum Associates.

Goffman, E. 1974. *Frame analysis: An essay on the organization of experience*. London: Harper & Row.

Graham-Harrison, E., and C. Cadwalladr. 2018. Cambridge Analytica execs boast of role in getting Donald Trump elected. *The Guardian*. http://www.theguardian.com/uk-news/2018/mar/20/cambridge-analytica-execs-boast-of-role-in-getting-trump-elected.

Gray, J., C. Sandvoss, and C. L. Harrington, eds. 2017. *Fandom: Identities and communities in a mediated world*. New York: New York University Press.

Hamari, J. 2011. Perspectives from behavioral economics to analyzing game design patterns: Loss aversion in social games. Paper presented at *The 2011 annual conference on human factors in computing systems, Vancouver, BC, Canada, May 7-12, 2011*.

Helmond, A. 2015. The platformization of the Web: Making Web data platform ready. *Social Media + Society* 1 (2). http://doi.org/10.1177/2056305115603080.

Hepp, A. 2012. Mediatization and the 'moulding force' of the media. *Communications* 37 (1): 1-28.

—. 2013. *Cultures of mediatization*. Malden, MA: Polity Press.

Hepp, A., S. Hjarvard, and K. Lundby. 2015. Mediatization: theorizing the interplay between media, culture and society. In *Media, Culture & Society* 37 (2): 314-324.

Hjarvard, S. 2008. The mediatization of society. A theory of the media as agents of social and cultural change. *Nordicom Review: Nordic Research on Media & Communication* 29 (2): 105-134.

—. 2013. *The mediatization of culture and society*. London: Routledge.

Huizinga, J. 1970. *Homo ludens: A study of the play-element in culture*. London: Temple Smith.

Iyengar, S. 1994. *Is anyone responsible? How television frames political issues*. Chicago, IL: University of Chicago Press.

Jahn-Sudmann, A., and R. Stockmann. 2008. *Computer games as a sociocultural phenomenon: Games without frontiers, war without tears*. Houndmills: Palgrave Macmillan.

Jarrett, K. 2008. Interactivity is evil! A critical investigation of Web 2.0. *First Monday* 13 (3): 34-41.

Jenkins, H. 2006a. *Fans, bloggers, and gamers: Media consumers in a digital age*. New York: New York University Press.

—. 2006b. *Convergence culture: Where old and new media collide*. New York: New York University Press.

—. 2012. *Textual poachers: Television fans and participatory culture*. New York: Routledge.

Juul, J. 2003. The game, the player, the world. In *Proceedings of Level Up: Digital games research conference, Utrecht, November 4-6, 2003*, eds. M. Copier and J. Raessens, 30-45. Utrecht: Utrecht University.

—. 2010. *A casual revolution: Reinventing video games and their players*. Cambridge, MA: The MIT Press.

King. 2012. *Candy Crush Saga*. [multiplatform]. King. Game.

Kiyohara, S. 2009. A study on how technological innovation affected the 2008 U.S. Presidential Election: Young voters' participation and Obama's victory. In *Proceedings of the 9th annual international symposium on applications and the internet, Bellevue, WA, 20-24 July 2009*, 223-226. Washington, DC: IEEE.

Krotz, F. 2007. The meta-process of 'mediatization' as a conceptual frame. *Global Media and Communication* 3 (3): 256-260.

Lakoff, G., and M. Johnson. 1980. *Metaphors we live by*. Chicago, IL: University of Chicago Press.

—. 1999. *Philosophy in the flesh: The embodied mind and its challenge to Western thought*. New York: Basic Books.

Latour, B. 1987. *Science in action*. Cambridge, MA: Harvard University Press.

—. 2005a. From Realpolitik to Dingpolitik or how to make things public. In *Making things public: Atmospheres of democracy*, eds. P. Weibel and B. Latour, 14-44. Cambridge, MA: The MIT Press.

—. 2005b. *Reassembling the social: An introduction to Actor-Network-Theory*. Oxford: Oxford University Press.

Law, J. 1992. Notes on the theory of the Actor-Network: Ordering, strategy, and heterogeneity. *Systems Practice* 5 (4): 379-393.

Lovink, G., and M. Tuters. 2018. They say we can't meme: Politics of idea compression. *Copyriot.com*. http://non.copyriot.com/they-say-we-cant-meme-politics-of-idea-compression.

Lundby, K. 2009. *Mediatization: Concept, changes, consequences*. New York: Peter Lang.

Manin, B. 1997. *The principles of representative government*. New York: Cambridge University Press.

Marres, N. 2006. Net-work is format work: Issue networks and the sites of civil society politics. In *Reformatting politics: Information technology and global civil society*, eds. J. Anderson, J. Dean, and G. Lovink, 3-17. New York: Routledge.

—. 2017. *Digital sociology: The reinvention of social research.* Malden, MA: Polity Press.

Marres, N., and R. Rogers. 2000. Depluralising the Web and repluralising public debate: The case of the GM food debate on the web. In *Prefered placement: Knowledge politics on the Web,* 113-135. http://dare.uva.nl/record/85893.

McCombs, M. E., and D. L. Shaw. 1972. The agenda setting function of mass media. *Public Opinion Quarterly* 36 (2): 176-187.

McGonigal, J. 2011. *Reality is broken: Why games make us better and how they can change the world.* New York: Penguin Press.

Meyrowitz, J. 2005. The rise of glocality. In *A sense of place: The global and the local in mobile communication,* ed. J. K. Nyíri, 21-30. Vienna: Passagen Verlag.

Mitchell, W. J. 2003. *Me++: The cyborg self and the networked city.* Cambridge, MA: The MIT Press.

Moore, C. 2011. The magic circle and the mobility of play. *Convergence: The International Journal of Research into New Media Technologies* 17 (4): 373-387.

Morozov, E. 2014. *To save everything, click here: The folly of technological solutionism.* New York: PublicAffairs.

Nagle, A. 2017. *Kill all normies: Online culture wars from 4chan and tumblr to Trump and the Alt-Right.* Winchester, UK: Zero Books.

Nagy, P., and G. Neff. 2015. Imagined affordance: Reconstructing a keyword for communication theory. *Social Media + Society* 1 (2).

Neiwert, D. 2017. *Alt-America: The rise of the radical right in the age of Trump.* London: Verso Books.

Nieborg, D. B. 2011. Triple-A: The political economy of the blockbuster video game. PhD thesis. Amsterdam: University of Amsterdam.

Nielsen, J., and K. Pernice. 2008. *Eyetracking web usability.* Berkeley, CA: New Riders Publishers.

Norman, D. A. 1988. *The psychology of everyday things.* New York: Basic Books.

—. 2002. *The design of everyday things.* New York: Basic Books.

Nunes, M. 2006. *Cyberspaces of everyday life.* Minneapolis, MN: University of Minnesota Press.

Ohlheiser, A. 2016. 'We actually elected a meme as president': How 4chan celebrated Trump's victory. *The Washington Post.* http://www.washingtonpost.com/news/the-intersect/wp/2016/11/09/we-actually-elected-a-meme-as-president-how-4chan-celebrated-trumps-victory.

O'Reilly, T. 2005. What is Web 2.0: Design patterns and business models for the next generation of software. http://www.oreillynet.com/pub/a/oreilly/tim/news/2005/09/30/what-is-web-20.html.

Pargman, D., and P. Jakobsson. 2008. Do you believe in magic? Computer games in everyday life. *European Journal of Cultural Studies* 11 (2): 225-244.

Pearce, C. 2008. The truth about baby boomer gamers. *Games and Culture* 3 (2): 142-174.

Philips, T. 2016. Discussions with developers: F2P and the changing landscape of games. In *Social, casual, mobile: Changing games*, eds. M. Willson and T. Leaver, 61-74. New York: Bloomsbury Academic.

Pick, C. Y. 2010. *Mobile strategies in political communication*. Washington: American University.

Poster, M. 2004. Digitally local communications: Technologies and space. Paper presented at *The global and the local in mobile communication: Places, images, people, connections, Budapest, June 10-12, 2004*.

Prior, M. 2007. *Post-broadcast democracy: How media choice increases inequality in political involvement and polarizes elections*. New York: Cambridge University Press.

Raessens, J. 2006. Playful identities, or the ludification of culture. *Games and Culture* 1 (1): 52-57.

—. 2014. The ludification of culture. In *Rethinking gamification*, eds. M. Fuchs, S. Fizek, P. Ruffino, and N. Schrape, 91-114. Lüneburg: meson press.

—. 2016. Game studies. In *The international encyclopedia of communication theory and philosophy*, eds. K. B. Jensen, R. T. Craig, J. D. Pooley, and E. W. Rothenbuhler, 1-5. Hoboken, NJ: Wiley.

Ritchey, R. 2008. Obama '08 IPhone Application Review. *Youtube*. http://www.youtube.com/watch?v=8X-FX58lfGs.

Rogers, R. 2002. Operating issue networks on the Web. *Science as Culture* 11 (2): 191-213.

—. 2013. *Digital methods*. Cambridge, MA: The MIT Press.

Roig, A., G. San Cornelio, E. Ardèvol, P. Alsina, and R. Pagès. 2009. Videogame as media practice. *Convergence: The International Journal of Research into New Media Technologies* 15 (1): 89-103.

Rovio Entertainment. 2009. *Angry Birds*. [Android/iOS/Windows Phone]. Chillingo. Game.

Sagolla, D. 2008. iOSDevCamp - Obama '08 iPhone App. *iOsDevCamp*. http://www.iosdevcamp.org/2008/10/02/obama-08-iphone-app.

Salen, K., and E. Zimmerman. 2004. *Rules of play: Game design fundamentals*. Cambridge, MA: The MIT Press.

Schäfer, M. T. 2011. *Bastard culture! How user participation transforms cultural production*. Amsterdam: Amsterdam University Press.

Scheufele, D. A., and D. Tewksbury. 2007. Framing, agenda setting, and priming: The evolution of three media effects models. *Journal of Communication* 57 (1): 9-20.

Schölzel, H. 2017. Backing away from circles of control: A re-reading of interpassivity theory's perspectives on the current political culture of participation. *Empedocles: European Journal for the Philosophy of Communication* 8 (2): 187-203.

Shaw, A. 2010. What is video game culture? Cultural studies and game studies. *Games and Culture* 5 (4): 403-424.

Shifman, L. 2014. *Memes in digital culture*. Cambridge MA: The MIT Press.

Sicart, M. 2014. *Play matters*. Cambridge, MA: The MIT Press.

Simon, B., K. Boudreau, and M. Silverman. 2009. Two players: Biography and 'played sociality' in Everquest. *Game Studies* 9 (1). http://gamestudies.org/0901/articles/simon_boudreau_silverman.

Sony Online Entertainment. 1999. *Everquest*. [Windows/MacOS]. Sony Online Entertainment. Game.

Steinkuehler, C. A. 2004. Learning in massively multiplayer online games. In *Proceedings of the 6th international conference on learning sciences*, eds. Y. B. Kafai, W. A. Sandoval, N. Enyedy, A. S. Nixon, and F. Herrera, 521-528. Mahwah: Erlbaum.

Sutton-Smith, B. 2005. Play and ambiguity. In *The Game design reader: A rules of play anthology*, eds. K. Salen and E. Zimmerman, 296-313. Cambridge, MA: The MIT Press.

Terranova, T. 2012. Attention, economy and the brain. *Culture Machine* 13 (1).

Tufekci, Z. 2017. *Twitter and tear gas: The power and fragility of networked protest*. New Haven, CT: Yale University Press.

Van Dijk, J. 2005. *The network society: Social aspects of new media*. London: Sage Publications.

Walz, S. P., and S. Deterding, eds. 2015. *The gameful world: Approaches, issues, applications*. Cambridge, MA: The MIT Press.

Whitlatch, A. 2015. A day with Edward Tufte. *Medium*. http://medium.com/@ashley_mw/a-day-with-edward-tufte-7b142cec760f.

Wilson, J. 2011. Playing with politics: Political fans and Twitter faking in post-broadcast democracy. *Convergence: The International Journal of Research into New Media Technologies* 17 (4): 445-461.

Woolgar, S. 1990. Configuring the user: The case of usability trials. *The Sociological Review* 38:58-99.

Zimmerman, E. 2015. Manifesto for a ludic century. In *The gameful world: Approaches, issues, applications*, eds. S. P. Walz and S. Deterding, 19-22. Cambridge, MA: The MIT Press.

About the author

Alex Gekker is a Lecturer in the departments of Media and Culture at the University of Amsterdam and Media & Communication at Erasmus University Rotterdam. He completed his PhD at Utrecht University in 2016, working on the relations between mapping, digital interfaces, and power. He is interested in ways socio-technical systems are designed to influence users, and his research has touched upon the quantification and datafication of society, the experience economy, and interface critique. Additionally, he has participated in the field of games and play studies throughout his career, both as a scholar and practitioner. He has launched an early prototype of a location-based game, was part of the co-founding team of the Games for Health Europe series of conferences, and now co-designs Playfields, a playful tool for teaching fieldwork.

Index of names

Index of subjects

For Product Safety Concerns and Information please contact our EU representative GPSR@taylorandfrancis.com
Taylor & Francis Verlag GmbH, Kaufingerstraße 24, 80331 München, Germany

www.ingramcontent.com/pod-product-compliance
Lightning Source LLC
LaVergne TN
LVHW010552300926
849162LV00002B/313
* 9 7 8 9 4 6 2 9 8 4 5 2 3 *